THE
CIVIL
WAR
DAY BY DAY

THE
CIVIL
WAR
DAY BY DAY

EDITED BY JOHN S BOWMAN
INTRODUCTION BY HENRY STEELE COMMAGER

DORSET PRESS

This edition published by
Dorset Press,
a division of Marboro Books Corp.,
by arrangement with Brompton Books
Corporation.

Produced by Brompton Books Corporation
15 Sherwood Place
Greenwich, CT 06830

ISBN 0-88029-332-2

Printed in Hong Kong

Page 1: General George Brinton McClellan,
one of the North's senior commanders,
strikes an heroic pose for the camera.
Pages 2-3: A scene from the Battle of
Gettysburg depicting the defeat of Pickett's
ill-starred attack on the Union line.
Pages 4-5: Union gunners practise their drill.

CONTENTS

INTRODUCTION
By Henry Steele Commager

How do we explain the perennial interest in the American Civil War? It has been more than a century now since that war ended in the farmhouse at Appomattox. But the fires of interest, if not of hostility, still burn and the stories of battles and leaders, and of the suffering and heroism of Johnny Reb and Billy Yank still have the power to elicit fascination and passion.

There are many explanations for this. The Civil War was, in many ways, the last of the old wars and the first of the new. It was General Sherman who said that 'war is hell,' and none will dispute that judgment. Yet to most Americans General Sherman's war has been, and still is, almost irresistibly romantic. The very names of this conflict, whether Civil War, or War Between the States or War for Southern Independence, conjure up a hundred images: Jackson standing like a 'stone wall' at First Bull Run (First Manassas); U S Grant becoming 'unconditional surrender' Grant; Lee upon Traveler saying, 'It is well that war is so terrible, or we should get too fond of it'; A P Hill, after a 30-mile march, breaking through the wheatfields at Antietam to save the day; Thomas standing like a rock at Chickamauga; Pickett's men streaming up the long slope of Cemetery Ridge, only to be mowed down by Union cannon; Farragut lashed to the mast at Mobile Bay, shouting 'Damn the torpedoes, full steam ahead'; Colonel Shaw leading his black regiment, the 54th Massachusetts, in a desperate charge against Fort Wagner, and dying on the ramparts; Sheridan pounding down the Winchester Pike; Lincoln pardoning the sleeping sentinels, reading Artemus Ward to his cabinet, dedicating the cemetery at Gettysburg, greeted by thousands of frantic blacks as he walks the streets of conquered Richmond, and, in the end, invoking 'with malice toward none, with Charity for all.'

It is romantic because of the youthfulness of so many of its officers and soldiers, and the desperate devotion of so many of them who seemed to have no real stake in the issues. The plain farmers of the South fighting for slavery, the German and Irish and Norwegian regiments fighting for their adopted country and, by contrast, the blacks (200,000 of them, no less) enlisting in the struggle for freedom.

It was almost the last war which was fought on foot, where soldiers marched, and marched to songs that have become part of our heritage: 'John Brown's Body,' 'Lorena,' 'Dixieland,' 'Marching Through Georgia'; and it still boasts a body of literature which no other war has produced, from Whitman's *Drum-Taps*, and Timrod's 'Ode to the Confederate Dead' and Lowell's noble 'Harvard Commemoration Ode' to twentieth century poetry and novels such as Benet's *John Brown's Body*, Margaret Mitchell's *Gone With The Wind*, Stark Young's *So Red The Rose* and MacKinlay Kantor's *Long Remember*. In Douglas Freeman's *Lee* and Carl Sandburg's *Lincoln*, it inspired the greatest scholarly and the most poetic of American biographies, and in Allan Nevin's *Ordeal Of The Union* one of the masterpieces of historical literature.

The Civil War was, too, almost the last war where combatants, on both sides, cherished notions of chivalry. That came readily enough to Southern planters who thought of themselves as descendants of the Normans and played at being knights in armor. It was to be found equally in the soldiers in blue. Listen to General Joshua Chamberlain of the 20th Maine describing the Confederate surrender at Appomattox:

Before us in proud humiliation stood the embodiment of manhood: men whom neither toils and suffering nor the fact of death, nor disaster, nor hopelessness could bend from their resolve; standing before us now thin, worn, and famished, but erect, and with eyes looking level into ours, waking memories that bound us together as no other bond: was not such manhood to be welcomed back into a union so tested and assured? How could we help falling on our knees, all of us together, and praying God to pity and forgive us all?

Yet, too, the Civil War has some claim to being the first modern war, the first to approach – certainly in the South – what we now call 'Total War'; the first in which ironclad warships and submarines fought; the first where soldiers dug trenches and put up wire entanglements; the first in which reconnaissance of enemy positions from balloons was made; the first to depend on railroads – and the destruction of which witnessed an even partial (and not very successful) attempt to control the national economy; the first where information and orders could be transmitted by telegraph. And if the Civil War pro-

Above, far left: President Abraham Lincoln, committed to preserving the Union.
Above left: President Jefferson Davis of the South.
Far left: The North's finest general, Ulysses Grant.
Left: Robert E Lee of the Army of Northern Virginia.
Right: The war's major campaigns.

duced in Lee a romantic commander who would himself lead a battlefield charge against the enemy, it produced also in Sherman and Grant modern generals whose tactics and strategy rested on continuous hammerblows and on the destruction of the enemy economy.

There is, too, a deeper explanation of our persistent interest in the Civil War: that it concerned issues not only of national, but of global importance, and that it settled these issues and settled them – as far as we now know – correctly. The first of these was the survival of the most interesting of all experiments in modern history – a nation which made, or contrived, itself. Could a nation 'so conceived and so dedicated . . . long endure?' No other nation had ever been created (Lincoln's phrase 'brought forth' is accurate); all others had grown over the centuries. And no other nation at that time had been created from below rather than organized from above – created, too, by an enlightened people, and 'dedicated to the proposition that all men are created equal.' No wonder that, in the 1860s, the whole of the Western World anxiously awaited the answer to that question of national survival.

The second issue was, like the first, put most eloquently by Lincoln: could the nation endure 'half slave and half free?' Would a nation, dedicated in theory to freedom and equality, but still mired in slavery, be able to emancipate, not only the slaves, but itself from thralldom?

Not many wars can plead such persuasive justification. What, after all, was the Spanish-American War about; what was the War of the Philippines about; what was the Vietnam War about? Were any of these necessary, or even justifiable? But we know, without doubt, what the Civil War was about: it was about union and freedom. And we know that the war settled (dare we say once and for all) the question of union. We know too that it settled, at least legally, the question of slavery. Here, too, the whole world was an interested party: would the people who had pioneered freedom and equality at last vindicate their commitment to these noble goals? We are still working out an answer to that question, but we can be certain that, thanks to the Union victory, the answer will eventually be that it can, and will.

This Almanac does not purport to be either a narrative or an interpretation of the Civil War. We have enough of these in battle histories, biographies, monographs and dramas.

What the Almanac provides is something at once practical and – shall we say – disciplined: a combination of a chronology, a statistical record, and an atlas. It is an encyclopedia which strives for accuracy, thoroughness and succinctness. Every student will, I think, be impressed by how much is condensed into such limited space. No previous chapter of our history has been quite so elaborately recorded as the Civil War: 70 volumes of *The Official Record of the War of the Rebellion*, plus 30 volumes of naval records and voluminous state records, joined by a hundred regimental histories. Yet even with all this we are still baffled by the inadequacy of documentation. We do not, for example, know just how many soldiers fought in the Union or Confederate forces. We do not have accurate figures on casualties (in this area Confederate figures are mostly guesswork), nor do we know how many soldiers deserted. Historians still quarrel over the effectiveness of the blockade; and the history of finances is all but chaotic.

Meanwhile the editors of this Almanac have done a heroic job of assembling whatever statistics are available, and providing us with a relevant factual background.

Henry Steele Commager
AMHERST, MASSACHUSETTS

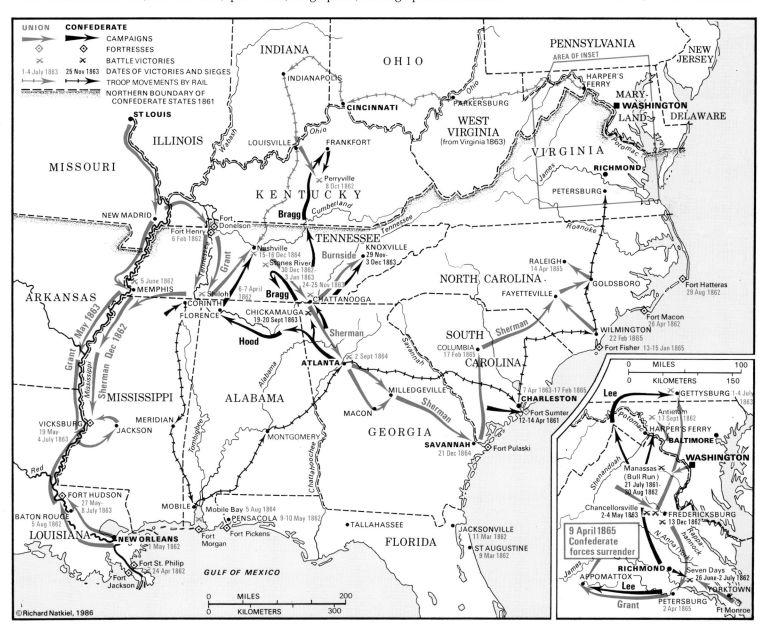

These pages: A Northern lithograph depicting the fate of runaway slaves. The Fugitive Slave Act, part of the 1850 Compromise proposed by Senator Henry Clay, did little to reduce the tension between the North and South.

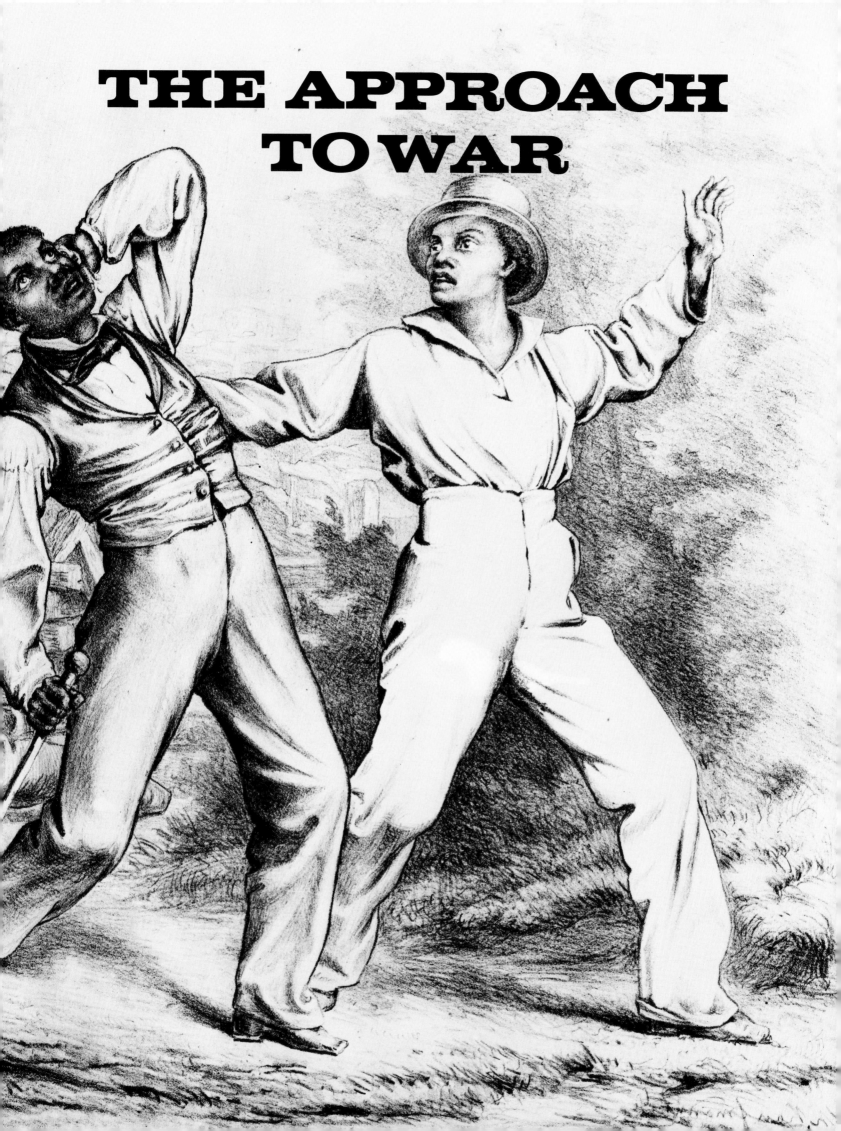

THE APPROACH
TO WAR

August 1619

English settlers in Jamestown, Virginia, purchase 20 black Africans from a Dutch frigate. Although these particular Africans are treated as indentured servants, it is not long before European colonists in North America are treating black Africans as slaves: they are imported, bought and sold as though material property, and their children are condemned to a life of slavery. Most of these black Africans are held in the Southern colonies, but many thousands are also held by Northerners – and many Northerners profit directly and indirectly from the slave trade. In the ensuing decades, as the number of slaves increases to hundreds of thousands, slavery itself evolves into a legally sanctioned system.

July 1776

The Declaration of Independence – with its resounding 'self-evident' truth 'that all men are created equal' – is adopted on 4 July. It is largely the work of Thomas Jefferson, himself a slaveowner, and it will be signed by many men who are also slaveowners.

1780-1804

In the Northern states, various laws are passed and court decisions handed down that effectively abolish slavery. In the South, however, where slavery has become inextricably involved in the economy and a total way of life, it remains legally sanctioned and sustained.

May-September 1787

In Philadelphia, 55 delegates from 12 states (Rhode Island refuses to participate) meet to draw up a Federal Constitution for a United States. The resultant document is in many ways a compromise among various conflicting views – sectional, economic, social, philosophical and otherwise. One of the major splits is between the Southern and the Northern states over the issue of allowing slavery to continue. But several Southern states refuse to join in any Union if slavery is not allowed, so despite the warning of George Mason, a

Below: The signing of the Declaration of Independence on 4 July 1776. Many of the signatories were slaveowners.

delegate from Virginia, that slaves 'bring the judgment of Heaven on a country,' the Constitution includes three clauses that effectively sanction the continuation of slavery: (1) Fugitive slaves are to be returned to their owners; (2) Slave trade (that is, new Africans from abroad) is to be permitted until 1808; and (3) For the purpose of apportioning congressional representatives on the basis of population, a slave is to be counted as three-fifths of a white person. In the debate that ensues in the states, most of the Northerners as well as Southerners who are opposed to ratifying the Constitution are simply against placing so much power in a national government and denying powers to the states.

July 1787

Meeting in New York City as the fading government under the Articles of Confederation, the Congress passes its last major act, the Territorial, or Northwest, Ordinance. One of its clauses states that 'there shall be neither slavery nor involuntary servitude in said territory.' Although immediately applicable only to the territory that will eventually be subdivided into the states of Ohio, Indiana, Illinois, Michigan and Wisconsin, the ordinance suggests a national policy of designating all new territories and states as 'free soil' – that is, as off limits to slavery.

December 1791

The first 10 amendments to the Constitution – known as the Bill of Rights – are put into effect. They guarantee many individual rights but say nothing about slavery or the rights of black Americans.

October 1793

Eli Whitney applies for a patent on a cotton gin, a device that greatly increases the speed and ease with which cotton fibers are separated from the seeds. This machine will soon increase the need for labor to produce more cotton, and since most of the cotton is grown in the Southern states, this will lead to the need for more slaves.

November-December 1798

The legislatures of Kentucky and Virginia adopt resolutions contending that the Alien and Sedition Acts are unconstitutional and

Above: Eli Whitney, creator of the cotton gin that greatly increased the demand for slaves.

that individual states retain the right to determine this. These acts are passed in June and July by a Congress controlled by the Federalist Party desirous of restricting the growth and freedoms of the Jeffersonian Republicans. What is particularly significant is that these resolutions, defiant expressions of states' rights, were written by Thomas Jefferson and James Madison, both of whom would become president of the United States.

November 1799

The Kentucky legislature passes another resolution reaffirming that of 1798 but adding that 'the remedy for [what states consider] infractions of the constitution' is 'nullification.'

August 1800

Gabriel Prosser, a black slave coachman, plans a revolt to liberate thousands of slaves in the Richmond, Virginia, area. On the day when the uprising is scheduled, a heavy thunderstorm washes away the bridge over which about 1000 armed slaves were to pass. Meanwhile, the state authorities have been following events thanks to an informer and they move in and arrest Prosser and many of his followers. Prosser and at least 37 others are executed. Although this is but one of more than 250 rebellions by slaves during some two centuries up to 1861, it is one of the more ambitious ones and convinces many Southerners that only strict measures can maintain the institution of slavery.

January 1808

From the first day of the new year, the importation of slaves from abroad into the United States is legally ended, as called for by the Constitution. But the buying and selling of slaves within the United States continues, and in practice many new slaves continue to be smuggled into the states. The enabling legislation itself provides that these smuggled slaves, when apprehended, are to be turned over to the state authorities and that the states may then sell the slaves.

December 1814-January 1815

A number of prominent New Englanders, strongly opposed to the war that the United States has been fighting against England since 1812, gather for secret meetings in Hartford, Connecticut. Various propositions are considered, including seceding from the Union, but by the end the only course those attending can agree on is to propose certain amendments to the Constitution. Meanwhile, on 14 December, the Treaty of Ghent is signed, ending the war, so the Hartford Convention's recommendations become moot. What is not moot, however, is the notion that representatives from a section of the United States might see their states' rights taking precedence over the Union and its federal Constitution.

December 1816-January 1817

The American Colonization Society is founded in Washington, DC, to aid in settling freed slaves in Africa. Although it will eventually obtain indirect aid from the United States government and will help in moving 11,000 blacks to the new African country of Liberia, the society is by no means endorsed by either black Americans or white abolitionists. Many from both of these groups see the goals of this society as merely avoiding the issue of slavery and the rights of blacks in America.

January-March 1820

The House of Representatives passes a bill calling for the admission of Maine to the United States. Since there are 11 free (that is, non-slave) states and 11 slave states, the admission of Maine as a free state would upset the balance that is jealously guarded by all parties in the Union. Therefore, the Senate adopts a bill that combines the admission of Maine with the admission of Missouri as a slave state. In addition, the Senate adopts a further compromise, an amendment that would bar slavery in the rest of the Louisiana Purchase north of 36° 30′ latitude. The House of Representatives then votes to accept the Senate bill with its amendment, and this legislation becomes known as the Missouri Compromise.

May 1822

Denmark Vesey, a former slave who had purchased his own freedom in 1800, is arrested, convicted and executed for planning an uprising of slaves in the area around Charleston, South Carolina. Vesey's original plan called for an attack on Charleston on a Sunday in July, a time when many white people would be out of the city. But Vesey is betrayed by a black slave and is apprehended before he and his followers can do much more than make a few weapons. Vesey is hanged along with 34 other blacks. As word of the planned revolt spreads, various slave states and border states pass 'black codes,' laws greatly restricting the freedom of movement and general conduct of slaves.

May 1824

Congress passes another Protective Tariff Act, but it still leaves the South feeling discriminated against even though Northern manufacturers are unsatisfied with the law. By 1827, this law will have prompted such

Above: Thomas Jefferson upheld the rights of individual states against Federal power.

protests as the anti-tariff meeting in Columbia, South Carolina, where Thomas Cooper, president of South Carolina College, will ask in his speech: 'Is it worth while to continue this Union of States, where the North demands to be our masters and we are required to be their tributaries?'

Below: The Battle of New Orleans (8 January 1815) was fought after peace had been declared.

Above: The capture in August 1831 of Nat Turner, the leader of a slave uprising in Southampton County, Virginia.

April-May 1828

Congress passes another Tariff Act, one calling for relatively high duties on a variety of goods but affecting raw materials more than manufactured goods. The promoters of the bill are motivated at least in part by a desire to embarrass President John Quincy Adams, but he ends up signing it. Very soon it becomes known to Southerners as the 'tariff of abominations' and leads to widespread protests and demands by some that the Southern states separate from the union.

December 1828

The South Carolina legislature adopts a series of resolutions condemning the Tariff Act of 1828 and questioning its constitutionality. Appended to the formal resolutions is an unsigned essay, 'South Carolina Exposition and Protest,' which argues that any federal laws considered unconstitutional may be 'nullified' by a state convention. What makes this document so significant, aside from its support for the absolute sovereignty of the individual states, is the fact that its author is John C Calhoun, previously a strong nationalist, and now the vice-president of the United States. The Georgia legislature also adopts a number of resolutions against the Tariff Act of 1828.

January 1830

The Senate is debating the issue of the sale of the vast lands of the American West, but it soon becomes apparent that the real subject under discussion is that of states' rights versus federal power. This sets Southern senators against Northern senators, and in his climax to his defense of the latter, Daniel Webster concludes, 'Liberty and Union, now and forever, one and inseparable!'

January 1831

William Lloyd Garrison, among the more radical of the abolitionists, begins publishing in Boston *The Liberator,* a newspaper dedicated to the abolition of slavery.

August 1831

Nat Turner, a pious but radical slave preacher, leads an uprising of slaves in Southampton County, Virginia. At least 60 whites are killed before soldiers put down the rebellion. Turner and 12 of his followers are executed, while about 100 blacks are killed during the search for the rebels.

July 1832

Another Tariff Act is adopted by Congress. Although more moderate than that of 1828, it still leaves the South dissatisfied.

November 1832

A special state convention meets in South Carolina, one of the most outspoken of the Southern states, and adopts an ordinance that nullifies the Tariff Acts of 1828 and 1832. The South Carolina legislature then adopts measures to enforce this ordinance – even allowing for secession if the Federal government resorts to force.

December 1832

President Jackson issues a proclamation – after reinforcing the Federal forts off Charleston – warning the people of South Carolina that no state can secede from the union 'because each secession . . . destroys the unity of a nation.'

January-March 1833

In the uproar that follows President Jackson's proclamation, the South Carolina legislature defies 'King Jackson' and even raises a volunteer unit to repel any 'invasion.' Jackson then asks Congress to adopt a 'force bill' to enable him to enforce the provisions of the Tariff Acts of 1828 and 1832. But Henry Clay, always anxious to work out a compromise that will save the Union, draws up a new tariff bill that is presented to the House of Representatives. The bill includes a gradual cutback in tariffs, and when word of its probable acceptance is passed to South Carolina, the legislature suspends its nullification ordinance. Congress then adopts both the tariff compromise and the force bill and President Jackson signs them within 24 hours. The confrontation is averted.

December 1833

The American Anti-Slavery Society is organized due primarily to the efforts of Arthur and Lewis Tappan, wealthy New York City merchants, and Theodore Weld, a prominent abolitionist minister. Weld, through his writings and speeches, will continue to play a major role in convincing many Americans of the necessity and justice of abolishing slavery.

October 1835

In Boston, a mob parades William Lloyd Garrison through the streets with a rope around his neck to express their disgust with his extreme views on slavery. And in Utica, New York, people meeting to organize an anti-slavery society are attacked by a mob (said to be led by a judge and a congressman).

December 1835

Santa Anna, president of Mexico, proclaims a unified constitution for all territories of Mexico. The North American settlers in

Below: Abolitionist Theodore Weld helped create the American Anti-Slavery Society in late 1833.

Theodore D. Weld

Texas announce that they intend to secede from Mexico rather than give up their 'right' to slavery, which Mexico has abolished.

February-March 1836

Santa Anna leads the siege of the Alamo, where 182 Texans are finally killed when the Mexicans overwhelm the fort. The heroic defense, however, inspires the North American settlers to meet in a convention, declare their independence from Mexico and draft a constitution.

Below: President John Adams was forced to sign the 'tariff of abominations' in 1828.

April 1836

Under General Sam Houston, Texans defeat the Mexicans and capture Santa Anna at the Battle of San Jacinto. The Texans ratify their own constitution, elect Sam Houston as president and send an envoy to Washington to demand annexation by the United States or recognition of the independent Republic of Texas. Since they intend to legalize slavery in any case, the debate that follows in Congress once again pits pro-slavery Southerners against anti-slavery Northerners.

May 1836

Southern members of the House of Representatives get a majority to vote for a 'gag' resolution, one that declares that all petitions or papers that in any way involve the issue of slavery should be 'laid on the table' – that is, there should be no discussion. The House of Representatives will continue to vote such a 'gag rule' at the outset of every session until 1844, but instead of burying the issue of slavery it only sharpens the difference between the two sides.

March 1837

On his last day in office, President Jackson recognizes the independent Lone Star Republic of Texas. Jackson has been avoiding this decision for many months, not wanting to aggravate the problems that already separate the South and the North. This leaves a Union of 13 free states and 13 slave states, but of the large territories that remain to be converted into states, only one – Florida – is controlled by slaveholders, while three non-slave territories still exist. A movement to admit Texas as a 'slave territory' to balance out these free territories is defeated.

Above: The heroic defense of the Alamo in 1836 paved the way for the admittance of Texas, a slave state, into the Union.

August 1839

The Spanish slave-ship *Amistad,* carrying 53 African slaves between two Cuban ports, is taken over in a mutiny led by Cinque, one of the slaves. They kill the captain and the crew except for two who are forced to navigate the ship to North American waters, where a United States warship brings the *Amistad* into a Connecticut port. Spain immediately demands that the slaves be returned, but Americans force the case into the courts. Eventually it will be taken all the way to the Supreme Court, where John Quincy Adams argues for their right to be freed. In March 1841 the Supreme Court rules, and Cinque and the others are returned to Africa.

April 1841

William Henry Harrison, ninth president of the United States, dies after one month in office and is succeeded by Vice-President John Tyler. When Tyler declares a Sunday as a 'day of national prayer,' various speakers use the occasion to speak out on the issue of slavery.

January 1842

The United States Supreme Court rules, in *Prigg v. Commonwealth of Pennsylvania,* that a Pennsylvania law forbidding the seizure of fugitive slaves in that state is unconstitutional. But the opinion goes on to state that the enforcement of fugitive slave laws is entirely a Federal responsibility, so various Northern states use this as a loophole and adopt personal liberty laws.

Above: James Polk defeated Henry Clay to the presidency in November 1844.

April 1844

A treaty agreeing to the annexation of Texas by the United States, negotiated by John C Calhoun, now secretary of state, is signed and President Tyler submits it to the Senate.

June 1844

The Texas Annexation Treaty is rejected by the Senate, where anti-slavery forces convince a majority that admitting a slave state

Below: A cartoon showing Polk (seated, right) surveying expansionists as they move to incorporate Oregon into the Union.

will simply lead to another confrontation between the South and the North.

November 1844

James K Polk defeats Henry Clay for the presidency. Polk is virtually an unknown politician, but his somewhat aggressive-expansionist views on acquiring Texas, Oregon and California strike a receptive chord among Americans. He owes his very nomination, in part, to the fact that the more obvious Democratic candidate, Martin Van Buren, had earlier in the year published a letter opposing the annexation of Texas. Clay had published a similar letter, and it is agreed that this contributed to his defeat.

February-March 1845

The House of Representatives and the Senate, acting on the proposal of President-elect Polk, adopt a joint resolution for the annexation of Texas. This is essentially a procedure to bypass the requirement of a two to three vote of the Senate alone, traditionally used to ratify a treaty. The resolution also authorizes the president to negotiate a new treaty with Texas that could be approved by either procedure, but the president does not immediately exercise this choice. Mexico, however, severs diplomatic relations with the United States as soon as the resolution is adopted.

July 1845

Texas formally agrees to annexation, so President Polk simply decides to treat it as a state, even though it remains Mexican territory under international law. Polk sends a detachment of the United States Army, led by General Zachary Taylor, to the south-western border of Texas to guard the state against an 'invasion' from Mexico.

March-April 1846

General Taylor takes his troops onto the left bank of the Rio Grande, always recognized as Mexican territory, on the orders of President Polk. Despite Mexico's evident desire to find some face-saving way of negotiating its way out of an armed conflict, President Polk persists in seeking an excuse for a war. It comes in late April when a small Mexican cavalry unit inflicts a few casualties on United States troops blockading a Mexican town.

May 1846

At the request of President Polk, Congress approves a declaration stating that 'By the act of the Republic of Mexico, a state of war exists between that Government and the United States.' But in the debate leading up to this declaration, and in the months to follow, it is clear that this war with Mexico is yet another divisive issue between the North and the South: Southerners tend to support the war as they see it leading to more territory to be worked by slaves, while Northerners oppose the war for that very reason.

June 1846

North American settlers in California, long seeking to break away from the rule of Mexico, proclaim the existence of the Republic of California. Meanwhile, there has long been simmering a dispute between the

United States and Great Britain over the border between the Oregon Territory and Canada. President Polk, anxious to gain support for the widening war with Mexico, submits to the Senate a treaty that extends the international boundary along latitude 49° to Puget Sound and then to the ocean through the Juan de Fuca Strait. In return for Southern support for the treaty, President Polk agrees to reduce certain tariffs. The Senate ratifies the treaty.

August 1846

President Polk asks Congress to appropriate $2 million to help purchase territory from Mexico in negotiations that he assumes will follow any fighting. The appropriation bill comes to the House where it is amended to include what is known as the Wilmot Proviso, so named after an otherwise obscure Pennsylvanian representative, David Wilmot, who introduces the amendment. Using words taken verbatim from the Northwest Ordinance of 1787, the Wilmot Proviso states that 'neither slavery nor involuntary servitude shall ever exist in any part of' the territories that might be acquired from Mexico. The House passes the appropriation with this amendment, but the lines between Northerners and Southerners are once more sharply drawn.

February-March 1847

The Senate takes up the appropriation bill with the Wilmot Proviso, and ends up passing the former without the latter. The House then approves the Senate version of the appropriation bill, so that the question of slavery within the territories remains open. But during the Senate's debate on the Wilmot Proviso, John Calhoun introduces four resolutions that attempt to provide justification for the Southern position. Essentially Calhoun argues that Congress has no right to limit existent or prospective states in matters of laws pertaining to slavery. Furthermore,

Below: General Zachary Taylor, hero of the war against Mexico in the 1840s.

Above: John Calhoun argued that Congress had no right to interfere with slave states.

since slaves are like any property that might be taken into a territory, Congress has the obligation to protect slavery. Calhoun's doctrine effectively sets aside the Missouri Compromise of 1820, and although the Senate in no way endorses it, the doctrine is in the air.

September 1847

General Winfield Scott marches victorious into Mexico City after a whirlwind campaign since landing at Vera Cruz in May.

December 1847

Senator Lewis Cass of Michigan, in a letter to A P Nicholson, a Tennessee politician, sets forth the doctrine that slavery should be left to the decision of the territorial government. Because Cass is an influential politician – he will run for president in 1848 – his proposal is given serious consideration. It will become known as the doctrine of 'popular sovereignty' and will attract many supporters anxious to sidestep either the constitutional or the moral issues of slavery.

February 1848

The United States signs the Treaty of Guadalupe Hidalgo, ending the war with Mexico. The United States gets over 500,000 square miles that include what will become the states of California, Nevada, Utah, most of New Mexico and Arizona, and parts of Wyoming and Colorado. Texas is also conceded to the United States, with the boundary at the Rio Grande. This makes the United States a transcontinental republic, but it also opens up new land to be disputed by pro- and anti-slavery forces.

March 1848

The Senate ratifies the treaty, and President Polk gets an appropriation bill to pay Mexico – but without the Wilmot Proviso.

August 1848

President Polk signs the bill organizing the Oregon Territory without slavery. The bill has passed with the support of Southern senators, who clearly are willing to concede Oregon to the 'free-soilers' with the understanding that other territory belongs to the slaveholders.

November 1848

Zachary Taylor, hero of the Mexican War, is elected president. Taylor is a slaveholder but is not especially committed to the principle of slavery.

September-October 1849

Californians gather at a convention in Monterey and adopt a constitution that establishes a state forbidding slavery. They then ask for admission into the Union.

December 1849

President Taylor asks Congress to admit California as a state. Southerners object because, as another free state, this will leave the slave states in a minority. There is talk again among some, such as Calhoun, of secession, but Taylor says he will crush secession even if he himself has to take to the field again.

January 1850

The aging Senator Henry Clay, who has dedicated his career to preserving the Union, is annoyed at the extremists from both the South and North who threaten to resort to force. He offers to the Senate a series of resolutions that he hopes all sides can agree to. The resolutions involve admitting California as a free state on the grounds that this is its people's own wish; meanwhile, no decision will be made at this time in regard to slavery in the other territory gained from Mexico – but the clear implication is that it will later be made according to the settlers' wishes. Other topics in Clay's resolutions include a strict

Below: Henry Clay dedicated his political life to preventing the break-up of the Union.

Above: A scene from *Uncle Tom's Cabin*. The anti-slavery message aroused strong feelings in both the North and South.

new fugitive slave law and the barring of trade in slaves – but not slavery itself – from Washington, DC.

February-March 1850

In opening the Senate debate on his resolutions, Clay pleads for a compromise by both sides. But the strongest advocates of both sides oppose compromise – Senator William Seward of New York arguing that 'there is a higher law than the Constitution which regulates our authority' while Senator John Calhoun of South Carolina argues that not only must the North concede the right of extending slavery but must also 'cease the agitation of the slave question.' (Calhoun is so ill that his speech is read for him by Senator James Mason of Virginia.) But the decisive speech is made by the senator from Massachusetts, Daniel Webster, long a political opponent of Clay and a moral opponent of slavery. 'I speak today for the preservation of

Below: Jefferson Davis, Secretary of War under Pierce; later leader of the Southern states.

the union,' he begins, and he proceeds to argue that the North must be ready to accept even slavery for this cause. Webster does not convert everyone immediately, but the spirit of compromise is now abroad.

June 1850

Leaders from nine Southern states convene in Nashville, Tennessee, to discuss the issues of slavery and states' rights. Although some delegates openly advocate secession, the moderates prevail. The convention ends when they adopt several modest resolutions, but one calls for extending the Missouri Compromise line of 36° 30' all the way across the new territories to the Pacific coast.

July 1850

President Taylor, who has opposed the compromise measures of Clay, dies and Vice-President Millard Fillmore assumes office.

September 1850

Congress adopts five bills based on the original resolutions of Henry Clay, and they come to be known as the Compromise of 1850. The one that continues to give Northerners the most trouble is the strict Fugitive Slave Act. President Fillmore signs all of the new acts.

November 1850

Southern leaders reconvene in Nashville, and since the more extreme delegates hold the majority there is much talk of the South's right to secede.

December 1850

A state convention in Georgia votes its desire to remain in the Union – but declares that the state will secede if the Compromise of 1850 is not observed by the North.

June 1851

Uncle Tom's Cabin by Harriet Beecher Stowe begins to appear as a serial in the *National Era,* an anti-slavery paper published in Washington, DC.

March 1852

The complete novel *Uncle Tom's Cabin, or Life Among the Lowly,* is published in Boston. Within a year it will sell over one million copies and its portrayal of slave life serves to arouse both Northerners and Southerners.

November 1852

Franklin Pierce defeats General Winfield Scott for the presidency on a Democratic Party platform that supports the Compromise of 1850.

January 1854

A national competition for the lucrative transcontinental railroad route has been underway for some time. Senator Stephen A Douglas of Illinois, hoping to have the route pass through the Great Plains region, supports a bill that he hopes will win over proponents of the southern route (promoted, among others, by Jefferson Davis, now secretary of war under President Pierce). Douglas agrees to divide the central territory into two, Kansas Territory and Nebraska Territory; the assumption is that one will be settled by pro-slavery people and the other by anti-slavery people. Since Douglas endorses the concept of 'popular sovereignty,' which means that the settlers will be able to decide for themselves, the bill effectively repeals the Missouri Compromise of 1820, as both Kansas and Nebraska lie above latitude 36° 30'. The debate that follows once again pits pro-slavery Southerners against anti-slavery Northerners.

February 1854

At Ripon, Wisconsin, anti-slavery opponents of the Kansas-Nebraska bill meet and recommend forming a new political party, the Republican Party. In the months that follow, others meeting in various Northern states join in the formation of the new party.

April 1854

The Emigrant Aid Society is formed in Massachusetts to encourage anti-slavery supporters to settle in Kansas and thus 'save' it as a free state. Relatively soon, about 2000 people go under the auspices of this project.

May 1854

The Kansas-Nebraska Act, creating the two new territories, is adopted by Congress with a clear majority, and President Pierce signs it. But many Northerners, even those who had previously advocated moderation, denounce this new development. In particular, Northerners threaten to stop obeying the Fugitive Slave Act of 1850.

July 1854

In Michigan, anti-slavery men meeting to join the new Republican Party demand that both the Kansas-Nebraska Act and the Fugitive Slave Act be repealed. In the Kansas Territory, the Federal government opens an office to supervise the distribution of land, but pro-slavery and anti-slavery settlers are staking claims and fighting each other with little regard for any laws.

March 1855

Elections for a territorial legislature are held in Kansas. Several thousand pro-slavery Missourians cross into Kansas and vote, thus electing a pro-slavery legislature. The election is recognized by the Federal governor of the territory.

Above: Senator Charles Sumner, an outspoken abolitionist, being attacked by South Carolina representative Preston Brooks in the Senate Chamber, May 1856.

July 1855

The Kansas legislature meets and not only adopts an extremely strict series of pro-slavery laws but also expels the anti-slavery legislators.

October-November 1855

Free-Soil Kansans hold a convention of their own in Topeka and adopt a constitution that outlaws slavery. (But they will also adopt a law that bars all blacks from Kansas.) A virtual civil war now exists, with frequent clashes between the pro- and anti-slavery elements in Kansas.

December 1855

The Free-Soil people of Kansas approve the Topeka constitution (and the law banning blacks).

May 1856

Charles Sumner, the senator from Massachusetts and an outspoken anti-slavery man, gives a vituperative speech against the pro-slavery elements in the Senate. Three days later, as Sumner is sitting at his Senate desk, a South Carolina representative, Preston Brooks, beats Sumner with a stick. It will be three years before Sumner fully recovers, but he is regarded as a martyr by Northern abolitionists – while many Southerners praise Congressman Brooks. In Kansas, late in May, pro-slavery men attack Lawrence, center of the anti-slavery settlers, and kill one man. In retaliation, a band of anti-slavery men, led by the fiery abolitionist John Brown, kill five pro-slavery men at Pottawotamie Creek.

July 1856

The House of Representatives votes to admit Kansas as a state with its anti-slavery Topeka constitution, but the Senate rejects this, so the issue is left open. Kansas, however, will later take an anti-slavery stance.

November 1856

James Buchanan, the Democratic candidate, defeats John Frémont, the Republican candidate, for the presidency in a contest that is fought quite openly along the lines of South versus North, pro-slavery versus anti-slavery.

March 1857

The Supreme Court hands down its decision in the Dred Scott case, and a majority declare that the Missouri Compromise of 1820 is unconstitutional. Scott is a black slave whose owner took him from the slave state of Missouri into the free state of Illinois and territory north of the latitude 36° 30', and then back to Missouri. Scott sued for his freedom, but the Court rules that he had never ceased to be a slave and so could not be considered a citizen with the right to sue in a Federal court. But the most far-reaching impact of the decision comes from the claim that Congress has no right to deprive citizens of their property – such as slaves – anywhere within the United States. An outburst of protest from Northerners and Republicans greets the decision.

December 1857

A pro-slavery constitution for Kansas is approved by the territorial legislature meeting at Lecompton, Kansas.

January-April 1858

Kansans reject the pro-slavery Lecompton constitution, but President Buchanan proceeds to ask Congress to admit Kansas as a state under this constitution. After considerable opposition by individual congressmen and several revisions, a bill is passed by both houses that allows for another popular vote by Kansans on their constitution.

June 1858

The Republican Party of Illinois nominates a former one-term representative, Abraham Lincoln, to challenge the incumbent, Senator Stephen A Douglas. Although personally opposed to slavery, Douglas has tried to straddle the issue in order to hold the Democratic Party together, but his promotion of popular sovereignty – that is, allowing each territory or state to decide the issue for itself – has only antagonized many staunch pro-slavery Democrats from the South. Lincoln, however, chooses to meet the issue head on, and in his acceptance speech at the convention he asserts, 'I believe this government cannot endure half slave and half free.'

Below: Dred Scott, a runaway slave, was returned to his owner after a Supreme Court ruling that provoked outrage in the North.

Above: Incumbent Republican Senator Stephen Douglas of Illinois attempts to stave off the challenge of Abraham Lincoln.

August-October 1858

Lincoln and Douglas meet in towns across Illinois in a series of seven debates. Although Lincoln is little known outside Illinois and Douglas is a national figure desperately trying to placate his own party, the debates help to define the most pressing issue confronting the nation. Lincoln takes a strong stand against slavery, on moral, social and political grounds, while Douglas defends not slavery as such but the right of Americans to vote their preference. Douglas will be elected senator by the Democratic majority in the Illinois legislature, but Lincoln emerges on the national stage as an articulate and respected spokesman for the anti-slavery position in the North.

March 1859

The Supreme Court reverses a decision of the Wisconsin Supreme Court in *Ableman v. Booth* and rules that state courts may not free Federal prisoners. Booth had been convicted in a Federal court for having rescued a fugitive slave, and in upholding this conviction, the United States Supreme Court confirmed the constitutionality of the Fugitive Slave Act of 1850. The Wisconsin legislature declares that 'this assumption of jurisdiction by the Federal judiciary . . . is an act of undelegated power, void and of no force.' Although in this instance it is an anti-slavery state defying the Federal authority, this is yet another case of a state asserting its rights. In any case, the Federal government rearrests and imprisons Booth.

May 1859

The Annual Southern Commercial Convention, an organization designed to promote economic development, after many years of considering the issue of re-opening the African slave trade, votes to approve the following: 'In the opinion of this Convention, all laws, State or Federal, prohibiting the African Slave Trade, ought to be repealed.'

October 1859

Kansans vote to ratify an anti-slavery constitution. At Harper's Ferry, Virginia, (now West Virginia) John Brown, one of the most radical of the abolitionists, leads an armed group (five black, 13 white men) that seizes the Federal arsenal. Although this is the first action in his vague plan to establish a 'country' for fugitive slaves in the Appalachians, there is no support from outside people. Within 24 hours he and four other survivors are captured by a force of United States Marines led by Colonel Robert E Lee. Within six weeks he is tried for criminal conspiracy and treason, convicted and hanged. Although most Northerners condemn the way that Brown went about his plan, Southerners note that many Northerners admire Brown and his goals. They see Brown's raid as confirming their worst fears about the violence and upheaval that would prevail if the blacks are not held down firmly.

February 1860

Jefferson Davis, the senator from Mississippi, presents a set of resolutions to the Senate to affirm that the Federal government cannot prohibit slavery in the territories but must actually protect slaveholders there. But Davis is less interested in getting the whole Senate's approval than that of the Democratic members, for he is anticipating the forthcoming Democratic Party convention and presidential election. Davis wants to commit the Democratic Party against Stephen Douglas and his concept of popular sovereignty.

April-May 1860

The Democratic Party holds its convention in Charleston, South Carolina. When the pro-slavery platform is rejected, delegates from eight Southern states depart. But the remaining delegates are unable to agree on a candidate, so the convention adjourns.

May 1860

In Chicago, the Republican Party, on its third ballot, nominates Abraham Lincoln as its presidential candidate. To gain the nomination, Lincoln has had to present himself as fairly moderate on the question of slavery, and the party's platform declares that it is for prohibiting it in the territories but against interfering with slavery in the states.

June 1860

The Democratic Party reconvenes, this time in Baltimore, and after another walkout by the anti-Douglas forces, he is nominated for the presidency. Later, the Southern Democrats convene in Baltimore and nominate Vice-President John C Breckinridge to run for president on a platform that calls for the protection of the right to own slaves.

Below: Abolitionist John Brown defying the Federal authorities at Harper's Ferry. His attempt to establish a 'country' for fugitive slaves failed; he was later executed.

July–October 1860

In the campaign the issues are reduced to slavery and sectionalism. Extremists on both sides do little except fan the fears of people, North and South. Only Stephen Douglas of the candidates even bothers to travel to all sections in an attempt to broaden his appeal, but even he soon realizes that his cause is lost because of the split within his own party. Various Southern spokesmen make it clear that secession will follow if Lincoln is elected.

November 1860

Abraham Lincoln is elected president with a clear majority of the electoral college votes but only a plurality of the popular votes. Although Lincoln had deliberately muffled his message of attacking slavery, there is no mistaking the fact that for the first time in its history the United States has a president of a party that declares that 'the normal condition of all the territory of the United States is that of freedom.' Within days of Lincoln's election Southern leaders are speaking of secession as an inevitable necessity.

December 1860

South Carolina, long a leader in threatening secession, holds a state convention that votes to secede from the Union. Meanwhile, Congress convenes and in an effort to work out some compromise each house appoints a special committee. A member of the Senate's committee, John J Crittenden of Kentucky, introduces a series of proposals, the chief of which calls for a constitutional amendment that restores the Missouri Compromise line across the continent and for all time. Although Crittenden's proposals and various others will eventually be brought before both houses, they will prove to be ineffectual in the face of events. Members of President Buchanan's cabinet are quitting in December to protest either his actions or inaction. And Major Robert A Anderson, in command of the Federal forts in the harbor of Charleston, South Carolina, moves his entire force to the larger and more defensible of the two, Fort Sumter. A delegation from South Carolina comes to Washington and demands that President Buchanan remove all Federal troops from Charleston. Buchanan, who has always been sympathetic to the Southern position on slavery and states' rights, cannot accede to such a demand. He announces that Fort Sumter will be defended 'against hostile attacks, from whatever quarter,' and authorizes preparation of a relief expedition by sea. In Illinois, President-elect Lincoln tries to avoid taking any position that will exacerbate the situation, but at the same time he has made himself clear: 'Let there be no compromise on the question of *extending* slavery.'

Right: A handbill announcing the secession of South Carolina from the Union – the final split leading to civil war.
Below: The violent expulsion of blacks and abolitionists from Tremont Temple, Boston, on 3 December 1860.

CHARLESTON

MERCURY

EXTRA:

Passed unanimously at 1.15 o'clock, P. M. December 20th, 1860.

AN ORDINANCE

To dissolve the Union between the State of South Carolina and other States united with her under the compact entitled "The Constitution of the United States of America."

We, the People of the State of South Carolina, in Convention assembled, do declare and ordain, and it is hereby declared and ordained,

That the Ordinance adopted by us in Convention, on the twenty-third day of May, in the year of our Lord one thousand seven hundred and eighty-eight, whereby the Constitution of the United States of America was ratified, and also, all Acts and parts of Acts of the General Assembly of this State, ratifying amendments of the said Constitution, are hereby repealed; and that the union now subsisting between South Carolina and other States, under the name of "The United States of America," is hereby dissolved.

THE

UNION

IS

DISSOLVED!

These pages: The bombardment of Fort Sumter, garrisoned by Northern troops under Major Robert Anderson, on 12-13 April 1861 signaled the opening of hostilities.

2 January 1861

Washington After South Carolina's vote to secede and Charleston's initiating war preparations, President Buchanan refuses to acknowledge officially a letter received from South Carolina commissioners. This letter, concerning Major Anderson's decision to hold Fort Sumter with a garrison of Federal troops, prompts the cabinet to order reinforcement of the fort.

Military The USS *Brooklyn* is readied at Norfolk, Virginia, despite General Winfield Scott's preference for a non-naval vessel to aid Fort Sumter. That same day, South Carolina seizes the inactive Fort Johnson in Charleston Harbor. Defense of the capital is placed in the hands of Colonel Charles Stone, who is charged with organizing the District of Columbia militia.

3 January 1861

Washington The compromise plan authored by Senator John J Crittenden is considered for submission to public referendum, an idea receiving only lukewarm support in Congress.

Military Former Secretary of War Floyd's orders to remove guns from Pittsburgh, Pennsylvania, on down through forts in the South are reversed by the War Department. With future defense in mind, Georgia state troops take over Fort Pulaski on the Savannah River.

5 January 1861

Washington In the nation's capital, senators from seven Southern states meet, afterward advising secession for their states – Alabama, Arkansas, Florida, Georgia, Louisiana, Mississippi and Texas.

Military Alabama further commits herself to the Southern course by seizing Forts Morgan and Gaines in order to defend Mobile. Meanwhile, 250 troops are on their way to Fort Sumter. The use of the *Brooklyn* having been vetoed by General Scott, the merchant ship *Star of the West* is called into service and sails from New York with those Federal troops.

6 January 1861

Military Florida troops seize the Federal arsenal at Apalachicola.

7 January 1861

Washington Senator Crittenden speaks for conciliation and moderation, although he is against secession. He addresses the Senate, saying 'I am for the Union; but, my friends, I must also be for the equal rights of my State under the great Constitution and in this great Union.'

Military The takeover of Fort Marion at St Augustine, Florida, is accomplished by state troops. Like all such actions, this meets with little, if any, opposition; most of the arsenals and forts are unmanned, and the Federal government is loath to provoke confrontation by making outright defense preparations for the moment.

8 January 1861

Washington President Buchanan urges adoption of the Crittenden Compromise, which would use the Missouri Compromise line to divide the proposed slave and non-slave territories. Jacob Thompson of Mississippi, Buchanan's secretary of the interior, resigns and is replaced by Chief Clerk Moses Kelley as acting secretary.

Military In Florida, Federal troops at Fort Barrancas open fire on a handful of men who advance on the Pensacola site.

9 January 1861

Secession Despite Buchanan's pleas, Southern sentiment runs high in favor of secession; Mississippi votes 84-15 to leave the Union, a move greeted with widespread public celebration.

Military The *Star of the West* approaches Charleston Harbor but is fired on prior to reaching Fort Sumter. No damage is done to the ship but it quickly retreats, heading back to New York. Although some officers at Fort Sumter are anxious to return the fire opened on the relief vessel, Major Anderson forbids this action. He complains to Governor Pickens about volleys fired on a ship bearing the United States flag. The South Carolina governor replies that a United States ship represents a hostile presence that the now-independent state cannot tolerate. Anderson soon appeals to Washington, but there is little change in the situation, although Charleston reacts excitedly to this near outbreak of war. Fort Sumter remains under United States control.

10 January 1861

Washington Jefferson Davis addresses the Senate, calling for a decisive response to Southern demands. He decries the use of 'physical force' to settle those demands, asking instead that United States authority be maintained 'by constitutional agreement between the States.'

Military Lieutenant A G Slemmer transfers Federal troops from Fort Barrancas to Fort Pickens on Santa Rosa Island after Florida votes 62-7 to secede. Orders to Major Anderson at Fort Sumter emphasize defensive preparations, despite the continual seizure, elsewhere, of Federal properties. Forts Jackson and St Philip in Louisiana are taken over by state troops, as is the large and valuable arsenal at Baton Rouge.

11 January 1861

Secession Furthering the Southern cause, Alabama's State Convention votes 61-39 to secede. Conversely, the New York legislature votes for pro-Union resolutions.

Military Louisiana's troops occupy the United States Marine Hospital near New Orleans. President-elect Lincoln writes a letter to James T Hale of Pennsylvania that 'if we surrender, it is the end of us, and of the government.'

12 January 1861

Washington Mississippi representatives leave the House. In an appeal to the Senate, New York's Senator Seward states, 'I do not know what the Union would be worth if saved by the use of the sword.'

Military In Florida, state troops demand the surrender of Fort Pickens and its garrison after having seized Fort Barrancas and its barracks, Fort McRee and the naval yard at Pensacola. Fort Pickens remains firmly in Federal hands, however.

Above: Former President John Tyler headed the Peace Convention in February 1861 in a last-minute attempt to save the Union.

13 January 1861

Washington Buchanan receives envoys from both Major Anderson and Governor Pickens concerning the disposition of Fort Sumter. The president emphasizes that the fort will not be turned over to South Carolina authorities.

14 January 1861

Military Fort Taylor at Key West, Florida, is garrisoned by United States troops. This effectively prevents its future takeover by the South. Fort Taylor represents a major Gulf Coast base for Union operations and will become an important coaling station for blockaders during the war. Fort Pike near New Orleans, Louisiana, falls into state hands.

16 January 1861

Washington The Senate, resolving that the Constitution should not be amended, virtually kills the Crittenden Compromise.

19 January 1861

Secession Georgia secedes on a vote of 208-89 despite indications of Union support. Moderate leaders in that state include Alexander Stephens, later to be vice-president of the Southern Confederacy. This type of moderate not withstanding, the move to secede is a strong one, prompted by the earlier election of Lincoln to the presidency.

20 January 1861

Military Mississippi troops take Fort Massachusetts on Ship Island in the Mississippi Gulf after several previously unsuccessful attempts at seizure of this important military installation.

21 January 1861

Washington Five senators representing the states of Alabama, Florida and Mississippi withdraw from the chamber. All make farewell speeches, Jefferson Davis among them, who asserts 'I concur in the action of the people of Mississippi believing it to be necessary and proper.' Davis is severely downcast by this exigency, that night praying for peace, according to his wife.

Slavery Boston, Massachusetts, is the site of an address by Wendell Phillips, an ardent abolitionist. His message hails the secession of slave states, for which he had little use or respect since they seemed to be only disruptive forces in the Federal Union.

24 January 1861

Military The arsenal at Augusta, Georgia, falls into state hands. Federal troops from Fort Monroe, Virginia, are sent to reinforce Fort Pickens in Florida.

26 January 1861

Secession An ordinance of secession passes the Louisiana State Convention 114-17.
Military In Savannah, Georgia, both Fort Jackson and the Oglethorpe Barracks are taken by state troops.

29 January 1861

Washington Kansas, with a constitution that prohibits slavery, receives the necessary congressional approval to become the Union's 34th state. This action is the outcome of several years of bitter fighting between pro- and anti-slavery factions in that former territory.

31 January 1861

Military New Orleans, Louisiana, is the scene of further takeovers. The United States Branch Mint and Customs House and the schooner *Washington* are seized by the state, ending a month of similar events throughout the South. The defiance of secessionists continues unabated and Washington seems unable, or unwilling, to still the confusion and unrest engendered by Southern actions.

1 February 1861

Washington William H Seward, secretary of state-designate, is the recipient of a letter from Lincoln in which the latter states, 'I am inflexible' in reference to extending slavery in the territories.
Secession With a vote of 166-7 at the State Convention, Texas secedes from the Union, the seventh state to do so.

4 February 1861

Washington The Peace Convention meets at the nation's capital, with 131 members from 21 states, although none of the seceded states send any delegates to this assembly. The convention is headed by former President John Tyler, who joins with others of like mind in a last desperate effort to compromise and save the Union.
Secession At Montgomery, Alabama, a convention of representatives assembles. This is the initial meeting of the Provisional Congress of the Confederate States of America, attended by many former United States senators, among them Louisiana's Judah Benjamin and John Slidell. Benjamin is later to become attorney general, then secretary of war, in Jefferson Davis' cabinet. He and Slidell have been law partners together in New Orleans. Slidell later becomes famous for his involvement in an international incident, the *Trent* affair.

5 February 1861

Washington Fort Sumter is again the subject of attention as the president summarily dismisses any notions held by South Carolina that the United States will give up its jurisdiction over the fort. Meanwhile, the Peace Convention attempts to arrange a settlement of differences between the secessionists and those who wish to uphold the Union. Speaking to the delegates, John Tyler indicates that 'the eyes of the whole country are turned to this assembly, in expectation and hope.'
Secession At Montgomery, Alabama, plans proceed for the establishment of 'a Confederacy of the States which have seceded from the Federal Union,' according to Christopher Memminger of South Carolina. Memminger is destined to be the Confederacy's treasury secretary.

8 February 1861

Secession A constitution is provisionally adopted by the Montgomery convention. With several significant changes, the document closely resembles the United States Constitution, those changes having to do with the right to own slaves, the treatment of fugitive slaves and the power of sovereign states in the South.

9 February 1861

Secession In a unanimous decision, Jefferson Davis of Mississippi is elected provisional president of the Confederate States of America. Alexander Stephens joins him as provisional vice-president. These two are moderate enough in their public views to please the border states and it is hoped that those states not yet seceded will soon do so now that the Confederacy has chosen able, and not fanatic, leaders. In a further move to preserve order and prevent a radical break, the Provisional Congress at Montgomery states that the laws of the United States of America are to remain valid unless they interfere with stated laws of the Confederacy. Tennessee declines the opportunity to hold a state convention which would rule on secession; the popular vote on this decision is 68,282 to 59,449.
Military Fort Pickens, Florida, does not receive the reinforcements that arrive on the USS *Brooklyn* because of the desire of both Federal and state authorities that the balance of power not be disturbed.

Below: The inauguration of Jefferson Davis as president of the Confederacy in front of Montgomery's State Capitol.

10 February 1861

Secession The arrival of a telegram announcing his election to the presidency of the newly-formed Confederacy catches Jefferson Davis by surprise in Mississippi. He is immediately involved in plans for a trip to the capital at Montgomery, Alabama, in order to take part in his inauguration, which the Confederacy clearly hopes to hold before Lincoln can take over the Federal government.

11 February 1861

Washington Preparations are made for the inauguration as President-elect Lincoln leaves Springfield, Illinois, on his journey to the Federal capital.
Secession Jefferson Davis leaves his Mississippi plantation, Brierfield, and at Montgomery, Alabama, Vice-President Alexander Stephens is sworn in but does not take advantage of the occasion to make any official statements.

12 February 1861

Secession As Lincoln travels to his inauguration in Washington, DC, he makes numerous stops along the way. Speaking before various groups, the president-elect is cautious in expressing his opinions. To German-Americans at Cincinnati, Ohio, he states his earlier intention of remaining silent about 'national difficulties.' Earlier, in that same city he asked the citizenry to remain loyal to the Constitution. Jefferson Davis is making his way to the Confederate capital and, like Lincoln, speaks to the crowds gathering along the way. He observes that a possible outcome of secession is war.
Military State troops take possession of United States munitions stored at Napoleon, Arkansas.

15 February 1861

Washington The Peace Conference drags on, attending to each detail with discussion and debate. Many Federal military officers, such as Raphael Semmes of the navy, are resigning their posts to become part of Southern military and naval forces.
Secession Again, Lincoln makes a cryptic observation, this time at Pittsburgh, Pennsylvania, that 'there is really no crisis except an *artificial* one!' Similar comments accompanied his address earlier to a crowd in Cleveland, Ohio.

18 February 1861

Secession At his inauguration, Jefferson Davis points out 'the American idea that governments rest on the consent of the governed.' It is clear that he would like to avoid armed conflict, but it is also apparent that he holds the Southern position to be sacred. His words – 'obstacles may retard, but they cannot long prevent, the progress of a movement sanctified by its justice' – leave little doubt as to his dedication. Elsewhere, Lincoln progresses from Buffalo eastward to Albany, New York.

19 February 1861

Secession A Confederate cabinet takes shape in Montgomery, Alabama. Secretaries of State, War and the Treasury, Toombs, Walker and Memminger are joined by Judah Benjamin as attorney general, Stephen Mallory as secretary of the navy, and John Reagan as postmaster general. At New York City, an estimated 500,000 persons greet Lincoln as he arrives in that Northern city.
Military Louisiana obtains control of the United States paymaster's office located at New Orleans.

20 February 1861

Military The Department of the Navy of the Confederacy is established. In addition, the Provisional Congress empowers President Davis to contract for the manufacture and purchase of war goods.

22 February 1861

Secession At a Washington's birthday celebration in Philadelphia, Pennsylvania, Lincoln points out that 'there is no need of bloodshed and war.' After having received an assassination threat the previous day, Lincoln leaves with a bodyguard for the nation's capital. It is arranged that he, detective Allan Pinkerton and a friend will travel by a revised schedule and route.

23 February 1861

Washington The president-elect arrives safely in the city at 0600 hours. Various delegations greet him throughout the day, including members of the Peace Convention.
Secession In Texas, voters respond favorably to appeals for secession in a popular public referendum.

27 February 1861

Washington At the Peace Conference, deliberations result in six proposed constitutional amendments. Although the proposals have no chance of acceptance, they are sincerely conceived. Meanwhile, United States representatives strike down plans for a constitutional convention, vote against amendments to interfere with slavery and against the Crittenden Compromise.
Secession Jefferson Davis, now head of the Confederacy, appoints three men to approach officials in the Federal capital with offers of peaceful negotiation of differences. Davis also receives missives from Governor Pickens in Charleston, South Carolina; the head of that state observes the need for Confederate takeover of Fort Sumter to preserve 'honor and safety.'

28 February 1861

Secession Missouri holds a State Convention: its purpose is to debate secession. North Carolina comes out in favor of the Union at its election concerning the possibility of a State Convention; secessionists garner 46,409 votes in favor of holding such a convention, those against the assembly tally 46,603 votes.
Military The stalemate at Fort Sumter continues, Major Robert Anderson staying in nearly constant communication with Washington. States that have seceded and formed the Confederacy grow increasingly more willing to confirm their independent status. With the inauguration only days away, the mood in Washington is expectant but subdued; there is little real action as the incoming administration awaits the beginning of its tenure. However, relations between the North and South are deteriorating, making war more likely.

Above: Charles Memminger, secretary of the treasury in the Confederate cabinet from 19 February 1861.

2 March 1861

Washington Senator John J Crittenden of Kentucky attempts to push a constitutional amendment through the Senate, but fails. This amendment, a culmination of Peace Convention efforts, is the final compromise issue supported by Crittenden, who now directs his energies at monitoring the inevitable conflict between North and South.

3 March 1861

Military General Winfield Scott, head of the United States Army, indicates in a letter to Secretary of State Seward that relief of Fort Sumter is not practical.

4 March 1861

Washington Abraham Lincoln is inaugurated as the 16th president of the United States of America at the nation's capital where some 30,000 people are assembled. Because of threats against the president's life, troops are everywhere. In his address to the nation on this momentous occasion, Lincoln emphasizes his position on slavery, stating that he is not opposed to the institution where it is already established. He further points out that the states voting for secession are in error, since 'the Union of these States is perpetual.' Taking the stance that acts against the Federal government are 'insurrectionary or revolutionary,' Lincoln vows to uphold the Union, saying to refractory Southerners, 'in *your* hands, my dissatisfied fellow countrymen, and not in *mine*, is the momentous issue of civil war.'

5 March 1861

Military Fort Sumter, again the subject of concern on both Northern and Southern sides, becomes a point of intense discussion between Lincoln and General Scott. It appears from Major Anderson's messages that the fort cannot be maintained without replacements and reinforcements, and the estimated number of troops needed at the South Carolina site hovers around 20,000. Both Scott and Lincoln agree that the disposition of Fort Sumter should be confronted soon.

6 March 1861

Washington Despite Lincoln's refusal to deal with them, the Confederate commissioners appointed by Jefferson Davis try to establish negotiations with the Republicans now in office.

7 March 1861

Washington Martin J Crawford, John Forsyth and A B Roman, the men Davis has sent to represent the Confederacy in the United States capital, continue to press for an appointment with Lincoln's administration. In addition, they contact influential individuals in Washington who express some support for the Southern position, or who are known to be on the side of peaceful negotiation rather than armed conflict.

11 March 1861

Military Lincoln is told by General Scott that the army can no longer be responsible for the immediate reinforcement of Fort Sumter. He tells the president that the situation at Charleston is reaching crisis proportions which the army alone cannot effectively handle.

13 March 1861

Washington Since Lincoln is averse to validating the Confederate nation in any respect, he counsels Secretary of State Seward to refuse meetings with Confederate ambassadors on any grounds. In avoiding such a conference, the president hopes to sidestep the question of whether or not those Southern states forming the Confederacy have actually left the Union.

15 March 1861

Military In the hope of avoiding armed conflict, Seward does not support the reinforcement of Fort Sumter since that move would, he feels, most definitely precipitate a response from the Confederacy. Lincoln, in the midst of the varying opinions of his cabinet, delays any final word concerning the issue in South Carolina.

16 March 1861

Secession Another state, Arizona, votes to leave the Union and join the Confederacy, in a convention at Mesilla. The Confederate government later establishes a territorial government for Arizona.

International The Confederacy, knowing that its future depends greatly on recognition, appoints commissioners to Britain.

18 March 1861

Secession A State Convention having turned down a move to secede 39-35, Arkan-

Below: A crowd of some 30,000 looks on as Abraham Lincoln is inaugurated as the 16th president of the United States.

sas agrees to an election later in the summer which will allow for public voting on the secession question.

Military While Confederate President Jefferson Davis hopes that Federal troops under Major Robert Anderson will withdraw, the president nevertheless communicates with Governor Pickens concerning the fortification of the area around Charleston, South Carolina. Davis points out that it is unlikely that 'the enemy would retire peacefully from your harbor.'

25 March 1861

Washington The capital is alive with rumors from Charleston, South Carolina, but there is little reliable information about the situation there. The next day, President Lincoln and his cabinet meet to discuss Fort Sumter and how to best deal with the mounting crisis.

29 March 1861

Washington The president finally announces his plan for Fort Sumter. An evacuation of that installation would not be attempted, but instead, a force would be sent to supply and support the troops already stationed there. It is Lincoln's preference that this force should be in readiness 'as early as the 6th April.' The cabinet's support of President Lincoln's decision to keep Fort Sumter in Federal hands is three to two in favor, Secretary of War Simon Cameron keeping silent about his wishes in this matter.

31 March 1861

Washington President Lincoln, having taken a stance on Fort Sumter, now prepares

Below: Major Robert Anderson, the commander of the Northern forces at Fort Sumter.

to act on Fort Pickens' dilemma. A force is ordered to Florida to relieve the latter military post, while rumors fly in the capital that Fort Sumter is to be abandoned; there is no truth to these rumors, as Lincoln's orders of 29 March prove.

Military Yet another Federal outpost, Fort Bliss in Texas, surrenders its jurisdiction to state troops. The toll of Federal property lost to Southern hands continues to mount, and the mood in both the Union and the Confederacy is pessimistic as to the outcome of the current problems. The Lincoln administration has taken steps which it feels are both emphatic yet non-provoking.

1 April 1861

Washington President Lincoln receives a message from Secretary of State Seward in which the latter speaks of relations between the United States and France, Britain, Spain and Russia. Seward indicates his willingness to assume responsibility for dealing with the Confederacy. In addition, the secretary of state tells the president that the issue with the Confederacy ought to center around union or disunion rather than slavery, and advises that Fort Sumter be abandoned while Federal occupation of other forts should continue. Lincoln's tactful yet firm response proves that he, and not Seward, will continue to make policy decisions. In a separate action, the president orders the USS *Powhatan* to proceed to Florida where it can then aid Fort Pickens. This effectively removes the *Powhatan* from the Fort Sumter rescue efforts. Secretary of State Seward has advised this course of action but it is not made clear to the Department of the Navy, introducing some later confusion when the Fort Sumter expedition is finally under way.

3 April 1861

Washington The president meets with his cabinet concerning Fort Sumter and issues related to the relief and reinforcement of that Federal installation.

Military In Charleston Harbor, the Federal schooner *Rhoda H Shannon* is fired on by Confederate batteries.

Above: A dramatic reconstruction of the bombardment of Fort Sumter in Charleston Harbor, South Carolina.

4 April 1861

Washington Lincoln writes to Major Anderson, informing him of the upcoming relief of Fort Sumter, saying 'the expedition will go forward.' Anderson is told to maintain the situation as it now stands, if possible, but he has been given the freedom to decide what the response would be to an attack by the Confederates.

Secession At its State Convention, Virginia votes 89-45 against holding a referendum on the most important secession question.

5 April 1861

Washington Formal orders are given by the secretary of the navy concerning the Fort Sumter expedition. Four vessels are told to provision the fort, but among these is the *Powhatan* which is already on its way to Fort Pickens, Florida, under direct orders from the president.

6 April 1861

Washington State Department Clerk Robert S Chew carries a message to South Carolina Governor Pickens regarding Fort Sumter: the Federal action will be one of provisioning rather than reinforcing on the condition that there be no resistance to or interference with the supply efforts. Lincoln directs Seward to reverse former orders concerning the USS *Powhatan* but it is too late to do so.

7 April 1861

Secession General Beauregard conveys the message to Major Anderson that no further communication between Fort Sumter and Charleston will be permitted by Confederate authorities.

8 April 1861

Secession In response to Lincoln's 6 April message concerning the supply of Fort Sumter, the Confederacy readies its forces in the vicinity of Charleston Harbor.

Military The Federal cutter *Harriet Lane* leaves New York for Fort Sumter.

9 April 1861

Military From New York, two more vessels sail for Charleston Harbor; one, the steamer *Baltic,* carries naval agent Gustavus Fox, a former officer who later becomes President Lincoln's assistant secretary of the navy.

10 April 1861

Military Beauregard receives word from Confederate Secretary of War Leroy Pope Walker that he is to require the surrender of Fort Sumter from the Federals. All around the fort, Confederate troops prepare for the expected conflict; a floating battery is stationed by rebels off Sullivan's Island in Charleston Harbor.

11 April 1861

Washington Three Confederate commissioners sent to the Federal capital leave for the South and carry with them the conviction that their government will not be recognized by Lincoln.

Military Major Anderson receives messengers from General Beauregard – Confederate Colonel James Chesnut, formerly a United States senator; Colonel A R Chisolm, Governor Pickens' representative, and Captain Stephen D Lee, formerly of the United States Army. These three men convey to Anderson that Beauregard is 'ordered by the Government of the Confederate States of America to demand the evacuation of Fort Sumter.' Anderson's refusal prompts Beauregard to contact War Secretary Walker; the latter encourages the Confederate general to wait and see whether Anderson evacuates so as to 'avoid the effusion of blood.' The Confederacy appears willing to hold its fire on Fort Sumter if the Federal garrison does nothing to further precipitate armed conflict.

12 April 1861

Military The three Confederate messengers to Fort Sumter, Chesnut, Chisolm and Lee, return to Major Anderson once more after speaking with General Beauregard. They try once more to ask for a time of probable evacuation of the fort by Federal troops. The major indicates 2400 hours 15 April as a target time in the event that he receives no supplies or orders from Washington. The Confederacy, knowing that help is undoubtedly on its way, refuses to accept this statement from Major Anderson and gives the Federal commander written notification of an attack to commence in one hour's time. At Fort Johnson, Captain George S James signals the other harbor batteries to open fire. At 0430 a rotation of fire proceeds against Fort Sumter, continuing through the day and at intervals through the night. The city of Charleston reacts with excitement, many people watching the bombardment from rooftops. The Federal vessels sent by Washington are visible at sea, prompting further speculation as to the outcome of the Southern attack. At Fort Pickens on Santa Rosa Island in Florida, the United States Navy lands troops to reinforce the existing garrison. This action prevents the Confederacy from gaining control of this important Gulf Coast fortification.

13 April 1861

Washington The president, as yet unaware of the battle at Fort Sumter, states that 'I shall hold myself at liberty to repossess places like Fort Sumter if taken from Federal control.

Military The Federal garrison at Fort Sumter is left with no option but to surrender to Confederate officers. This action is declared at 1430 hours. Major Robert Anderson, with no remaining food and an insufficient number of men, concludes that further conflict is purposeless and that his troops have done their best under difficult conditions. No lives have been lost and the wounded are few on both sides, despite the firing of some 40,000 shells during the battle.

14 April 1861

Washington The cabinet and President Lincoln meet after receiving official notice of the surrender at Fort Sumter. The chief executive calls for 75,000 volunteers, and also for a session of Congress to meet on 4 July 1861.

Military Major Anderson and his men leave Fort Sumter and proceed northward by sea after a ceremony of surrender. On this occasion, an accidental blast kills two and injures four Union soldiers as a stockpile of ammunition is inadvertently detonated.

15 April 1861

Washington Lincoln issues a public proclamation calling for 75,000 militia to still the insurrection in South Carolina, eliciting an in-

Below: With little hope of being relieved, the troops inside Fort Sumter were forced to surrender on 13 April.

Above: A photograph showing members of Company K, 4th Georgia Volunteers, one of the militia regiments raised to protect the Confederacy in the early stages of the war.

stant supportive response from Northern states. Border states such as Kentucky, Maryland, Missouri, North Carolina and Virginia are areas of discontent and uncertainty. Kentucky and North Carolina ultimately refuse to respond to Lincoln's appeal while the New York legislature commits $3 million in aid for the Northern cause.

17 April 1861

Secession   Baltimore, Maryland, is the setting for a meeting held by secessionists. Missouri and Tennessee decide against meeting Lincoln's requests for volunteers, and at Richmond, Virginia, the State Convention passes 88-55 a secession ordinance. A public referendum is to be held in that state on 23 May for a final decision on the secession question. For all intents and purposes, Virginia is now viewed by the rest of the nation as a part of the Confederacy.
The Confederacy   President Jefferson Davis announces that the Confederate government will accept applications for letters of marque, a move which will permit privateering, a practice that to many seems little better than legalized piracy.
Naval   At Indianola, Texas, the steamer *Star of the West* is taken in Gulf waters by Confederate troops under General Van Dorn; the ship will later become a receiving vessel in the Confederate navy.

18 April 1861

Washington   At the capital, the president is informed by eyewitnesses as to the events at Fort Sumter. It is alleged that Lincoln has approached Colonel Robert E Lee and has asked him to command the Union army; Lee has purportedly declined the offer. It is clear that while there are staunch supporters for

both the Union and the Confederacy, there are also those who prefer to avoid further conflict.

19 April 1861

Washington   The president makes one of his strongest moves up to this time, ordering the blockade of all ports in the Confederate states. This order immediately causes the Federal Department of the Navy to place its ships outside all critical ports, and the blockade is soon extended to include North Carolina and Virginia. It is one effort which proves effective, though in varying degrees, throughout the war.
The North   In New York, the 6th Massachusetts Regiment travels toward Washington, pausing at Baltimore, Maryland. A vital railroad nexus, this city is important for both the supply and defense of the Federal capital. As the Massachusetts troops move through Baltimore on their way to the Washington depot, they are attacked by rioters carrying Confederate flags. Nine civilians and four soldiers are killed in the melee. The troops reach the capital and are ultimately quartered in the Senate Chamber. It appears that Washington will lose a railroad link with the North as a result of this Baltimore riot, causing the Federal navy to carry troops to Washington via Philadelphia and Annapolis.

20 April 1861

The North   A move later censured by Union officials is that of Commandant Charles S McCauley giving orders to burn the Federal Gosport Naval Yard near Norfolk, Virginia. Calculated to prevent the property from falling into Confederate hands, the base has been an important Federal military installation and its loss creates difficulty for Union operations along the coast. The 4th Massachusetts Regiment arrives to support Fort Monroe.
The Confederacy   Robert E Lee resigns his post with the Federal army, choosing to side

with the South. Many Confederate merchants are now repudiating debts to the North.

21 April 1861

The North   In Baltimore, Maryland, rioting continues while the president meets with that city's mayor to discuss ways of ending the violence.
Secession   Monongahela County in the western part of Virginia hosts meetings of anti-secessionists, who resolve to support the Union despite the stand taken by the remainder of the state.

22 April 1861

Washington   The difficulties in Baltimore have continued to threaten the Federal capital because troops heading for Washington must go through Maryland. Lincoln's words to the Baltimore YMCA – 'you . . . would not lay a straw in the way of those who are organizing . . . to capture this city' – indicate his concern for the defense of Washington.
The Confederacy   Jefferson Davis is in communication with Virginia's Governor John Letcher and hopes that the latter will be able to 'sustain Baltimore if practicable.'
Western Theater   Cairo, Illinois, is garrisoned by state troops.
Trans-Mississippi   Arkansas Governor H M Rector refuses to send troops to support the Union. The Federal arsenal at Fayetteville, Arkansas, is taken by North Carolina state troops.

24 April 1861

Washington   The president continues to worry about the security of the capital city as invasion from the South looms on the horizon. In writing to Reverdy Johnson, a Maryland political leader, Lincoln says, 'I do not mean to let them invade us without striking back.'

25 April 1861

Washington   The 7th New York Regiment arrives in Washington, much to President Lincoln's relief.
Trans-Mississippi   In a secret action against the pro-secessionists in Missouri, Captain James H Stokes of Chicago, Illinois, goes to St Louis from Alton, Illinois. Upon arrival, he and his men remove 10,000 muskets from the arsenal, returning to Alton the next morning with munitions for Illinois troops.

27 April 1861

Washington   In a bold action, Lincoln suspends the writ of habeas corpus in an area stretching from Philadelphia, Pennsylvania, to Washington, DC, and then leaves General Scott in charge of supervising any incidents arising out of that suspension. Lincoln does this in part to provide for a cessation of the turmoil that has been plaguing Baltimore, Maryland, and causing troop transport to be severely disrupted because of it. In addition, the president extends the Federal blockade of Southern ports to include Virginia and North Carolina.
The Confederacy   Richmond is offered by the Virginia Convention as a possible site for a new capital for the Confederacy to replace Montgomery, Alabama.

29 April 1861

Secession   The state legislature of Maryland repudiates secession with a vote of 53-13.
The Confederacy   Jefferson Davis speaks at the second session of the Confederate Provisional Congress. Explaining reasons for secession, the Confederate leader says, 'we protest solemnly in the face of mankind that we desire peace at any sacrifice save that of honor and independence.'

30 April 1861

Washington   Complying with orders from the president, Federal troops evacuate Indian Territory forts, leaving the Five Civilized Nations – Cherokees, Chickasaws, Choctaws, Creeks and Seminoles – virtually under Confederate jurisdiction and control.

1 May 1861

The North   Soldiers killed in the Baltimore riots are honored at ceremonies in Boston, Massachusetts. A call for volunteers to support the Union is publicized in the Nebraska Territory.
Eastern Theater   Confederate troops under Colonel T J Jackson are sent to Harper's Ferry, Virginia, by General Robert E Lee.
Naval   Federals seize two Confederate ships in Atlantic waters, and the United States Navy blockades the mouth of the James River.

3 May 1861

Washington   Making preparations for the war which now appears inevitable, Lincoln sends out a call for 42,000 volunteers and another 18,000 seamen. He also forms the Department of the Ohio, to be commanded by George Brinton McClellan. General Winfield Scott, the general in chief of the Federal army, explains that, with the aid of a powerful blockade, it is possible to 'envelop' the states along the entire length of the Mississippi River and provide for the subjugation of insurgents in this way. The arrangement is known as the Anaconda Plan.
International   The Confederacy has sent commissioners to London, England, to meet with the British foreign minister in the attempt to gain recognition for their government in the South. The United States complains to the British ministry about this meeting although it is an unofficial one, according to the British, who are not interested in upsetting their delicate relations with the United States.

Above: Rioters with pro-Southern sympathies attack members of the 6th Massachusetts Regiment as they pass through Baltimore.

Below: A view of Norfolk after it was wrecked and abandoned by its Union garrison on 20 April, a loss that was deemed unnecessary.

5 May 1861

The Confederacy State troops abandon, temporarily, the city of Alexandria, Virginia, which lies across the Potomac River from the Federal capital.

6 May 1861

Secession At Little Rock, Arkansas, the state legislature votes 69-1 in favor of secession. Elsewhere, Tennessee votes to set a public referendum on secession; while the 8 June deadline for this election is one month away, the state legislature's 66-25 vote in favor of secession confirms the direction that Tennessee will take in the upcoming conflict.
The Confederacy Jefferson Davis gives approval to the Confederate congressional bill declaring a state of war between the United States and the Confederate States.

7 May 1861

Washington Major Robert Anderson, who had gained national recognition as the commander in charge of Union forces at Fort Sumter, South Carolina, is assigned to recruit

Right: US Marines return to barracks after a parade through Washington, DC.
Below: The death of Union officer Elmer Ellsworth during an attempt to remove a Southern flag provoked outrage on both sides.

troops for the Federal cause. President Lincoln asks Anderson to obtain Union volunteers from Kentucky and western Virginia.
Border States Conflicting sentiments cause a riot at Knoxville, Tennessee; pro-secessionists clash with Union supporters, resulting in injuries and one fatality.

9 May 1861

The North At Newport, Rhode Island, the USS *Constitution* and the steamer *Baltic* are preparing to set up the United States Naval Academy since it can no longer be based in Annapolis, Maryland, due to the uncertain nature of that area's political sentiments. It seems important to locate the academy in an area which is solidly pro-Union.
The Confederacy James D Bullock is charged with purchasing arms and vessels from the British for the Confederate cause.
Naval The Virginia blockade precipitates gunfire between Confederate batteries on shore at Gloucester Point and the Federal vessel *Yankee*.

10 May 1861

The Confederacy President Jefferson Davis orders the purchase of warships and munitions for the Confederacy. Naval Secretary Mallory suggests ironclads as logical additions to the small Confederate navy, hoping that this will favor the Southerners, for their Union opponents have a much larger and more diverse fleet.
Secession A riot in St Louis, Missouri, results when United States troops clash with pro-secessionist state militia. While Federal forces do not provoke the attack, under the leadership of Captain Nathaniel Lyon they march to the state militia barracks at Camp Jackson where armaments for secessionists are allegedly stored. The state forces led by General D M Frost surrender peacefully, but during the ensuing march, curious crowds

trigger further violence. In the fracas, a reported 29 are killed or fatally injured.

11 May 1861

The North Both Wheeling in western Virginia and San Francisco, California, are scenes of pro-Union demonstrations, even though a strong secessionist element remains in the latter area.
Secession At St Louis, the unrest continues. Fights between civilians and the 5th Reserve Regiment result in seven more deaths. Eventually, Federal control is resumed and the secessionists slowly back down.

13 May 1861

The North General Benjamin F Butler moves Federal troops into Baltimore without official authorization. Butler has received notice of possible riots in that Maryland city.
International Britain's Queen Victoria announces her nation's position of neutrality. She further states that the British will assist neither side, but will give each the rights accorded belligerents.

14 May 1861

The North General Butler continues his occupation of the city of Baltimore.
Western Theater Major Robert Anderson receives word from President Lincoln that Kentucky Unionists are to be given aid, despite their state's neutral position.

16 May 1861

Washington Orders go out to Commander John Rodgers to take charge of the United States naval operations on rivers in the West.
Secession In Kentucky, the legislature proposes its intention that the state retain its neutral status.

18 May 1861

Eastern Theater In its first offensive against the South, the Union engages rebel batteries at Sewall's Point, Virginia.
Naval The blockade of Virginia is complete with the sealing off of the Rappahannock River.

20 May 1861

Secession North Carolina assembles a convention at Raleigh, voting for secession.
The North In order to reveal pro-secessionist evidence, United States marshals in the North appropriate the previous year's telegraph dispatches.
The Confederacy Confederate provisional congressmen vote to relocate their nation's capital at Richmond, Virginia.

23 May 1861

Secession In a vote of 97,000 to 32,000, Virginia moves in favor of secession. The western portion of the state, however, is clearly pro-Union and has been for some time contemplating a formal break with the rest of the state.

24 May 1861

Eastern Theater Alexandria, Virginia, is occupied by Federal troops moving quietly across the Potomac River. In this way the Union begins to defend Washington. Virginia troops display little resistance. The first

Union combat fatality of the Civil War occurs during this move: 24-year-old Elmer Ellsworth, head of the 11th New York Regiment, dies in an attempt to remove a Confederate flag from a hotel roof. The man who shot Ellsworth, the hotel keeper James Jackson, is then shot by a Union soldier. Both the North and the South have martyrs for their respective causes. Newspapers give full play to the emotions in reporting the events – 'Jackson perished amid the pack of wolves' was the way one Southern newspaper chose to describe the killing.
Slavery In an action provoking questions as to the disposition of slaves by the North, General Benjamin F Butler holds three slaves at Fort Monroe. The issue is quickly interpreted as one of whether slaves are to be regarded as contraband. This will become an increasingly difficult controversy, ultimately ruled on by Secretary of War Cameron in July 1861.

26 May 1861

Washington Lincoln's Postmaster General Blair announces the cutting of postal connections with the Confederate States as of 31 May 1861.
Naval Additional blockades are established: one at Mobile, Alabama, and one at New Orleans, Louisiana.

27 May 1861

Washington In a case concerning the legality of Lincoln's suspension of the writ of habeas corpus, Chief Justice Roger B Taney decrees the arrest of John Merryman illegal. Merryman was imprisoned for recruiting Confederate soldiers; the arrest was made by General Cadwalader, who argued that Lincoln's proclamation allowed such action. It is Lincoln's view that in time of rebellion such moves are required in order to preserve public safety.

29 May 1861

Washington Dorothea Dix is received by Secretary of War Cameron, who accepts her offer of help in setting up hospitals for the Union Army.

30 May 1861

The North Grafton, Virginia, in the western part of the state, is occupied by Union troops who are sent to protect citizens and to guard the Baltimore & Ohio Railroad line.

31 May 1861

The North Union troops, which have evacuated forts in Indian territory, reach Fort Leavenworth, Kansas. The path they travel is later known as the Chisholm Trail after one of their guides, Jesse Chisholm.
The Confederacy General Beauregard is given command of the Confederate forces in northern Virginia.

1 June 1861

Eastern Theater Northern Virginia is the scene of fighting at Arlington Mills and Fairfax County Courthouse. A Confederate captain, John Q Marr, is killed in this minor skirmish, one of the early Southern fatalities.
International British territorial waters and ports are proclaimed off-limits to belligerents carrying spoils of war.

3 June 1861

The North Forty-eight-year-old Stephen A Douglas dies, probably of typhoid fever. The Democrats lose a staunch, committed leader, and the Union, a strong supporter. In the nation's capital, President Lincoln mourns the 'Little Giant' who defeated him in the race for a Senate seat, but who lost his bid for the presidency.
Eastern Theater Western Virginia is again the focus of conflict, Union forces surprising Confederates at Philippi. The rebels, under Colonel G A Porterfield, flee. This Northern triumph, so easily accomplished, came to be known as the 'Philippi Races' due to the Confederates' rapid retreat under fire. It was in some ways responsible for western Virginia's later break with the main part of the state. With Confederate troops no longer in

Below: The scene inside a Northern recruiting office. Lack of a standing army ensured that both North and South would have to rely on civilians to fill the ranks.

the vicinity, the majority of western Virginians, who were pro-Union, could more easily express their support for the North.

5 June 1861

The North   Arms and gunpowder are seized by Federal marshals at the Du Pont works in Delaware and at Merrill & Thomas, a gun factory in Baltimore.

6 June 1861

Washington   Lincoln's cabinet declares that the Union government will pay for all war expenses that are incurred once the states have mobilized their volunteers.

8 June 1861

Washington   The United States Sanitary Commission is given executive approval. This board will help maintain healthy conditions for Union troops.
Secession   In a public referendum, Tennessee favors secession by 104,913 votes to 47,238. This popular action serves to formalize the course already chosen for the state by its legislature.

10 June 1861

Eastern Theater   At Bethel Church, Virginia, Federal troops are forced into retreat by aggressive Confederates. Union fatalities total 18, with 53 wounded. The Southerners lose only one man and sustain seven injured. Colonel Charles Stone and his forces head out on an expedition which is part of the planned defense of the Federal capital.

11 June 1861

Trans-Mississippi   Troubles in St Louis, Missouri, continue as General Nathaniel Lyon meets with a pro-Southern state government. Lyon is angered over what he feels is local intervention in orders given to Federal troops.

Below: Professor Thaddeus Lowe, an enthusiastic proponent of hot-air balloons in warfare.

12 June 1861

Trans-Mississippi   In a further effort to promote the Confederacy in his state, Governor Claiborne Jackson of Missouri puts out a call for 50,000 volunteers. He hopes to repel what he perceives as attempts by Federals to take over the state.

14 June 1861

Eastern Theater   Harper's Ferry, Virginia, is abandoned by rebels hoping to avoid being cut off by McClellan and Patterson who are advancing from the west and the north.

17 June 1861

Washington   The president observes Professor Thaddeus S C Lowe demonstrate the use of a hot-air balloon. Some military advisors hope to employ balloons for observation of enemy movements during the war.
Trans-Mississippi   In Missouri, Union troops establish themselves in the state capital at Jefferson City. Elsewhere, pro-Confederate troops are defeated at Boonville, thus providing Federals with further control of the Missouri River.

19 June 1861

The North   A meeting of Virginians loyal to the Union elects Francis H Pierpont as provisional governor of what will soon be West Virginia.

24 June 1861

Eastern Theater   At Mathias Point, Virginia, Confederate batteries are attacked by Federal gunboats. Three days later, Confederates repel spirited Union attempts to land troops at this position.

27 June 1861

Washington   In order to plan military strategies for the Southern coast, delegates from the army, navy and coast survey convene in the Federal capital. This body was later to make valuable recommendations throughout the war.

29 June 1861

Washington   President Lincoln and his cabinet meet with key military leaders to examine the future course to be taken by Union forces. Generals McDowell and Scott describe their plans, recognizing the importance of maintaining widespread public support and enthusiasm.

30 June 1861

Naval   The CSS *Sumter* successfully slips past the Union blockade, despite efforts by the USS *Brooklyn* to prevent it.

1 July 1861

Washington   In order to fill the need for Federal troops, the War Department decrees that both Kentucky and Tennessee are to be canvassed for volunteers. This despite the fact that Tennessee has joined the Confederacy, having voted to secede at the 6 May State Convention, a vote confirmed by public referendum in June. Kentucky has, at this point in time, voted to remain neutral.

2 July 1861

Washington   General John Frémont meets with President Lincoln. The two discuss Fré-

mont's upcoming command of the Missouri forces in an area of violent unrest.
The North   At Wheeling, West Virginia, the new legislature convenes, having been recognized by the United States.
Eastern Theater   Federal troops under General Robert Patterson head for the Shenandoah Valley where they intend to curtail the movement of Confederates toward Manassas, Virginia. At Hoke's Run in West Virginia Union forces clash with rebel troops resulting in a Federal victory.

3 July 1861

Eastern Theater   Patterson's soldiers march to Martinsburg, Virginia, causing the Confederates, who are commanded by General Joseph E Johnston, to pull back.

4 July 1861

Washington   It is Independence Day and in the Federal capital a special session of the 27th Congress meets. Called by the president, this session is to handle war measures partially sketched out by Lincoln in a message directed to the assembled body. According to the president, the North has done everything in its power to maintain peace and has attempted to solve problems precipitated by the South without resorting to war. Blaming Southerners for the Fort Sumter affair, the chief executive emphasizes that the questions facing the nation have to do with the United States maintaining 'its territorial integrity, against its own domestic foes.' Lincoln reiterates his position concerning the indivisibility of the Federal Union, once again making clear his stance on declar-

Above right: Uniforms of Northern and Southern forces at the outset of war.
Right: The Governor of Pennsylvania inspecting Union volunteers.
Below: John Bankhead Magruder, an experienced officer, sided with the Confederacy and was responsible for the victory at Bethel Church, Virginia, in June 1861.

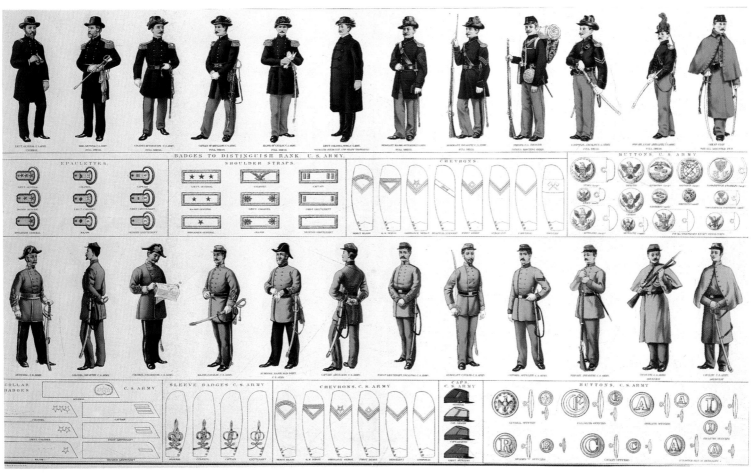

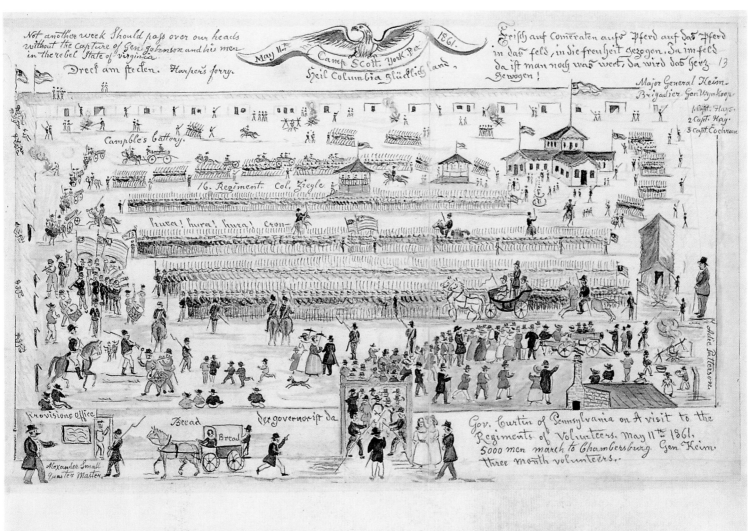

Above: Troopers of the 1st Virginia Cavalry at a halt during the last few days before the First Battle of Bull Run.

ing war against the Confederacy. He makes a request for an additional 400,000 men to aid the Union.

Eastern Theater Harper's Ferry is the site of a brief engagement between Confederates and Northern troops as the latter stream into the Shenandoah Valley.

5 July 1861

Trans-Mississippi Carthage, Missouri, witnesses an attack by Federal forces on prosecessionist Missouri troops under the command of Governor Claiborne Jackson, a staunch Confederate. While the Missouri troops are less well organized than the Union forces, they outnumber the latter three to one. As the Southern cavalry attacks both sides of the Union line, the Northern troops under Franz Sigel fall back. Total losses are tallied at 40 to 50 Confederates killed and 120 wounded, while the Union reports 13 deaths and 31 wounded. In spite of this, the battle is considered a Confederate victory. It slows considerably the Federal push into southwest Missouri and provides the South with a triumph important to Confederate morale.

8 July 1861

Trans-Mississippi The Confederacy, anxious to remove all Federal presence from the New Mexico Territory, places General Henry Hopkins Sibley in command of rebel troops in that area. In Florida, Missouri, an encampment of Confederates is attacked and dispersed by Federal troops.

10 July 1861

Washington President Lincoln, in a letter to the Inspector General of Kentucky's militia, Simon B Buckner, indicates that the Union forces will not enter that neutral state.

Eastern Theater General McClellan in West Virginia sends troops forward to meet Confederates at Rich Mountain. This force of four

regiments and a cavalry unit is under the command of General William S Rosecrans. In addition to this movement, General T A Morris is sent by McClellan to meet rebels at Laurel Hill, Virginia.

11 July 1861

Eastern Theater The road to Beverly, Virginia, is opened by General Rosecrans' troops. Attacking Colonel John Pegram's Confederates, Rosecrans forces the rebels to surrender at Rich Mountain. At Laurel Mountain, General Garnett's forces have evacuated their posts, heading for the Cheat River valley after General Morris attacks the Laurel Mountain position. Altogether the Union fatalities for these two engagements are listed at 12, with 49 wounded. The Confederate estimates are not available.

12 July 1861

Western Theater As McClellan occupies Beverly in West Virginia, the Confederate troops retreat from Laurel Hill. To the west and south of this position, another group of Union soldiers, under the command of Jacob Cox, is moving in to meet with rebels in the Great Kanawah valley. These Southern troops are under the command of former Virginia Governor General Henry Wise.

13 July 1861

Washington Missouri representative John Clark is expelled from the House by a vote of 94 to 45.

Western Theater At Carrickford, Virginia, Union troops crush the Confederate forces of General Robert S Garnett who is killed in the ensuing battle. McClellan has now enabled Federals to take control of the entire area in West Virginia, an important move forward for the Union due to the communications links, including railroads, found there. It also provides Union troops with a base of operations from which to launch raids into Virginia proper. The number of rebels killed at Carrickford totals 20 compared to a grand total of 53 Union lost.

Above: Confederate Simon Bolivar Buckner, the inspector general of Kentucky's militia in the first months of the civil war.

14 July 1861

Western Theater After the Rich Mountain and Laurel Hill battles, the North is anxious to press farther into Virginia. Toward this end, General McDowell advances on Fairfax Courthouse, Virginia, with 40,000 Union troops.

Naval In the harbor at Wilmington, North Carolina, the USS *Daylight* establishes a blockade. This effort is only partially effective and soon demands additional ships to make it successful.

17 July 1861

Western Theater General Beauregard requests aid in repulsing the Federal advance into Virginia. Beauregard is stationed near Manassas, Virginia, with a force of about 22,000 men. Confederate President Jefferson Davis orders General Joseph Johnston to Manassas so as to meet Beauregard's request for more troops.

18 July 1861

Eastern Theater Blackburn's Ford, Virginia, proves to be a test for the upcoming battle at Manassas, Virginia. McDowell's Union forces are encamped at nearby Centreville, and a small party of soldiers is sent forward to examine the area around Blackburn's Ford. The men meet Confederates under the command of James Longstreet and heavy skirmishing ensues during which the Federals lose 19 men and sustain 38 wounded. The rebels have 15 fatalities and 53 injured but succeed in pushing the Union troops back. In addition, a small clash occurs at Mitchell's Ford. Jefferson Davis, upon hearing of the Confederate success at Blackburn's Ford, says to Beauregard, 'God be praised for your successful beginning.' Blackburn's Ford is, however, only the first round in the campaign; a major battle has yet to be fought by both sides.

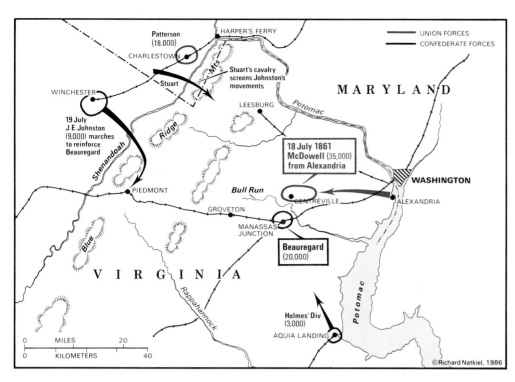

20 July 1861

Eastern Theater   Both Union and Confederate forces prepare for the imminent battle, Johnston's 1400 troops having joined those 2500 of Jackson at Manassas. McDowell is situated with around 1300 men near Sudley Ford on Bull Run, a creek running by Manassas; this creek will make the battle known as First Bull Run to Northerners, while Southerners know it as First Manassas – a second battle at this locale being fought in August 1862. Other Union troops are to travel by the Stone Bridge over Bull Run. There is little time left – one Union soldier comments on the 'ominous stillness.'

21 July 1861

Eastern Theater   Unknown to McDowell's troops, which are situated at Sudley Ford on Bull Run, Johnston has combined forces with Jackson. McDowell hopes to surprise the

Left: The movement of the rival forces prior to the Bull Run engagement.
Below: General Thomas Jackson wins his nickname of 'Stonewall' during a perilous moment for the South during the Bull Run battle.

rebels by striking them on the left flank of their position at the Stone Bridge, but after Northern artillery begins at about 0500 hours, the Confederates learn of the Union advance. Accordingly, General N G Evans meets McDowell's troops as the latter approach from Sudley Ford, holding the Southern position until around noon. The Confederates then fall back to Henry House Hill where Evans and others, Jackson among them, make a strong stand. (It is because of his unit's stout defense that Jackson will thereafter be known as 'Stonewall'.) McDowell's forces advance on this Confederate position at Henry House Hill around 1400, Beauregard and Johnston aiding Evans' beleaguered troops. Despite Union attempts to charge this position, the rebels hold fast and are successful in driving the Federals back in defeat. As McDowell's men pull away, panic strikes when a shell destroys a wagon; the main road of retreat is blocked and the Union troops scatter. The Confederate victory is observed by Jefferson Davis from Manassas, Virginia. It is a costly triumph: the rebels list 387 dead, 1582 wounded, 13 missing; Union troops lose 460 men, sustain 1124 injuries and list 1312 as missing. Lincoln, learning of the defeat, immediately closets himself with his cabinet, and throughout the North runs the conviction that the war has begun in earnest.

Below: Bull Run (Manassas) was the first major land battle of the civil war.

22 July 1861

Secession   Confusion continues in Missouri as the State Convention meets at Jefferson City, voting to uphold the Union and providing for a new government to be established at St Louis. Pro-South Governor Claiborne Jackson continues to claim that his administration is the only legal body in the state.

Above: Irish troops under the command of Colonel Michael Corcoran lead a Union attack during the Battle of Bull Run.

24 July 1861

Eastern Theater   In West Virginia, Union General Jacob Cox attacks Confederates who are commanded by General Henry Wise. This action at Tyler Mountain causes Wise to evacuate the area around Charleston and to pull back to Gauley Bridge.

25 July 1861

Washington   The Crittenden Resolution passes, 30-5. This bill states that the war is to be fought to preserve the Union and uphold the Constitution, not to alter slavery in its established form.

Trans-Mississippi   Missouri remains an area of unrest. Fighting breaks out at Harrisville and at Dug Springs. Confederates in the New Mexico Territory clash with Union troops from Fort Fillmore; the rebels, under Captain John Baylor, hope to press the Federals to leave the Southwest, which would open the area to Confederate control. The Union soldiers are able to push the rebels back, however. The following day, the same Union troops, under the command of Major Isaac Lynde, are confronted at Fort Fillmore by Baylor's troops and Lynde abandons the position. This despite the fact that Lynde's forces outnumber Baylor's, the rebels having but 250 men to the Federals' 500. Lynde is subsequently discharged from the army for this action, but after the war is placed on the retirement list.

27 July 1861

Washington   At the Northern capital, President Lincoln hands over command of the Federal Army of the Potomac to General

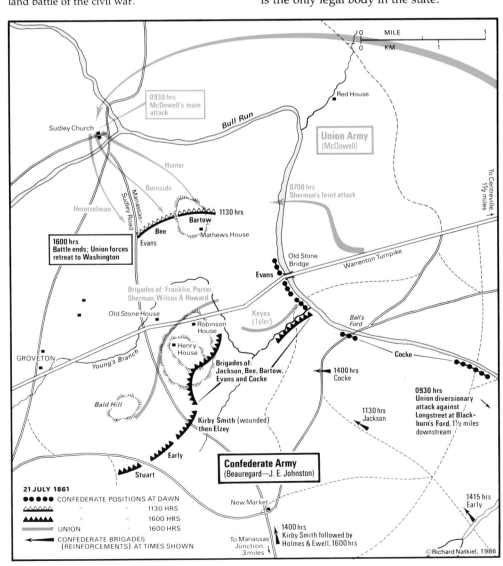

Above right: Major-General Irwin McDowell, the ill-fated Union commander at Bull Run.
Above, far right: George Brinton McClellan, Union general-in-chief from November 1861.
Right: Union troops on the retreat at Bull Run. Although the Union forces had a clever plan, the raw troops were unable to carry it out.

Above: Union troops attempt to prevent the widespread retreat from Bull Run turning into a complete rout.

George McClellan. The latter replaces McDowell, whose forces had been so badly beaten at Bull Run. Lincoln indicates that Union forces should push toward Tennessee by seizing Manassas Junction, Virginia, and Strasburg, Kentucky, in the strategically vital Shenandoah Valley.

30 July 1861

Washington   Secretary of War Simon Cameron is pressed by General Benjamin Butler at Fort Monroe, Virginia, to make a determined policy concerning former slaves now in Federal hands. Butler by now has about 900 former slaves and is unclear as to their status as property. He asks Cameron, 'What shall be done with them?'

Secession   In Missouri, the State Convention votes 56-25 to declare the governor's office open. In addition, the secretary of state and lieutenant governor's offices are now vacant, as are the seats in the legislature. Most of those holding office in Missouri were pro-Confederate. The following day, Hamilton Gamble is elected governor of pro-Union Missouri.

31 July 1861

Washington   President Lincoln names Ulysses S Grant stationed in Illinois as a general of volunteers. The month has seen a variety of military activity at Bull Run and elsewhere. The Federal blockade is fairly successful, although Confederate privateers are still quite active. Throughout the North and the South civilians and soldiers alike prepare for further action as it becomes clear that the war will not be over in a short time but is likely to continue for some months.

1 August 1861

The Confederacy   Captain John Baylor, who successfully routed Union troops at Fort Fillmore, decrees that all territory in Arizona and New Mexico south of the 34th parallel belongs to the Confederate States of America. There is some dissent among pro-Unionists in New Mexico who object to the wholesale takeover of their territory. Advising General Johnston to take advantage of 'the weakness' which would be felt by the Union forces after their defeat at Bull Run, Confederate President Jefferson Davis urges further action in Virginia. He sends General Robert E Lee to take top command of forces in the area of West Virginia after General Garnett's defeat at Carrickford.

2 August 1861

Washington   For the first time in United States history, the Congress passes a national income tax bill which provides also for tariffs to aid in the war effort. These congressional measures are to raise $500 million for Union support. The income tax of three percent is applicable to incomes exceeding $800 per year, but is never actually put into effect.

Trans-Mississippi   Another fort in the Southwest, Fort Stanton, in the New Mexico Territory, is evacuated by Federal troops as a result of Baylor's Confederates. Further disturbances occur in Missouri; Dug Springs is the site of a small clash between Federals led by Nathaniel Lyon and pro-secessionists under General McCulloch's command. General Frémont sends reinforcements to General Lyon who anticipates continued unrest in southwestern Missouri.

5 August 1861

Trans-Mississippi   In Missouri, General Nathaniel Lyon pulls his troops out of Dug Springs as reports indicate that Confederates are advancing in large numbers.

Naval   The USS *Vincennes* captures a rebel blockade-runner, the *Alvarado*, and burns it off the coast of Florida near Fernandina.

6 August 1861

Washington   Lincoln is empowered by Congress to pass measures concerning army and navy actions. The president decides that slaves used by the South against the North will be freed. Since there is some dispute as to Kentucky's neutral position, a Union military camp is established near Lexington in a show of Federal force.

7 August 1861

Eastern Theater   In Virginia, where General Benjamin Butler is in command at Fort Monroe, the town of Hampton is burned by Confederates. The commander, General John Bankhead Magruder, indicates that the action is partially in response to Butler's quartering of runaway slaves.

Naval   In a further attempt to improve Union naval operations, a new version of ironclad is put into production and later proves to be a vital part of Union operations.

8 August 1861

Washington In further reply to General Butler's queries, Secretary of War Simon Cameron points out the need for Union troops to adhere to fugitive slave laws, but only in Union territory. Those states in insurrection were exempt from this protection. Further, Cameron tells Butler that escaped slaves cannot be returned to owners in the Confederate states.

10 August 1861

Trans-Mississippi General Nathaniel Lyon is killed at Wilson's Creek, Missouri, where he has led 5200 men to meet rebel troops under the command of General Benjamin McCulloch. The Confederates are joined in this encounter by pro-southern Missouri militia under the command of Sterling Price. While Union troops are defeated at Wilson's Creek, they put up a valiant fight, pushing back two rebel charges on Bloody Ridge, the spot where Lyon falls. After this fatality, the Federals pull back, commanded now by Major Samuel Sturgis, and march to Rolla, Missouri, to the southwest of St Louis. The Confederates' force of 15,000 was depleted by 421 deaths and 1300 wounded as compared to Federal losses of 263 fatalities and 721 injuries. The Battle of Wilson's Creek is the second important clash between the two enemies and gives the South another significant victory over the North following that of Bull Run in Virginia.

12 August 1861

Trans-Mississippi In Texas, Confederates are attacked by Apache Indians who kill 15. It is not Confederate practice to make war with the Indians, engaged as they are in efforts to gain control of the Southwest for the benefit of the Confederacy.

14 August 1861

Eastern Theater Grievances among the troops of the 79th New York Regiment provoke mutiny by these volunteers. Among other things, the men requested, and had been denied, a furlough, precipitating an action that results in several arrests and places the entire unit under armed guard.

Trans-Mississippi Due to the unsettled conditions in St Louis, Missouri, General John Frémont issues a declaration of martial law in that city.

15 August 1861

Eastern Theater Another group of soldiers, the 2nd Maine Volunteers, mutinies. Altogether 60 men are assigned to duty on Dry Tortugas off Key West, Florida, as a disciplinary measure.

Trans-Mississippi General Frémont fears continuing conflict in Missouri, so he requests aid from Washington. Lincoln recognizes threats posed by McCulloch and Price, who can easily invade with Confederate forces. The president therefore directs the War Department to arrange reinforcements for Frémont.

16 August 1861

The North In several separate cases, certain newspapers in the Union states are brought to court for alleged pro-Confederate leanings, among them the Brooklyn *Eagle*, the New York *Journal of Commerce* and the New York *Daily News*.

Trans-Mississippi Missouri continues to experience clashes between Northern and Southern forces, this time near Fredericktown and Kirkville.

19 August 1861

The North Seizure of pro-South newspapers continues as offices in West Chester and Easton, Pennsylvania, are attacked by loyal Unionists. An *Essex County Democrat* editor in Haverhill, Massachusetts, is tarred and feathered for similar Southern sympathies expressed in the newspaper.

The Confederacy In an action which does little to settle the discord in Missouri, the Congress of the Confederacy allies with that state, essentially providing for the establishment of a Confederate state government.

20 August 1861

The Confederacy President Jefferson Davis approves the addition of more commissioners to represent the Confederacy in Europe. It is hoped that supplies and armaments so necessary to Southern victory will be obtained from France, Britain and Spain.

Trans-Mississippi Skirmishing continues in Missouri: Jonesboro is the site of fighting which follows clashes between Union and Confederate forces at Klapsford several days earlier.

24 August 1861

The Confederacy At Richmond, Virginia, three new Confederate commissioners to Europe are appointed: John Slidell to France; James Mason to Britain; and Pierre Rost to Spain.

26 August 1861

Eastern Theater Virginia is a scene of much action as skirmishing breaks out at Wayne Court House and Blue's House in the western regions of the state.

Naval At Hampton Roads, Virginia, Union vessels move out toward Cape Hatteras, North Carolina, in preparation for a Federal assault on Confederate fortifications there. This operation is under the command of Commodore Silas Stringham and General Benjamin Butler who have eight vessels and 900 men at their disposal.

27 August 1861

Eastern Theater The Union expeditionary force at Cape Hatteras, North Carolina, lands troops under fire. Confederate batteries attempt to prevent a Federal takeover of the area, without sucess. The rebels had established two positions, Fort Clark and Fort Hatteras, but abandon the former, enabling the Union to occupy it with no resistance. The following days sees the surrender of Fort Hatteras, which sustains considerable damage from Federal batteries. There are few casualties among Union or Confederate troops. The successful takeover by the Federals of this strategic point on Hatteras Inlet gives the North an important advantage in its efforts to crush the blockade-runners, since the area commands control of an important route used by those Confederate vessels. The blockade is rapidly becoming one of the North's best strategies in the war.

30 August 1861

Trans-Mississippi General John Frémont, in an action which Lincoln later terms 'dictatorial,' declares martial law throughout Missouri. In an unauthorized act, Frémont allowed for the confiscation of property belonging to 'those who shall take up arms against the United States,' and also makes an emancipation proclamation concerning slaves of pro-Southerners: 'their slaves . . . are hereby declared free men.' In defense of this extremely unpopular move, Frémont explains that Missouri suffers from 'helplessness of civil authority and total insecurity of life.'

1 September 1861

Eastern Theater Western Virginia is again an area of light military activity, Blue Creek, Boone Court House and Burlington all witnessing their share of brief skirmishing.

Trans-Mississippi Jefferson County, Missouri, is the focus of action in the West. At Cape Girardeau in Missouri, General Ulysses S Grant assumes command of Federal forces.

2 September 1861

Washington In response to General Frémont's proclamations concerning martial law and emancipation of slaves, President Lincoln communicates to the general his concerns that the actions are precipitate. The president feels that there is a danger of alienating Southern Federal sympathizers and 'perhaps ruin our rather fair prospect for Kentucky.'

3 September 1861

Western Theater General Polk orders Southern troops into Kentucky in order to hold Confederate positions there. These forces are under the command of Gideon Pillow, and the move effectively terminates Kentucky's neutral status. General Polk's orders result in part from the belief held by Confederates that the Union would soon attempt to take military control of Kentucky.

Below: Union officer General Nathaniel Lyon was killed at Wilson's Creek, Missouri, in a battle with Confederates under McCulloch.

Above: Generals Nathaniel Lyon and Franz Sigel confer during operations to secure Missouri for the Union.

5 September 1861

Washington The president and the cabinet confer with General Scott, discussing General Frémont's conduct and future position in the Army.

Western Theater General Grant, upon hearing of Polk's move into Columbus, Kentucky, begins preparations for an expedition to Paducah, Kentucky, which is near the mouth of the Cumberland River.

6 September 1861

Western Theater General Grant's forces move into Paducah, Kentucky, in order to prevent Confederates from seizing the city. The action, provoking no fighting or bloodshed, proves to be strategically critical as it allows Federals an important foothold in an area that will be central to the western river campaign in the upcoming year. General Charles F Smith is given command of forces in western Kentucky as General Grant leaves for his headquarters at Cairo, Illinois.

9 September 1861

Washington General Frémont's conduct in Missouri continues to worry President Lincoln, who is advised by some military officials to relieve Frémont of his command there. The president directs General David Hunter to go to Missouri to provide Frémont with aid.

Eastern Theater General Rosecrans' troops advance on Confederates near Carnifex Ferry, Virginia, where skirmishing has been continuing, indicating the probability of a battle in that area in the future.

10 September 1861

Washington The president receives Mrs John Frémont, wife of the general; she has traveled to the Union capital to provide support for her husband's position in Missouri. She is concerned about Lincoln's being in-

fluenced against General Frémont, and the interview, by some accounts, is not a calm one.

Eastern Theater Confederates at Carnifex Ferry, Virginia, fall back after being attacked by General Rosecrans. The Union troops outnumber the Southerners, and the Northern victory is instrumental in helping to preserve western Virginia for the Union.

11 September 1861

Washington The proclamations issued by General Frémont concerning property confiscation and the emancipation of slaves in Missouri, issued on 30 August 1861, prompt President Lincoln to write to the general. Lincoln tells Frémont that the proclamations must be altered in order to align them with Federal Acts of Congress, otherwise they remain unacceptable.

Eastern Theater Fighting breaks out at Cheat Mountain, western Virginia, between General Lee's forces and those of General John Reynolds. Although Lee has planned a surprise attack on Reynolds' Union forces at Cheat Mountain and at Elkwater, severe precipitation and the difficult terrain prevent Confederates from carrying out the assault as designed. Federal troops hold their ground as the rebels pull back, and this Union victory at Cheat Mountain secures the area of West Virginia for the North. Estimates of Confederate casualties total near 100; Federals killed and wounded tally only 21 men.

12 September 1861

Washington Lincoln communicates with Mrs Frémont about her husband, assuring her that he, the president, is not 'acting in any hostility' toward the general. Accordingly, he dispatches Judge Joseph Holt to St Louis, Missouri, with instructions to urge moderation and modification of Frémont's proclamation of 30 August.

16 September 1861

Western Theater In Kentucky, the Cumberland River is the scene of intensified action as the USS *Conestoga* takes two Confederate ves-

Below: Southern recruits head off their initial military training.

sels. Ship Island, Mississippi, is evacuated by rebel forces, leaving the area open to subsequent occupation by Union troops. The North is to use Ship Island as an operating base for action along the Gulf Coast.
Trans-Mississippi In Missouri, Confederate General Price continues to press Colonel Mulligan's troops at Lexington; the latter is waiting for help from General Frémont.

18 September 1861

Washington The president meets with his cabinet; General Frémont is once again the topic of discussion as reports concerning his command in the West are presented. The secretary of the navy receives word that Federal expeditions to the Southern coast are to commence within the month.
The North Another publication, the Louisville, Kentucky, *Courier,* is prevented from using the postal service. The newspaper has indicated an alleged hostility to the Union

Below: A Union call for volunteers. Bull Run shattered the myth that the war would end within a few months.

cause and several employees are arrested by Federal officials when the headquarters of the *Courier* are seized.

19 September 1861

Western Theater In Kentucky, the Confederates are making a strong defense along a line including the area around Cumberland Gap, Bowling Green and Columbus. Pro-Union Kentucky troops are driven out of the vicinity of Barboursville, Kentucky, by General Felix Zollicoffer's rebel forces.
Trans-Mississippi Beleaguered Union troops at Lexington, Missouri, are acutely aware of their precarious position as Price's forces continue to lay siege to the city. Unless reinforcements appear, surrender is clearly inevitable.

20 September 1861

Trans-Mississippi General John Frémont's inaction in bringing relief to Colonel Mulligan's troops at Lexington, Missouri, leads to the enforced surrender of those forces after more than a week of siege. General Sterling Price, the Confederate officer who led the

offensive, lost 25 men out of 18,000 troops, while Mulligan's force of 3600 Federals was reduced by 39 fatalities. Because of Frémont's failure to send reinforcements, the general receives further criticism of his already questionable behavior in handling matters.

23 September 1861

Trans-Mississippi General Frémont's sensitivity to criticism provokes him to close the offices of the St Louis *Evening News* and to arrest the editor of that publication. The latter raised some questions about Frémont's inaction during the recent siege of Lexington, Missouri.

25 September 1861

Eastern Theater Forces led by General Lee and General Rosecrans continue to converge on the Kanawha Valley of western Virginia.
Western Theater Minor clashes occur between Union and Confederate troops near the Cumberland River in Kentucky and also near Lewinsville, Virginia; and at Canada Alamosa, New Mexico Territory.

27 September 1861

Washington In a meeting with the cabinet, President Lincoln and General McClellan confer over plans for an offensive in Virginia. There is much public pressure for increased action in this area.

30 September 1861

Washington After four weeks of brief engagements but no major battles between Union and Confederate forces, President Lincoln is left anxious to establish firm control in Kentucky and settle matters with General Frémont in Missouri. In addition, the lack of military action in Virginia continues to draw criticism from both civilian and military observers.

1 October 1861

Washington President Lincoln appoints General Benjamin Butler to the post of commander of the Department of New England; this branch of the army is used largely to recruit and train soldiers for upcoming campaigns. The cabinet confers with Generals Scott and McClellan. In addition, the chief executive directs his cabinet to make preparations for the implementation of an east coast expedition to commence in November. This eventually is known as the Port Royal, South Carolina, operation under the command of General Thomas S Sherman.
The Confederacy Centreville, Virginia, is the site of a strategy planning session between Confederate President Jefferson Davis and Generals Johnston, Beauregard and Smith. They meet to discuss a possible solution to problems posed by the Southern offensive in Virginia which is what the citizenry of the Confederate nation are currently demanding. An assessment of the army's capabilities leads to the conclusion that such a move to attack the North at this time would be foolhardy. Southern troops are neither sufficiently provisioned nor available in the numbers necessary for an offensive; the consensus is to wait until spring and watch further developments on all fronts, not just in Virginia.
Naval Confederates seize the Federal sup-

FOURTH REGIMENT
NEW HAMPSHIRE

DOWN WITH THE REBELLION.

VOLUNTEERS.

ABLE BODIED MEN WANTED
FOR THE FOURTH REGIMENT.

The subscribers having been appointed Recruiting Officers, will open a Recruiting Office at

Where they will enlist all who would like to rally around the OLD STARS AND STRIPES, the emblem of America's Freedom.

$10 BOUNTY WILL BE ALLOWED!

Regular Army pay and Rations to commence on taking the oath.

Lieut. J. M. CLOUGH,
Sergt. W. B. ROWE.

Sept. 1861.

Fogg, Hadley & Co., Printers, Concord.

Above: Naval designer John Ericsson was the creator of the *Monitor*, the world's first battle-tested ironclad and a vessel which heralded a new era of sea warfare.

ply steamer *Fanny* at Pamlico Sound, North Carolina. In this capture, 31 Union soldiers are taken, along with a large amount of military supplies.

2 October 1861

Eastern Theater   Confederates are defeated at Chapmansville, Virginia; there is also skirmishing at Springfield Station in that same state.

Trans-Mississippi   Union troops succeed in disrupting a rebel camp at Charleston, Missouri, where clashes between pro-Union and secession groups have been occurring for several days.

3 October 1861

The Confederacy   The governor of Louisiana, Thomas O Moore, bans the shipment of cotton to Europe in order to place pressure on European nations. It is hoped that this may sway opinion in favor of recognizing the Confederacy.

Eastern Theater   Greenbriar, Virginia, sees the rout of Confederate troops. This victory enables the Northern forces, which have made this reconnaissance from their Cheat Mountain encampment, to take possession of valuable cattle and horses. The Pohick Church, Virginia, area is occupied by Federal forces.

4 October 1861

Washington   The president observes another balloon ascension by Thaddeus Lowe. The chief executive also meets with military and government officials concerning General Frémont's duties in the Department of the West. John Ericsson of New York submits a contract, which is approved by the cabinet, to build ironclad warships for the Union navy. The vessels ultimately constructed include the *Monitor*, which is later to take part in the first naval battle involving ironclads.

The Confederacy   Treaties are signed by the Confederates with the Cherokee, Shawnee and Seneca Indian tribes; this enables the rebels to utilize willing Indians in their confrontations with Union troops.

Naval   Two more Confederate vessels fail in an attempt to slip by the Federal blockade. The USS *South Carolina* seizes the rebel ships off Southwest Pass near New Orleans, Louisiana. The Southern forces attack Federal troops near the Hatteras Inlet forts, but with no success in their attempt to retake those critically positioned bases now in Union hands.

5 October 1861

Trans-Mississippi   In California, Federal troops carry out an expedition to Oak Grove and Temecula Ranch; their objective is to reveal the position of alleged pro-Confederates in the state.

International   Disputes about whether the British should or should not support the Confederacy's claim are in evidence as the London *Times* shows sympathy with the Union; the London *Post* speaks out in favor of recognizing the Confederacy.

7 October 1861

Washington   After discussion with his cabinet and military advisors, President Lincoln has sent Secretary of War Simon Cameron to investigate conditions in the West. Cameron carries a letter to General Samuel R Curtis from the president in which the latter asks for an assessment of General Frémont's ability to command.

Trans-Mississippi   In Missouri, General Frémont has gathered troops and set out on a mission to intercept Confederate General Sterling Price. This belated action ultimately does little to redeem Frémont in the eyes of the president and his advisors.

8 October 1861

Eastern Theater   General Robert Anderson, the former hero of Fort Sumter and currently in command of the Union Department of the Cumberland, is relieved of his post and replaced by General Sherman. Anderson has for a period of time been suffering from nervous strain and is unable to continue his military duties; after his departure from this last post, he never again resumes military active duty. Soon, General Sherman experiences similar exhaustion in the demanding position of head of the Cumberland troops, although Sherman remains in command at Louisville, Kentucky.

9 October 1861

Western Theater   Santa Rosa Island in Pensacola Bay, Florida, is the scene of a Confederate assault on Union batteries. A force of 1000 troops under the command of General Richard Heron Anderson tries unsuccessfully to destroy the Federal shore batteries and is obliged to withdraw. Troops from Fort Pickens on Santa Rosa Island are instrumental in the rebuff of this Southern force.

10 October 1861

The Confederacy   Confederate President Jefferson Davis expresses his concerns about troop organization, railroad transportation in the South and the use of blacks as laborers for the Confederate army, in a letter to General G W Smith. Later to come out in favor of their employment by the military, Davis at this early date is unable to speak with conviction for the use of slaves as regular soldiers.

12 October 1861

Trans-Mississippi   Minor clashes take place in Missouri which continues to be in an uproar, partly as a result of Frémont's orders. Fighting goes on for two days near Clintonville and Pomme de Terre, Missouri, and

Below: Confederate vessels attempt to break through the Union blockade at the mouth of the Mississippi, 12 October 1861.

Southern raiders under former Virginian and now partisan fighter, Jeff Thompson, push into the Ironton area of the state from Stoddard County.

Naval At the mouth of the Mississippi River the Confederate ironclad *Manassas* confronts the USS *Richmond* as well as the USS *Vincennes*. Despite the fact that both the *Richmond* and the *Vincennes* are run aground, they manage to escape. The Federal blockade resumes after a short time, but the clash is one that puts the Union at a psychological disadvantage.

International John Slidell, Confederate commissioner to France, and James Mason, commissioner to Britain, successfully slip past the Union blockade of Charleston, South Carolina, on the *Theodora*. Their next stop is Cuba, but they are en route to Europe in order to help their government buy armaments and to work for recognition of the Confederacy by European powers.

14 October 1861

Washington President Lincoln once again places himself in a vulnerable position, although one that he feels is defensible, when he orders General Winfield Scott to suspend the writ of habeas corpus. Scott is given the authority to implement suspension from points in Maine to the Federal capital.

Trans-Mississippi Jeff Thompson, one-time mayor of St Louis and now a pro-secessionist in the Missouri state militia, establishes southeastern Missouri as an area which he and his troops are determined to rid of Federal 'invaders.'

15 October 1861

Trans-Mississippi In Missouri, Thompson's raiders again strike a party of Union soldiers near Potosi, capture 50 and burn the Big River Bridge.

Naval In order to overtake the vessel that allegedly carries John Slidell and James

Mason, three Union gunboats leave New York in search of the *Nashville*, despite the fact that the commissioners are sailing to Cuba on the *Theodora*.

16 October 1861

The Confederacy Jefferson Davis encounters difficulties with Confederate army soldiers who are concerned with their states' defenses. The Confederate president is besieged with requests from regular soldiers who want to return home to aid their state militia. Davis feels it a matter of principle and public interest to deny these requests.

Eastern Theater Near Harper's Ferry, Virginia, there is a clash between Federals and rebels.

Trans-Mississippi Lexington, Missouri, is taken over by Union forces. The town had been under the control of a rebel garrison, although most of the Confederates have already evacuated the area.

18 October 1861

Washington The president meets with his cabinet to discuss General Winfield Scott's future military service. The aging commander of the army is now being considered for retirement of a voluntary nature, although it is clear that there are those who would be glad to see Scott leave active military duty, General McClellan among them. Lincoln is called upon to settle disagreements between McClellan and General Sherman; a coastal expedition to the South is being planned and McClellan is reluctant to furnish Sherman with the necessary troops for such a foray.

Western Theater Federals make a gunboat expedition down the Mississippi River, and minor fighting breaks out in Kentucky near Rockcastle Hills.

Trans-Mississippi Jeff Thompson's forces in Missouri clash with Northern troops from Cape Girardeau as the Ironton area continues

to experience the effects of a great deal of action and unrest.

20 October 1861

Eastern Theater The Potomac River area, under the command of Union General Nathaniel Banks, contains several important crossings, among them Edward's Ferry and Conrad's Ferry. Both of these are situated near Leesburg, Virginia, where Confederate General Nathan Evans is positioned. Federal activity in the area includes the occupation of Drainesville, Virginia, by General George McCall's troops. General Charles Stone is ordered by General McClellan to engage in a 'slight demonstration' so as to provoke the Confederates at Leesburg to some action. Although Stone complies, taking troops into the area, he pulls back after no conclusive engagement has taken place.

21 October 1861

Eastern Theater Leesburg, Virginia, witnesses battling between rebels and Federal troops, the latter under General Charles Stone's command. Stone is pushing toward Leesburg on orders from Washington and is assisted by Colonel Edward Baker, who is shuttling troops across the Potomac River from Ball's Bluff and Edward's Ferry. When fire from Confederate troops succeeds in pushing the Union troops back at Ball's Bluff and a retreat is in order, Colonel Baker is killed. The men attempt to withdraw but panic and confusion, as well as steep and hilly terrain along the river bank, prevent an orderly retreat. Men are drowned and shot as boats swamp and as the Union troops attempt to escape via the steep cliffs. Losses are severe: 49 killed, 158 wounded, 714 missing and presumed drowned; Confederates

Above: Union General Frémont's cavalry charge through Springfield, Missouri. Frémont was later sacked for excessive lethargy.

tally their casualties at 36 dead, 117 wounded, 12 missing. The disorderly and costly defeat of the Union troops causes a public outcry against General Stone who was charged by the press as being an inept commander, friendly toward the enemy and a traitor to the Northern cause. Colonel Baker, a former senator from Oregon and a friend of President Lincoln, is considered a martyr. There is little criticism aimed at General McClellan under whose orders the entire operation was carried out. The South is overjoyed at the victory and General Nathan Evans is given wide public acclaim as the hero of this Battle of Leesburg, or Ball's Bluff, Virginia.

22 October 1861

Washington The cabinet and President Lincoln meet to confer about General Frémont's situation in the west, and also to discuss the defeat at Ball's Bluff. In addition, it is learned that the Confederates are in control of all important points on the Potomac River south of Alexandria.

23 October 1861

Washington The writ of habeas corpus is suspended in the District of Columbia for all military-related cases.
Western Theater Skirmishing breaks out in Kentucky near West Liberty and at Hodgenville. This line of Confederate troops in Kentucky is a matter of grave concern to the Union and to General Sherman in particular as he does not want the Confederates to advance deeper into Kentucky.

24 October 1861

Washington President Lincoln reaches a decision concerning the termination of General John Frémont's command in the Western Department. Via General S R Curtis, he sends orders that relieve Frémont of his position and hand over control of the western troops to General David Hunter. Lincoln advises Curtis to withhold delivery of these orders if Frémont should 'be in the immediate presence of the enemy, in expectation of a battle.' Lincoln attends the funeral of Colonel Baker who was killed at Ball's Bluff, Virginia.

25 October 1861

Trans-Mississippi In Missouri, General Frémont's forces are on an expedition to rout Confederates under Sterling Price and are occupying Springfield, far from Price's location near Lexington. Frémont is aware that orders are on their way from Washington which will remove him from his command, and he is anxious to prevent or delay their delivery for as long as possible.
Naval An important project begins at Greenpoint, Long Island, with the laying of the keel of the USS *Monitor*. Although it is not the first ironclad vessel for either side, the *Monitor* will later earn a role in naval history because of its crucial battle with the Confederate ironclad, *Merrimack* (9 March 1862).

26 October 1861

Eastern Theater South Branch Bridge in western Virginia is an area of some minor skirmishing between Union and rebel soldiers. Romney, in the northern reaches of western Virginia, is the scene of Union action against Confederate forces, which are cleaned out with few casualties.

27 October 1861

Trans-Mississippi General Frémont is now in pursuit of Confederate General Sterling Price, whom Frémont believes to be moving toward Springfield, Missouri. In actuality, Price is not in that area, and Frémont's intended confrontation is not an immediate possibility.

29 October 1861

Eastern Theater An expedition to the Confederate coast leaves Hampton Roads, Virginia, under the command of Federal General Thomas W Sherman and Flag Officer Samuel Du Pont. This fleet of 77 vessels carries one of

Below: General Winfield Scott tenders his resignation to Lincoln and his cabinet on 1 November 1861.

Above: General George McClellan, Scott's replacement as head of the Union forces.

the largest forces yet assembled by the United States, consisting of about 12,000 men. The ships soon experience difficult weather in storms off Cape Hatteras, North Carolina.

31 October 1861

Washington General Winfield Scott makes a formal petition to President Lincoln concerning resignation from his position as general in chief of the Union army. Despite his experience – he is a veteran of both the War of 1812 and the Mexican War – Scott is prompted to this action by his advancing age and personality clashes with younger, ambitious military personnel. Scott convinces Lincoln to grant his retirement request and is succeeded by General McClellan.

Western Theater Fighting of a minor nature breaks out in Morgantown, Kentucky, with an attack on a Federal encampment by rebel soldiers. The Union troops are able to withstand this attack although the Confederates suffer moderate losses. The month ends with no major realignment on the part of either the North or the South; both sides are waiting for spring weather. Frémont continues to pursue Price's Confederates in Missouri.

1 November 1861

Washington General Winfield Scott voluntarily relinquishes his post as general in chief of the United States Army. Scott's decision allows 34-year-old General George Brinton McClellan to assume control of the army; President Lincoln and the cabinet bid General Scott farewell as the aging war hero makes his way to retirement at West Point. There is a great deal of enthusiasm for the younger McClellan, who appears to be eminently suited for the position he now assumes.

Eastern Theater In western Virginia, near Gauley Bridge and Cotton Hill, Confederates attack General Rosecrans' troops. The rebel force, under the command of General John B Floyd, clashes with Federals for three days but ultimately withdraws without achieving success.

Trans-Mississippi General Frémont, in Missouri, communicates with General Price's messengers, agreeing to exchange prisoners. This decision is made without Lincoln's authorization and the president later abrogates the arrangement.

Naval Off Cape Hatteras, North Carolina, a storm has scattered the Port Royal expedition ships, leaving a badly damaged fleet to make its way to its destination as best it can. The USS *Sabine* is lost in this heavy weather, the marines aboard escaping to safety before the vessel goes down.

4 November 1861

The Confederacy President Davis and General Beauregard continue to disagree over what was appropriate at Manassas, or Bull Run, Virginia. Davis contacts Generals Lee and Cooper in order to gain their support for his position as the president is aware of rumors circulating about his administration's ineptitude.

6 November 1861

The Confederacy The South holds elections, and the results of these prove that Jefferson Davis is as popular and respected a leader as when first chosen provisional president. He is elected to a six-year term of office as president of the Confederacy and is once again joined by Alexander Stephens as vice-president.

7 November 1861

Western Theater Cairo, Illinois, sees the departure of a force of 3500 Union soldiers under the command of General Ulysses S

Below: Union vessels bombard Southern forts at Port Royal; a successful operation that saw the Confederates abandon their positions at considerable cost.

Grant, which leaves for a point near Columbus, Kentucky, on the Mississippi. The troops travel in two gunboats and four other vessels, disembarking at Belmont, Missouri, opposite Confederate defenses at Columbus. Rebel General Leonidas Polk quickly crosses the river with a force of Confederates and pushes the Union troops back to their boats which carry them northward again. This inconclusive raid was accompanied by another reconnaissance from Paducah, Kentucky, to Columbus, but neither of these two actions results in gain for the North. There are casualties, however; Federal losses tally at 120 killed and 383 wounded. The rebels lose 105, with 494 wounded. The strategic value of this operation at Belmont, Missouri, is insignificant but it does allow General Grant to exercise his military capabilities without having to deal with the stress and danger of a major battle with the Confederates.

Naval   The Port Royal operation under Flag Officer S F Du Pont is under way, the Union squadron easily evading the relatively weak Confederate defenses as it sails into Port Royal Sound between Forts Beauregard and Walker. The ensuing exchange of fire between the Federal vessels and the shore batteries sees the rebels retreat from the two fortifications to take up positions inland. The North loses eight men in the battle, with 23 wounded, and Confederate losses are similarly light – 11 killed, 48 wounded, three captured, four missing. The Port Royal expedition is considered a success as it places Union troops in a strategically critical area between Savannah and Charleston, and Port Royal

Below: Union troops land at Fort Walker to carry out mopping-up operations after the retreat of the Southern garrison.

proves to be important as a refueling depot for the large number of Federal blockaders operating in the area.

8 November 1861

Western Theater   In Kentucky, pro-Unionists rise up against rebel troops in the eastern region of the state. The Confederate commander in charge there, General Felix Zollicoffer, is obliged to request reinforcements due to the disruption caused by these ardent mountaineer Unionists.

The Confederacy   The Port Royal operation causes telegraph offices in the South to be besieged with people wanting information about the Union invasion. Newspapers seize

Above: Confederate batteries at Fort Walker reply to Union fire during the fighting around Port Royal, 7 November 1861.

the opportunity to promote unity for the cause. The Charleston *Mercury* states, 'Our Yankee enemies will, sooner or later, learn to their cost the difference between invaders for spoils and power.' Despite this bravado, many civilians fear the possible outcome of this recent military action and hundreds prepare to evacuate the Atlantic coastal area.

International   The USS *San Jacinto,* under the command of Captain Charles Wilkes, stops at Havana, Cuba, and finds the two Confederate commissioners, James Mason

and John Slidell, awaiting passage to Europe on the British packet *Trent*. As the *Trent* sails into open waters in the Old Bahama Channel, the *San Jacinto* forces the British vessel to stop. Wilkes demands that Mason and Slidell be turned over to him. This accomplished, the *San Jacinto* sails to Hampton Roads, Virginia, with the two commissioners under armed guard. The British captain and crew make their way back to Britain with the families of Mason and Slidell still aboard the *Trent*. More immediately it becomes an international *cause célèbre* of such magnitude as to provoke the possibility of armed conflict between the United States and Britain, and it also creates an incident which the Confederacy can use against the Federals.

11 November 1861

Washington A celebration in honor of the new general in chief of the United States Army, General George Brinton McClellan, includes a torchlight parade in the nation's capital. On the Potomac, further balloon ascents take place under the direction of Professor Thaddeus Lowe.

13 November 1861

Washington President Lincoln calls on General McClellan at his home, waiting to speak with the new commander of the Union army. McClellan retires without acknowledging the president.

15 November 1861

Washington The war effort on the home front receives aid from the Young Men's Christian Association. A committee known as the US Christian Commission will help provide nurses for war hospitals, supplies and various other services to the Union forces.
International The larger ramifications of the *Trent* affair become apparent to both the North and South as the USS *San Jacinto* arrives at Fort Monroe, Virginia. Slidell and Mason are to be transferred to a prison at Fort Warren in Boston Harbor, Massachusetts. Captain Wilkes, the hero of the hour for his courageous and daring action in seizing the Confederate commissioners, is soon to receive more subdued acclaim as the cabinet and other advisors to the president recognize the seriousness of Wilkes' action. Not only does this *Trent* affair provide the Confederacy with an incident which might garner foreign support, it also places relations between Britain, France and the United States in a precarious position.

16 November 1861

Washington Postmaster General Montgomery Blair speaks out against Wilkes' action in capturing James Mason and John Slidell. He is joined in this protest by Senator Charles Sumner of Massachusetts; both men urge the surrender of the two Confederate commissioners.

18 November 1861

Washington In order to arrange for a Federal expedition to New Orleans, Commodore David Dixon Porter is charged with obtaining and provisioning gunboats for the Union.
Secession At Hatteras, North Carolina, a convention of pro-Union delegates from 42 counties meets and repudiates the order of 20 May 1861 concerning that state's secession from the Union. The convention appoints Marble Nash Taylor as provisional governor of North Carolina. In Kentucky, Confederate soldiers convene at Russellville and adopt a secession ordinance which results in Kentucky's having two state governments, one pro-North and the other pro-secession, just as in Missouri.
The Confederacy The Provisional Government of the Confederate States of America convenes in its fifth session at Richmond, Virginia.

20 November 1861

Washington General McClellan reviews some 60,000 troops in the nation's capital.
Trans-Mississippi Brief confrontations break out at Butler, Missouri. In California, Federal forces begin pursuit of a Confederate group, the Showalter Party, and several days later the troops capture 18 men including the leader, Daniel Showalter, southeast of Los Angeles, California
Eastern Theater Confederate General John B Floyd pulls his troops out of an encampment near Gauley River, Virginia, destroying tents and equipment in his quick withdrawal from the area.

21 November 1861

The Confederacy Reorganization of the Confederate cabinet places Judah Benjamin in the post of secretary of war. Benjamin succeeds Leroy Pope Walker in this slot, the latter having encountered a fair amount of criticism for what was considered an ineffectual handling of some military issues. The attorney general's position goes to Thomas Bragg. General Lloyd Tilighman is appointed commander of Forts Henry and Donelson on the Tennessee and Cumberland Rivers. These two positions are strategically located and are important to the Confederates because of their value to the South's defense against invasion.

Above: The fall of Port Royal allowed Union blockaders to use its facilities during the operations against Charleston and Savannah.

22 November 1861

Naval An engagement begins between Federal batteries at Fort Pickens, Florida, and Confederates at Forts McRee and Barrancas as well as the Pensacola Naval Yard. The Union ground forces are aided by the USS *Niagara* and the USS *Richmond* on the first day of the barrage. There is damage to both sides but it proves to be an ultimately inconclusive exchange.

24 November 1861

Washington Lincoln and his cabinet meet to discuss the *Trent* affair and its significance to the Northern war effort. The two Confederate commissioners, Slidell and Mason, arrive at Fort Warren in Boston, Massachusetts, on the USS *San Jacinto*.
Western Theater Federal troops achieve a foothold on Tybee Island in Georgia. This location on the Savannah River is of great strategic importance as it controls the entrance to the harbor and access to Fort Pulaski, the main fortification protecting Savannah from attack.

25 November 1861

Naval The Confederate Naval Department prepares to convert the former USS *Merrimack*, now the CSS *Virginia*, to an ironclad vessel. The CSS *Sumter* seizes a Federal ship while Union vessels succeed in capturing a blockade-runner in an action off the coast of South Carolina.

26 November 1861

The North At Wheeling in western Virginia a convention adopts a new constitution calling for the formation of West Virginia after that area's secession from the rest of the state. In Boston, Captain Wilkes, the instigator of the *Trent* affair, is honored for his accomplishments at a special banquet.

Above: A Southern zouave dressed in his French-inspired uniform.
Above right: A Louisiana Tiger zouave, a member of a unit with a fearsome reputation.

Naval The CSS *Sumter* seizes yet another Federal vessel in the Atlantic, while at Savannah, Georgia, rebels try without success to engage Union ships in fire from Fort Pulaski.

27 November 1861

Western Theater Ship Island, Mississippi, is the destination of a Union expeditionary force from Hampton Roads, Virginia. The intent is to set up a base of operations against New Orleans, Louisiana, and the general Gulf Coast area.
International The *Trent* affair is becoming more serious as word of the unlawful seizure of Confederate diplomats reaches Great Britain. In London, signs reading 'Outrage on the British Flag' begin to appear.

28 November 1861

The Confederacy The Provisional Congress at Richmond formally admits Missouri to the Confederacy.
Eastern Theater Federal officials in the Port Royal, South Carolina, vicinity are given authorization by Washington to seize agricultural products and slaves. The latter will work for the Federal defense of the area.

30 November 1861

International In a letter to Great Britain's minister to the United States, Lord Lyons, the British Foreign Secretary, Lord John Russell, communicates Britain's displeasure at the seizure of Confederate diplomats John Slidell and James Mason. He further requests that the Union apologize for the seizure and release the two diplomats to Britain's jurisdiction. The British navy is placed on alert but is told to avoid any hostilities. Lyons is directed to leave Washington, DC, in one week's time if there is no satisfactory response to Britain's request for redress of the affair.

1 December 1861

Washington In a communication to General McClellan, President Lincoln questions the new chief about the army's movement. The president is somewhat concerned that little action has taken place. He asks of the Army of the Potomac, 'How *long* would it require to actually get it in motion?'
Naval Successfully preventing the blockade-runner *Albion* from carrying supplies to the Confederates, the United States gunboat *Penguin* seizes the vessel and its cargo, which includes armaments, various foodstuffs, tin, copper, and military equipment valued near $100,000.

2 December 1861

Washington The 37th Congress meets in the nation's capital for its regularly scheduled session. The mood here is a less positive one than it had been in July when the Congress last met. There is continued concern over repercussions stemming from the *Trent* affair and there are some who feel that the army in Virginia ought to have made an offensive prior to the coming of winter. In general, there are criticisms of Lincoln's current military plans which are made up of a three-fold strategy: the plans call basically for the re-accession of Tennessee to facilitate the position of the army in the heart of the Confederacy; taking control of the Mississippi River and focusing on the eastern theater of war, especially between Richmond, Virginia, and Washington, DC.
Western Theater Federal General Henry Halleck is authorized to suspend the writ of habeas corpus in the area commanded by the Department of the Missouri.
Naval Newport News, Virginia, is the setting for a naval skirmish between four Union gunboats and the Confederate vessel *Patrick Henry*. As a result of the exchange, the *Patrick Henry* sustains considerable damage.

3 December 1861

Washington President Lincoln makes his State of the Union address to Congress. In this message the chief executive stresses that 'the Union must be preserved, and hence all indispensable means must be employed.'
Western Theater At Ship Island, Mississippi, the first of the troops in General Butler's expedition to the Gulf Coast area are landed. The Federal steamship *Constitution* carries this initial offensive force, made up of the 26th Massachusetts Regiment and the 9th Connecticut Regiment.

4 December 1861

Washington Another Federal office holder, Senator John Breckenridge of Kentucky, is expelled from his position, in this case by a vote of 36-0. Formerly Buchanan's vice-president, Breckenridge had joined the rebel army in November after exhausting all possibilities for the negotiation of peace between the two opposing forces.
Trans-Mississippi General Henry Halleck authorizes the arrest of any persons found helping the pro-secessionist movement in St Louis, Missouri. Those arrested for aiding the enemy are to be executed by the military.
International Britain's Queen Victoria issues a statement prohibiting any exports to the United States including armaments or materials for their production.

5 December 1861

Washington Congress considers several bills which would abolish slavery, particularly in territory 'in rebellion.' The secretary of war reports that the regular army has 20,334 men, and volunteers total 640,637. Naval Secretary Gideon Welles shows that the Federal navy tallies 22,000 sailors and marines.

7 December 1861

Eastern Theater The Potomac River Dam Number Five is the site of a small clash between Federals and rebel soldiers.
Western Theater Further military activity takes place as a group of Confederate troops takes Glasgow, Missouri.
Naval In a move to prevent the Confederate evasion of the blockade, the USS *Santiago de Cuba* stops the English ship *Eugenia Smith*. The Union vessel, under the command of Daniel Ridgely, succeeds in seizing J W Zacharie of New Orleans, Louisiana. Zacharie is a known Confederate purchasing agent and this incident serves to increase the agitation engendered by the *Trent* affair.

8 December 1861

Naval The Northern whaling industry is now affected by the conflict: the CSS *Sumter* seizes the whaler *Eben Dodge* in Atlantic waters.

9 December 1861

Washington To replace John Breckenridge as senator from Kentucky, Garret Davis is elected. As a result of criticism and debate over military defeats such as that at Ball's Bluff, the United States Senate calls for the establishment of the Joint Committee on the Conduct of the War. In a vote of 33-3, the approval of this committee paves the way for a series of investigations and interrogations which are uneven, though useful, in terms of resulting reports.

The Confederacy Along the southern Atlantic coast, plantation owners burn their cotton crops to prevent confiscation by the Union. Seizing every opportunity to enlarge upon the significance of such acts and the threats posed by the anticipated Union advance, the Charleston *Courier* asserts that by destroying the cotton, planters prevent the North from enjoying 'the extensive spoils with which they have feasted their imagination, and the obtainment of which was one of their chief objects.'

Trans-Mississippi Missouri remains the scene of brief and minor encounters between the Union and the Confederacy. Union Mills, Missouri, witnesses skirmishing, and in the Indian Territory, pro-South forces made up largely of Indians push pro-Union Creek Indians out of the vicinity of Chusto-Talasah, or Bird Creek, later to be known as Tulsa,

Below: Judah Philip Benjamin, holder of several cabinet posts under President Jefferson Davis during the civil war.

Oklahoma. The Confederate efforts are soon briefly discontinued, however, due to a shortage of adequate provisions and to the tenacity of the Creeks.

10 December 1861

Washington The proposal which will set up the Joint Committee on the Conduct of the War is finally approved by the Federal House of Representatives.

The Confederacy The Congress of the Confederacy admits Kentucky to the rebels' jurisdiction as their 13th state. This despite the sentiment of a majority of Kentucky's citizens against such a move. The tenure of Kentucky in the Confederacy is short-lived; barely one month later, the rebel forces have virtually relinquished claim on that state, preferring to try to hold Tennessee.

11 December 1861

The Confederacy Charleston, South Carolina, is ravaged by fire, and half of the city is destroyed, including much of the business district. Such an occurrence does psychological damage to the Confederacy, as Charleston is an important center of operations in the South. Combined with the Hilton Head Island occupation by Union troops and the relatively effective Federal blockade, the fire

proves to be extremely fortuitous to the strategy of the North.

13 December 1861

Eastern Theater Heavy fighting breaks out at Camp Allegheny, Buffalo Mountain, in western Virginia. Union troops under General R H Milroy attack the rebel encampment. Casualties in the Federal camp total 137, causing the force to fall back to Cheat Mountain. The Confederates suffer equally heavy losses (146 casualties) and they, too, retreat to Staunton, Virginia, in the Shenandoah Valley.

14 December 1861

International Britain falls into mourning at the unexpected death of Queen Victoria's husband and consort, His Royal Highness Prince Albert. Two weeks previously the prince had prepared correspondence relevant to the *Trent* affair and the seizure of Confederate diplomats Mason and Slidell; he had recommended a moderate course of action and the avoidance of outright hostilities with the United States over the affair. Despite this, there remains great apprehension over possible war between the United States and Britain.

17 December 1861

Eastern Theater Various military operations of a minor nature occur on this day. At Chisolm Island, South Carolina, there is skirmishing, and at Rockville in that state confrontations between Union soldiers and rebels take place. The Union garrison at Hilton Head poses such a threat to Confederates at Rockville that the Southerners leave the vicinity. Near Harper's Ferry, General 'Stonewall' Jackson carries out maneuvers along the Potomac River with his Confederate troops.

Naval Savannah Harbor is the scene of efforts by Federals to prevent shipping access: seven stone-laden vessels are sunk in the harbor entrance. On Green River in Kentucky, there is a battle which leaves 10 Union soldiers dead and 17 wounded. Confederate losses in this exchange total 33 killed and 55 wounded.

18 December 1861

Washington President Lincoln and his cabinet meet to discuss the *Trent* affair. Meanwhile, Lord Lyons, the British minister in Washington, receives his orders from London concerning Britain's demands for Slidell and Mason's immediate release. General McClellan and the president confer at the general's house about upcoming military strategy concerning the Union army.

19 December 1861

International A meeting between United States Secretary of State Seward and the British Minister Lord Lyons results in an exchange of information and terms over the *Trent* affair. Lyons explains Britain's position and gives the United States seven days in which to respond to those demands.

20 December 1861

Naval In the shipping lanes off Charleston, North Carolina, 16 outmoded whaling vessels are sunk in order to prevent access to the

city harbor by blockade-runners. Although the Union efforts in this respect were often repeated, they were of only limited effectiveness overall.

International The British navy sends two ships to Canada in order to have forces in readiness if the *Trent* affair should necessitate formal military action against the United States.

21 December 1861

Washington Further meetings between Lord Lyons and Secretary of State Seward result in a communication several days later to Lord Russell, British foreign minister. In this letter, Lyons asserts: 'I am so concerned that unless we give our friends here a good lesson this time, we shall have the same trouble with them again very soon . . . Surrender or war will have a very good effect on them.' It appears that there is, in fact, some sentiment in favor of a stepped-up confrontation between the two countries, although Britain continues to exhibit restraint in the matter. The Confederacy's attitude is one of hopeful anticipation, newspapers in the South promoting the possibility of armed conflict between the United States and Britain, and commenting on its favorable effects for the Confederacy.

Left: Battery Rogers on the Potomac, one of an impressive series of forts placed to prevent any seaborne assault against the Union capital.
Below: The 24-pounders of the 1st Connecticut Artillery protect Fort Richardson, Virginia.

23 December 1861

Washington Once again, Lord Lyons requests the surrender of Slidell and Mason in a communication with Seward. The cabinet meets with President Lincoln to discuss the matter further. After the latter conference, Massachusetts Senator Charles Sumner counsels the president on the advisability of releasing the two Confederate commissioners as soon as possible.

24 December 1861

Washington In the Federal capital, Congress passes duties on such luxury items as coffee, tea, sugar and molasses. At the War Department orders are given which suspend enlistment of cavalry soldiers. The president prepares for a full Christmas day, with expected meetings between members of the cabinet and himself on means of resolving the *Trent* affair.

25 December 1861

Washington Although the president and Mrs. Lincoln entertain guests for Christmas dinner, a decision concerning the disposition of Mason and Slidell is the focus of the day. The decision is to be forthcoming within the next 24 hours.
Eastern Theater The fighting continues at Cherry in western Virginia and near Fort Frederick, Maryland.

26 December 1861

Washington The United States agrees to surrender Confederate commissioners James

Mason and John Slidell into the keeping of Great Britain. After many meetings the cabinet acknowledges the seizure of the diplomats as illegal and terms the action a misunderstanding on the part of Captain Charles Wilkes. Lord Lyons receives the statement made by United States officials, and Secretary of State Seward orders the men released from their incarceration at Fort Warren in Massachusetts.
Trans-Mississippi St Louis, Missouri, is placed under martial law, a ruling which also extends to all railroads in that state. General Henry Halleck gives this order, which is unpopular at best. Clashes between pro-Union Creek Indians and Confederates occur at Christenahlah in Indian Territory. The retreating Creeks flee to Kansas after suffering extensive losses.
Naval Union blockaders are attacked by a small group of Confederate vessels at the mouth of the Savannah River. Despite its intent, the rebel offensive succeeds in dislodging the blockade only temporarily.

27 December 1861

Trans-Mississippi Skirmishes break out at Hallsville. Missouri, and a clash between rebels and Union soldiers, under the command of General Benjamin Prentiss at Mount

Above: Secretary of the Navy Gideon Welles was the mastermind behind the Union blockade of the South's major ports.

Sion, Missouri, results in the dispersion of the 900 Confederates who had been stationed there.

29 December 1861

Trans-Mississippi In Missouri, Jeff Thompson's rebels continue to be active against pro-Union forces in that state. The rebels there fight forces in Commerce and also attempt an attack against the steamer *City of Alton*.

30 December 1861

International James Mason and John Slidell are transferred to the custody of Lord Lyons, the British minister to the United States.

31 December 1861

Washington President Lincoln, due to the fact that General McClellan is ill, contacts General Halleck in Missouri. The chief executive is concerned that the Union army seems to lack direction and focus. He asks Halleck, 'are General Buell and yourself in concert?' hoping that the Western Department will be pressed into action of some sort.

These pages: A Northern propaganda poster depicting a column of triumphant 'Uncle Sams' marching through the South.

1862

1 January 1862

Eastern Theater   From Fort Pickens, Florida, Union troops fire on Confederate batteries at Pensacola. At Fort Barrancas there is a similar exchange of fire. The Port Royal area in South Carolina witnesses skirmishing as Federals continue their move to establish a permanent base at this important coastal location; this latter conflict results in rebel batteries being pushed out of their positions on Port Royal Island, South Carolina.

Western Theater   While skirmishes at Dayton, Missouri, cause some extensive damage to that town, General Halleck receives communications from Washington concerning the army's inactivity. Halleck is encouraged to advance with his own troops, as well as with forces under General Buell, on Nashville, Tennessee, and Columbus, Kentucky.

International   James Mason and John Slidell, the two Confederate commissioners seized on the *Trent* and now released by the Union government, board a British schooner off Provincetown, Massachusetts, in the first leg of their journey to England. The British vessel *Rinaldo* will take the two men to London where they will continue their interrupted attempt to gain recognition and support for the Confederacy. With their departure, the *Trent* affair, which caused so much consternation in Washington, DC, and which carried with it the possibility of a serious conflict between the British and American governments, is effectively closed.

3 January 1862

The Confederacy   The Confederate president, Jefferson Davis, expresses worry over the Union presence on Ship Island, Mississippi. In a letter to that state's governor, the president says that the troops stationed at Ship Island have planned an offensive which 'no doubt, is intended against Mobile or New Orleans.'

Eastern Theater   There is some movement of Union troops in Virginia as General Jackson's forces leave Winchester. The object of

Below: Edwin Stanton replaced Simon Cameron as Union war secretary on 15 January 1861.

this winter march, termed the Romney campaign, is the destruction of the lines of the Baltimore & Ohio Railroad and the dams along the Chesapeake and Ohio Canal. There is skirmishing at Big Bethel, Virginia, as the Union troops seize the town and Confederates fall back, evacuating the area.

5 January 1862

Eastern Theater   The operations around Hancock, Maryland, continue unabated as Confederate troops try to rout the Federals who have retreated to this position. The rebel batteries are located at positions along the Potomac River.

6 January 1862

Washington   There is growing sentiment in official circles against General McClellan as he appears to be reluctant to commit troops to any concerted action. Accordingly, a group of senators approach President Lincoln with the suggestion that McClellan be replaced. Lincoln rejects this proposal, and in like concern over what seems to be a general lack of intent, the president communicates with General Buell, who is positioned in Kentucky. The president makes strong recommendations that the Union forces advance in order to provide support for 'our friends in East Tennessee.'

7 January 1862

Eastern Theater   The troops which have been positioned at Hancock, Maryland, are now directed away from the vicinity of the Potomac, moving toward Romney, Virginia. A result of this is skirmishing between Federals and rebel soldiers at Blue's Gap, Virginia, where Colonel Dunning's Northern troops rout Confederates and seize two of their cannon.

9 January 1862

Washington   It is a matter of intense concern to the president that neither General Buell nor Halleck has responded to the administration's urging that the western troops advance. Lincoln discusses the issue with General McClellan who continues to recuperate from probable typhoid fever. The United States Congress is absorbed by discussions of the slavery problem, petitions being submitted which would curtail or terminate that institution. Some measures suggested include the possible colonization of former slaves elsewhere in the world; reimbursing owners for the loss of their property; emancipation of slaves; and various combinations of all these solutions.

10 January 1862

Western Theater   At Cairo, Illinois, General Grant's troops make preparations for an expedition into Kentucky by way of the Mississippi River. Near Prestonburg, Kentucky, Union forces under General Garfield clash with Humphrey Marshall's Confederates at the forks of Middle Creek. The result of this encounter is not completely decisive; both sides retreat but feel that they have won.

Eastern Theater   Romney, Virginia, is evacuated as General Jackson's troops push into the vicinity of western Virginia. The town is taken over by Confederates who will camp there during the cold weather.

11 January 1862

Washington   After considerable difficulty with the War Department's administration, President Lincoln accepts the resignation of Simon Cameron as war secretary. As a conciliatory gesture, Lincoln suggests appointing him to the post of minister to Russia. While Cameron and his department have been under considerable criticism for fraudulent actions and general incompetence, there has been little actual evidence that Cameron himself is a corrupt individual.

Eastern Theater   The Northern navy carries 15,000 troops under the command of General Ambrose Burnside to the coast of North Carolina. Commodore Louis Goldsborough is in charge of the naval squadron consisting of approximately 100 ships. These forces will augment the troops which have already established a firm hold in the Port Royal environs, causing further threat to Confederates in that area.

13 January 1862

Washington   To fill the position in his cabinet vacated by Simon Cameron, the president chooses Edwin Stanton. He was the attorney general in Buchanan's administration and is now a lawyer in the nation's capital. In a continuing effort to spur General Buell and General Halleck to action in the West, President Lincoln writes to both men, stating his wish to press the Confederacy, 'menacing him with superior forces at *different* points, at the *same* time.'

15 January 1862

Washington   Edwin Stanton receives the Senate's approval and becomes Lincoln's secretary of war. Stanton is an anti-slavery man and is a personal friend of General McClellan.

Western Theater   General Grant moves into the Kentucky-Tennessee area as gunboats on the Tennessee River reach toward Fort Henry. Both the naval and land forces work in tandem for a period of 10 days, pressing farther into Confederate territory, gathering information about enemy positions.

16 January 1862

Western Theater   Confederate troops under General Felix Zollicoffer are positioned north of the Cumberland River despite General Crittenden's orders to the contrary. This arrangement proves later to be an unsatisfactory one. Union troops are said to be pushing forward toward this rebel encampment.

Naval   Cedar Keys, Florida, sees the burning of blockade-runners, as well as dockside property, by the Federal navy.

17 January 1862

Naval   General Charles Smith attacks the area around Fort Henry on the Tennessee River.

18 January 1862

Western Theater   Union troops are beginning to close in on Confederate troops at Mill Springs and Somerset on the Cumberland River in Kentucky. General Crittenden's troops should be partially protected by Zollicoffer's soldiers, but they are not because of the latter's careless positioning of his men north of the Cumberland River.

19 January 1862

Western Theater   Rebels are defeated at Mill Springs, Kentucky, by Northern soldiers in a battle that claims 39 Union lives, wounds 207 and totals 15 Federals captured. The Southern forces indicate 125 killed, 309 wounded and 99 missing. Due to Zollicoffer's poor strategy, the rebels are obliged to retreat across the Cumberland River when Union General Thomas' men force them to fall back. Zollicoffer is killed in this battle; Crittenden, as senior officer, is castigated for having lost control of the positioning of troops. This exchange is perhaps most significant because the rebel defeat means a gap in the Confederate line of defense in the Tennessee-Kentucky area. This clash proves invaluable to the North as it enables the capture of 10 cannon, 100 wagons, over 1000 horses and a large number of boats as well as munitions and provisions.

20 January 1862

Naval   Federals attempt to disrupt rebel blockade running by sinking stone-laden vessels in the harbor at Charleston, South Carolina. Off the coast of Alabama, a Confederate ship trying to run the Union blockade is halted; running the *J W Wilder* ashore, Federals make an effort to board the vessel but are prevented from doing so by rebel troops in the area. However, the blockade-runner is put out of commission.

Above: Union troops disembark near Port Royal, a move which threatened the Confederate forces on Roanoke Island.
Right: Confederate General Henry Wise was placed in command of Southern forces on Roanoke Island on 22 January 1862.

21 January 1862

Western Theater   Union forces under General McClernand return to the Columbus, Kentucky, vicinity. Although this group of about 5000 men had only minimal contact with the rebels, their presence served to alert the Confederacy as to the strength of the Federal army in the area; in this respect it was a significant operation.

22 January 1862

Eastern Theater   The Port Royal force poses an important threat to Roanoke Island near Hatteras Inlet, South Carolina. The Union troops under General Burnside are gathering strength and it is thought that, by naming General Henry Wise to the rebel command on Roanoke, the Federals may be deterred from seizing yet another position in Confederate territory.

23 January 1862

Trans-Mississippi   Martial law in St Louis provides for seizure of pro-South property in the event that its owners have refused to support pro-Union fugitives. General Halleck,

Above: General Grant directing the Union assault on Fort Donelson near Dover, Tennessee. Its capture heralded Grant's rise to power.

who has strengthened these martial law orders, allows for the arrest of persons attempting to subvert the law.

Naval Another group of stone-laden ships is sunk in Charleston Harbor to prevent Confederate shipping from entering the port. A clash between Union blockaders and the rebel vessel *Calhoun* near the mouth of the Mississippi River results in that vessel being taken by the North. The following day two more Confederate ships are run aground and burned as they try to slip away from Federals at this Mississippi point near the Southwest Pass.

27 January 1862

Washington After months of delay and frustration, President Lincoln issues *General War Order Number One*: 'that the 22nd February 1862, be the day for a general movement of the Land and Naval forces of the United States against the insurgent forces.' The president does this only after exhortations by military and civilian advisors and in the hope that the Union armies as well as the Gulf naval forces will come to some conclusive action with the Confederates.

30 January 1862

The North In a brief ceremony at Greenpoint, Long Island, the ironclad *Monitor* is launched. John Ericsson, the Swedish-born designer of this ship and others like it, states that such vessels are critical to the Northern efforts and 'will admonish the leaders of the Southern Rebellion that the batteries on the banks of their rivers will no longer present barriers to the entrance of the Union forces.'

International The two Confederate commissioners from the *Trent* affair, James Mason and John Slidell, arrive in England after their delayed voyage is completed.

31 January 1862

Washington Another statement, the president's *Special War Order Number One*, is issued in the Federal capital (this special order supplemented Lincoln's *General War Order Number One* of 27 January 1862). Lincoln hopes to press the Army of the Potomac to confront the Confederates in Virginia as the Union troops in the area are told to take possession of 'a point upon the railroad south westward of what is known as Manassas Junction.'

International In Britain, Queen Victoria makes known once more the position of neutrality being observed by her country in the matter of the American Civil War. This statement does little to encourage the Confederacy, which hopes for support from European powers and which is now experiencing further doubts and diminished expectations as Federal forces seem to gather strength on all fronts.

1 February 1862

Western Theater Cairo, Illinois, sees preparations for an expedition under General Grant. This campaign will aim for the seizure of Fort Henry, a Confederate position on the Tennessee River. General Halleck in St Louis, Missouri, has approved of this movement and Grant's troops are now readying for the upcoming action.

3 February 1862

Washington President Lincoln communicates with General McClellan, who continues to disagree, both in public and private, with the chief executive. The two men have different preferences for the disposition of the Virginia forces: Lincoln favors a direct overland movement, his general in chief wishes to land troops on the coast and then march inland to the Confederate capital at Richmond, Virginia.

Western Theater General Grant's operation to Fort Henry gets under way as a Federal fleet moves up the Tennessee River and transports head for Paducah, Kentucky, from Cairo, Illinois.

International At Southampton in England, the Confederate steamer *Nashville* prepares to leave port for the United States. A Federal gunboat, the *Tuscarora*, sets off to capture the Southern vessel. Such an action is prevented, however, by the British ship HMS *Shannon*. The question of Southern blockade-runners using British ports remained contentious.

4 February 1862

The Confederacy Confederate House Delegates at the capital in Richmond, Virginia, enter into a debate concerning free blacks' enlistment in the Southern army. The *Examiner*, a Richmond newspaper, exhorts citizens to support the cause by re-enrollment in the army and a stronger commitment to the struggle between the North and South. Some observers are worried that Southerners are becoming tired and are 'not sufficiently alive to the necessity of exertion.'

5 February 1862

Western Theater General Grant's force is scheduled to open its attack on Fort Henry on the Tennessee River within 24 hours. General Charles Smith's men seize an evacuated Fort Heiman near Fort Henry, establishing Union troops there. Meanwhile, 3000 Confederates under General Lloyd Tilighman prepare as best they can for the upcoming attack on Fort Henry.

6 February 1862

Western Theater The Confederate position at Fort Henry is attacked by Federals. The Southern General Tilighman removes the bulk of his troops from the fort and remains behind with a handful of men to try to defend the post. At around 1100 hours the Union forces strike, shelling the fort from gunboats. The troops at the fort respond with their artillery, striking both the *Essex* and the *Cincinnati*; by 1400 hours the battle is over as the Confederate guns are destroyed by Union fire. Tilighman surrenders 78 soldiers and 16 hospital patients to Flag Officer Andrew Foote. Southern losses tally at five killed, 11 wounded and five missing; the Federals lose 11 men and sustain 31 injuries. The ground troops, some 15,000 strong, under General

Below: Andrew Foote led the Union gunboats during the attack on Fort Henry.

Grant, arrive too late to engage in the fighting. Having sent the major portion of his garrison to Fort Donelson on the Cumberland River, General Tilighman has at least prevented the Union force from easily taking immediate possession of the entire area. The Federals move from the vicinity to fortify their vessels as Confederate General Bushrod Johnson assumes command of Fort Donelson and makes a request for reinforcements and provisions.

7 February 1862

Western Theater   Federal troops under General Grant himself start an expedition to Fort Donelson near Dover, Tennessee, in preparation for the upcoming attempt to seize that Confederate position. Confederate troops are ordered into the area as the Kentucky defenses further deteriorate. Meetings among Confederate Generals Johnston, Beauregard and Hardee attest to the severity of this most recent military development between North and South. Roanoke Island sees the advance of General Burnside's forces. Commodore Goldsborough succeeds in overcoming some minor Southern positions there, and later in the day Burnside's troops land. On the Tennessee River, Union guns destroy two Confederate transports.

8 February 1862

Washington   Lincoln confers with General McClellan, asking for information about the Department of the West, and for reports on vessels sent toward Harper's Ferry on the Potomac River. The president, beset with worry over the nation's military strength, is also filled with concern for his son, Willie, who lies ill with typhoid.

Western Theater   The Confederates at Roanoke Island are moved to the northern end of their position as General Burnside's 7500 Union soldiers attack. Colonel Shaw's Confederates are seriously outnumbered and their regular commander, General Henry

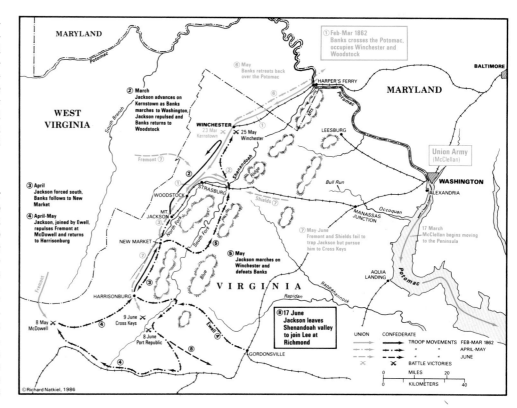

Above: 'Stonewall' Jackson's Valley campaign, one of the greatest feats of arms during the civil war. For more than three months his small force outwitted and outmaneuvered a succession of larger Union armies.
Below: Union troops under the leadership of General Ambrose Burnside storm the Confederate defenses on Roanoke Island. Its loss proved a serious setback for the South.

Wise, is too ill to be in charge, necessitating the temporary command of Shaw. The latter makes an attempt to hold the Southern position, but it is an exercise in futility. He surrenders after 23 men are killed and 62 are wounded. The Confederates relinquish 30 guns in this takeover and lose an important position on the Atlantic coast, a severe blow to the Southern war effort. Union losses in this exchange are totaled at 37 killed, 214 wounded and 13 missing.

Naval   Two Confederate vessels, the *Sallie Wood* and the *Muscle,* are taken by the Federals at Chickasaw, Mississippi. In a follow-up of Confederates fleeing the Roanoke Island battle, 13 Union gunboats traverse the Pasquotank River in the direction of Elizabeth City, North Carolina.

10 February 1862

Western Theater   Clean-up operations at Roanoke Island, North Carolina, are finished and General Burnside, now firmly established at this position, prepares for further campaigning against the Confederates in the area of New Berne. General Grant completes preparations for his offensive against Fort Donelson.

Naval   Gunboats under Union control meet Confederates at Elizabeth City, North Carolina, and demolish the remaining vessels in the Confederate fleet. On the Tennessee River, Union gunboats capture three Confederate vessels while six more are burned by secessionists to prevent their falling into Union hands.

11 February 1862

Western Theater   The action against Fort Donelson commences as General Grant's troops begin to march and General McClernand's Union forces move out from their position at Fort Henry. Federal gunboats travel up the Cumberland River. This Union activity provokes the evacuation by Confederates of Bowling Green, Kentucky, and

Below: Men of the 9th New York Regiment, one of the North's zouave units, storm a Southern entrenchment on Roanoke Island.

renders the previously fortified Kentucky line defenseless; only Columbus, Kentucky, remains relatively secure.

12 February 1862

Western Theater   As Grant's force of 40,000 encircles the hills around Fort Donelson and the town of Dover, Tennessee, the Federal gunboats move into position to attack from the river. Confederates at the fort number about 18,000. Further action in the Roanoke Island vicinity results in the possession of Edenton, North Carolina, by Union forces.

13 February 1862

Western Theater   The awaited attack on Fort Donelson occurs. The Confederate command has transferred to General John Floyd, whose arrival with Confederate reinforcements proves to be ultimately useless. The Federal attack from the right and left is led by General C F Smith and General McClernand, respectively, and Grant receives further aid from auxiliary troops by the end of the day. Fort Heiman nearby sees some brief action and portions of Bowling Green, Kentucky, are burned as the Southern evacuation of the area continues.

Above: Union vessels bombard Fort Donelson prior to the Confederates' unconditional surrender to General Grant's forces on 16 February.

14 February 1862

Washington   The war secretary, with the president's approval, issues orders releasing political prisoners who will take the oath of allegiance to the United States. A general amnesty is proclaimed for all those who comply with the oath and who agree to give no further aid to the rebellion.

Western Theater   The battle at Fort Donelson in the Cumberland River area is expanded by the arrival of four Union ironclads and several wooden vessels, although the easy victory which Grant anticipated is not forthcoming. The Union general sees a temporary withdrawal of this river force as shore batteries threaten serious damage to the Federal vessels. The Union ironclads *St Louis* and *Louisville* are badly hit and rendered virtually useless. Flag Officer Andrew Foote, who so ably performed at Fort Henry, is wounded in this rain of Southern shelling. Bowling Green, Kentucky, is taken by Federals. A meeting of Confederate commanders recommends that Gideon Pillow's forces attack the Federal right flank which lies to the south of Fort Donelson.

15 February 1862

Western Theater   Fighting continues on the Cumberland River as Confederates under General Gideon Pillow attempt to break through Federal lines which surround Fort Donelson. The Southerners succeed in this effort, providing their troops with an escape route toward Nashville, Tennessee. Hesitation on the part of several commanders places the Confederates back at their posts, while Grant tries to close the line with the help of Generals Smith and McClernand. He is partially successful in this attempt. In Dover, Tennessee, Confederate generals discuss their options; surrender seems inevitable but there is resistance from General Floyd. In the end, Floyd does leave the battle area with General Pillow, placing General Buckner in the position of having to surrender the fort. Given Union local superiority the garrison can do little to prevent the fort's capture.

16 February 1862

Western Theater In a statement which leaves the Southerners no room for negotiation, General Grant issues his terms for the disposition of Fort Donelson: 'No terms except unconditional and immediate surrender can be accepted. I propose to move immediately upon your works.' General Buckner is left with no alternative, and so relinquishes possession of the military position which had proved to be a costly one to hold. Estimates of Southern casualties hover around 1500, and it appears that somewhere near 1200 soldiers surrendered. Union troops under General Grant show losses of 500 killed, 2100 wounded and 224 missing out of a total fighting force of 27,000. Needless to say, this victory for the North is of major importance and proves to be similarly significant a defeat in Southern eyes. Tennessee and Kentucky are lost and the Cumberland and Tennessee Rivers are in Union control now. The following day, news of the battle reaches Washington, DC, where there is rejoicing over the outcome. The battle proves to be important to General Grant's career – he is now promoted to major general of volunteers. The Confederacy sees disruption throughout Tennessee as civilians attempt to flee the area occupied by Federal troops.

18 February 1862

The Confederacy The dismissal on the previous day of the Provisional Congress of the Confederacy is followed by the initial meeting of the 1st Congress of the Confederate States of America. Structured now as a two-part government, the Congress is composed of representatives exclusively from slaveholding states in the South, with the exception of Delaware and Maryland.

20 February 1862

Washington President and Mrs Lincoln suffer the tragedy of losing their 12-year-old son, Willie, to typhoid fever. This personal stress is compounded by news of fatalities at Fort Donelson; the president seems engulfed by sorrow.

Western Theater Further pullbacks of Confederate troops result in the evacuation of Columbus, Kentucky. In Tennessee, the Confederate Governor Isham Harris decrees that the state capital will be fixed at Memphis as Nashville is in the line of Union troop advances. At the latter location, the Southern army is commanded by General Albert Johnston to move to a position southeast of the city near Murfreesboro. A group of 1000 late arrivals to the Southern defense at Fort Donelson is captured by Union troops.

21 February 1862

The North The convicted slave trader Nathaniel Gordon is hanged at New York City, the first time the Union has ever imposed this punishment.

Trans-Mississippi A Confederate victory results when the forces of General H H Sibley attack Union troops near Fort Craig at Valverde, New Mexico Territory. The Federals under the command of Colonel E R S Canby lose 68 men, with 160 wounded and 35 missing out of a total of 3810 men. Southerners

Above: Confederate troops pull back through the Cumberland Gap after Grant's victory at Fort Donelson.

numbering 2600 suffer 31 deaths, 154 wounded and one missing. The Confederates move toward Santa Fe after seizing six pieces of Union artillery.

22 February 1862

The Confederacy After his election to the presidency of the Confederacy (up to now he has been provisional president), Jefferson Davis' inauguration is held at Richmond, Virginia. In his address to the Confederate nation, Davis says, 'We are in arms to renew such sacrifices as our fathers made to the holy cause of constitutional liberty.'

24 February 1862

Eastern Theater Harper's Ferry is taken over by General Banks' Union soldiers. Near Pohick Church, Virginia, there is minor skirmishing between Southern and Northern troops.

Western Theater At Nashville, Tennessee, Buell's Federals take over and the Confederate cavalry troops there under General Nathan Forrest are forced to retreat.

27 February 1862

The Confederacy Jefferson Davis is given authorization by the Confederate Congress to suspend the privilege of habeas corpus. The Confederate president issues a call for martial law in both Norfolk and Portsmouth, Virginia.

Naval The Federal ironclad *Monitor* leaves its New York harbor under sealed orders.

28 February 1862

The Confederacy Southerners hold a day of fasting at the request of President Davis. In writing to his commander of the Army of Northern Virginia, General Joseph Johnston, Jefferson Davis observes that there is a need for thoughtful, planned defense. He tells Johnston that 'traitors show the tendencies heretofore concealed, and the selfish grow clamorous . . . at such an hour, the wisdom of the trained, and the steadiness of the brave, possess a double value.'

Eastern Theater Charleston, Virginia, is occupied by Federal troops.

1 March 1862

The Confederacy Richmond, Virginia, witnesses the arrest of John Minor Botts for treason against the Confederacy. Botts, a former Virginian congressman and avowed neutral, is seized along with 30 others, among them the Reverend Alden Bosserman, a Universalist minister. The latter has prayed for an end to 'this unholy rebellion.' The Confederate capital is now under martial law, President Jefferson Davis placing General John Winder in control of the city.

Western Theater General Beauregard positions troops along the Mississippi River while General Henry Halleck directs General Grant to take his forces toward Eastport, Mississippi. There are brief clashes between Union and Confederate soldiers at Pittsburg Landing, where gunboats have traveled up the Tennessee River. They destroy a Confederate battery positioned there by General Beauregard's troops.

3 March 1862

Western Theater Accusations are leveled at General Ulysses Grant by General Henry Halleck concerning Grant's tardy appearance

Below: The clash at Pea Ridge, Arkansas, ended after a series of spirited Southern attacks were repulsed by Union forces under General Curtis.

Above: The CSS *Merrimack* steams toward the USS *Monitor* during the Battle of Hampton Roads, the first encounter between ironclads.

during the Fort Donelson takeover. Halleck is given permission by President Lincoln to transfer General C F Smith to command the troops going up the Tennessee River out of Fort Henry; it is felt that Grant's recent conduct does not warrant his taking responsibility for the upcoming action.

4 March 1862

Washington General Andrew Johnson receives Senate approval as the military governor of Tennessee.

The Confederacy General Robert E Lee is replaced by General John Pemberton as commander of the Confederate Department of South Carolina, Georgia and East Florida. Lee has been called to Richmond by President Jefferson Davis to assume duties as a military advisor in Virginia. The Confederate president runs into problems with various congressmen dissatisfied with the defense of the Mississippi River. These congressmen demand additional batteries to cover the river

despite the efforts of Davis' administration to provide the best defenses possible.

5 March 1862

Western Theater At Jackson, Tennessee, General Beauregard takes charge of defenses along the Mississippi valley. Federals begin to position themselves around Savannah, Tennessee, as General Johnston's Confederates begin a move to prevent the further entrenchment of Union forces in the area. General C F Smith's Federals at Savannah are quickly joined by three gunboats and 80 troop transports.

Trans-Mississippi Fighting continues in Arkansas as Sterling Price's Southerners combine with General Van Dorn's forces against Union General Samuel Curtis. An attack is imminent, Van Dorn positioning his troops just past Fayetteville and Elm Springs, Arkansas.

6 March 1862

Washington President Lincoln, in part responding to suggestions from various senators, requests the states' cooperation in devising ways to abolish slavery. This message to Congress indicates the availability of Federal financial funding for aiding emancipation efforts in individual states.

The Confederacy A proclamation is issued by the Confederate Congress concerning the destruction of valuable cotton and tobacco crops in the event that Northern troops advance farther into Virginia. Military authorities are charged with the responsibility for carrying out this disposal of Confederate property if the need arises.

Trans-Mississippi In Arkansas, near Fayetteville, forces under Confederate General Earl Van Dorn clash with Union soldiers under General Samuel Curtis. While this fighting is limited, it presages an upcoming battle. Van Dorn is anxious to gain an optimum position and therefore moves his troops to Pea Ridge.

Above: Albert Johnston, one of the South's best-remembered generals.
Right: The Battle of Hampton Roads saw Southern hopes of smashing the Union blockade dashed due to the arrival of the USS *Monitor*.

7 March 1862

Eastern Theater McClellan takes the Federal Army of the Potomac toward the southwestern region of Virginia where General Joseph Johnston's Confederates are encamped at Manassas. The Union soldiers are well positioned and are prepared to do battle with the Confederates whom they expect to vanquish easily. In Winchester, Virginia, there is skirmishing.

Trans-Mississippi The Federal forces at Pea Ridge, or Elkhorn Tavern, Arkansas, are surprised by General Van Dorn's Confederate troops in an attack from the latter's northern position. About 17,000 Confederates, including some Indian troops, make valiant attempts to rout the Union soldiers, but the North is ultimately victorious. Van Dorn's forces are made up of Missouri state guards under Sterling Price, as well as General McCulloch's division and General Pike's troops which are comprised of three Indian regiments.

8 March 1862

Washington The president and General McClellan discuss plans for the Army of the Potomac, and other military advisors concur with McClellan's desire to enter Virginia by way of the peninsula southeast of Richmond. In *General War Order Number Two*, the chief executive provides for certain of the Union troops to be positioned for defense of the Federal capital during the upcoming campaign, despite the fact that this will draw off troops from the offensive.

Trans-Mississippi The Battle of Pea Ridge, Arkansas, the most significant of Civil War battles in the Trans-Mississippi west, sees the death of both Generals McCulloch and McIntosh, depriving the Confederacy of two able commanders. Federals under General Curtis continue to hold out for a second day of fighting, which ends as Van Dorn and his

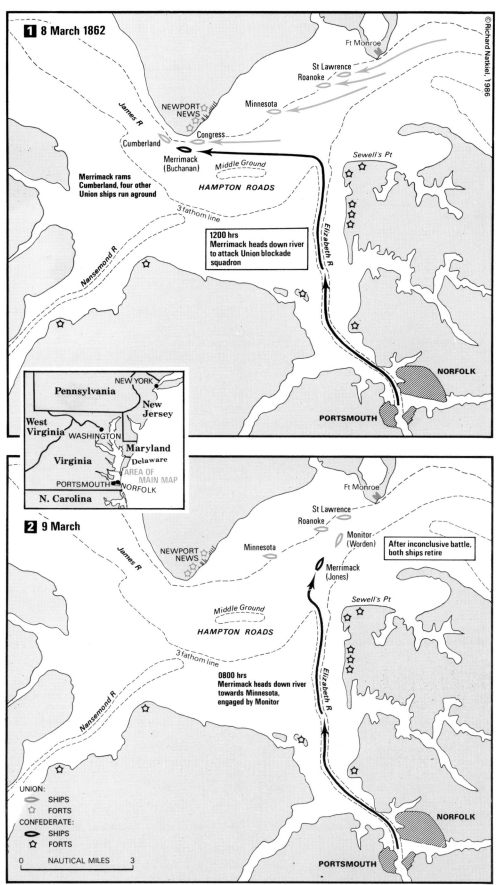

men retreat to the Arkansas River with orders to leave the state and head for the Mississippi River to aid in the defense of Confederate positions there. The tally of casualties shows that the Confederacy has lost around 800 men, while the North suffers 1384 dead and wounded.

Naval In Virginia, at Hampton Roads, the ironclad *Merrimack* approaches a squadron of Federal vessels, all much less well defended and ill-equipped to battle with the heavily armored Confederate ship. In the ensuing encounter, two Union vessels are put out of commission – the USS *Cumberland* and the USS *Roanoke* – and the USS *Minnesota* is heavily damaged. Flag Officer Franklin Buchanan of the *Merrimack* is slightly wounded during the fight, though in

Above: The USS *Monitor* (foreground) and the CSS *Merrimack* exchange broadsides at close quarters on 9 March.

general, few Confederates suffer serious injury. The Union forces suffer a greater number of casualties and damage to their ships is especially severe. A Confederate military observer notes, 'Pains, death, wounds, glory – that was the sum of it.' Late in the day of the battle between the *Merrimack* and these various Federal vessels, the USS *Monitor* appears in the harbor at Hampton Roads after a difficult journey south from New York.

9 March 1862

Eastern Theater   The Confederate army in Virginia under General Joseph Johnston moves near a position at Rappahannock Station close to the Rappahannock River. Union soldiers under McClellan move out, but do not engage rebels in any fighting. They soon return to Alexandria after finding only empty camps left behind by the Confederates.
Naval   In a battle of special significance to naval warfare, the CSS *Merrimack* and the USS *Monitor* clash in the harbor at Hampton Roads. Beginning around 0900 hours fighting continues for nearly two hours until injuries force both commanders to pull back. While the exchange of fire is impressive, there is relatively little damage done to either vessel and the battle has no real victor. Federals are considered to have a stronger position as the *Merrimack* is unable to easily maneuver due to its unwieldy construction. There is concern that the Confederate vessel may make its way to Washington, DC, or New York City, but this worry is soon dispelled.

11 March 1862

Washington   In issuing another major military order, *General War Order Number Three*, President Lincoln removes General George McClellan from his command as general in chief of the Union army. McClellan is given the Army of the Potomac and he, along with other generals, will be under the direction of the secretary of war; no general in chief is yet to be appointed.
The Confederacy   After their flight from the military action at Fort Donelson, Generals Floyd and Pillow submit reports to Confederate President Jefferson Davis. The president does not accept these reports and removes both Pillow and Floyd from their commands.
Eastern Theater   Manassas Junction, Virginia, is investigated by Union troops, who find little of value left in the wake of retreating Confederate soldiers. At Winchester, Virginia, 4600 Confederates are under the command of General Jackson who takes his troops southward.

13 March 1862

The Confederacy   General Robert E Lee is given the responsibility of overseeing Confederate military positions. Confederate President Jefferson Davis does not define the specific nature of this advisory post held by Lee.
Eastern Theater   Meetings between General McClellan and his staff provide a clearing house for plans concerning placement of the Army of the Potomac. General Johnston is situated near the Rappahannock and there is great concern to avoid direct confrontation there as Federals march on Richmond, Virginia. McClellan intends to bring troops to the Confederate capital via the York and James

Rivers. McClellan, intent on moving via the peninsula, is warned by President Lincoln's secretary of war that Washington, DC, must remain protected, as must Manassas Junction, Virginia. General McClellan is told to 'at all events, move such remainder of the army at once in pursuit of the enemy.'
Western Theater   General Burnside's troops disembark at New Berne, North Carolina, on the western branch of the Neuse River.
Trans-Mississippi   Skirmishing occurs at Point Pleasant, Missouri, leading to the area's capture by General Pope who also provokes the evacuation of New Madrid by his military actions. In this move, the Confederates abandon large quantities of arms and provisions estimated at a value of $1 million.

14 March 1862

Washington   In a continuing discussion of his position concerning slavery, President Lincoln attempts to justify the proposed financial compensation to slaveholders. Lincoln feels that such recompense 'would not be half as onerous as would be an equal sum, raised *now*, for the indefinite prosecution of the war.'
Western Theater   In North Carolina, the town of New Berne is taken by General Burnside's 11,000 men, who push General Branch's 14,000 Confederates out. This position is maintained by Federals for the duration of the war, proving an effective point of departure for inland expeditions. There are some 600 Confederate casualties after this battle, including 64 deaths. Union troops suffer 90 killed with 380 wounded.
Trans-Mississippi   The capture of New Madrid, Missouri, by General John Pope's Federals places the Northern forces in a posi-

tion which will enable them to make an assault on Island Number Ten in the Mississippi River. This latter Confederate post defends east Tennessee.

15 March 1862

Western Theater   General Grant resumes command of field forces in Tennessee after General Halleck absolves Grant of charges of misconduct at Fort Donelson.

17 March 1862

Eastern Theater   General McClellan and the Army of the Potomac move out on the Peninsular campaign, heading for the James and York Rivers.

18 March 1862

The Confederacy   Jefferson Davis names Judah Benjamin secretary of state. Benjamin has up until now served as war secretary and has been under criticism in that position.
Eastern Theater   At Aquia Creek, Virginia, Confederates occupy the town.
Western Theater   General Albert Johnston's Confederates begin arriving in Corinth, Mississippi, from Murfreesboro.

20 March 1862

Eastern Theater, Peninsular Campaign   At Strasburg, Virginia, where the day before there had been some action, there is a general pullback of Federals as General Jackson's forces advance. At Philippi, western Virginia, there is light skirmishing.

22 March 1862

Eastern Theater, Peninsular Campaign   Light fighting takes place at the town of Kernstown, Virginia, between General Shields' Union soldiers and General Jackson's advancing Confederates.

23 March 1862

Eastern Theater, Peninsular Campaign   About 9000 Union troops clash with 4200 Confederates at Kernstown, Virginia. Skirmishing of the previous day has led the Confederates to assume a smaller enemy force but, although outnumbered, Jackson's

Above: Despite several hours of heavy firing neither the *Monitor* nor the *Merrimack* suffered major damage at Hampton Roads.

troops perform admirably. They retreat, ultimately, after suffering 80 killed, 375 wounded, 263 missing, compared to Union losses of 118 killed, 450 injured and 22 missing. This battle is the preliminary to the Shenandoah Valley campaign. Militarily import-

Below: The ruins of Manassas Junction, Virginia, abandoned by Confederate troops on 11 March in the face of larger Union forces.

ant, the battle provides a diversion central to Southern strategy: Lincoln, now fearing an offensive on the Federal capital, issues orders that General McDowell's troops remain as part of Washington's defense. This means fewer troops for the peninsular campaign. In addition, this assault at Kernstown suggests the possibility of a threat on Harper's Ferry, and General Banks' troops are ordered to return to that vicinity rather than join forces with McClellan.

Western Theater Fort Macon at Beaufort, North Carolina, is the object of the next move by Burnside's Federals. The following day sees General John Parke's soldiers approach Fort Macon and request its surrender. The subsequent refusal results in a Union siege of that Confederate position.

24 March 1862

Slavery The emancipation issue continues to be one fraught with emotion. In Cincinnati, Ohio, the abolitionist Wendell Phillips speaks and is greeted with a barrage of eggs and rocks. Lincoln, commenting on the prospect of compensated emancipation, notes in a letter to newspaperman Horace Greeley that 'we should urge it persuasively, and not menacingly, upon the South.'

26 March 1862

Trans-Mississippi State militia in Missouri clash at Hammondsville with Confederate forces; at Warrensburg pro-Unionists con-

Below: Union and Confederate troops exchange volley fire at the height of the fighting at Shiloh, one of the war's most costly battles.

front Confederates; the latter are repelled in both cases. In Colorado Territory there is an encounter between Southern cavalry and Union forces near Denver City resulting in the capture of 50 Confederate cavalrymen. In New Mexico Territory, Confederates meet a troop of Union soldiers coming toward Santa Fe from Fort Union. There is a fight between the two forces at Apache Canyon, resulting in a victory for Union troops who fall back to an area near Glorietta. Confederate troops regroup after the skirmish and follow the victorious Union forces.

Above: Union reinforcements arrive to stem a Confederate attack during the bloody Battle of Shiloh, or Pittsburgh Landing.

28 March 1862

Eastern Theater, Peninsular Campaign Brief fighting occurs along the Orange and Alexandria Railroad in Virginia over a period of several days. Shipping Point, Virginia, is occupied by Federal troops.

Trans-Mississippi The New Mexico Territory sees a major battle between North and South at La Glorietta Pass. Union troops

under Colonel John Slough clash with Confederates under Colonel W R Scurry, pushing the Federals back. Confederate supply wagons at nearby Johnson's Ranch are attacked by Major John Chivington's men, causing the Confederates to fall back to Santa Fe and effectively stopping the Southern invasion. Of 1100 Confederates, 36 are killed, 60 wounded; Union troops totalling 1324 lose 31 with over 50 wounded.

29 March 1862

Eastern Theater, Peninsular Campaign In western Virginia, William Rosecrans' command of the Mountain Department is given over to General Frémont. Middlebury, Virginia, witnesses a cavalry charge by Union troops in pursuit of a fleeing Confederate detachment.

Western Theater General Albert Johnston pulls the Confederate forces together at Corinth, Mississippi; General Beauregard is his next in command. Generals Polk, Bragg, Hardee and Crittenden are also there with their troops.

1 April 1862

Eastern Theater, Peninsular Campaign General John Wool's force of 12,000 men at Fort Monroe, Virginia, is supplemented by General McClellan's movement of 12 divisions from the Northern Army of the Potomac. In addition, the Federal Shenandoah forces are pushing toward General Jackson's troops in position near Woodstock and Edenburg, Virginia.

Naval Northern troops move, via gunboats, up the Tennessee River and Federal forces are able to complete a mission at Island Number Ten on the Mississippi River.

2 April 1862

Washington President Lincoln's suggestions about compensated emancipation receive favorable attention in the United States Senate. This plan – which would allow Federal financial support to Northern states willing to provide compensation – is intended as a means to encourage the freeing of slaves. Although proposed by Lincoln it is a plan which will never be implemented.

Western Theater Shiloh, or Pittsburgh Landing, in Tennessee, is the goal that General A S Johnston's Confederates have in mind as they are ordered to move out to the Federal position from Corinth, Mississippi. Confederate troops succeed in encircling a portion of the 2nd Illinois Cavalry at Farmington, Mississippi. The Northern troops are able, however, to break through the enemy lines and escape.

Trans-Mississippi In Missouri, various military actions continue as Confederates and Northern soldiers skirmish at Walkersville, and as a Union reconnaissance force sets out for Jackson, Whitewater and Dallas from Cape Girardeau. Along the Mississippi River, from Cairo, Illinois, to New Madrid, Missouri, there is a great deal of damage done to various installations as a result of severe tornadoes.

3 April 1862

Washington The United States Senate passes a bill, 29-14, to abolish slavery in the District of Columbia. President Lincoln is

gravely concerned about the defense of the nation's capital. He finds that General McClellan has arranged for the distribution of troops so as to leave less than 20,000 men in the Washington area. Accordingly, the chief executive orders the retention of an additional corps to ensure the safety of the Northern capital; the impact on McClellan's troop strength for the peninsular campaign is negligible, as McClellan has nearly 112,000 men for his siege of Yorktown.

Western Theater General A S Johnston's Confederates move to attack Shiloh on the Tennessee River, where General Grant's Northern troops are encamped. Apalachicola, Florida, surrenders to Federal troops.

4 April 1862

Eastern Theater, Peninsular Campaign The campaign continues to take shape as General McClellan proceeds to bear down on Yorktown. The Southern forces are greatly outnumbered; General Johnston's troops total around 17,000 as compared to McClellan's enormous Army of the Potomac consisting of over 100,000 troops. Much of the Confederate Army of Northern Virginia has been shifted into position on the Peninsula to afford some increased defense of the Southern position there. The Confederate line of defense stretches along an eight-mile front; the prospects for the South are not good.

5 April 1862

The North Difficulties over the oath of allegiance to the Union occur between the military governor of Tennessee, Andrew Johnson, and city officials of Nashville. The result is the suspension of the mayor, aldermen and councilmen of that occupied area.

Eastern Theater, Peninsular Campaign In a valiant, but seemingly futile effort, General Joseph Johnston's troops continue to gather reinforcements for the imminent conflict at Yorktown, Virginia. The Confederates are outnumbered by McClellan's stronger and larger Army of the Potomac.

Western Theater General Grant's forces continue to be relatively unaware of the Confederate troops bearing down on their position at Shiloh, Tennessee.

Above: Union infantry recapture an artillery battery at the point of the bayonet during the Shiloh battle.

6 April 1862

Western Theater The Battle of Shiloh, or Pittsburgh Landing, comes after several days of Confederate preparations which have gone largely unnoticed by the Federals. General Grant's troops fall back after several hours, despite the fierce defense of their position at the Hornet's Nest, a defense orchestrated by General Prentiss' division. While the initial force of Confederates under General Johnston presses General William Nelson's Federals to breaking point, the day ends without any conclusive victory for either the North or the South. The following day sees the destruction of Prentiss' division and the concurrent wearing down of Beauregard's troops. The Confederate command has been assumed by Beauregard after General Johnston was killed on the previous day. Fresh troops from Union General Wallace's division and from Generals Nelson and Crittenden give Grant's forces the necessary reinforcement and bolstering. In like manner, General Beauregard is waiting for 20,000 men under General Van Dorn, hoping to make another offensive for the Confederates; without Van Dorn's forces this is clearly impossible. Unfortunately for the Confederates, Van Dorn's men do not arrive; Beauregard orders a retreat to Corinth, Mississippi, leaving Northern troops to remain in much the same position they had occupied prior to the Battle of Shiloh. While it is unclear whether or not the Union has gained a great deal from the two-day clash, the Federals have maintained a firm hold on positions that they had previously taken, and they also achieve a splitting of the rebel forces along the Mississippi River and an evacuation of much of the Confederate force in Tennessee. Losses at the Battle of Shiloh total 13,047 for the North; 10,694 for the Confederates.

7 April 1862

Naval The Federal gunboats *Carandolet* and *Pittsburgh* run the Confederate installations at Island Number Ten in the Mississippi

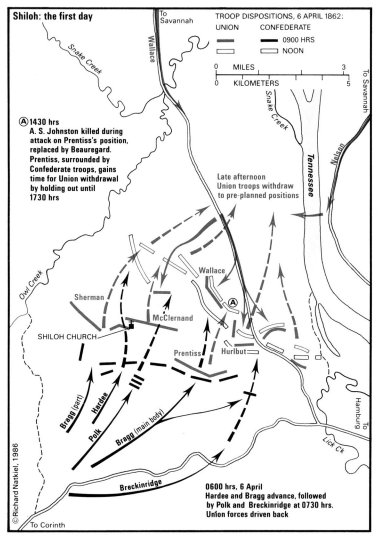

Shiloh: the first day

To Savannah

TROOP DISPOSITIONS, 6 APRIL 1862:

UNION   CONFEDERATE

⬛ 0900 HRS

⬜ NOON

MILES
0   3
KILOMETERS
0   5

(A) 1430 hrs
A. S. Johnston killed during attack on Prentiss's position, replaced by Beauregard. Prentiss, surrounded by Confederate troops, gains time for Union withdrawal by holding out until 1730 hrs

Late afternoon Union troops withdraw to pre-planned positions

Wallace

Sherman

McClernand

(A)

SHILOH CHURCH

Prentiss

Hurlbut

Bragg (part)

Polk

Hardee

Bragg (main body)

Breckinridge

© Richard Natkiel, 1986

0600 hrs, 6 April
Hardee and Bragg advance, followed by Polk and Breckinridge at 0730 hrs. Union forces driven back

To Corinth

Snake Creek

Owl Creek

Tennessee

Nelson

Lick Ck

To Hamburg

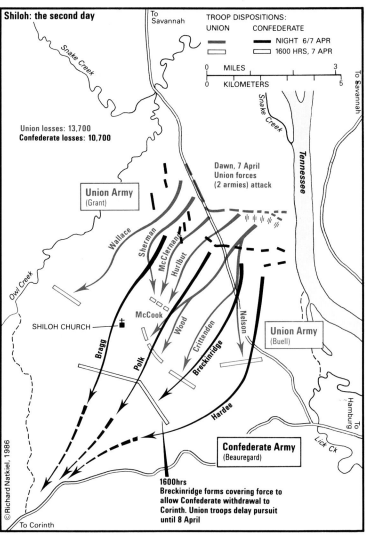

Shiloh: the second day

To Savannah

TROOP DISPOSITIONS:

UNION   CONFEDERATE

⬛ NIGHT 6/7 APR

⬜ 1600 HRS, 7 APR

MILES
0   3
KILOMETERS
0   5

Union losses: 13,700
Confederate losses: 10,700

Dawn, 7 April
Union forces (2 armies) attack

Union Army
(Grant)

Wallace

Sherman

McClernand

Hurlbut

SHILOH CHURCH

McCook

Wood

Crittenden

Nelson

Bragg

Polk

Breckinridge

Hardee

Union Army
(Buell)

Confederate Army
(Beauregard)

1600hrs
Breckinridge forms covering force to allow Confederate withdrawal to Corinth. Union troops delay pursuit until 8 April

© Richard Natkiel, 1986

To Corinth

Snake Creek

Owl Creek

Tennessee

Lick Ck

To Hamburg

River near New Madrid, Missouri. Under the direction of General John Pope, troops succeed in cutting a canal through the marshy area near the island, thus allowing the Federal vessels to go southward around the island and land four regiments in Tennessee below the Confederate position on Island Number Ten.

10 April 1862

Western Theater Skirmishing occurs at Fernandina, Florida, and in Illinois. Union General W H L Wallace succumbs to injuries he received at the Battle of Shiloh. In the harbor of Savannah, Georgia, Fort Pulaski readies itself for an attack by Federals. Commanded by General Quincy Adams Gillmore, the Northern assault takes place from a position opposite the fort on Tybee Island. The Confederates have about 40 guns but the Federals' long range guns and penetrating shells are a match for the masonry fort, which sustains heavy damage. The bombardment at Fort Pulaski begins at 0800 hours and continues throughout the night, the Federal guns at Tybee Island being stilled the following day at around 1400. Three hundred and sixty Confederates are taken prisoner; one Union soldier is killed, as is one Southerner.

11 April 1862

Washington In a vote of 93-39, the House of Representatives passes a bill which calls for the gradual abolition of slavery in the District of Columbia.
Western Theater In Tennessee, several hundred Confederates are captured when the town of Huntsville is occupied by Federals. The Memphis and Charleston Railroad is near to this site. The South is slowly losing its grip on Tennessee. The Union begins to marshal its forces for a push toward Confederate positions at Corinth, Mississippi. General Henry Halleck has assumed command of these troops with Generals Buell, Grant and Pope directly beneath him.
Naval At Newport News, Virginia, the *Merrimack*, the South's ironclad, seizes three small merchant ships but does not engage in conflict with the Federal vessel *Monitor* as anticipated. The *Monitor* has been awaiting the approach of the Confederate vessel, but then gives no indication of desiring an actual encounter.

12 April 1862

The North James Andrews, a spy for the Union, had led a group of 21 men through the Confederate lines in order to seize a train on the Western and Atlantic Railroad. Taking the locomotive, the *General*, Andrews and his men head northward, followed by Confederates in the locomotive *Texas*. Andrews and his men are caught by the Southern forces and are eventually executed, with the exception of 14 who are imprisoned.
Eastern Theater, Peninsular Campaign General Joseph Johnston sends troops to support besieged Yorktown, Virginia. The

Above left: General Grant leads infantry and cavalry during the decisive phase of the Battle of Shiloh.
Left: The Battle of Shiloh, showing the initial Southern advance and the subsequent attacks of Grant's Northern forces.

situation in the peninsular campaign is still one which bodes ill for the vastly outnumbered Confederates.

13 April 1862

Western Theater Fort Pulaski, Georgia, is termed a free area by General David Hunter, providing for the confiscation and setting free of all salves in the vicinity.
Trans-Mississippi The evacuation of New Mexico Territory by Confederates continues with Union soldiers pressing Southern troops back as far as El Paso.

16 April 1862

Washington President Lincoln signs a bill which will prohibit slavery in the District of Columbia.
The Confederacy In a culmination of several weeks' preparations, President Jefferson Davis gives his approval to a congressional proposal that will require a military draft in the Confederate states. This law states that 'all persons residing within the Confederate states, between the ages of 18 and 35 years . . . shall be held to be in the military service.' This action, while believed to be necessary by many due to the critical need to upgrade the military strength of the Confederacy, is nevertheless a move which is at variance with the generally accepted traditions embracing states' rights and the rugged individualism endorsed by many people in the Confederacy.

17 April 1862

Western Theater Confederate attention is focused on the increase in military strength of Federal troops at Ship Island, Mississippi, which is now supplemented by Union vessels on the Mississippi River. The latter include a fleet under Flag Officer David Farragut and Commander David Porter with a mortar fleet. The intention of these Union forces is the takeover of New Orleans, Louisiana, which is situated in what is rapidly becoming a vulnerable and defenseless position up-river.

Above left: Ormsby MacKnight Mitchel, commander of the Federal forces that captured Huntsville on 11 April 1862.
Above: Commander, later Admiral, David Porter, the North's outstanding naval leader.

18 April 1862

Eastern Theater, Peninsular Campaign Northern troops under General McDowell occupy Falmouth, Virginia, and at Yorktown a Confederate attack on Union troops is unsuccessful, the latter forces pushing the Southern troops back.
Naval As they had feared, the Confederates at Ship Island are subject to a barrage of mortar fire from Federal gunboats.

20 April 1862

Naval In a continuing bombardment of the Fort Jackson and Fort St Philip area, Federal troops attempt to open the river by removing obstructions placed there by Confederates.

23 April 1862

Naval Flag Officer David Farragut orders the Federal fleet on the Mississippi River to move past Forts Jackson and St Philip. Due to the inconclusive nature of the recent attacks on these two fortifications, it seems appropriate that the North push onward to its ultimate goal of New Orleans, Louisiana.

24 April 1862

Naval Farragut's fleet is able to slip past the Confederate forts on the Mississippi despite valiant attempts on the part of Southern forces to prevent this. The Union force makes its way up-river toward New Orleans. Encountering further Confederate resistance in the form of a ram, *Manassas,* Federals counter with their own fire, ultimately losing only the ship *Varuna* and 36 men. The Confederates lose eight ships and 61 men.

25 April 1862

Western Theater North Carolina's Fort Macon under Confederate Colonel Moses White surrenders to the Federal forces which

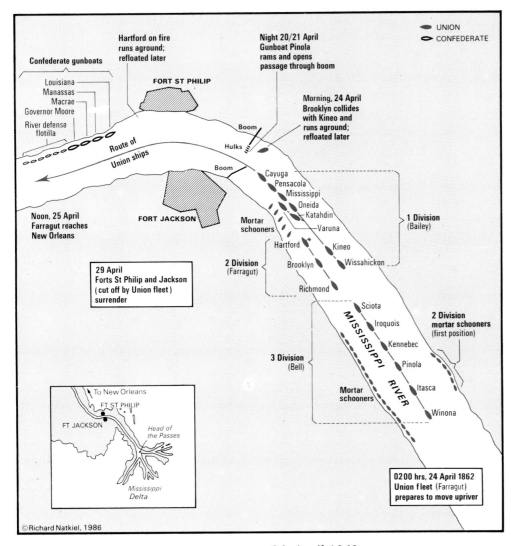

Confederate gunboats
Louisiana
Manassas
Macrae
Governor Moore
River defense flotilla

Hartford on fire runs aground; refloated later

FORT ST PHILIP

Night 20/21 April Gunboat Pinola rams and opens passage through boom

Morning, 24 April Brooklyn collides with Kineo and runs aground; refloated later

● UNION
◗ CONFEDERATE

Route of Union ships

Boom
Hulks
Boom

Cayuga
Pensacola
Mississippi
Oneida
Katahdin
Varuna

1 Division (Bailey)

Noon, 25 April Farragut reaches New Orleans

FORT JACKSON

Mortar schooners

Hartford
Kineo

2 Division (Farragut)

Brooklyn
Wissahickon

Richmond

29 April Forts St Philip and Jackson (cut off by Union fleet) surrender

Sciota
Iroquois

2 Division mortar schooners (first position)

3 Division (Bell)

Kennebec
Pinola

MISSISSIPPI RIVER

Mortar schooners
Itasca
Winona

To New Orleans
FT ST PHILIP
FT JACKSON
Head of the Passes

Mississippi Delta

0200 hrs, 24 April 1862 Union fleet (Farragut) prepares to move upriver

© Richard Natkiel, 1986

Above: The Battle of New Orleans, a successful Union attempt to force the Mississippi.

have been besieging it for nearly a month. The next day, formal ceremonies relinquish Southern jurisdiction of Fort Macon to Union General John Parke, and 400 Confederate soldiers become Northern prisoners-of-war.
Naval Farragut's forces seize the city of New Orleans, Louisiana, which has been left defenseless after Confederate General Mansfield Lovell and his 4000 troops withdraw. There is little resistance to the Union takeover by the civilian population and four days later, on 29 April, New Orleans is formally surrendered to Federal forces.

27 April 1862

Western Theater As a result of the capture several days earlier of New Orleans, four Confederate forts – Livingston, Quitman, Pike and Wood – surrender to the North. At Fort Jackson to the south, Confederate troops mutiny against their own officers and many flee in the face of their impending imprisonment. The following day both Forts Jackson and St Philip surrender, totally removing any Confederate resistance to Northern action on the Mississippi River as far up as New Orleans. General Benjamin Butler arrives with troops, landing just north of Fort St Philip. Butler will see to the management of the captured city which is, according to his written observation of several days later, a 'city under the dominion of the mob.'

28 April 1862

Western Theater In Mississippi, General Halleck is preparing to move on General Beauregard's position at Corinth.

29 April 1862

Western Theater General Halleck continues to ready his army of over 100,000 troops so as to attack Beauregard, whose forces are considerably smaller. Skirmishing breaks out at Cumberland Gap, Kentucky, and near Bridgeport, Alabama. The conquering Federals at New Orleans post a United States flag on the New Orleans Custom House and on the City Hall, much to the sorrow and anger of the citizenry.

1 May 1862

Eastern Theater, Peninsular Campaign The siege of Yorktown, Viriginia, continues as Federals under McClellan prepare to attack. Guns are readied for the assault scheduled to begin in several days.

3 May 1862

Eastern Theater, Peninsular Campaign Yorktown, Virginia, is evacuated by General Joseph Johnston's troops. The enormous force of the Army of the Potomac has overwhelmed the Confederates without a major battle, and the Southern troops now move toward Richmond. McClellan's forces have been successful with their siege tactics, and they enter Yorktown the following day.
Western Theater Near Corinth, Mississippi, where General Beauregard's troops are stationed, there is minor skirmishing at Farmington. General Halleck's Federals are moving now in the direction of Corinth, hoping to arrive there on the following day.

5 May 1862

Washington President Lincoln and his Secretaries of War and the Treasury, Stanton and Chase, leave the capital. They travel by ship to Fort Monroe where they will observe the Federal troops' advance into Virginia.
Eastern Theater, Peninsular Campaign As a result of the Confederate evacuation of Yorktown, there is serious fighting between advancing Federals and retreating Confederates at Williamsburg. In all, 1703 Southern soldiers are lost during the encounter which claims 456 Union troops, with 373 listed as missing.

7 May 1862

Eastern Theater, Peninsular Campaign Further clashes occur in the Shenandoah Valley; General Franklin's Federals are attacked by General G W Smith's Confederates who hope to keep the road from Williamsburg to Yorktown protected. This clash at Eltham's

Below: A Union 13-inch mortar battery prepares to open fire on Yorktown during the Peninsular campaign.

Above: The Union gunboats *Mound City* and *Cincinnati* (background) were sunk by Southern vessels on 10 May 1862.

Landing, Virginia, foreshadows the events of the upcoming week. In order to boost morale and to help encourage General McClellan to move on to Richmond, President Lincoln visits the *Monitor* and meets with various military officials.

8 May 1862

Eastern Theater   The Battle of McDowell, a major encounter in the Shenandoah Valley Campaign, sees General Stonewall Jackson's Confederates repulse an attack by Federals under the command of General Robert Schenck. The Southern troops, numbering around 10,000, outfight the 6000 Union troops. Jackson's forces pursue the fleeing Federals toward Franklin, West Virginia, but continue only for several days before returning to the Shenandoah.

9 May 1862

Eastern Theater, Peninsular Campaign President Lincoln meets with General McClellan, who is advancing slowly toward Richmond, Virginia. The chief executive admonishes McClellan for his difficulties in maintaining cooperation between himself and his corps leaders. Norfolk, Virginia, is evacuated by Confederates in a costly move. While they destroy much of their supplies and equipment, they still leave a large amount of valuable material to the Federals pushing into the area the following day. **Western Theater**   At Hilton Head, South Carolina, General David Hunter, commander of the Department of the South, frees slaves in South Carolina, Florida and Georgia. This move, not given congressional authorization or approval by President Lincoln, is later repudiated by the chief executive. Mississippi is the scene of clashes between Confederates and advancing Federals near Corinth. Pensacola, Florida, is evac-

uated by Confederates and within three days the Union army has taken hold of the area.

10 May 1862

Eastern Theater   The Federal push to gain further control in Virginia continues unabated. Jackson moves in on Franklin, West Virginia; Norfolk and Portsmouth are occupied by 5000 Union troops. This operation began with troops landing at Willoughby Point and involved, among other things, the burning of the naval yard at Gosport, Virginia. President Lincoln is personally involved in this action in that he superintends the movement of this Federal expeditionary force.
Naval   At Fort Pillow, Tennessee, on the Mississippi River, a Confederate force of eight gunboats attacks seven Union vessels, the latter made up of sturdy ironclads. The Confederate flotilla is singularly ill-equipped to make this offensive at Plum Run Bend a successful one, but Captain James Montgomery commands the Confederates in a valiant manner and under his direction the Southern boats succeed in sinking the Union ironclads *Cincinnati* and *Mound City*. Despite this, the Confederate gunboats are forced, ultimately, to retreat to Memphis, Tennessee, after the Union guns disable their ships.

11 May 1862

Naval   The Confederate ironclad *Merrimack,* after having confronted the Union ironclad *Monitor* in a spectacular stand-off on 9 March 1862, is destroyed by the Confederate navy. The Union troops advancing on Virginia have placed the Confederates in a situation requiring destruction of a valuable naval vessel, which would otherwise fall into enemy hands.

12 May 1862

Washington   In a reversal of his blockade order, President Lincoln issues a proclamation which opens the ports of Beaufort, North Carolina; Port Royal, South Carolina; and

New Orleans, Louisiana. This order will take effect on 1 June 1862 and will provide for the resumption of commercial operations at these formerly Confederate-held ports.

13 May 1862

The Confederacy   The situation at the Confederate capital of Richmond, Virginia, assumes crisis proportions in the face of advancing Federal troops. As McClellan's Army of the Potomac presses the Southerners, President Davis' wife, Varina, joins many others who leave the city.
Eastern Theater   General Jackson prepares to confront Federal General Nathaniel Banks and his troops at Strasburg, Kentucky, as part of the Shenandoah Valley campaign.
Naval   The Confederate steamer *Planter* is seized in Charleston Harbor by eight blacks. They pilot the vessel, which has seven guns, out of the harbor. At Natchez, Mississippi, Union gunboats under David Farragut take over jurisdiction of the city.

15 May 1862

Eastern Theater, Peninsular Campaign Land forces pressing in on Richmond, Virginia, move closer to the Confederate capital. Nearby, General Joseph Johnston's troops are moving back across the Chickahominy River. In West Virginia, at Ravenswood and Princeton, minor skirmishing occupies Confederate and Federal troops. Major fighting breaks out at Drewry's Bluff in Virginia, where Federals moving near the Confederate capital deal with gunfire from Fort Darling.
Naval   The battle at Drewry's Bluff involves the Northern ironclad *Monitor* and the gunboat *Galena*. The Union force is eventually forced to retreat as the Confederate defenses at Fort Darling prove adequate.

Below: Union General Robert Schenck led his forces to defeat at McDowell during Jackson's campaign in the Shenandoah Valley.

Above: Front Royal, West Virginia, scene of a Southern victory during Jackson's onslaught against Union troops in the area.

16 May 1862

Western Theater   In one of his most controversial actions to date, General Benjamin Butler at New Orleans, Louisiana, issues what is known as the 'Woman Order.' The full text of this *General Order Number 28* is indicative of Butler's complete disregard for convention and his, at times, tyrannical attitude toward the citizens of this vanquished city. The order reads, in part, 'As the officers and soldiers of the United States have been subjected to repeated insults from the women (calling themselves ladies) of New Orleans . . . when any female shall . . . show contempt for the United States, she shall be regarded as a woman of the town plying her avocation.' The Woman Order, while not revoked by the Lincoln administration, helped to set the stage for Butler's removal from the military governorship of New Orleans on 16 December 1862. The day after the issuance of the Woman Order, Butler stops the New Orleans newspapers *Bee* and *Delta* under the control of Federal authorities.

17 May 1862

Eastern Theater, Peninsular Campaign   General McDowell is at Fredericksburg, Virginia, and receives orders to advance toward the Confederate capital in order to be in concert with McClellan's forces.

18 May 1862

Eastern Theater, Peninsular Campaign   In Virginia, Union troops press closer to Richmond, taking Suffolk and occupying that town 17 miles south of Norfolk. In the Shenandoah Valley, Confederate General Stonewall Jackson continues to harry the Federals, clashing with General Nathaniel Banks.
Naval   Vicksburg on the Mississippi River is the object of David Farragut's advance with a Federal fleet, the city being under the protection of Confederate General M L Smith who will not surrender jurisdiction to the North. It is important to the Federals to take possession of this large Confederate city since it

commands an important strategic position on the Mississippi.

19 May 1862

Washington   In an action reversing an earlier decision made by General David Hunter, President Lincoln countermands the order of 9 May 1862 which liberated slaves in the Department of the South. Lincoln's position is that General Hunter had exceeded his official authority in issuing such a liberation order, and that such decisions are to be made only by the chief executive.
The Confederacy   President Jefferson Davis, in continued communication with his wife, indicates the Confederate position concerning preparation for the Federal offensive on Richmond, Virginia: 'We are uncertain of everything except that a battle must be near at hand.'
Eastern Theater, Peninsular Campaign   There is little change in the continuing build-up of Union troop strength in the area surrounding Richmond, Virginia.

20 May 1862

Washington   President Lincoln signs a bill authorizing the Homestead Act. Designed to aid the private citizen who wishes to obtain quality land at affordable rates, the Homestead Act also makes 160-acre quarter sections available for a nominal fee to those who can improve the parcel of land for five years. This is later to be considered a critical instrument in the settlement of the West and the development of western agricultural lands.
Eastern Theater, Peninsular Campaign   The Army of the Potomac under General McClellan is now only eight miles from Richmond, Virginia, the Confederate capital. In an attempt to prevent Union General Nathaniel Banks from moving troops to meet and support McClellan, Confederate Generals Stonewall Jackson and Richard Ewell take their 16,000 men into the Luray Valley area of the Shenandoah. By moving north Jackson hopes to block Banks' path out of the western reaches of the Shenandoah. The Virginia Central Railroad is attacked by Union troops at Jackson's River Depot.

21 May 1862

Eastern Theater, Peninsular Campaign   General McClellan continues to ask President Lincoln for more troops to augment the Army of the Potomac; this time he requests help from McDowell's forces which are en route to Richmond, Virginia.

22 May 1862

Eastern Theater, Peninsular Campaign   General Stonewall Jackson pushes nearer Front Royal, West Virginia, in preparation for a major engagement with Federals on the following day.
Western Theater   General Henry Halleck continues to direct his troops in the skirmishing which occurs at Corinth, Mississippi, between the Federals and the Confederate forces under General Beauregard.

23 May 1862

Eastern Theater   After having journeyed to Fredericksburg, Virginia, President Lincoln confers with General McDowell who is positioned at Aquia Creek and Fredericksburg. The following day, Lincoln sends orders to McDowell, telling the general to direct 20,000 troops into the Shenandoah area in order to prevent Confederates from moving their forces any closer to Banks' troops of the Army of the Potomac. Lincoln tells McDowell, 'Your object will be to capture the forces of Jackson and Ewell.' At Front Royal, West Virginia, General Jackson's troops encounter 8000 Union soldiers and take the area from Federal control. This victory is a relatively easy one and does little to improve Banks' position, which is now seriously threatened.

24 May 1862

Washington   President Lincoln confers with his cabinet; the result of this discussion is the issuance of new military orders to General Frémont. The general is instructed to

Below: Union General Benjamin Butler, the highly unpopular officer in charge of affairs in New Orleans, Louisiana.

advance against General Jackson's forces in the Shenandoah Valley. Because of Lincoln's new orders to General McDowell, also concerning Jackson, the president communicates the information to General McClellan that an increase in his strength is impossible.

25 May 1862

Washington Communications between the president and General McClellan continue as Lincoln presses his general in chief to 'either attack Richmond or give up the job and come to the defense of Washington.' The Union Secretary of War Edwin Stanton puts out a call for additional men to be supplied by any state that can spare more troops. Orders go out to give military transport top priority on railroad lines in the North.

Eastern Theater In the Shenandoah Valley, at Winchester, Virginia, General Stonewall Jackson attacks Federal positions. While the Federals maintain their stance for a time, the offensive on the right, by troops under the command of Jackson, and on the left by Ewell's troops, eventually compel General Nathaniel Banks' forces to pull back in a retreat toward Harper's Ferry, Virginia. This encounter at Winchester claims 400 Confederate casualties – 68 dead, 329 wounded, three missing. General Banks' troops had totaled nearly 8000 at the start of this clash; he lost 62 men, with 243 wounded and 1714 either missing or captured.

26 May 1862

Washington The discussion over allocation of troop strength and movement continues as President Lincoln asks General McClellan,

'Can you get near enough to throw shells into the city?'

Eastern Theater There is little that Union General Nathaniel Banks can do but continue to move back away from Jackson's Confederates after the defeat at Winchester, Virginia. Banks moves the following day across the Potomac River into Federal territory near Williamsport.

29 May 1862

Eastern Theater, Peninsular Campaign Various actions occur to consolidate the Federal position near Richmond, Virginia. Approximately 40,000 Union troops gather near Jackson's Confederates at Harper's Ferry. There is skirmishing at the South Anna River in Virginia, where Federals burn a 500-foot bridge and ultimately capture the nearby town of Ashland.

Western Theater The pressure that General Halleck's Federals have put on General Beauregard's troops at Corinth, Mississippi, has finally caused the Confederate general to give orders for his men to retreat toward Tupelo, Mississippi.

30 May 1862

Eastern Theater, Peninsular Campaign At Front Royal in West Virginia Union troops under General Shields occupy the town after a minor clash with General Jackson's retreating Confederates. Jackson is pulling away from the Harper's Ferry area so as to avoid being cut off by Frémont and McDowell.

Western Theater At Corinth, Mississippi, over 2000 prisoners are taken by Federal troops moving into the city. General Beaure-

Above: The Battle of Fair Oaks, Virginia, did little to ease the pressure on Richmond despite being a Southern victory.

gard's Confederates have destroyed much of value that could not be taken out of Corinth; General Halleck's success in occupying the city is a real one but it is a success which lacks some degree of triumph simply because the campaign has taken over one month to reach fruition.

31 May 1862

Eastern Theater, Peninsular Campaign Movements by Confederate General Joseph Johnston and McClellan's Army of the Potomac result in a major operation at the Battle of Fair Oaks, or Seven Pines. This somewhat delayed offensive by Johnston is only marginally effective strategically, causing the Federal troops to pull back on the following day, but doing little to lessen the threat posed to the Confederate capital at Richmond, Virginia. In all, Confederate losses are 6134 while Union troops lose 5031. General Johnston is wounded in this battle, causing Confederate President Jefferson Davis to name General Robert E Lee as commander of the Army of Northern Virginia.

1 June 1862

Washington President Lincoln sends a telegram to General McClellan concerning the situation at Richmond, Virginia. He tells the general: 'Hold all your ground, or yield any only inch by inch and in good order.'

Eastern Theater, Peninsular Campaign General Jackson's Confederate troops meet those of Union General McDowell as Jackson continues to retreat to a position near Harrisonburg, Virginia.

3 June 1862

Western Theater   The Confederate garrison at Fort Pillow near Memphis, Tennessee, evacuates its position, leaving the city helpless in the face of advancing Union troops which have already taken Corinth, Mississippi. McClellan's forces meet and skirmish with Confederates on James Island, South Carolina. This is a position near Charleston, which is the object of the Federal advance in that area.

4 June 1862

Eastern Theater, Peninsular Campaign Richmond, Virginia, remains threatened by the Army of the Potomac which is resting after the Fair Oaks battle earlier in the week. Some skirmishing does occur, however, mainly in West Virginia, near Big Bend. General Stonewall Jackson and his Confederate troops continue to pull back into the Shenandoah Valley.

5 June 1862

Eastern Theater, Peninsular Campaign   Inclement weather prevents General McClellan's forces from pushing toward Richmond, Virginia, where the Confederates anticipate attack from the Union army and where Confederate General Robert E Lee is preparing a defensive operation with the Army of Northern Virginia.
Trans-Mississippi   Skirmishing breaks out at various locations – Sedalia, Missouri; Round Grove, in Indian Territory; and near the Little Red River in Arkansas.
Naval   The Federal fleet which is moving toward Memphis, Tennessee passes Fort Wright and Fort Randolph unharrassed. The

Below: Frame House, the site of a Union field hospital during and after the Battle of Fair Oaks, Virginia.

five ironclads and four rams making up the Union flotilla are under the direction of Commodore Charles Davis. They come to rest at anchor two miles above Memphis.

6 June 1862

Naval   Confederate Captain James Montgomery, with an inadequate force of gunboats, engages the Union flotilla at a point near Memphis, Tennessee. Commodore Davis' resources far exceed those of the Confederates, who have only 28 guns compared to the Union strength of 68 guns. As crowds gather in the pre-dawn hours, the Federals and Confederates clash, and within two hours the latter force has been almost completely disabled. The one vessel, *Van Dorn*, left to the Confederates after the river battle,

Above: General George Stoneman and his staff pose for the camera in the vicinity of Fair Oaks in June 1862.

escapes. Triumphant Federals accept the surrender of Memphis shortly before noon. This battle is significant in that it opens the Mississippi region.

7 June 1862

Eastern Theater, Peninsular Campaign   As Confederates retreat, coming closer to Harrisburg, skirmishing breaks out at Union Church, Virginia, when they meet advancing Northern troops. Reconnaissance efforts on the part of Federals at Chickahominy Creek bring those troops close to the Confederate capital of Richmond, where General Lee is readying his Confederates for an offensive, as well as for the defense of the city.
Western Theater   The difficult relations engendered by Union General Benjamin Butler's treatment of New Orleans citizens are made even more uncomfortable when Butler orders William Mumford hanged. Mumford, having removed and destroyed the United States flag on display over the New Orleans Mint, was seized, imprisoned, tried and found guilty of treason against the Federal government.

8 June 1862

Eastern Theater, Peninsular Campaign Near Port Republic, Virginia, the Battle of Cross Keys nearly causes the retreat of Confederate forces. While Jackson's troops are advancing against General Frémont's Federals, Confederate General R S Ewell is the commander of forces which are able to hold off the Union troops and defend General Jackson's men. The Federals, numbering 10,500, are held off by 6500 of Ewell's troops.

9 June 1862

Eastern Theater, Peninsular Campaign Fighting continues in the area of Cross Keys, Virginia, but the battle today between Jack-

Above: A Union observation balloon rises into the sky to carry out intelligence duties during the Peninsular campaign.

son's troops and those of Frémont and Shields takes place at Port Republic. The Confederates make a strong stand and eventually push the Northern troops back. General Ewell's Confederates are an important resource in this offensive as they hold Frémont's men away from Jackson's main force. The battle here at Port Royal and the previous day's encounter at Cross Keys signal the end of Jackson's current campaign in the Shenandoah.

12 June 1862

Eastern Theater, Peninsular Campaign In one of the more flamboyant moves of the war, Confederate General J E B Stuart takes a force of cavalry and artillery out on a reconnaissance of the Federal positions on the Peninsula. This action, which covers a period of several days, is an important one as it disturbs supply and communication networks. Riding completely around McClellan's Union army force, General Stuart seriously undermines the morale of the Federals who feel threatened by what is a seemingly larger enemy force than actually exists. This move (which comes to be known as Stuart's First Ride Around McClellan) is responsible for encouraging Southerners who have been suffering from numerous defeats and invasions over the past months. Stuart's move is buttressed by Jackson's forces who are reinforced at Lee's command and add to the threat posed by cavalry under Stuart.

16 June 1862

Western Theater At James Island, South Carolina, Federal troops engage in a battle at Secessionville. The losses are significant, Union General H W Benham's forces losing 107 men, with 487 wounded and 89 missing. The Confederates under General N G Evans lose 52, with 144 injured and eight missing. The Union force is repulsed despite its vigorous assault on a position which is critical to the control of Charleston Harbor. In Winchester, Tennessee, skirmishes break out.

17 June 1862

Washington President Lincoln oversees the reorganization of commands in the East. Resentful at being placed under General John Pope, General John Frémont resigns from the new Army of Virginia. General Franz Sigel steps into the vacancy created by Frémont's resignation. This move by Frémont places him in a position of ambiguity and he spends the remainder of the war in New York, hoping for further orders.
Naval In Arkansas, on the White River, Union gunboats draw fire from Confederate batteries positioned at St Charles. The Federal steamer *Mound City* is severely damaged when her boiler explodes, killing and wounding 125 men.

19 June 1862

Washington President Lincoln outlines his controversial Emancipation Proclamation which outlaws slavery in all the states which continue to be in rebellion against the Federal government.

20 June 1862

Western Theater The Federal advance against Vicksburg, Mississippi, has begun under the command of General Thomas Williams. Admiral David Farragut aids in the attempt by providing gunboat protection. Confederates under General Van Dorn, who commands the Department of Southern Mississippi and Louisiana, attempt to further fortify the city.

21 June 1862

Eastern Theater, Peninsular Campaign While the Richmond, Virginia, area remains calm and quiet as a whole, there is some minor skirmishing between Federals and Confederates at the Chickahominy Creek. The Northern and Confederate armies are both awaiting the inevitable battle; as President of the Confederacy Jefferson Davis points out in a letter, 'A total defeat of McClellan will relieve the Confederacy of its embarrassments in the East.'

Below: Union engineers put the finishing touches to a bridge on the Chickahominy, 18 June 1862, prior to the Seven Days campaign.

Above: President Lincoln reads a draft of his Emancipation Proclamation to members of his government.

23 June 1862

Washington   President Lincoln leaves the Federal capital on a trip to New York and West Point. The president intends to discuss current and future military strategies with the retired General Winfield Scott.

24 June 1862

Eastern Theater, Peninsular Campaign White House, Virginia, is evacuated as McClellan's troops press forward, and at Mechanicsville there is minor skirmishing between Confederate and Union soldiers.

Western Theater   General Van Dorn's troops are at beleaguered Vicksburg, Mississippi, where 3000 Federals are encamped close-by.

25 June 1862

Eastern Theater, Peninsular Campaign   An effort by Confederates to deflect what they fear will be a crippling blow to Richmond, the Confederate capital, begins with the Seven Days campaign. The first of a series of engagements, at Oak Grove, sees Confederate General John Magruder conduct operations calculated to confuse Federals into assuming a larger Confederate force than is actually assembled. While Magruder attempts this, General Lee attacks McClellan's forces gathered east of Richmond; despite a relatively ineffective assault on the Union troops, General McClellan is considerably more concerned than he had previously been about his army's safety. A total of 51 killed, 401 wounded and 64 missing on the Federal side results from this engagement; Confederates lose 40 men with 263 injuries and 13 missing.

27 June 1862

Eastern Theater, Peninsular Campaign The Battle of Gaines' Mills, the third in a series in the Seven Days campaign, sees General Lee's troops break through Federal lines and follow the Northern force as it heads for Harrison's Landing, Virginia. The Federals are undaunted, however, and the Confederate command is not able to take advantage of the weaknesses in the Union lines. General Porter takes his Federal troops back across the Chickahominy to rejoin McClellan's main army. General Magruder, south of the Chickahominy, continues to press the Union troops there with a greatly outnumbered force of Confederates. The results of the Gaines' Mills battle is a total of 6837 casualties for the North as compared to 8750 for the South. As McClellan pulls his army back, the Confederates see some relief in the strain placed on their defenses at Richmond.

28 June 1862

Eastern Theater, Peninsular Campaign   At Garnett's and Golding's Farms, fighting between Confederate and Union troops continues in Virginia. The Northern forces are pulling away from Richmond in the direction of the Potomac River. At White House Landing, Northern troops destroy supplies and equipment as they complete their evacuation of the area.

Naval   Admiral David Farragut takes his fleet past Confederate shore batteries at Vicksburg, Mississippi, losing 15 men and sustaining injuries to 30 others. All but three Federal vessels succeed in slipping past the Confederate fortifications but this in no way indicates an easy victory over the Confederates at Vicksburg. The Northern offensive will continue for over a year.

29 June 1862

Eastern Theater, Peninsular Campaign The Seven Days campaign continues as Southern troops clash with Union forces at Savage's Station. This battle sees Federals withdraw east of Richmond, Virginia, toward the James River, leaving behind over 2000 injured and ailing soldiers. It is a battle that can only be considered inconclusive.

30 June 1862

Eastern Theater, Peninsular Campaign   At White Oak Swamp, Virginia, the sixth in a series of battles occurs as Union soldiers under General McClellan attempt to consolidate their positions, succeeding to a certain degree in comparison to Longstreet's and Jackson's troops which seem plagued by confusion. It is in part this confusion and lack of coordination which allows McClellan to assume a safely entrenched position on Malvern Hill to the north of the James River.

1 July 1862

Washington   President Lincoln signs into law a Federal tax which levies a three percent rate on annual incomes of $600 to $10,000 and five percent on incomes above $10,000. Unlike a similar act passed in the previous year, this one actually goes into effect.

Eastern Theater, Peninsular Campaign The defeat of Confederate troops after a short battle at Malvern Hill spells the end of the Seven Days campaign in Virginia. Confeder-

Below: A sign of war weariness in the South during the second year of the conflict; the issue of conscription was hotly debated on both sides during the civil war.

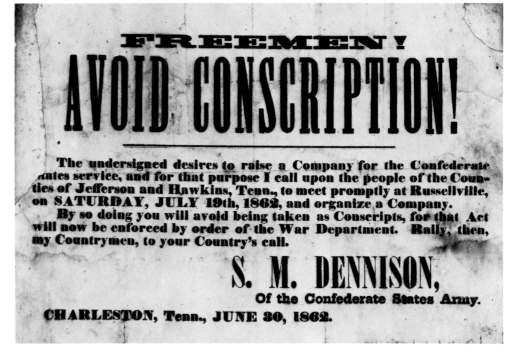

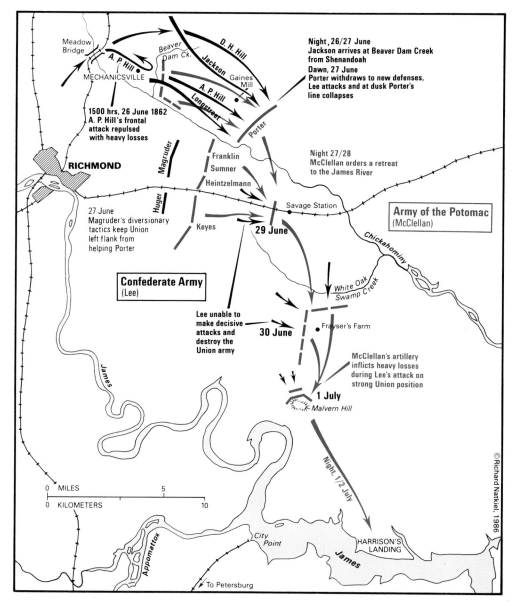

Above: Union attempts to capture Richmond during the Seven Days battles.

ate troops under General Lee attack McClellan's Army of the Potomac at a point north of Richmond, Malvern Hill. In this battle, the Confederate forces appear disorganized and make only minimal impact on Union troops which are equipped with better guns. Despite this final assault which goes badly for the South, the Northern army is prevented from taking the Southern capital of Richmond, Virginia. And despite the ability of Lee's forces to hold the Federals at bay, the Union Army of the Potomac is not destroyed or even seriously disabled. Throughout the Seven Days campaign there are thousands of casualties – the North tallying nearly 16,000 dead, injured and missing. Confederates estimate over 20,000 casualties.

2 July 1862

Washington In a move which is later to become important to the further development of vast agricultural lands in the West, President Lincoln signs the Morrill Land Grant Act. This law will give states apportionments of public land on which to build agricultural colleges. This important act is introduced in Congress by Senator Justin Morrill of Vermont.

Eastern Theater, Peninsular Campaign Harrison's Landing, Virginia, is the goal of McClellan's army which is retreating from its recent battle at Malvern Hill. Some minor skirmishing breaks out as the Union forces pull away.

4 July 1862

Washington This 86th celebration of Independence Day is observed with more than the usual enthusiasm.

Western Theater In Kentucky, Confederate Colonel John Hunt Morgan begins a series of raids which later earn him recognition from the Confederate Congress for his 'varied, heroic and invaluable services in Tennessee and Kentucky.'

7 July 1862

The North General McClellan, having reached Harrison's Landing on the James River, is visited by President Lincoln. In view of the recent difficulties faced by the Army of the Potomac which were, in McClellan's opinion, exacerbated by Lincoln's refusal to send more troops to aid in the peninsular campaign, the general delivers a letter to the president. In this letter, General McClellan points out what he perceives as weaknesses in Lincoln's current military and political strategies. He attempts to persuade the president to maintain a more conservative approach in conducting the war, urging that the war 'should not be at all a war upon population, but against armed forces and political organizations.'

9 July 1862

Western Theater Confederate John Hunt Morgan seizes Tompkinsville, Kentucky. The Confederate colonel and his cavalry unit are continuing to carry out a series of raids against Federal positions.

Naval At Hamilton, North Carolina, Confederate positions on the banks of the Roanoke River fall into Federal hands. Several Confederate vessels are taken by the North, and about 35 Southerners are killed. The Federals lose two men and sustain 10 injuries.

10 July 1862

Eastern Theater The Northern Army of Virginia commanded by General John Pope is positioned in the Shenandoah Valley.

Below: A scene from the inconclusive Battle of White Oak Swamp during the Union drive to reach the Confederate capital.

General Pope makes clear that civilians in the area are obligated to give aid to and prevent disruption of the Federal military efforts there. Pope prescribes harsh treatment in response to any resistance from the people in the Shenandoah Valley.

Western Theater Colonel Morgan and his raiders press Federals in Kentucky, and the Southern commander urges the people of the area to 'rise and arm, and drive the Hessian invaders from their soil.'

11 July 1862

Washington President Lincoln appoints General Henry Halleck to the position of general in chief of the Federal army. Halleck has proven to be an able and far-sighted leader, and his most recent actions at the successful seizure of Corinth, Mississippi, suggest that he will continue to exhibit sound judgment in military matters.

Below: General Henry Halleck was promoted to the position of Union general-in-chief by Lincoln on 11 July 1862.

13 July 1862

Washington President Lincoln is in correspondence with General McClellan over the allotment of soldiers for the attempted seizure of Richmond, Virginia. It is becoming increasingly difficult for Lincoln to ignore the fact that McClellan has yet to launch an effective offensive on the Peninsula.

Eastern Theater Movement of General Lee's Confederates away from Richmond, Virginia, suggests the beginning of another campaign against the threatening Northern forces. A bridge near Rapidan Station, Virginia, is destroyed by Northern troops as they skirmish with Confederates at this point on the Rapidan River.

Western Theater At Murfreesboro, Tennessee, Federal forces are defeated by General Nathan Bedford Forrest's 1000 troops. Northern General Thomas Crittenden and his men make a valiant defense but are overpowered and nearly all are captured by the Confederates. The North loses a large amount of valuable military equipment and supplies in this raid on their position at Murfreesboro.

Above: Union General John Pope, commander of the North's Army of Virginia during the Shenandoah Valley battles.

14 July 1862

Washington President Lincoln asks Congress to approve a law which will compensate 'any state which may abolish slavery within its limits.' The congressional approval that Lincoln seeks is not forthcoming, however, as 20 border states disagree with the president's plan. In a separate action, Congress passes a law creating the state of West Virginia which has seceded from the state of Virginia as a result of the split between North and South.

Eastern Theater The Union Army of Virginia under General John Pope's command receives orders from him concerning its conduct toward the enemy. In this famous address to the Northern troops, General Pope makes clear his stance and that which he expects his army to take: 'The strongest position a soldier should desire to occupy is one from which he can most easily advance against the enemy.'

15 July 1862

Naval In a spectacular battle on the Mississippi, the Southern ironclad *Arkansas* engages three Federal vessels, and proceeds down river. Near the City of Vicksburg, Admiral David Farragut atttacks the *Arkansas* with the Federal fleet but to no avail. The Union loses 18 men, sustains 50 injuries and lists 10 men as missing. Confederates tally 10 killed and 15 wounded.

17 July 1862

Washington The Second Confiscation Act is signed into law by President Lincoln. This act provides for the freedom of those slaves coming into Federal jurisdiction from outside the Union, and also gives the president certain powers to grant amnesty and pardon in cases where he deems such actions appropriate. (This act supplements, in many ways, the Emancipation Proclamation as it deals with slaves outside the Confederacy. The Emancipation Proclamation is concerned

with the disposition of those slaves who are in the territories in rebellion.)

Western Theater Confederate raiders under Colonel John Hunt Morgan make a surprise attack on Northern troops at Cynthiana, Kentucky. After several hours of fighting to defend their positions there, the Federals are overcome and Southern troops occupy the town. At this engagement, 17 Federal soldiers and 24 Confederates are killed. Skirmishing also occurs at Columbia, Tennessee.

20 July 1862

Western Theater Colonel Morgan's Confederate raiders are surprised by Union cavalry near Owensville, Kentucky, with the result that the Southern soldiers are dispersed, the Federals taking horses and equipment from them.

22 July 1862

Washington President Lincoln presents his Emancipation Proclamation to his cabinet. This action produces surprise in most quarters. The War Department announces that the military is empowered to employ as paid laborers any persons of African descent.

23 July 1862

Eastern Theater Confederates near Carmel Church, Virginia, are attacked by Federal cavalry. In Northern Virginia, General John Pope announces that all disloyal citizens within his jurisdiction are to be arrested.

Western Theater Confederate troops under General Braxton Bragg are advancing on Chattanooga, Tennessee, from their base at Tupelo, Mississippi.

27 July 1862

Trans-Mississippi There is skirmishing at various points between Federals and Confederates: near Brown's Spring, Missouri; in Carroll, Ray and Livingston counties in that state; and in Indian Territory.

28 July 1862

Trans-Mississippi Confederates lose 10 men at Bollinger's Mills, Missouri, as Federal forces make a successful assault on the Southern position there.

29 July 1862

Trans-Mississippi At Moore's Mills in Missouri, Confederates are routed by Union guerrillas. Southern losses tally at 62 dead, 100 wounded. Federals lose 16 men and sustain 30 injuries.

International Union officials in England are unsuccessful in an attempt to prevent the Confederate vessel *Alabama* from sailing out of Liverpool. Commanded by Captain Raphael Semmes, the *Alabama* will inflict much damage on Federal vessels in Atlantic waters, and is the ship responsible for a series of claims against the British government brought by United States ambassador Charles F Adams.

1 August 1862

Eastern Theater Federal troops under General McClellan, stationed at Harrison's Landing, Virginia, are bombarded by Confederate batteries. The Federals return the fire and silence the Confederate guns.

Trans-Mississippi Skirmishing breaks out in Missouri at Ozark, Grand River and Carrolton. In addition, at Newark, Missouri, Northern soldiers battle unsuccessfully with Southern troops resulting in the former's capitulation after several hours. About 70 Federals surrender to the Confederates in this action, while Southern casualties tally over 100 dead and injured.

2 August 1862

Washington Secretary of State Seward communicates the Federal government's position on mediation offers from Britain. Seward counsels United States ambassador to Britain, Charles F Adams, to decline any suggested mediation of the ongoing civil conflict in the United States.

Eastern Theater Orange Court House, Virginia, having been occupied by several Southern cavalry regiments, is seized by troops from General John Pope's Army of Virginia. These forces cross the Rapidan River, clashing with Confederates who lose 11 men and see 52 taken as prisoners; the Federals sustain five casualties in this encounter. Malvern Hill, Virginia, is retaken by troops from General McClellan's Federal Army of the Potomac.

3 August 1862

Washington General in Chief Henry Halleck sends orders to General McClellan that the Army of the Potomac is to be relocated. In order to better provide for the defense of the Federal capital, McClellan's troops are to be stationed at Alexandria and at Aquia Landing in Virginia. This conflicts with McClellan's views of the military needs of the Peninsula, and the general clashes bitterly with Halleck over this order.

4 August 1862

Washington The president issues military orders which are to provide for a draft of upwards of 300,000 men. This order never goes into effect, but in a separate action Lincoln makes provision for the recognition and promotion of competent military personnel. President Lincoln also declines the opportunity to enlist two black regiments from Indiana.

5 August 1862

Western Theater At Baton Rouge, Louisiana, Confederate forces attack Union troops stationed there. General John Breckenridge and about 2600 Southerners fight with 2500 Union soldiers under the command of General Thomas Williams, who is subsequently killed. The Confederates are eventually pushed back to a point some 10 miles out of the city, due in part to the inability of the Southern gunboat *Arkansas* to relieve the land forces. At this battle, Federals lose 383 men, the South tallies 453 dead. In Tennessee, Fort Donelson is attacked and the Union troops garrisoned there push the Southerners back after a fierce fight.

7 August 1862

Eastern Theater Confederate troops in Virginia push toward Union positions at Culpeper Court House and Madison Court House. Federals pull back from their recently recovered position at Malvern Hill, and there

Above: Captain Raphael Semmes commanded the successful Southern commerce-raider *Alabama* during the civil war.

is skirmishing between Federals and Southern troops at Wolftown, Virginia.

Trans-Mississippi Fort Fillmore in the New Mexico Territory witnesses the routing of Confederate troops in the area by Federal forces under Colonel E R S Canby. Montevallo, Missouri, is the site of skirmishing.

8 August 1862

Washington Secretary of War Stanton orders that anyone attempting to evade military service shall be subject to arrest.

Western Theater At Cumberland Gap in Tennessee, Confederates and Federals engage each other in fighting which ultimately leaves the Southern troops the losers – they tally 125 killed and injured as compared to Union casualties of three dead and 15 wounded.

9 August 1862

Eastern Theater, Second Bull Run Campaign At Cedar Mountain, Virginia, General Jackson's Confederates are positioned near Culpeper, and intend to strike the Union forces under General John Pope. In what is ultimately an unsuccessful action, General Banks and his Federals attack Jackson. This attack is foiled by General A P Hill's arrival; the Confederate troops under Hill manage to push Banks' forces back. It is by now clear to General Jackson that McClellan's Army of the Potomac will be moving into the region with reinforcements for Pope's troops. At this Battle of Cedar Mountain, the beginning of the Second Bull Run campaign (also known as Second Manassas) that lasts until September 1862, Union losses tally at 314 dead, 1445 injured, 622 missing. Southern forces report 1341 casualties.

11 August 1862

Western Theater Various actions occur – near Columbia, Tennessee, there is minor fighting between Southern troops and

Above: General Ambrose Hill, one of the key figures in the South's victory at the Battle of Cedar Mountain, Virginia.

Northern forces while similar clashes occur near Williamsport, also in Tennessee. In Corinth, Mississippi, an announcement by Union General Ulysses Grant states that those fugitive slaves in the area under his jurisdiction shall be employed by the military authorities.

12 August 1862

Western Theater   Confederate Colonel John Hunt Morgan carries out a raid on Gallatin, Tennessee, the result of which is the capture of the town where a Federal garrison, composed of four companies, is stationed. This takeover is short-lived, however, as Gallatin falls back into Union hands within 24 hours.

Below: Union troops storming Southern positions on the edge of a wood during the Cedar Mountain battle.

13 August 1862

Eastern Theater, Second Bull Run Campaign   Various minor skirmishes occur between Southerners and Northern troops in Virginia near Orange Court House. General Robert E Lee's forces begin to advance on Gordonsville, where this Army of Northern Virginia will soon be immersed in the Second Battle of Bull Run.

Trans-Mississippi   Confederates clash with, and are defeated by, Northern forces at Yellow Creek in Missouri. Around 60 Southern soldiers fall into Union hands after this engagement.

Naval   The Potomac River is the site of a collision between two Federal steamers, the *George Peabody* and the *West Point*. A total of 83 lives is lost in this accident.

16 August 1862

Eastern Theater, Second Bull Run Campaign   Following orders, General McClellan moves out of Harrison's Landing in Virginia with his Army of the Potomac. He proceeds northward to meet General Pope's Federals near Alexandria. Skirmishing breaks out in West Virginia at Wire Bridge.

17 August 1862

Trans-Mississippi   Minnesota sees the beginning of a six-week uprising of Sioux Indians, who are in revolt because of living conditions on their reservations. After nearly 300 whites are massacred by the Indians, Federal forces led by General H H Sibley are finally able to quell the uprising which continues until 23 September 1862.

18 August 1862

Eastern Theater, Second Bull Run Campaign   In order to protect his troops from Lee's advancing forces while waiting for the arrival of McClellan's army, General John Pope retreats to the north. At this time, information regarding Lee's movements has been captured by the Federals. Pope is now situated across the Rappahannock River from Lee's Army of Northern Virginia. Skirmish-

ing breaks out at Rapidan Station and Clark's Mountain in Virginia.

The Confederacy   At Richmond, Virginia, the Second Session of the Confederate Congress assembles. President Jefferson Davis makes a statement concerning the Southern nation's progress. While railing against the Union army's treatment of Southerners, Davis also speaks encouragingly about 'our final triumph in the pending struggle against despotic usurpation.'

Western Theater   In Tennessee, Clarksville is surrendered to Confederate forces. The Union commander there, Colonel R Mason, puts up no resistance to Southern troops prior to surrendering the city; he is later to be removed from military duty 'for repeated acts of cowardice.'

19 August 1862

The North   Editor of the *New York Tribune* Horace Greeley speaks out on the slavery issue, criticizing President Lincoln's stance. In his letter to the *Tribune,* titled 'The Prayer of Twenty Millions,' Greeley says, 'All attempts to put down the Rebellion and at the same time uphold its inciting cause are preposterous and futile.'

Trans-Mississippi   The Sioux Indians continue their uprising, creating major difficulties in Minnesota; the following day, Fort Ridgely is attacked by Indians but manages to withstand the assault.

20 August 1862

Eastern Theater, Second Bull Run Campaign   General McClellan's Army of the Potomac continues to advance toward a position near Alexandria, Virginia, in order to reinforce General Pope's troops. The latter have encountered Jackson's men at various points in the area between Culpeper and the Rappahannock.

21 August 1862

Eastern Theater, Second Bull Run Campaign   Confederate troops crossing the Rappahannock encounter strong resistance from

Federals; over 700 Southern soldiers lose their lives in this operation and nearly 2000 are captured by Union troops.

Western Theater In Tennessee, Confederate General Braxton Bragg moves his forces to a position above Chattanooga, and Gallatin is surrendered to the South by Union troops.

22 August 1862

Washington Responding to Horace Greeley's *New York Tribune* letter, 'The Prayer of Twenty Millions,' President Lincoln speaks in defense of his strategy. He points out his main objective, which is to preserve the Union, and that any and all efforts to achieve this preservation are, in his eyes, appropriate: 'I would save the Union. I would save it the shortest way under the Constitution . . . If I could save the Union without freeing *any* slave I would do it, and if I could save it by freeing *all* the slaves I would do it.'

23 August 1862

Eastern Theater A heavy barrage of Federal artillery opens along the Rappahannock, fire which is returned promptly by Southern batteries. After about five hours, this firing stops. Skirmishing occurs at Beverly Ford, Fant's Ford and at Smithfield Springs, all in Virginia.

25 August 1862

Washington Orders go out from Edwin Stanton, secretary of war, to the Southern Department. These orders provide for the enlistment of black soldiers, 'up to 5000 in number and to train them as guards for plantations and settlements.'

Eastern Theater, Second Bull Run Campaign At Waterloo Bridge, Virginia, there is heavy skirmishing between Confederates and Federals. The Southern forces under General Stonewall Jackson proceed out from their position on the Rappahannock, camping at Salem the following day and preparing for the impending battle with Union troops.

26 August 1862

Eastern Theater, Second Bull Run Campaign Also known as the Second Manassas, the campaign takes full shape as Confederates under General Jackson move in on Union General John Pope's troops. Manassas Junction and the railroad line there are seized by Southern forces. As Jackson divides his troops and encircles Pope's position, it becomes apparent to the latter that despite twice as many men, he may be forced to withdraw. Jackson's attempts to 'always mystify, mislead and surprise the enemy if possible' appear to be proving successful. General Pope does little while Jackson's men move into position near Sudley Mountain, on Stony Ridge. McClellan continues to move in to provide support for Pope's forces.

Trans-Mississippi In an effort which combines both land and naval forces, Union troops seize the Southern steamer *Fair Play* which is laden with arms and ammunition. This takeover occurs on the Yazoo River in Arkansas and is the result of an expedition led jointly by General Samuel Curtis and Commodore Charles Davis. In this venture, the Federals are rewarded with the acquisition of 1200 Enfield rifles, 4000 muskets and nearly 7000 pounds of powder.

Above: Union General Daniel Sickles directs his forces during Second Bull Run, a hard-fought encounter that saw the initially outnumbered Confederates repulse a succession of attacks before the Northerners finally conceded the battle to General Jackson's troops.

27 August 1862

Eastern Theater, Second Bull Run Campaign Kettle Run, Virginia, is one of several places which sees heavy skirmishing. General Hooker and his Federal troops are able to rout the Confederates at this point. Other sites of fighting in Virginia include Bull Run Bridge, Buckland Bridge and Waterford. The Confederates have now been able to interrupt communications between President Lincoln and General Pope. The latter is exhibiting some confusion as he pulls back from the formerly held positions along the Rappahannock River and moves slightly northward.

28 August 1862

Eastern Theater, Second Bull Run Campaign General Jackson's forces prepare to proceed to a point near Groveton, Virginia, and they engage Federals there who are commanded by General Rufus King. The fighting is extremely fierce at this Battle of Groveton, and many casualties are sustained by both North and South. General John Pope, operating under the mistaken assumption that Jackson is retreating toward the Shenandoah Valley, directs his troops to Groveton in order to rout the Confederates who remain there after the battle. Fredericksburg, Virginia, is evacuated by Union troops.

Above: Union troops assault a Confederate-held railroad embankment during the height of the fighting at Bull Run.

29 August 1862

Eastern Theater, Second Bull Run Campaign   In a strategic error, General Pope allows his men to attack Jackson's Confederates so as to cut off the latter's retreat. Pope is unaware that the Southern forces have no intention of withdrawing, even though there are 20,000 Confederates to repel 62,000 Federals. This imbalance is soon minimized by the arrival of additional Southern troops under General Longstreet. Pope's somewhat disorganized troops are no match for the Confederates who have been anticipating and preparing for this, the Second Battle of Bull Run, or Manassas, for several days. Union General John Pope, oblivious to the fact that Longstreet has arrived with reinforcements, intends to pursue the fight further the following day. Unfortunately for the Northern troops, this gives Longstreet an opportunity to crush a portion of Pope's left flank, causing a retreat over the Bull Run but also saving a number of Federal soldiers.

31 August 1862

Eastern Theater, Second Bull Run Campaign   There is minor skirmishing in the aftermath of the Union defeat at the Second Battle of Bull Run. General Pope consolidates his forces near Centreville, Virginia. Weldon, Virginia sees fighting – 110 Confederates were left dead and five Union soldiers were killed at this engagement.
Western Theater   Minor fighting occurs in Alabama and Kentucky.

1 September 1862

Eastern Theater, Second Bull Run Campaign   A battle at Chantilly, or Ox Hill, Virginia, proves to be the final clash between North and South in the Second Battle of Bull Run. The day-long engagement between 1300 Federals and 800 Confederates results in victory for the South. The defeat of the North is compounded by the deaths of Union Generals J J Stevens and Philip Kearney. General Pope finally retreats toward Washington, DC.

Western Theater   In Kentucky, General E Kirby Smith and his Southern troops cause apprehension at Lexington since it is expected that the Confederates will try to take the city. The state legislature in Kentucky adjourns and moves to a more secure location at Louisville.

2 September 1862

Washington   In an important command change, President Lincoln orders General McClellan to take over the Union Army of Virginia and the forces now defending Washington, DC. This is a move made without the full support of Lincoln's cabinet; notably, Secretary of War Edwin Stanton withholds his approval.

3 September 1862

Washington   General Halleck is the recipient of a report made by General John Pope concerning the action of various officers at the Second Battle of Bull Run. Pope charges McClellan with lack of support, pointing out the need for reinforcements at the time Jackson was attacking and the tardiness with which McClellan's men arrived.
Western Theater   Frankfort, Kentucky, is occupied by General E Kirby Smith's Confederates, and in the Geiger's Lake area there is minor skirmishing.

4 September 1862

Eastern Theater   Various minor engagements occur as the Confederate Army of Northern Virginia under General Robert E Lee moves toward Maryland. General A G Jenkins conducts raids in West Virginia near Point Pleasant.
Naval   The Federal blockade off Mobile Bay, Alabama, is unsuccessful in preventing the Confederate steamer *Oreto* from making it safely to port, despite the valiant efforts of the Union *Oneida*.

7 September 1862

Washington   Due to the Confederate army's positioning itself at Frederick, Maryland, the Union capital at Washington, DC, is in turmoil. Many fear an immediate invasion there and citizens of other nearby cities – Baltimore and Hagerstown, Maryland, and

Harrisburg, Pennsylvania – make various arrangements to arm themselves against the alleged invaders. Many people evacuate their homes.
Western Theater   Minor skirmishing breaks out at Murfreesboro and Pine Mountain Gap, Tennessee. General Bragg advances with his Confederates, Kentucky being their goal; Bowling Green is occupied by Union forces.

8 September 1862

Eastern Theater   The Confederate Army of Northern Virginia under General Lee creates fear and confusion among the citizens of Maryland where Lee and his forces are encamped. In response to these feelings, Lee makes an attempt to explain the Southern position: 'We know no enemies among you, and will protect all, of every opinion. It is for you to decide your destiny freely, and without constraint. This army will respect your choice, whatever it may be.' Close to the Federal capital, General Nathaniel Banks takes charge of defense forces.

9 September 1862

Eastern Theater, Antietam Campaign   Williamsburg, Virginia, is attacked by Confederates but Union troops there successfully repel the advance. General Longstreet receives orders to approach Boonesboro, Maryland, with his Confederates. Skirmishing occurs at Monocacy Church and Barnesville, both in Maryland.

10 September 1862

Eastern Theater, Antietam Campaign   Gauley, Virginia, witnesses an attack on Union forces by Confederates posted in the area. Fayetteville, West Virginia, sees military action which results in a Southern victory. General McClellan continues to advance on Lee's army which is positioned near Frederick, Maryland.
Western Theater   Cincinnati, Ohio, anticipates an invasion by Confederates and prepares to make defense of the city. Militia is called out to repel the imminent invasion.

12 September 1862

Eastern Theater, Antietam Campaign   General McClellan pushes toward Frederick, Maryland, with the Army of the Potomac which has absorbed the Army of Virginia. Skirmishing continues in the vicinity.

13 September 1862

Eastern Theater, Antietam Campaign   In what proves to be a stroke of luck for the Union forces, General Lee's orders for the Maryland invasion are discovered by Union soldiers. Due to this, General McClellan is able to approach with more accuracy the Confederate positions near Harper's Ferry, where Jackson has been posted; Hagerstown, where General Longstreet is to be stationed; and South Mountain, the location of Jeb Stuart's cavalry. It is now clear that McClellan can take advantage of the divided strength of Lee's army.

14 September 1862

Eastern Theater, Antietam Campaign   The Battle of Crampton's Gap, the first of several engagements making up the Antietam campaign, occurs. As Confederate troops under

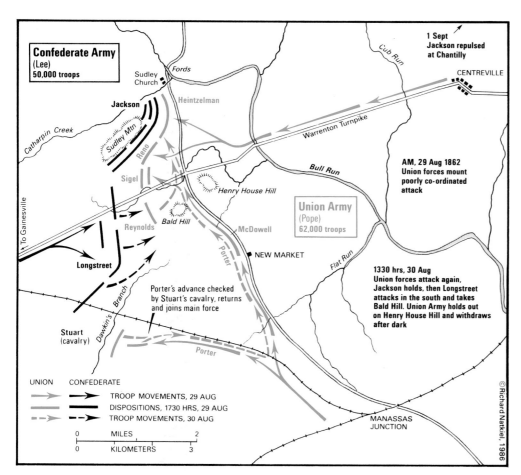

Confederate Army
(Lee)
50,000 troops

Sudley
Church

Fords

Jackson

Heintzelman

Catharpin Creek

Sudley Mtn

Reno

Sigel

To Gainesville

Reynolds

Bald Hill

Longstreet

Stuart
(cavalry)

Dawkin's Branch

Porter's advance checked
by Stuart's cavalry, returns
and joins main force

Henry House Hill

McDowell

Porter

NEW MARKET

Porter

Warrenton Turnpike

Bull Run

Cub Run

CENTREVILLE

1 Sept
Jackson repulsed
at Chantilly

AM, 29 Aug 1862
Union forces mount
poorly co-ordinated
attack

Union Army
(Pope)
62,000 troops

Flat Run

1330 hrs, 30 Aug
Union forces attack again,
Jackson holds, then Longstreet
attacks in the south and takes
Bald Hill. Union Army holds out
on Henry House Hill and withdraws
after dark

© Richard Natkiel, 1986

UNION   CONFEDERATE
———→   ——→   TROOP MOVEMENTS, 29 AUG
- - - -   ———   DISPOSITIONS, 1730 HRS, 29 AUG
- - -→   - - →   TROOP MOVEMENTS, 30 AUG

0   MILES   2
0   KILOMETERS   3

MANASSAS
JUNCTION

the command of General LaFayette McLaws prepare to attack Harper's Ferry, Virginia, Union troops move in on them. Under General William Franklin this Union force is able, after a day of fighting, to cause the Confederates to pull back. The Union general is overcautious in his judgment of the Southern forces' abilities, even after their retreat. This results in the eventual capture of Harper's Ferry by the Confederates since Franklin's reluctance to engage McLaws again permits the latter to regroup and support Lee's assault on Harper's Ferry the following day. In a separate battle, that of South Mountain, Federals under General Alfred Pleasonton attack Confederates at Turner's Gap, Virginia. The engagement results in the Southern forces being pushed out of the higher ground. At this battle, the Union troops lose 325 men and sustain 1403 injuries. Likewise, the South sees 325 soldiers killed and 1561 wounded. The latter forces report 800 missing while Northern soldiers missing tally only 85.

15 September 1862

Eastern Theater, Antietam Campaign The fighting in northern Virginia continues as General Lee's Confederates, under General

Left: The movements of the rival armies prior to the Second Battle of Bull Run. Longstreet's sudden arrival helped the South win the battle. *Below:* Union troops advance on the Southern line at the Battle of Antietam.

Stonewall Jackson's leadership, attack Harper's Ferry. This episode in the Antietam campaign sees Federal troops unable to withstand the fierce assault and nearly 12,000 Union soldiers are captured after relatively brief defense. The Federal commander at Harper's Ferry, General Dixon S Miles, is killed during this battle. At Sharpsburg, Southern forces arrive after having been pushed out of their position at South Mountain, Virginia. The Confederate Army under General Lee is now preparing to confront the Northern forces near Sharpsburg.

17 September 1862

Eastern Theater, Antietam Campaign
Despite the fact that the Southern forces are greatly outnumbered by General McClellan's Army of the Potomac, General Lee positions his troops for an attack along Antietam

Left: Artillery in action during the heavy fighting at Antietam.
Below: Union forces recross Burnside bridge after an attempt to turn the Southern flank at Antietam.

Creek. The Northern assault coming early in the day is disorganized and it allows the Confederates to rally somewhat. Union General Burnside attacks the southern right flank, pushing the Southern troops aside, crossing Burnside Bridge and advancing on Antietam, a movement which is halted by General A P Hill's arrival. The latter has been dealing with the surrender of Harper's Ferry and has only been able to join the rest of Lee's forces late in the day. Hill's advent on the battle scene prevents any further movements by the Federals and saves the Confederate right. At this Battle of Antietam, or Sharpsburg, the Confederates suffer heavy losses, as do the Union forces. However threatened General Lee's troops are in terms of manpower or positioning, they continue to hold their ground, a withdrawal not being considered until the following day. Casualties for the North are

Left: Lincoln confers with McClellan at Harper's Ferry after Antietam.
Below: Confederate dead litter the floor of 'Bloody Angle,' scene of heavy fighting during the Battle of Antietam.

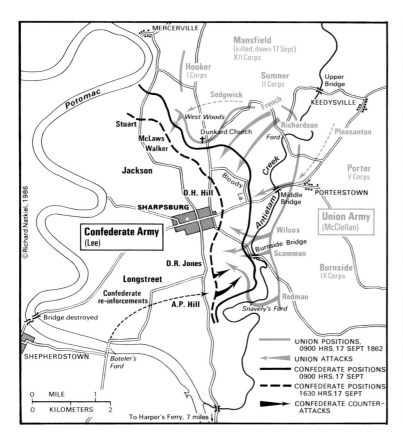

tallied at 2108 killed, 9549 wounded, 753 missing; for the South, estimates list 2700 killed, 9024 wounded, and 2000 missing. Antietam is considered by many to be 'the bloodiest single day of the war.'

Western Theater   In the West, General Braxton Bragg accepts the surrender of Mumfordsville, Kentucky, as the Union commander, Colonel John Wilder, relinquishes control of that city.

18 September 1862

Eastern Theater, Antietam Campaign   Late in the day, General Robert E Lee and his Army of Northern Virginia move out of Maryland after the engagement at Antietam the previous day. With this invasion of the North via Maryland in a shambles, the Confederates once more find themselves in a defensive posture.

19 September 1862

Eastern Theater   Portions of Harper's Ferry, Virginia, are burned by retreating Confederates. Skirmishing occurs near Sharpsburg and Williamsport, Maryland.

Western Theater   In a battle which claims 782 Federal casualties, Southern troops attack Union forces at Iuka, Mississippi. The Confederates, under General Sterling Price, number nearly 17,000. The Federals have around 9000 and are attacked as Union General Rosecrans leads a movement into the town. After several hours the Northerners have overwhelmed Price's forces and the latter retreat toward the south.

21 September 1862

Eastern Theater   In Virginia, Federals crossing the Potomac engage in skirmishing with Southern troops at Shepherdstown. This results ultimately in a retreat by Union forces, which lose about 150 men.

Western Theater   In Kentucky, General Braxton Bragg takes his Southern troops to Bardstown. The purpose of this is to enable Bragg's men to join with General E Kirby Smith's troops, but it allows Union General Buell to push forward to Louisville, Kentucky. At Mumfordsville, Kentucky, Union troops retake the town which had previously fallen to Confederates.

22 September 1862

Washington   President Lincoln makes a move which is to help terminate slavery as a United States institution. In presenting the Emancipation Proclamation to his cabinet, Lincoln has chosen a time, after the Union success at Antietam, which he hopes will prove most advantageous.

24 September 1862

Washington   President Lincoln suspends the writ of habeas corpus for any individuals who are deemed guilty of 'discouraging volunteer enlistments, resisting militia drafts, guilty of any disloyal practice or affording comfort to Rebels.'

Above, far left: The Battle of Antietam.
Above left: Union General 'Fightin' Joe' Hooker at Antietam.
Left: Confederate troops launch an assault against the Union Battery Robinett during the Battle of Corinth.

1 October 1862

Washington   President Lincoln travels to Harper's Ferry to discuss the future of the Army of the Potomac with General McClellan.

The Confederacy   At the Confederate capital of Richmond, Virginia, the newspaper *Whig* voices an opinion concerning Lincoln's recent Emancipation Proclamation, 'It is a dash of the pen to destroy four thousand millions of our property, and is as much a bid for . . . insurrection, with the assurance of aid from the . . . United States.'

2 October 1862

Western Theater   Columbia, Mississippi, is the scene of a major battle between Federals and Confederates. The latter forces, under the command of Generals Van Dorn and Sterling Price, press Northern troops northwest of Corinth. On this first day of fighting, the Federals are forced on to the defensive.

4 October 1862

Western Theater   Another day of intense fighting at Corinth, Mississippi, sees Federals under General Rosecrans hit hard by Van Dorn's Confederate troops. Despite this intense offensive, the Southerners are forced to withdraw before nightfall. Van Dorn's men are positioned, after this retreat, at Chewalla, Mississippi. Casualties at the close of the battle tally as follows: Union soldiers killed, 355; wounded, 1841; missing, 324. The Confederates estimate that they have lost 473 men here, have 1997 injured, and 1763 missing. The result of this battle at Corinth, Mississippi, does not give the South the satisfaction of securing the railroad center there, nor does it cause General Rosecrans to pull back toward Ohio. There is minor fighting in Kentucky at Bardstown and Clay Village. Middleton, Tennessee, also sees a brief engagement between rival forces of Federals and Confederates.

5 October 1862

Western Theater   Outside of Corinth, Mississippi, Federals under General Rosecrans' command follow retreating Confederates, although Van Dorn's men are able to slip away from this Northern force. They are apprehended, however, by Federal General E O C Ord's men near the Hatchie River in Tennessee. This results in fighting of an intense, albeit brief, nature. The fighting associated with Corinth, Mississippi, ends as Confederates break free of Ord's troops and head for Holly Springs. In Kentucky, General Braxton Bragg and his Southern troops move away from Bardstown and are followed by General Buell's Federals.

6 October 1862

Western Theater   General Braxton Bragg and his Confederates pull back toward Harrodsburg, Kentucky, pursued by General Buell's Northern troops. The latter occupy Bardstown, Kentucky.

8 October 1862

Eastern Theater   Minor fighting breaks out near Fairfax in Virginia.

Western Theater   The Battle of Perryville, Kentucky, occurs involving General Braxton Bragg's Confederates and General Don Car-

Above: General Earl Van Dorn led the Southern forces during the prolonged battle at Corinth, Mississippi, in October.

los Buell's Northern troops. The result of this encounter, the most significant of the battles fought in Kentucky, is that Bragg is compelled to retreat southeastward. Casualties are listed for the Federals at 845 dead, 2851 wounded, 515 missing, out of a total of 36,940 men. Confederates tally 510 killed, 2635 injured, 251 missing out of a total troop strength of 16,000.

9 October 1862

Eastern Theater   At Chambersburg, Pennsylvania, Confederate General J E B Stuart begins several days of raiding which he carries as far as Cashtown, Pennsylvania. Stuart has crossed Federal lines in order to accomplish this and has ridden his 1800 troops in a circle around General McClellan's inactive Army of the Potomac.

10 October 1862

The Confederacy   A request is made by Confederate President Jefferson Davis to draft 4500 blacks. The purpose of this is to further aid the Confederate army in its construction of fortifications around Richmond, Virginia.

11 October 1862

The Confederacy   In Richmond, Virginia, the Confederate Congress passes a bill, approved by President Jefferson Davis, which amends the military draft law. According to the new regulations, anyone owning 20 or more slaves is exempt from service in the Confederate army. This law is publicized amid much controversy due to its selective nature, and serves to heighten a sense of class conflict in the Confederacy, some viewing the military situation as a 'rich man's war and a poor man's fight.'

Eastern Theater   Chambersburg, Pennsylvania, witnesses the continued raiding by J E B Stuart's Confederates. They seize around

500 horses and destroy several trains before crossing the Potomac and returning to Virginia near Poolesville several days later.

12 October 1862

Trans-Mississippi Ozark, Missouri, is the jumping-off point for a Northern expeditionary force headed for Yellville, Arkansas. This mission lasts for seven days. There is light fighting near Arrow Rock in Missouri.

15 October 1862

Eastern Theater Part of the Army of the Potomac under General McClellan is involved in an expedition from Sharpsburg, Maryland, to Smithfield, West Virginia. They also take part in a reconnaissance beginning at Harper's Ferry and ending in Charlestown, West Virginia.

18 October 1862

Western Theater Confederate John Hunt Morgan with 1500 men routs Federal cavalry forces outside Lexington, Kentucky. The Southerners enter the city and seize an estimated 125 prisoners.

20 October 1862

Western Theater There are various episodes of minor skirmishing. Hermitage Ford, Tennessee, sees light action as does Wild Cat, Kentucky. Near Nashville, Tennessee,

Below: 'Teazer' gun on a Confederate gunboat. Such vessels were used in a wide variety of roles by both sides.

Union troops push back Confederates under the command of General Nathan Bedford Forrest. Near Bardstown, Kentucky, Southern forces manage to attack and destroy a line of 81 Federal wagons. The Confederates are subsequently able to seize yet another train of wagons several hours later in Bardstown itself.

21 October 1862

Washington An announcement by President Lincoln urges support in Tennessee for state elections. Lincoln entreats both civilian and military personnel to move to elect state government officials, a legislature and members of Congress.

22 October 1862

Western Theater Confederate General Braxton Bragg is successful in withdrawing Southern troops from Kentucky where Federals under General Buell continue to make their presence felt following the Battle of Perryville on 8-9 October 1862. There is a Union reconnaissance to Waverly, Tennessee, leaving from Fort Donelson. This expedition encounters Confederate forces, skirmishing several times during the next three days. Loudon, Kentucky, is seized by a force of Confederate cavalry under the command of Southern General Joseph Wheeler.

Trans-Mississippi At Maysville, Arkansas, what is known by some as the Second Battle of Pea Ridge is fought. Union forces are successful in pushing 5000 Confederates out of the area into the valley of the Arkansas.

Above: Confederate General Braxton Bragg managed to beat a skilful retreat after the Battle of Perryville.

Southerners suffer losses of artillery and horses at this encounter.

24 October 1862

Washington Because of his failure to prevent Bragg's Confederates from escaping from Kentucky, General Don Carlos Buell is relieved of command of Federal troops in Kentucky and Tennessee. President Lincoln

authorizes General William Rosecrans to take over the responsibility for these troops as well as Federal forces in the Department of the Cumberland.

Western Theater In Brownsville, Tennessee, Confederate forces are routed by Federals. At Morgantown, Kentucky, Union troops seize 16 Southern soldiers. On St Helena Island in South Carolina there is a brief skirmish between Union and Confederate troops.

Trans-Mississippi Fayetteville,Arkansas, sees light fighting and there is a Federal expedition from Independence, Missouri, which, in the course of its three-day maneuver, encounters several guerrilla forces around the settlements of Greenton, Chapel Hill and Hopewell.

25 October 1862

Washington President Lincoln is again in communication with General McClellan over the Army of the Potomac. The chief executive is becoming increasingly annoyed with the general's seeming inability to launch any major assault against Confederates in Virginia. As a telegram to McClellan indicates, Lincoln is not above venting his anger at the general's delays: 'Will you pardon me for asking what the horses of your army have done since the battle of Antietam that fatigue anything?' This is in response to a communication from McClellan about 'sore tongued and fatigued horses.'

26 October 1862

Eastern Theater General McClellan moves the Federal Army of the Potomac across the river into Virginia, causing the president to write from Washington, DC, that he 're-joiced' in this overdue action.

27 October 1862

Western Theater In Louisiana, the Battle of Labadieville takes place on Bayou Lafourche. Confederates are routed at this action, losing six men, sustaining 15 wounded and reporting 208 taken prisoner. Federals report 18 dead and 74 wounded.

Naval Federal blockaders on Bull's Bay in South Carolina successfully seize the British steamer *Anglia*.

28 October 1862

Eastern Theater General McClellan is moving his Potomac Army troops toward Warrenton, Virginia, and this causes Confederate General Robert E Lee to push his troops slightly to the south. Lee wishes to prevent his forces from being encircled by McClellan's men. Union forces occupy Halltown, Virginia, and there is light skirmishing at Snicker's Gap.

Trans-Mississippi At Fayetteville, Arkansas, there is a clash between 1000 Union soldiers and about 3000 Confederates encamped there. The Federal forces follow the retreating Southerners into the area around the Boston Mountains.

31 October 1862

Western Theater The upcoming Federal action against Vicksburg, Mississippi, is foreshadowed by the gathering of Northern troops at Grand Junction, Tennessee. These troops are moving in from Corinth, Missis-

sippi and Bolivar, Tennessee. Union forces scheduled to act as relief for the garrison at Nashville, Tennessee, move through Bowling Green, Kentucky.

1 November 1862

Western Theater In New Orleans, Louisiana, military governor General Benjamin Butler tightens restrictions on movement to and from the city. In addition, Butler allows for the freeing of all imprisoned 'slaves not know to be the slaves of loyal owners.' Vicksburg, Mississippi, is the target of a campaign being planned by General Ulysses Grant.

4 November 1862

The North Congressional elections in Northern states prove advantageous to Democrats in New York, New Jersey, Illinois and Wisconsin. New York elects a Democrat as governor, Horatio Seymour. There are some Republican victories in border states, in California, Michigan and New England, however, which help the Republicans maintain control of the House of Representatives.

Western Theater In Mississippi, General Grant's Federals successfully occupy La Grange. This occupation, as well as a similar one at Grand Junction, Tennessee, is in preparation for the upcoming Vicksburg campaign. Union troops in Georgia destroy the Southern saltworks at Kingsbury.

5 November 1862

Washington In one of the more significant command changes of the war, President Lincoln removes General George Brinton McClellan from his post as head of the Army of the Potomac. After months of attempting to support McClellan, Lincoln is alleged to have said, 'sending reinforcements to McClellan is like shovelling flies across a barn.' The general has been extremely reluctant to make any offensives against Lee's army in Virginia, and any of his efforts in that direction are so minimal as to be virtually unnoticed. The official orders read: 'By direction of the President, it is ordered that Major General McClellan be relieved from the command of the Army of the Potomac; and that Major General Burnside take the command of

that Army.' In another shift in command, General Fitz John Porter is replaced by General Joseph Hooker.

7 November 1862

Eastern Theater General George McClellan is notified of his removal from the command of the Army of the Potomac. Completely surprised by this turn of events, he makes an extreme effort to prevent those around him from seeing how amazed he is to receive this news: 'I am sure that not the slightest expression of feeling was visible on my face.'

8 November 1862

Washington Further command changes see General Benjamin Butler replaced as head of the Department of the Gulf. Butler is succeeded by General Nathaniel Banks, whose orders include the directive that 'The President regards the opening of the Mississippi River as the first and most important of our military and naval operations.'

9 November 1862

Eastern Theater Virginia witnesses some light action in Greenbrier County, and at Warrenton, Virginia, General Burnside officially takes over command of the Army of the Potomac. A Union cavalry charge into Fredericksburg results in the taking of 34 Confederates as prisoners of war. Federals lose only one man out of a force of 54.

10 November 1862

Eastern Theater At Warrenton, Virginia, General George Brinton McClellan says his farewell respects to the Army of the Potomac there. Well-liked and respected by the troops, McClellan's departure is an occasion marked by near-idolization of 'Little Mac.'

13 November 1862

Western Theater Military actions of a minor, inconclusive nature continue. At Nashville, Tennessee, Union and Confederate soldiers engage in skirmishing. A railroad

Below: General Brinton McClellan takes his leave of the Army of the Potomac after being dismissed by Lincoln.

depot near Holly Springs, Mississippi, is taken by Federals. General Braxton Bragg, intent on joining forces with General Breckenridge, pushes his Army of Tennessee toward Murfreesboro from Chattanooga, Tennessee.

14 November 1862

Eastern Theater The newly-appointed chief of the Army of the Potomac, General Burnside, reorganizes his troops placing Generals Sumner, Hooker and Franklin in charge of three main divisions of the army. This is in preparation for an assault on the Confederate capital at Richmond, Virginia.

Western Theater General Braxton Bragg has positioned his Confederate troops at Tullahoma, near Nashville, Tennessee.

15 November 1862

Eastern Theater General Burnside moves his Potomac Army troops out of Warrenton, Virginia, and advances on Fredericksburg. There is an exchange of artillery fire between Union and Southern forces at Fayetteville, Virginia.

17 November 1862

Naval The Southern steamer *Alabama*, under the command of Captain Raphael Semmes, sails into the harbor at Martinique followed by the USS *San Jacinto*, although the latter vessel quickly leaves the harbor in order to lie in wait for the Confederate ship.

Left: General Ambrose Burnside, McClellan's replacement as head of the Army of the Potomac.
Below: Union troops embark on pontoons to begin the attack on Fredericksburg.

18 November 1862

Eastern Theater, Fredericksburg Campaign General Burnside and his Army of the Potomac arrive in Falmouth, Virginia, on the banks of the Rappahannock River across from Fredericksburg. Skirmishing breaks out between Union and Confederate soldiers at Rural Hill, Virginia.

Naval Despite the efforts of the *San Jacinto*, the Confederate *Alabama* manages to leave Martinique.

19 November 1862

Eastern Theater Both Union and Confederate forces are taking positions in the vicinity of Fredericksburg, Virginia. General Longstreet is established near Culpeper; General Burnside near Falmouth. The Confederate cavalry under J E B Stuart is positioned at Warrenton Junction, Virginia.

Western Theater General Ulysses Grant sends out reconnaissance forces to ascertain the strength of Confederate troops defending Vicksburg, Mississippi. Federal forces leave Grand Junction, Tennessee, on a two day expedition to Ripley, Mississippi.

20 November 1862

Eastern Theater The Confederates in Virginia stationed near Fredericksburg are heartened by the arrival of General Robert E Lee. Charlestown, Virginia, sees some minor skirmishing between North and South.

21 November 1862

Eastern Theater As military strength builds in the vicinity, the mayor of Fredericksburg, Virginia, is issued a request for surrender by General Burnside. Refusing to give in, the mayor is told to evacuate women, children and injured or infirm people from the town.

22 November 1862

Washington In the Federal capital orders go out from Secretary of War Stanton to release all those imprisoned for political reasons – those who had been found guilty of draft evasion, of discouraging others to enlist in the armed service and for other similar actions.

Eastern Theater In a reversal of Burnside's orders of the previous day, General Sumner tells the mayor of Fredericksburg, Virginia, that he will not fire on the town. This agreement is made in exchange for a promise of 'no hostile demonstrations' from the townspeople.

26 November 1862

Washington In order to meet with his recently-appointed general of the Potomac Army, President Lincoln leaves the Federal capital for Aquia Creek, Virginia.

27 November 1862

Eastern Theater President Lincoln confers with General Burnside. The two are not in total agreement about the proper strategy to employ in the current situation along the Rappahannock. The general ultimately decides not to defer to the president's wishes and instead follows his own plan for an assault on Fredericksburg where most of Lee's forces are concentrated. In the forthcoming campaign Burnside will be outfought by Lee's forces.

28 November 1862

Eastern Theater At Frankfort, Virginia, Confederate troops are routed by Union forces and some 110 Southerners are taken prisoner.

Trans-Mississippi General James Blunt and his Federals stage an attack on Confederate positions at Cane Hill, Arkansas. The 8000 Southern troops there are under the command of General John Marmaduke. Blunt's 5000 men pursue Marmaduke into the Boston Mountains after beating them back, but this chase is called off due to the strategic danger it creates for the Union forces. At this encounter, Federals tally losses at 40 men while the Southern total is considerably higher at 435.

30 November 1862

Naval The Confederate steamer *Alabama* continues to be elusive as it sails Atlantic waters and threatens Northern shipping. The Federal vessel *Vanderbilt* makes an attempt to capture the Southern vessel, but is unsuccessful.

1 December 1862

Washington Congress meets in the Federal capital; President Lincoln addresses this, the third session of the 37th Congress, giving his State of the Union message. In addition to remarks made about the North's progress in the war and the positive condition of the Federal economy, the chief executive discusses several constitutional amendments. These proposed amendments center around slavery, suggesting plans for colonization, and for financial compensation to previous slave owners as well as cooperating states. Lincoln points out that '. . . *we* cannot escape history, . . . In *giving* freedom to the *slave*, we *assure* freedom to the free.'

3 December 1862

Western Theater Near Nashville, Tennessee, Confederates attack Northern soldiers along the Hardin Pike. Grenada, Mississippi, is seized by General Hovey's Federals, who number about 20,000. This takeover occurs after Southerners have destroyed 15 locomotives and approximately 100 railroad cars.

Above: Northern forces crossing the Rappahannock in the first stages of the Battle of Fredericksburg.

4 December 1862

Eastern Theater, Fredericksburg Campaign Winchester, Virginia, falls into Union hands, resulting in the capture of 145 Southern soldiers. Near Fredericksburg, Virginia, Northern troops clash with Confederates on the Rappahannock River and also on Stone's River, near Stewart's Ferry.

6 December 1862

Washington As a result of the Indian uprisings in Minnesota during September, President Lincoln orders the execution of 39 Indians, the hangings to take place on 19 December 1862.

Trans-Mississippi There is an attack on Federal troops at Cane Hill, Arkansas.

7 December 1862

The Confederacy Confederate General John Pemberton receives a communication from President Jefferson Davis concerning

Below: John Hunt Morgan was renowned as a Confederate guerrilla leader.

the defense of Vicksburg, Mississippi. The Confederate president is worried about Pemberton's ability to hold out against an attack by Grant's men. Davis asks Pemberton: 'Are you in communication with General J E Johnston? Hope you will be reinforced in time.'

Western Theater Hartville, Tennessee, is the scene of yet another raid by John Hunt Morgan and his men. Federal forces under Colonel A B Moore suffer losses tallied at 2096, 1800 being taken prisoner by the Southern raiders.

Trans-Mississippi In Arkansas, the Battle of Prairie Grove takes place as Confederate General Thomas Hindman surprises 10,000 Northern troops. The latter, commanded by Generals James Blunt and Francis Herron, are unable, despite their combined forces, to repel the Confederates, who also number 10,000. The South suffers 164 fatalities, 817 injuries and reports 336 missing at this battle, whereas Federals report 175 dead, 813 wounded, 263 missing.

10 December 1862

Washington A bill creating the state of West Virginia passes the United States House of Representatives on a vote of 96-55. This follows a similar action by the Senate on 14 July 1862.

Eastern Theater, Fredericksburg Campaign The Union troops under General Burnside's command around Fredericksburg, Virginia, increase their preparation for an advance on that city. Port Royal, Virginia, is bombarded by Federal gunboats in retaliation for an attack on the latter by Confederate shore batteries.

11 December 1862

Eastern Theater, Fredericksburg Campaign Fredericksburg, Virginia, is occupied by Union forces under General Burnside. The Confederates in the vicinity are poised in readiness for the upcoming attack.

Below: Wave after wave of Union troops attempt to storm the Southern entrenchments on Marye's Heights behind Fredericksburg.

Western Theater More skirmishing breaks out near Nashville, Tennessee. At Columbia, Tennessee, Confederate General Nathan Bedford Forrest moves out with nearly 2500 men in an attempt to disrupt General Grant's lines of communication.

13 December 1862

Eastern Theater, Fredericksburg Campaign Approximately 72,000 Confederates under General Stonewall Jackson's command are attacked at Fredericksburg, Virginia, by Union troops totaling about 106,000. The forces under General William Franklin attack Southern positions just across the Rappahannock to the south of the city. Meanwhile, General Sumner advances on positions north of the city and is able initially to break through the Confederate defenses, but the result is that Union soldiers are now forced to attack Southern troops placed at the foot of Marye's Heights. The Confederates are firmly entrenched and it is impossible for Federals to do more than struggle along the base of the ridge where the South is positioned. The attempt by Northern troops is a genuine but futile one. One Union soldier comments: 'It was a great slaughter pen . . . they might as well have tried to take Hell.' The casualties are high – 12,700 killed and wounded among the Federals. The Confederates report 5300 dead or injured, among them, Generals Cobb and Gregg. General Robert E Lee remarks of this day's fight, 'I wish these people would go away and let us alone.'

Western Theater At Tuscumbia, Alabama, there is a clash between Federal and Southern troops as Union soldiers attack and rout Confederates there. Mississippi sees a six-day offensive staged by Federal forces on the Mobile and Ohio Railroad which runs between Tupelo and Corinth.

14 December 1862

Eastern Theater, Fredericksburg Campaign The Northern Army of the Potomac in and around Fredericksburg, Virginia, makes preparations to move back across the Rappahan-

nock River. Despite the Union army's vulnerable position after the Battle of Fredericksburg, the Southern forces under the command of General Lee do not attack Burnside's troops prior to their withdrawal.

15 December 1862

Western Theater In Tennessee, General Grant's forces, which are on their way to Vicksburg, Mississippi, experience difficulties with Confederate forces under General Nathan Bedford Forrest. The latter has, with approximately 2500 soldiers, started toward Vicksburg intending to interfere with the Federal communications along the way. New Orleans, Louisiana, sees the departure of General Benjamin Butler, who has been forced to step down as military governor. Few of the citizens of New Orleans are sorry to see him leave.

16 December 1862

Washington The execution of Sioux Indians, slated for 19 December 1862, has been delayed by President Lincoln. A new date of 26 December 1862 has been set.

Eastern Theater West Virginia witnesses an outbreak of skirmishing at Wardensville. General Burnside and the Army of the Potomac occupy Falmouth, Virginia. The general has made a statement concerning his part in the failure at Fredericksburg, a failure for which he assumes total responsibility.

Western Theater After General Butler's departure from New Orleans, Louisiana, General Nathaniel Banks takes command there, assuming responsibility for the Federal Department of the Gulf. Tennessee is the site of Confederate General N B Forrest's march against Grant. North Carolina sees skirmishing in various places, among them White Hall and Goshen Swamp.

17 December 1862

Washington President Lincoln experiences difficulties with the Federal cabinet. Secretary of the Treasury Salmon Chase is in conflict with Secretary of State Seward and also with Seward's son who is the latter's assistant. The result is that both Sewards submit their resignations to the chief executive although Lincoln will not accept them.

Western Theater General Grant makes public *General Order Number Eleven* concerning speculation but specifically singling out Jews as the object of the declaration against illegal trade: 'The Jews, as a class violating every regulation of trade established by the Treasury Department and also department orders, are hereby expelled from the department within twenty-four hours from the receipt of this order.' While the order is rescinded several weeks later, on 4 January 1863, Grant's reputation is damaged by the adverse publicity.

18 December 1862

Western Theater Lexington, Tennessee, is the site of a skirmish between cavalry under the command of Confederate Nathan Bedford Forrest and Union cavalry troops. The Confederates report 35 casualties compared to 17 listed by the Federals as killed or wounded. New Berne, North Carolina, sees the return of Northern expeditionary forces after eight days of minor skirmishing.

Above: The scene at the foot of Marye's Heights after the struggle for Fredericksburg, 13 December 1862.

19 December 1862

Washington President Lincoln convenes his cabinet to discuss the tendered resignation of Secretary of State Seward. Also at this meeting are members of the Senate Republican caucus committee.

Western Theater At Spring Creek in Tennessee there is an encounter between Northern and Southern troops, and another at Jackson in that same state.

20 December 1862

Washington Compounding the crisis in Lincoln's cabinet triggered by Seward's abruptly proferred resignation, Secretary of the Treasury Salmon Chase also submits a request to be permitted to step down from his post. After discussing the situation at length with his advisors and with the remaining cabinet members, Lincoln makes a decision not to accept the resignations. This effectively prevents any further upheaval but does little to alleviate the pressures stemming mainly from political differences experienced by the cabinet as a whole.

Western Theater Grand Junction, Tennessee, is attacked by Confederates with the result that the Federals tally 50 casualties. In Mississippi, at Holly Springs, Northern troops under General Grant are surprised by General Earl Van Dorn's Southerners. The latter capture an enormous supply of stores worth over $1 million and take about 1500 Northern soldiers prisoner. To prevent such a valuable commodity from falling into enemy hands, Confederates burn over 4000 bales of cotton. This attack on Holly Springs, Mississippi seriously hampers Union General Grant's efforts to move on Confederate positions near Vicksburg.

23 December 1862

The Confederacy Due to Union General Benjamin Butler's military governorship of New Orleans, Louisiana, and the intensely bitter feelings resulting from his tenure there, Confederate President Jefferson Davis brands the general a felon and an enemy of

mankind. The chief executive suggests immediate execution of Butler if he should be seized by Confederates, and further states that any Federal army officers imprisoned by the Confederacy shall not be released prior to Butler's punishment.

25 December 1862

Washington As part of their observation of the Christmas holiday, the president and Mrs Lincoln pay visits to several military hospitals in the Federal capital where injured soldiers convalesce.

Western Theater In Tennessee, near Brentwood, there is some inconclusive fighting and similar activity along the Edmondson Pike. John Hunt Morgan's raiders clash with Union troops near Bear Wallow in Kentucky. Glasgow, Kentucky, is seized and occupied by Confederate troops. In Mississippi, north of Vicksburg, Sherman's forces conduct operations.

26 December 1862

Western Theater Vicksburg, Mississippi, is the goal of advancing Federal forces. These troops, under the command of General William Sherman, are positioned on the Yazoo River to the north of Vicksburg. In Tennessee, General William Rosecrans pushes toward the Confederate encampment at Murfreesboro. There is some minor fighting along the way, near La Vergne, Franklin and Knob Gap.

Trans-Mississippi As a result of the Sioux Indian uprising in Minnesota, causing the death of over 450 white settlers, 38 Indian participants in the uprising are executed at Mankato, Minnesota.

27 December 1862

Western Theater Near Vicksburg, the Federal advance troops of General Sherman clash with Confederates. In addition, Northern gunboats fire on Southern shore batteries positioned at Haine's Bluff, Mississippi. Efforts to disrupt communications between the Vicksburg troops and reinforcements include the destruction of the Vicksburg and Shreveport Railroad. In Kentucky, there is an attack on Confederate forces resulting in 17 dead or wounded, and 57 taken prisoner by

the Federals. John Hunt Morgan's Confederate raiders complete a successful attack on Elizabethtown, Kentucky, which results in the capture of the Federal garrison there.

28 December 1862

Western Theater Mississippi witnesses minor fighting near Vicksburg, as General William T Sherman pushes closer to the city. In Kentucky, Confederate John Hunt Morgan and his men blow up a bridge at Muldraugh's Hill. Baton Rouge, Louisiana, is heavily damaged by fire.

Trans-Mississippi In Van Buren, Arkansas, there is an outbreak of fighting between Confederates and Federals. The latter are under the command of General James Blunt. The Union troops are successful in seizing 100 prisoners as well as many supplies and some equipment. In Missouri, Federal troops evacuate New Madrid.

29 December 1862

Western Theater The Federal forces gathering north of Vicksburg, Mississippi, clash with Confederates at Chickasaw Bayou. While Northern troops make a concerted effort to break through the Confederate defenses there at Chickasaw Bluffs, it is an operation that meets with no success. General Sherman, whose men are outnumbered by the Southern troops, says later: 'I reached Vicksburg at the time appointed, landed, assaulted and failed.' The Federal forces of 31,000 are reduced by 208 fatalities, 1005 wounded and 563 missing at this battle. Southern losses tally 63 dead, 134 injured, 10 missing out of a total fighting force of 14,000.

30 December 1862

Washington President Lincoln makes final preparations for the announcement of his Emancipation Proclamation. He submits drafts of the document to his cabinet in the hopes that he will be given practical advice as to the final wording.

Western Theater Confederate raider John Hunt Morgan and his men clash with Union troops as they pull out of the town of New Haven, Kentucky.

Naval In stormy waters off Cape Hatteras, the USS *Monitor* is lost after severe difficulties; this results in the death of 16 men and officers. The USS *Rhode Island* manages to rescue another 47 men.

31 December 1862

Washington President Lincoln meets with General Burnside to discuss the latter's role in the Union defeat of Fredericksburg, Virginia. In addition to this meeting, the president confers once again with his cabinet about the Emancipation Proclamation and signs a bill establishing West Virginia as the nation's 35th state.

Western Theater The Battle of Stone's River, or Murfreesboro, Tennessee, commences on the last day of the year as General Rosecrans' Federals face General Bragg's Confederates. The Southern attack on the Federal position comes at dawn and by noon, despite several vigorous counterattacks by the Union forces, the latter are on the defensive. By night time, General Rosecrans' troops are undefeated and awaiting a resumption of fighting on the following day.

These pages: Union batteries help repulse Pickett's Charge during the Battle of Gettysburg, 3 July 1863. The defeat of Lee's forces ended hopes of an outright Southern victory in the civil war.

1863

1 January 1863

Washington President Lincoln signs the Emancipation Proclamation, stating that 'all persons held as slaves within said designated States, and parts of States, are, and henceforward shall be free.' Reactions are, for the most part, enthusiastic. The provisions for freed slaves include assurances that former slaves are to be permitted to serve in the military. Continued difficulties with General Burnside over the aftereffects of the Fredericksburg defeat still plague the president. After meeting with the chief executive, Burnside states in an open letter that he has felt little support from fellow officers and that he considers retirement in order to 'promote the public good.' Lincoln persuades Burnside to reconsider.

Western Theater Murfreesboro, Tennessee, is relatively stable after the previous day's fighting. Both Generals Bragg and Rosecrans re-position their troops and there is some minor skirmishing as the troops assume a more advantageous stance. In Mississippi, Union General Sherman makes preparations to pull troops out of the area north of Vicksburg, and elsewhere in that state there is a minor clash between Federals and Confederates at Bath Springs.

2 January 1863

Western Theater The second day of major fighting in the Battle of Stone's River, or Murfreesboro, Tennessee, sees General Breckenridge's Confederates badly defeated after

Below: Southern warships attempt to pierce the Union blockade outside Galveston, Texas, on 1 January 1863.

their attempt to establish a hold on high ground. Both of the armies pause once again, each anticipating a withdrawal by the other. General Sherman pulls away from the Yazoo River in Mississippi, putting aside any further attempts to seize the area north of Vicksburg.

3 January 1863

Western Theater General Braxton Bragg moves his Confederate Army of Tennessee away from Murfreesboro. This is in spite of the fact that the South remained in relative control after the Battle of Stone's River, or Murfreesboro, on 31 December 1862. This move is later to garner Bragg considerable criticism from military advisors.

4 January 1863

Western Theater Fort Hindman, Arkansas, is the goal of 30,000 Federal troops which, under the command of General McClernand, are transported north on the Mississippi in an unauthorized movement intended to implement seizure of the Confederate post. Skirmishing occurs in Tennessee in the wake of General Bragg's withdrawal from the area around Murfreesboro.

Naval The Union blockade continues to reap rewards as the USS *Quaker City* seizes yet another Confederate blockade-runner off the coast of Charleston, South Carolina.

7 January 1863

Trans-Mississippi There is a major attack on Springfield, Missouri, by Confederate troops under the command of Generals Marmaduke and Price. They move on and capture Ozark, Missouri.

8 January 1863

Western Theater Ripley, Tennessee, witnesses the capture of 46 Southern soldiers by Captain Moore's Union troops. In the skirmish there, the Union suffers three wounded. The Confederates, under Colonel Dawson's command, tally eight dead and 20 injured plus those taken prisoner. In a separate action, a six-day expedition and raid under Confederate General Joseph Wheeler threatens Mill Creek, Harpeth Shoals and Ashland.

9 January 1863

Eastern Theater Suffolk, Virginia, sees the defeat of Confederate forces under the command of General Pryor. Federals, under General Corcoran's command, lose 104 during this encounter. At Fairfax Court House, Virginia, there is minor skirmishing.

International The French minister to the United States confers with the minister of foreign affairs in France in order to clarify their country's role in a possible mediation attempt between the Confederacy and the Union.

10 January 1863

Washington President Lincoln writes to General Curtis in Missouri about the various ways to handle the slave problem in St Louis. In a separate action General Fitz John Porter is court-martialed and cashiered from the Federal army. This is due to Porter's failure to follow orders at the Battle of Second Manassas on 29 August 1862.

Trans-Mississippi At Galveston, Texas, Union gunboats positioned there bombard the city. An important operation under

Above: General John Breckenridge led Southern forces to defeat at Stone's River.

General McClernand proceeds as Fort Hindman, on the Arkansas River, is surrounded by Union troops and gunboats effectively silence any Confederate artillery from the fort. Southern forces there are under the command of General T J Churchill. Elsewhere there is skirmishing of a minor variety near Carrollton, Arkansas.

11 January 1863

Trans-Mississippi Fort Hindman, Arkansas, is seized by Federal troops under General McClernand and Admiral David Porter. During this battle, the Union loses 134 men, suffers 898 wounded and 29 missing while Confederates tally 28 killed, 81 wounded and 4720 prisoners taken. In Missouri, Union Colonel Merrill engages Confederates under General Marmaduke in battle with a resulting 35-man loss for the Federals, who defeat the Southern troops. The latter lose 150 men.

Naval In three separate operations, the Confederacy is involved in confrontations with the Union. Off the coast of Memphis, Tennessee, the South sinks the USS *Grampers Number Two*. At Bayou Teche, Louisiana, the Confederate gunboat *Cotton* is seized and destroyed by General Weitzel. Again, proving its superiority, the Confederate cruiser *Alabama* attacks and sinks the Federal vessel *Hatteras* in waters off the coast of Texas.

12 January 1863

The Confederacy At the Confederate capital, Richmond, Virginia, the third session of the First Confederate Congress meets. President Jefferson Davis addresses the assembly, emphasizing his hopes for European recognition of the Southern nation.

15 January 1863

The Confederacy In a letter to General Braxton Bragg concerning the Confederate position in the Murfreesboro-Tullahoma area of Tennessee, President Jefferson Davis advises that the general should seek to 'select a strong position and fortifying it, to wait for an attack.'

16 January 1863

Western Theater In Alabama, the Confederate privateer *Florida* slips through the Union blockade and makes its way safely out of Mobile Bay. The vessel subsequently is responsible for the capture and destruction of 15 Federal ships before its own capture in waters off Bahia, Brazil.

19 January 1863

Eastern Theater The Federal Army of the Potomac is about to engage in its second attempt to gain control of Fredericksburg, Virginia. General Burnside makes preparations to cross the Rappahannock River with his troops and is aided by division commanders Hooker and Franklin. There is some minor skirmishing elsewhere in Virginia, near Williamsburg and Burnt Ordinary.

20 January 1863

Eastern Theater The Army of the Potomac continues its plans to sweep down on Fredericksburg, Virginia. A change in the weather conditions from snow to rain creates transportation difficulties. Reflecting on this change, General Burnside reports, 'From that moment we felt that the winter campaign had ended.' It becomes increasingly more difficult for the Federal forces to make any significant progress on this front.

21 January 1863

Washington President Lincoln communicates with General Halleck concerning orders given by General Grant. These orders, which are being revoked, concerned the expulsion of Jews from the Department of the Mississippi. Lincoln's position in this controversy is that revocation of such orders is necessary 'as it in terms proscribed an entire religious class, some of whom are fighting in our ranks.' The president, in a separate order, formally dismisses General Fitz John Porter from military service. (This presidential order will later be revoked after an 1879 review, and Porter subsequently is reinstated as a colonel in the Federal army.)

Eastern Theater The Federal Army of the Potomac is still stalled along the banks of the Rappahannock River in Virginia. General Burnside is soon to be faced with a decision concerning effective withdrawal from the area, since the rain has been steadily falling for 30 hours. It is only a short time before Burnside realizes that crossing the river is impossible.

22 January 1863

Eastern Theater General Burnside, faced with extremely bad weather and mud everywhere, prepares to pull the Army of the Potomac back from its position – an admission that the Fredericksburg, Virginia, mission was not to be fruitful. Known as the 'mud march,' this withdrawal is described by a private in the 118th Pennsylvania Volunteers: 'Further progress was impracticable . . . It was some twelve miles back to the nearest camp. Pontoons, artillery trains could not be moved.'

Western Theater General Grant takes overall responsibility for Union troops in the region of Arkansas and its general vicinity. The upcoming push to take Vicksburg, Mississippi, is the goal of General Grant and he begins the preparations by resuming Federal efforts to dig a canal through the marshy area across from Vicksburg.

23 January 1863

Eastern Theater In an abrupt and stinging move, General Burnside issues orders which will take Generals Hooker, Franklin, Newton and Brooks out of command in the Army of the Potomac. Motivated in part by the frustration at the difficulties encountered because of poor weather, Burnside has not evidenced a total commitment to the command forced on him three months prior to now. The orders he has served on the generals are never actually approved by President Lincoln.

25 January 1863

Washington In a meeting with General Burnside, President Lincoln discusses the general's plans for the dismissal of Generals

Below: The Confederate raider *Alabama* uses a burning Union vessel to lure further Union ships into cannon range.

Above: An imaginative, if somewhat impractical, attempt to protect Union railroad workers from Confederate raiding parties.

Hooker, Franklin, Newton and Brooks. Later, the president confers with his cabinet and with General Halleck. The outcome is the removal of General Burnside from the command of the Army of the Potomac. In his place, General Joseph Hooker is appointed as general in chief of the Potomac Army. Burnside is apparently not displeased with this change, and will assume military responsibilities in the West.

26 January 1863

Eastern Theater   General Joseph Hooker, 48-years-old and a West Point graduate, officially assumes command of the Union Army of the Potomac. It is hoped by the president as well as by the soldiers themselves, that 'Fightin' Joe' will prove to be both able and assertive, qualities which seemed lacking in the sincere but militarily inept General Burnside. In a letter to General Hooker, the president offers encouragement and cautions the general to avoid mixing 'politics with your profession.' Lincoln praises Hooker's confidence, 'which is a valuable, if not an indispensable quality.'

27 January 1863

The North   A Philadelphia newspaperman, A D Boileau, is arrested on charges that his *Journal* is publishing anti-Union matter.
The Confederacy   In a message to Georgia Governor Brown, President Jefferson Davis makes note of the urgent need to step up the cultivation of cotton and other produce. 'A short supply of provisions presents the greatest danger to a successful . . . war.'
Naval   In a fierce bombardment from the ironclad USS *Montauk*, the Confederate Fort McAllister in Georgia sustains some damage. Firing from the Federal vessel in the Ogeechee River lasts for a better part of the day.

29 January 1863

The Confederacy   Defense of Vicksburg, Mississippi, is uppermost in President Jefferson Davis' mind, since this city is critical to the control of an important stretch of the Mis-

sissippi River. Accordingly, the president sends a cable to General Pemberton at Vicksburg asking, 'Has anything or can anything be done to obstruct the navigation from Yazoo Pass down?' The Confederate president is well aware that General Grant means to press his Union troops on the city as soon as possible.
Eastern Theater   Near Suffolk, Virginia, Union troops engage in minor skirmishing with Confederate forces. There is similar light fighting at Turner's Mills, also in Virginia.
Naval   The Stono River in South Carolina is the site of an exchange between Confederate shore batteries and the Union gunboat *Isaac Smith*. The result is that the vessel first runs aground during the encounter and is then captured by the Confederates.

31 January 1863

Western Theater   Despite the Confederate pullback from Murfreesboro, Tennessee, earlier in the month, there continues to be a series of minor confrontations between Union and Confederate soldiers in that vicinity. While on a reconnaissance mission from Murfreesboro to Franklin, Federals engage Southern troops at Unionville, Middleton and Dover. At the latter location, the North sustains five injuries while Confederates report 12 dead and 300 taken prisoner.
Naval   At Charleston, South Carolina, there is a spectacular battle between Southern gunboats and Northern blockaders. The Confederate vessels *Chicora* and *Palmetto State*, both ironclads, succeed in damaging the Federal *Mercedita* and *Keystone State* extensively. The former vessel's crew suffer four killed and three injured, many of these casualties being the result of steam explosions from broken boilers. Despite this action, which does no damage to the Confederate ironclads, the harbor remains under the Federal blockade – although the South declares otherwise.

1 February 1863

The Confederacy   Wartime inflation has made a serious impact on the Confederate currency so that it is estimated that the Confederate dollar has a buying power of only 20 cents.

Western Theater   In Tennessee, Franklin is taken and occupied by Union troops. The Federal forces in New Berne, North Carolina, set off on an expedition which will last for 10 days and will take them to Plymouth.

2 February 1863

Eastern Theater   The Union Army of the Potomac under the command of General Joseph Hooker encounters hostile fire as it gathers information about the area surrounding the Rappahannock River. There is skirmishing at Rappahannock Station.
Naval   Vicksburg, Mississippi, is again the focus of action taken by the Union. The Federal vessel *Queen of the West* makes its way past Vicksburg, although the ram was fired on by Confederate shore batteries and sustained minor damage. The commanding officer of the vessel, Captain Charles Ellet, was hoping to destroy the Southern vessel *City of Vicksburg* and to put Confederate shipping in jeopardy. While unable to do this, Ellet succeeds in slipping by the shore batteries without losing his ship.

3 February 1863

Washington   The Federal Congress recognizes naval Commodore John Worden's contribution to the Union war effort. Worden was the officer in charge of the USS *Monitor* at the time it battled the CSS *Merrimack* in March 1862. Worden was also in command of the *Monitor* when it foundered and was lost off Cape Hatteras, North Carolina, in December 1862. Secretary of State Seward confers with the French minister about the latter's handling of possible mediation. These mediation proposals are ultimately declined.
Western Theater   In Tennessee, Fort Donelson is once again under attack, this time by Confederates under Generals Wheeler and Forrest. The Union troops garrisoned at the fort, under Colonel Harding, are able to hold out against the Southerners. Losses after the battle there indicate Northern dead at 12, with 30 injured. The Southern reports list 100 killed and 400 wounded, with 300 prisoners. Vicksburg, Mississippi, sees the *Queen of the West* attack and seize three Southern vessels. More Federal troops move out of Murfreesboro on a reconnaissance mission.
Trans-Mississippi   In Missouri, Federal troops under Major Reeder engage in skirmishing with Southern forces at Mingo Swamp. The casualties reported by Confederates indicate nine dead and 20 wounded. At Yazoo Pass in Arkansas, Union soldiers are able to break through the levee, providing a passage for troops along the Yazoo River north of Vicksburg, Mississippi. It is intended that this channel will facilitate the Northern force's taking of the city at a date in the near future.

4 February 1863

Western Theater   Union troops at Lake Providence, Louisiana, are routed by the forces of the Confederate 3rd Louisiana Division. The latter, however successful in this, sustains 30 casualties.

5 February 1863

International   Queen Victoria makes an official statement concerning Great Britain's refusal to enter into mediation attempts between the Union and the Confederacy at this time. The reasons given include the observation that such matters cannot be 'attended with a probability of success.'

Eastern Theater General Joseph Hooker, appointed commander of the Union Army of the Potomac, reorganizes the force and makes a variety of command changes. There continues to be reconnaissance efforts around Rappahannock Bridge and Grove Church, Virginia. In West Virginia, Union troops embark on a four-day mission to Wyoming County from Camp Piatt.

6 February 1863

Washington After the re-establishment of the Federal Department of Washington, the command of said department is given to General S F Heintzelman. Secretary of State Seward makes official the Federal government's refusal of mediation offers from Napoleon III's government in France. Seward conveys this information to the French minister, M Mercier.

7 February 1863

Eastern Theater At Williamsburg, Virginia, Confederates ambush a Federal cavalry unit, resulting in the death and injury of 11 Union soldiers.

Naval Despite its secure hold on Southern ports, the Federal blockade fails in preventing three Confederate raiders from slipping through its cordon. The three vessels make it safely to port at Charleston, South Carolina. At Galveston, Texas, the South manages to remove the threat of the blockade, announcing the port there and at Sabine Pass to be open.

10 February 1863

Eastern Theater At Chantilly, Virginia, there is minor fighting between Union and Southern soldiers. In West Virginia, Northern troops embark on a three day reconnaissance, leaving from Beverly and heading for Pocahontas County. There is continued reconnaissance and exploration along the Rappahannock River as the Army of the Potomac reorganizes and assesses its position.

Western Theater Camp Sheldon, Mississippi, is once again the site of desultory skirmishing. In Louisiana, at Old River, Federal troops under Captain Tucker are successful in pushing back a force of Confederates. The resulting casualty list indicates that the South has 11 killed and wounded, with 25 men taken prisoner. The North reports eight dead and wounded.

12 February 1863

Western Theater Bolivar, Tennessee, witnesses the defeat of Union forces, resulting in four dead and five injured. At Sandy Ridge, North Carolina, some Union troops skirmish with Confederate troops.

Naval Captain Ellet's *Queen of the West* manages to fire on and destroy a number of Confederate wagon trains carrying supplies and ammunition, this taking place on the Red River. In Arkansas, the USS *Conestoga* takes two Southern steamers on the White River. The blockade-runner CSS *Florida* manages to seize and destroy the Yankee clipper *Jacob Bell* in the waters of the West Indies. The *Jacob Bell* was carrying a cargo of Chinese tea and other goods of an estimated value of $2 million; the entire cargo is lost. Off Vicksburg, Mississippi, the Union ironclad gunboat *Indianola* successfully runs past Confederate shore batteries.

14 February 1863

Eastern Theater Annandale, Virginia, sees the defeat of a Federal cavalry unit at the hands of Confederate troops. Skirmishing breaks out along the Hillsborough Road and at Union Mills.

Trans-Mississippi Cypress Bend, Arkansas, is the site of light skirmishing between Federal and Confederate troops.

Naval Despite its recent success in avoiding serious damage or capture, the Union vessel *Queen of the West*, under the command of Captain Charles Ellet, finally suffers defeat. At first its operation on the Red River is successful and it manages to seize the Southern vessel *New Era Number Five*. Subsequently, however, the Federal ship runs aground and is abandoned by its crew when the boiler threatens to explode. The USS *De Soto* is in the vicinity and provides a safe escape vehicle for the *Queen of the West*'s crew who then transfer to the captured *New Era Number Five*. Ellet and his men take this vessel downstream where they connect with the ironclad *Indianola* on the following day, at a point just south of Natchez, Mississippi.

15 February 1863

Western Theater Minor fighting breaks out in Tennessee near Nolensville. The Federal force there under the command of Sergeant Holmes manages to defeat the Southern forces, killing eight, wounding 20 and taking four prisoners. There is also skirmishing at Cainsville, Tennessee, where Union Colonel Monroe is successful in holding off cavalry under Confederate General John Hunt Morgan. The tally of casualties shows two Federals killed, 12 injured; 20 Confederates dead, a large number wounded and six taken prisoner. Morgan's men were far from beaten in the fighting.

16 February 1863

Washington The Federal Senate passes the Conscription Act, which has yet to be signed into law by President Lincoln but which has the chief executive's full support. This new draft law is intended to fill the ranks of the Union army which is not adequately served by voluntary enlistment. In addition, desertion is found to be an increasingly serious problem. Late in 1862, Provost-Marshal General Simeon Draper estimated that around 100,000 soldiers had deserted their posts. This new draft law will, it is hoped, better provide for the interests of the Union than was the system in use until now.

Western Theater Skirmishing occurs at Yazoo Pass, Mississippi, as General Grant's men encounter Confederate opposition to the Federal preparation for a campaign against Vicksburg.

17 February 1863

Western Theater Lexington, Tennessee, is the starting point for a Federal expedition which will last five days and will take troops to Clifton, Tennessee. In Memphis, there is skirmishing between Union forces and Confederates.

Naval The Federal vessel *Indianola* is now in position near Vicksburg at the juncture of the Red and the Mississippi Rivers. The *Indianola* will carry on a harassing campaign against the Southern vessels headed upriver to Vicksburg. The USS *Hercules* is attacked by Confederates which prompts the burning of nearby Hopefield, Arkansas, in retaliation.

18 February 1863

Eastern Theater The Army of Northern Virginia sees several divisions of its Confederate troops removed from the vicinity of Fredericksburg, Virginia. These troops are to position themselves near Richmond, in order to protect the Southern capital from attack.

Below: The scene in a Southern camp during a lull in the fighting – a typical sight on both sides of the line.

19 February 1863

The North   In Iowa, Federal troops convalescing in a hospital in Keokuk become angry over the anti-Union sentiment expressed in the local newspaper the *Constitution*. Accordingly, the soldiers break into and ransack the news office.

The Confederacy   President Jefferson Davis sends a letter to General Joseph Johnston, and in it the Confederate chief executive comments on his reluctance to remove General Braxton Bragg from command. Davis says to Johnston, 'It is scarcely possible for him to possess the requisite confidence of the troops.' Bragg's officers have expressed extreme dissatisfaction in his manner of command.

Western Theater   At Coldwater, Mississippi, Southern troops under the command of Colonel Wood lose a minor confrontation with Federals. The results are six Confederate dead, three wounded, 15 taken prisoner.

20 February 1863

Western Theater   Yazoo Pass, Mississippi, sees Union troops hold off an attack on their positions by Confederates. The casualty lists record five Northern soldiers wounded, six Confederates killed and 26 taken prisoner.

23 February 1863

Washington   At the Federal capital, former War Department Secretary Simon Cameron hands in his resignation as minister to Russia.

Western Theater   Skirmishing occurs at Athens, Kentucky, and in the vicinity of Fort Caswell in North Carolina.

24 February 1863

Western Theater   In an unlooked-for blow to its river operations, the Federal navy suffers from the capture of its ironclad gunboat

Right: John Singleton Mosby, one of the South's greatest leaders of irregular forces.
Below: The destruction of the USS *Jacob Bell* by the Confederate raider *Florida* in West Indian waters, February 1863.

Indianola. After repeated ramming by the Confederates, the *Indianola* is forced to surrender, its commander Commodore George Brown terming it 'a partially sunken vessel.'

25 February 1863

The Confederacy   Inflated prices continue to plague the Confederate nation, and reports from Charleston, South Carolina, indicate that a half-pound loaf of bread costs $25.00 and that flour is selling for $65.00 a barrel.

Eastern Theater   There are repeated incidents of minor skirmishing in Virginia. These outbreaks between Federal and Confederate forces occur in Strasburg, Chantilly, near Winchester, and also at Hartwood Church.

26 February 1863

The North   In an affirmation of support for the Union, the Cherokee Indian National Council repeals its former ordinance of secession.

The Confederacy   President Jefferson Davis informs General T H Holmes that he is concerned for the welfare of Confederate citizens in the Trans-Mississippi District. The chief executive feels that it is necessary to be diligent in both crop cultivation and military matters if the South wishes to maintain its hold on the area.

Eastern Theater   Skirmishing occurs in Germantown, Virginia. At Woodstock, in that same state, Confederate forces clash with Union troops but are defeated, the latter suffering losses of 200 killed and wounded. General Longstreet takes command of Southern troops in the Confederate Department of Virginia and North Carolina.

28 February 1863

Western Theater   On Georgia's Ogeechee River, the USS *Montauk* attacks and destroys the Confederate steamer *Nashville*. The *Montauk* is under the command of Commodore J L Worden, who commanded the Union's ironclad *Monitor* during its famous encounter with the Southern vessel *Merrimack*.

1 March 1863

Washington   In order to discuss upcoming military appointments, some of which will be submitted for congressional approval within a few days, President Lincoln meets with Secretary of War Edwin Stanton and other advisors.

Western Theater   In North Carolina, Union troops leave New Berne on a five-day reconnaissance to Swan Quarter. During the course of this expedition, there are numerous incidents of skirmishing.

2 March 1863

Washington   While Congress approves several hundred military promotions and appointments that the president has submitted, actions are also taken to dismiss 33 army officers from the service as a result of their court-martials for a variety of charges.

Eastern Theater   There is minor skirmishing in Virginia at Neosho and Aldie. The Army of the Potomac, under General Hooker, continues to make preparations to advance against General Robert E Lee's positions in Virginia.

Western Theater   Tennessee sees skirmishing near Petersburg, the results of which are reports that Confederates suffer 12 dead and 20 wounded. Union troops set out on a three-week reconnaissance mission that begins in New Orleans, Louisiana, and will take them to the Rio Grande in Texas.

3 March 1863

Washington   A number of comprehensive measures are passed by Congress, the most important of which is the new Enrollment Act, often called the Conscription Act, which calls for the enlistment in military service of all able-bodied male citizens between 20 and 45 years of age. This service will be for a three-year period, and the law also provides for these forces to be called up by Federal decree, without state intervention. On the whole, the Enrollment Act is well-received at least by the military. It passes both Houses of Congress. Generals Rosecrans, Sherman and Grant are particularly pleased about the prospect of receiving fresh troops as a result of this bill; the estimate of how many men would actually be drafted hovers around three million, but in reality, the first 10

months of 1863 sees a total of only 21,331 new soldiers. The final tally of men enrolled during 1863-64 is about 170,000 – falling far short of original estimates but clearly benefitting the military in a moderate way. The Financial Bill passed by Congress at this time is intended to aid the Federal economy in part by the issuance of treasury notes. In addition, Congress authorizes suspension of the writ of habeas corpus throughout the entire Union. This measure is controversial and 36 Democratic representatives express their desire to go on record as protesting against such a sweeping move to curtail individual freedom, although this protest is not formally lodged. The Territory of Idaho is formed in the area which had previously been a portion of Washington.

4 March 1863

Washington   The 37th Congress of the United States adjourns after completing its legislative activities. Among the final measures passed is one establishing the National Academy of Sciences to be based in Washington, DC.

Western Theater   In Tennessee, near Spring Hill, General Van Dorn succeeds in capturing several of General Rosecrans' regiments. At Unionville, there is minor skirmishing, and a 10-day reconnaissance sets out from Murfreesboro, encountering considerable hostile fire from Confederates in the area.

5 March 1863

The North   A newspaper office in Columbus, Ohio, that of the *Crisis*, is ransacked by Union troops after the publication of anti-Union sentiments.

Western Theater   Vicksburg, Mississippi, continues to prepare and fortify against the inevitable battle looming ahead. Union forces are involved in constructing a canal across from the city; operations are occasionally interrupted by fire from Confederate shore batteries. Near Franklin, Tennessee, the Federal troops under Colonel Coburn's command are attacked and defeated by Confed-

Above: Members of the US 107th Colored Infantry Regiment pose for the camera outside their camp's guardhouse.

erates. The latter occupy the town, and Union losses are reported at 100 dead, 300 injured, 1306 taken prisoner. Southern casualties are tallied at 180 dead, 450 wounded.

7 March 1863

Western Theater   The preparations for a campaign against Vicksburg, Mississippi, continue as Union General Banks advances toward Baton Rouge, Louisiana, in order to connect with General Ulysses Grant's plans for Vicksburg.

8 March 1863

Eastern Theater   Fairfax County Court House in Virginia is the temporary headquarters of Union General E H Stoughton. The general and his men are captured there by Colonel Mosby's Confederates. This proves to be a valuable takeover for the South; they seize a number of prisoners, 58 horses, and large quantities of equipment and ammunition.

9 March 1863

Western Theater   There are various incidents of minor skirmishing – at St Augustine, Florida, and in Tennessee near Salem. In Louisiana, near Port Hudson, General Nathaniel Banks' troops encounter Confederates as the former continue to move toward General Grant's position.

Trans-Mississippi   Arkansas continues to see action near Chalk Bluff, and in Missouri a Federal expedition moves out from Bloomfield for a six-day reconnaissance mission which will take them to the towns of Kennett and Hornersville.

10 March 1863

Washington   A proclamation of general amnesty is read by President Lincoln in order to encourage soldiers who are absent without leave to return to their regiments. This agreement is that if these men report back to their units and active duty by 1 April 1863, they will not suffer any adverse consequences. The alternative is that these soldiers would be charged with desertion and arrested.

Western Theater   Union forces commanded by Colonel Higginson and made up of predominantly black regiments occupy Jacksonville, Florida. Skirmishing breaks out in Tennessee near Covington, where Federal Colonel Grierson is successful in defeating Colonel Richardson's Southern troops.

11 March 1863

Western Theater   In an effective action against the Northern preparations to move against Vicksburg, Mississippi, Confederate troops construct a defensive outpost known as Fort Pemberton. Union forces attempting to move past this position on the Yalobusha River, find that their gunboats are unable to withstand the fire from shore batteries at Fort Pemberton, where Confederates are under the command of General W W Loring. After six days of exchanging fire, the Union troops under General Grant are finally obliged to give up this preparatory effort of the Vicksburg campaign.

13 March 1863

The Confederacy   Due to the carelessness of a factory worker who accidentally detonated a device on which she was working, the Confederate Ordnance Laboratory at Brown's Island near Richmond, Virginia, is the site of an explosion. As a result, 69 factory workers, of whom 62 are women, are either killed or injured. The fact that such a high proportion of casualties at an industrial site are women is a direct result of the Confederacy's response to wartime needs: not only are women taking the place of men on the farms, but when needed, they are taking over in both clerical and industrial roles to release men for military service.

14 March 1863

Naval   Port Hudson, Louisiana, where Confederate troops are positioned north of Baton Rouge, is subject to bombardment from Union gunboats under Admiral David Farragut's command. This attempt by Federals to move past a Southern defense and head toward Vicksburg costs the navy the USS *Mississippi* which runs aground and is eventually burned. The USS *Hartford* and the *Albatross* are successful in making it past Port Hudson, but two other vessels in the flotilla, the *Monongahela* and the *Richmond*, sustain considerable damage and are forced to turn back. During this bombardment and destruction of one Federal ship, 65 men are listed as killed or missing.

15 March 1863

Western Theater   In Mississippi, where Vicksburg residents and troops garrisoned there brace themselves for the seemingly inevitable Northern attack, Federal forces attempt to pass by Haines' Bluff but are unsuccessful.

Naval   In the continuing blockade of Southern ports, the Federal navy is foiled once more as the *Britannia*, a British vessel, slips through the cordon off Wilmington, North Carolina. The Union blockade has been much

more successful during the opening months of 1863, however, and authorities are pleased with their record of captures.

17 March 1863

Eastern Theater   The Army of the Potomac sends a cavalry corps under the command of General William Wood Averell, to attack General Fitz Lee at Culpeper, Virginia. Taking 2100 men and six pieces of artillery, Averell engages 800 Southerners and four guns at the Battle of Kelly's Ford. After a full day of fighting, the Federals pull back from the site. Losses are tallied at 78 Union casualties to 133 for the Confederates.

19 March 1863

Naval   Admiral Farragut has successfully maneuvered past Natchez, Mississippi, and is now moving past Confederate batteries at Grand Gulf with his two vessels, the *Hartford* and the ironclad *Albatross*. Farragut is now positioned just below Vicksburg.

20 March 1863

Western Theater   In Florida there is some skirmishing at St Andrew's Bay. In Tennessee, near Milton, Confederates are attacked and defeated by Colonel Hall's Union troops who lose seven men and sustain three injuries. The South reports 40 dead, 140 wounded and 12 missing after this encounter. In Mississippi another Union attempt to reach Vicksburg, this time via Steele Bayou, proves unsuccessful as Admiral Porter takes 11 vessels along this water route, encountering Confederate fire at Rolling Fork. General Sherman has provided land reinforcements to help Porter's expedition and these reinforcements prove critical to the defense of Porter's fleet while it is under fire at Rolling Fork.

21 March 1863

Western Theater   Tennessee witnesses various outbreaks of skirmishing: Union troops headed for Saulsbury on a reconnaissance from La Grange encounter hostile fire from Confederate forces, and there is fighting at Salem. Southern troops attack a Federal railroad train between Bolivar and Grand Junction, Tennessee. In Kentucky, Mount Sterling is seized by Confederates under the

Above: Confederate shore batteries pound a Union flotilla attempting to reach Vicksburg, 14 March 1863.

command of Colonel Cluke. Several Federal expeditions begin – one from New Orleans headed to Ponchatoula, and one going from Bonnet Carre to the Amite River in Louisiana.

22 March 1863

Western Theater   The area around Murfreesboro, Tennessee, continues to see much action between Federals and Confederate troops. In Kentucky there are several encounters between North and South as General John Hunt Morgan's cavalry attacks Federal positions there, and John Pegram's Confederates conduct operations against Union troops. These operations will continue throughout the rest of the month.

Trans-Mississippi   In Missouri, Union forces are attacked and defeated by some irregular raiders near Blue Spring. In the sharp skirmishing, nine are killed, several are injured and five are taken prisoner.

23 March 1863

Western Theater   The Union vessels *Hartford* and *Albatross*, positioned in waters just south of Vicksburg, make an attack on Confederate shore batteries at Warrenton. In Kentucky Union troops attack Mount Sterling where two days previously Confederates had seized the area. After brief fighting, Northern forces are once again in control there. Jacksonville, Florida, is the site of Federal reconnaissance efforts.

24 March 1863

Western Theater   Northern troops attempt to make progress in their move toward Vicksburg, Mississippi, this time using Black Bayou as a passageway. This attempt is fruitless, however, both the geography and the Confederate troops posted in the area causing interminable delays. General Grant decides to terminate these efforts, and orders General Sherman to withdraw from the area in the final expedition in the Steele's Bayou area, the last of several endeavors to reach Vicksburg. Although fighting in the area draws to a close, Grant will later resume his efforts to capture the city.

25 March 1863

Washington President Lincoln approves command changes as General Burnside assumes responsibility for the Department of the Ohio. Burnside, formerly chief commander of the Army of the Potomac in Virginia, takes this new command after it is vacated by General Horatio Wright, who is transferred to the Army of the Potomac as a division commander.
Naval The final Union expedition to Vicksburg, that via Black Bayou, causes the North some difficulty as Confederates bombard the *Lancaster* and the *Switzerland*, two Northern rams, with artillery from shore. The *Lancaster* is destroyed and sinks; the *Switzerland* escapes, although it is badly damaged. Elsewhere, it is reported that Union ironclad vessels have left Hilton Head, North Carolina, and are making their way toward the habor at Charleston, South Carolina.

26 March 1863

Washington In a letter which reveals some of Lincoln's private sentiments concerning the former slave population, the chief executive says to Governor Andrew Johnson of Tennessee: 'The colored population is the great *available*, and yet unavailed of, force for restoring the Union. The bare sight of fifty thousand armed and drilled black soldiers on the banks of the Mississippi would end the rebellion at once.'
The North In West Virginia the citizens vote on and approve a referendum which will provide for the emancipation of slaves to be effected over a period of months.

27 March 1863

Washington President Lincoln meets with members of several American Indian tribes, advising them to turn to 'the cultivation of the earth' in order to provide economic stability for their people.

29 March 1863

Eastern Theater At Point Pleasant, West Virginia, there is some brief skirmishing which results in one Northern soldier dead, 12 Southerners killed and 14 wounded. There is also fighting at Williamsburg and Kelly's Ford, Virginia, where Confederates and Union troops clash.
Western Theater General Grant, anxious to establish a successful route to Vicksburg, Mississippi, directs General McClernand to open such a route from Milliken's Bend to an area just south of Vicksburg at New Carthage. McClernand is joined in this effort by Admiral Porter, who is to provide naval support - both troop transport and supply delivery. By combining both his naval and land forces, Grant is developing a strategy that will ultimately lead to the fall of Vicksburg.

30 March 1863

Washington President Lincoln announces the establishment of a day of fasting and prayer throughout the Union. This is set for 30 April 1863.
Western Theater Kentucky sees an encounter between North and South at Dutton Hill, where Confederates fight valiantly for five hours only to be defeated by a stronger Federal force. In North Carolina there is skirmishing at Rodman's Point.

31 March 1863

Eastern Theater Drainesville, Virginia, sees Union cavalry clash with Southerners under Colonel Mosby with the result that the Federals are defeated and lose 60 men.
Western Theater Union troops evacuate Jacksonville, Florida. At Eagleville, Tennessee, there is skirmishing and at Lexington in that state Northern forces begin a four-day reconnaissance mission heading for the Duck River.
Naval The CSS *Nashville* attempts to run the Union blockade in waters of the Savannah River. The vessel is sunk by a Northern ironclad. On the Mississippi, Union Admiral David Farragut is successful in taking the *Hartford*, the *Switzerland* and the *Albatross* past Confederate shore batteries at Grand Gulf, Mississippi.

2 April 1863

The Confederacy The Confederate capital of Richmond, Virginia, is the site of a bread riot – instigated by various factors, chief among them the very real specter of hunger facing many in the city and other parts of the Southern nation. A mob of people initially demand bread from a bakery wagon but soon harass nearby shops, destroying property and necessitating the call-out of local police; one store reports losses of $13,000 in merchandise. President Jefferson Davis makes a brave move, placing himself in the middle of the gathered crowd and stating, 'We do not desire to injure anyone, but this lawlessness must stop. I will give you five minutes to disperse, otherwise you will be fired upon' (this, in reference to the assembled militia nearby). When the mob recognizes that the intent of the militia is to fire, the crowd disperses and the riot ends without bloodshed, although a number of arrests are made.

3 April 1863

Washington The president makes preparations to visit the Army of the Potomac, where he will meet with General Hooker.
The Confederacy There are concerns on the part of President Jefferson Davis that the Trans-Mississippi area will fall into Federal hands unless the eastern bank of the Mississippi River can be adequately defended. In a letter to Arkansas Governor Harris Flana- gin, Davis says, 'The defense of the fortified places on the Eastern bank is therefore regarded as the defense of Arkansas quite as much as that of Tennessee, Mississippi and Louisiana.'

4 April 1863

Washington President Lincoln leaves the Federal capital for Fredericksburg, Virginia, where he will meet with generals of the Army of the Potomac.

5 April 1863

International The British take action against several Confederate vessels, detaining them at Liverpool. One of these, the *Alexandria*, has been undergoing construction in preparation for its use as a blockade-runner in Confederate waters. The indication by this action is that Great Britain is changing its views regarding active support of the Federals. While the *Alexandria* is ultimately released, its seizure and detention serve to notify the Confederacy that they can expect less and less from Palmerston's government in terms of recognition or support.

6 April 1863

Washington After conferring with General Hooker at Potomac Army headquarters, President Lincoln notes, 'our prime object is the enemies [sic] army in front of us, and is not with, or about, Richmond.'
Western Theater As General Grant has ordered, General McClernand has proceeded to New Carthage, Mississippi. There is some brief fighting between Federals and Confederate troops as a result of this advance toward Vicksburg, Mississippi.

7 April 1863

Western Theater There are various episodes of minor skirmishing as Southern forces under General Wheeler conduct raids on several railroads in Tennessee. The Louisville and Nashville line and the run between Nashville and Chattanooga are the targets of these surprise Confederate attacks occurring for four days.

Below: The USS *Mississippi* burns after running aground during an unsuccessful attempt to pass the Southern batteries at Port Hudson.

Above: Nine Union ironclads under Flag Officer DuPont bombard Fort Sumter in an unsuccessful attempt to close Charleston harbor.

Naval The Union vessel *Barataria*, plying the waters of the Amitie River in Louisiana, is attacked and seized by Southern troops. At Charleston, South Carolina, Federal naval forces attack Fort Sumter with a fleet of nine ironclad vessels. These forces are led by Flag Officer Samuel DuPont, and the attack provokes both Fort Sumter and Fort Moultrie to retaliate. The USS *Weehawken* is hit, along with the *Passaic*, the *Montauk*, the *Nantucket* and the *Patapsco*. The Federals are unable to return the Confederate fire in any effective way, being too severely disabled. DuPont withdraws the remaining vessels, and both Confederates and Federals sustain extensive damage; the South reports seven dead, the North, two killed and 13 injured. The USS *Keokuk* is hit so badly as to be unsalvable and it sinks the following day. This action indicates to Federals that, despite their hopes, the important Southern port of Charleston cannot be taken by naval action alone, but will require an operation of combined land and sea forces.

8 April 1863

Western Theater McClernand's Union troops in Mississippi engage in skirmishing in the vicinity of New Carthage, near Milliken's Bend. The troops were carrying supplies and preparing a route for General Grant's upcoming operations against Vicksburg. A particularly sharp skirmish occurs at James' Plantation between McClernand's men and Southern forces in the area.

10 April 1863

Washington President Lincoln, after spending the morning reviewing Potomac Army troops at Falmouth, Virginia, disembarks at Aquia Creek and returns to the Federal capital late in the day.
The Confederacy In an emphatic statement concerning his beleaguered nation's needs, President Jefferson Davis points out that 'We must not forget . . . that the war is not yet ended.' He advises Confederates to concentrate their agricultural efforts on crops other than tobacco and cotton; these cash crops are considered less critical now than 'corn, oats, peas, potatoes and other food for man and beast.' It has become obvious to Davis, government authorities and the general citizenry, that the Southern economy is nearly at breaking point, that to purchase food and industrial products from abroad will be less and less feasible. The nation must redouble its efforts at self-sufficiency, as the recent bread riot in Richmond, Virginia, points out. Several months prior to this, a newspaper in the Confederate capital, the *Dispatch*, indicated that the cost of feeding a family increased over the first two years of the war from $6.65 to $68.25 per week.
Western Theater In Tennessee, near the town of Franklin, General Granger's troops attack Confederate forces under General Van Dorn and defeat the latter in a brief battle which leaves 100 Northern soldiers dead and injured. Confederate losses are tallied at 300 killed or wounded.

11 April 1863

Washington Having recently met with General Hooker and other Potomac Army officers in Virginia, President Lincoln now holds meetings with his cabinet and with General Halleck. At these meetings, the president discusses strategies for both the Eastern and Western Theaters with emphasis on the upcoming Vicksburg campaign under General Grant.
Eastern Theater In Virginia there is skirmishing near Williamsburg and near the Blackwater River. Confederate troops under Longstreet begin a month-long siege of Suffolk, Virginia.
Western Theater In Louisiana Federal General Nathaniel Banks takes 17,000 troops on an expedition toward the Red River, where Confederates are at Fort de Russy.

12 April 1863

Washington In a letter to President Lincoln, General Hooker indicates his desire to cross the Rappahannock River and outflank General Robert E Lee and his Confederates.
Western Theater The Amitie River in Louisiana is the site of a minor skirmish between Federals and Confederates. Stewartsborough, Tennessee, is the scene of brief skirmishing as Federal reconnaissance efforts are conducted in the area.

13 April 1863

Western Theater General Burnside, commander of the Department of the Ohio, issues a proclamation stating that Confederate sympathizers in the vicinity are to be deported to Southern lines. In addition he states that the death penalty is to be meted out to those convicted of aiding the Southern cause.

14 April 1863

Western Theater In Louisiana, at Bayou Teche, Union troops confront Confederates, resulting in 150 Northern casualties. The Southern tallies are not definitive, but in general it is agreed that their losses are much more substantial than Federal casualty figures. At this engagement, the *Queen of the West*, formerly a Union vessel but now in Confederate hands, is bombarded and destroyed by Northern fire.

15 April 1863

Eastern Theater In an estimate of troop strength, General Hooker, head of the Army of the Potomac, reports that he has nearly 130,000 men at his disposal. This contrasts with General Lee's forces in the area which number about 60,000. There is , once again, skirmishing at Norfleet House near Suffolk, Virginia.
Naval Two Federal whaling ships are seized by the CSS *Alabama* which continues

Below: General Grenville Dodge commanded the Northern forces during the Battle of Tuscumbia, Alabama, on 24 April 1863.

to ply Atlantic waters. The *Alabama* takes the two Union vessels off the coast of the Brazilian island of Fernando de Noronha.

16 April 1863

The Confederacy   President Jefferson Davis puts his signature to a bill passed by Congress which will allow soldiers below the age of majority to hold military commissions.
Naval   In a successful venture involving 12 vessels, Admiral David Porter runs the Confederate batteries at Vicksburg, Mississippi. There is but one ship lost as Porter's fleet sails through a heavy bombardment from the shore. The fleet comes to rest at Bruinsburg, Mississippi.

17 April 1863

Western Theater   Colonel Benjamin Grierson leads 1700 men on a 16-day raiding mission that leaves La Grange, Tennessee, at dawn. Intended to divert Confederate strength and attention from the buildup of Federal forces near Vicksburg, Grierson's raid ultimately covers a 600-mile area of Mississippi.
Trans-Mississippi   A raiding party that sets out from Arkansas is led by Confederate General John Marmaduke. These forces harass Federal positions throughout Missouri for a 16-day period.

18 April 1863

Western Theater   There is minor activity near New Iberia, Louisiana, the location of a Southern saltworks. Federal troops seize and destroy this position. In Hartsville, Tennessee, there is continued skirmishing. Grierson's Union raiders encounter the first dis-

ruption in their line of march near the town of New Albany, Mississippi, where light skirmishing breaks out.
Trans-Mississippi   Arkansas is the site of fighting as Southern troops attack Northern forces at Fayetteville, but with little success. In Missouri, Union troops conduct several reconnaissance missions.

19 April 1863

Washington   In order to gather further information about the status of the Potomac Army, President Lincoln takes General Halleck and War Secretary Edwin Stanton to Aquia Creek, Virginia, on a one-day fact-finding mission.
Western Theater   There is continued skirmishing in Mississippi connected with Grierson's raid, Pontotoc seeing a brief encounter between Federals and Confederates. In Tennessee there is skirmishing at Coldwater, where Colonel Bryant's Union forces successfully subdue Southern troops there.

20 April 1863

Washington   After its approval by Congress, the bill allowing West Virginia to enter the Union is declared by President Lincoln as taking effect on 20 June 1863.
Western Theater   In Louisiana, General Nathaniel Banks and his Northern troops successfully take Opelousas. During this ground operation, the Federal naval forces operating in the area take Butte-a-la-Rose. In Tennessee there is a Union reconnaissance from Murfreesboro to the area around McMinnville in an operation lasting for a 10-day period.
Trans-Mississippi   In Missouri, there is an

Above: Union gunboats under Admiral David Porter run the Confederate blockade at Vicksburg on the Mississippi.

encounter between Northern and Southern troops at Patterson. The result of this action is the defeat of Federals under Colonel Smart, with an approximate 50 casualties. Bloomfield, Missouri also sees minor skirmishing.

22 April 1863

The Confederacy   President Jefferson Davis communicates with General John Pemberton at Vicksburg, Mississippi. The Confederate president advises the general to consider disrupting Federal naval operations by sending fire rafts down the Mississippi River.
Eastern Theater   In Virginia, near the town or Strasburg, Confederate troops are defeated by Majors McGee and White. The results of this minor encounter are that the Southerners lose five men, with nine injured and 25 taken prisoner. There are also outbreaks of fighting near Belle Plain, Virginia, as Union troops set out from there to Port Royal on a reconnaissance lasting three days.
Naval   At Vicksburg, Mississippi, Federals make an attempt to send 18 vessels past Confederate shore batteries. There is some success in this venture; although the Union loses one transport and six barges, General Grant's troops receive the supplies carried by the 11 remaining vessels.

24 April 1863

The Confederacy   In a controversial move, the Confederate Congress approves a fiscal measure which places an eight percent tax on all agricultural products grown in the pre-

Above: Union reinforcements arrive to complete the defeat of the South at the Battle of Tuscumbia, Alabama.

vious year. In addition, there is a 10 percent tax placed on profits made from the purchase or sale of most food, clothing and iron . Taxes on licenses are included in this bill, and a graduated income tax is instituted. Estimates of the revenues generated from the 10 percent tax-in-kind levied on agricultural products grown or slaughtered in 1863 hover around $62 million. This last component of the tax law is considered to be particularly difficult, some terming it confiscatory.
Western Theater   In Alabama, Confederate troops encounter Northern forces under General Grenville Dodge at Tuscumbia, and

Below: Two scenes from the engagement at Chancellorsville, showing the repulse of Jackson's Southerners.

are defeated there. In Mississippi, Grierson's Federal raiders push deeper into Confederate territory and engage in fighting near Birmingham.
Trans-Mississippi   On the Iron Mountain Railroad in Missouri, the North successfully routs Southern troops near St Louis. In addition, Confederate General John Marmaduke and his forces skirmish at Mill Creek in Missouri.

25 April 1863

Eastern Theater   Fighting in West Virginia at Greenland Gap sees Federals clash with Southern forces. The former tally losses of 15 dead with 60 taken prisoner; the Confederates estimate close to 100 killed and a large but undetermined number of prisoners.
Western Theater   In Mississippi the forces of General Grant, intent on taking possession of Vicksburg, engage in skirmishing near Hard Times Landing.

26 April 1863

Western Theater   General Streight sends troops on a raid, leaving from Tuscumbia, Alabama. In Kentucky a band of Southern troops known as the Texan Legion surrenders at Franklin. There is a raid on Deer Creek, Mississippi, staged by Union forces.
Trans-Mississippi   The Federal garrison at Cape Girardeau, Missouri, is attacked by Confederate raiders under the command of General John Marmaduke. The Union troops there successfully repel the Southern forces and the latter suffer 40 dead, 200 wounded. Union troops under the command of General John McNeil report six dead and six wounded at this encounter.

27 April 1863

Eastern Theater, Chancellorsville Campaign
The Federal Army of the Potomac under General Hooker's command moves along the Rappahannock River, heading in the direction of Chancellorsville, Virginia. Hooker has approximately 70,000 men with him. Staying behind is General Sedgwick, with 30,000 men, in position near the Confederate camp at Fredericksburg.

28 April 1863

Eastern Theater   The Army of the Potomac crosses the Rappahannock River.
Western Theater   In Georgia, there is a clash between Union and Confederate cavalry at Sand Mountain. The result of this is the defeat of the Southern forces.

29 April 1863

Eastern Theater, Chancellorsville Campaign
There is a severe threat to General Robert E

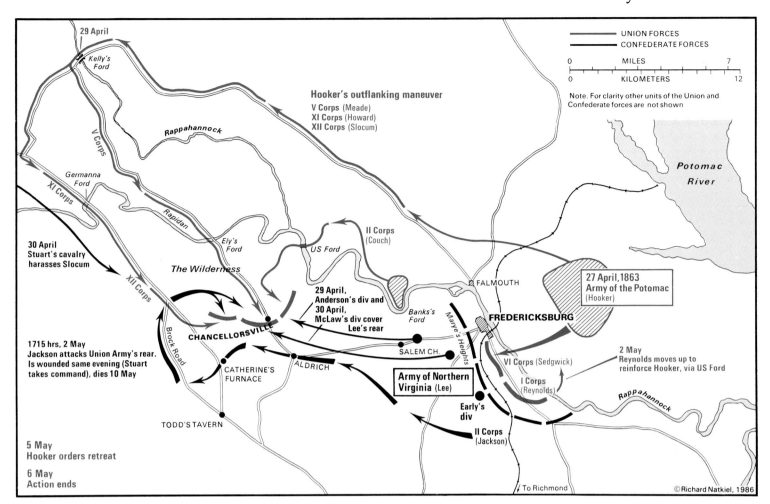

UNION FORCES
CONFEDERATE FORCES

0 ____ MILES ____ 7
0 ____ KILOMETERS ____ 12

Note. For clarity other units of the Union and Confederate forces are not shown

29 April

Kelly's Ford

V Corps

Rappahannock

Germanna Ford

XI Corps

30 April
Stuart's cavalry harasses Slocum

XII Corps

Rapidan

Ely's Ford

The Wilderness

Hooker's outflanking maneuver
V Corps (Meade)
XI Corps (Howard)
XII Corps (Slocum)

US Ford

II Corps (Couch)

Potomac River

1715 hrs, 2 May
Jackson attacks Union Army's rear. Is wounded same evening (Stuart takes command), dies 10 May

Brock Road

CHANCELLORSVILLE

29 April, Anderson's div and 30 April, McLaw's div cover Lee's rear

Banks's Ford

FALMOUTH

27 April, 1863
Army of the Potomac (Hooker)

FREDERICKSBURG

SALEM CH.

CATHERINE'S FURNACE

ALDRICH

Army of Northern Virginia (Lee)

Marye's Heights

VI Corps (Sedgwick)

I Corps (Reynolds)

2 May
Reynolds moves up to reinforce Hooker, via US Ford

TODD'S TAVERN

Early's div

II Corps (Jackson)

Rappahannock

5 May
Hooker orders retreat

6 May
Action ends

To Richmond

©Richard Natkiel, 1986

Lee's Confederates as the major portion of the Federal Army of the Potomac continues to cross the Rappahannock River. There is minor skirmishing near Fredericksburg and at Crook's Run near Kellysville, Virginia.

Western Theater Union troops conduct a reconnaissance that leaves La Grange, Tennessee, and moves into Mississippi several days later. At Vicksburg, Mississippi, Union troops under General Sherman stage an attack near Snyder's Mill in order to distract Confederate forces in the area.

Naval Union gunboats fire on Southern positions at Grand Gulf, Mississippi, although the effort, headed by Admiral David Porter, is ultimately useless in providing a clear route for the passage of General Grant's forces to Vicksburg.

30 April 1863

The Confederacy In order to try to save Vicksburg, Mississippi, from General Grant's imminent attack, President Jefferson Davis advises General Joseph E Johnston of General Pemberton's situation at the beleaguered city: 'General Pemberton telegraphs that unless he has more cavalry, the approaches to North Mississippi are almost unprotected.'

Eastern Theater, Chancellorsville Campaign General Stoneman and his detachment of Union cavalry lead a raid on the Confederate Army of Northern Virginia, destroying portions of the Virginia Central Railroad and cutting General Robert E Lee's communication lines. As a result of this operation, which lasts for seven days, the Union force, totaling about 10,000, suffers around 150 casualties. The South tallies its losses at about 100 killed

and injured, with 500 soldiers taken prisoner. General Hooker, encamped near Chancellorsville with the Army of the Potomac, reports that 'the operations of the last three days have determined that our enemy must ingloriously fly, or come out from behind their defenses.'

Western Theater In Mississippi, General McClernand's Union troops cross the Mississippi River near Bruinsburg. Near Vicksburg, General Grant prepares to push inland with his Federal forces stating, 'All the campaigns, labor, hardships . . . were for the accomplishment of this one object.'

1 May 1863

The Confederacy The First Confederate Congress establishes a provisional navy and draws up a resolution that will provide for the punishment of white Northern army officers captured while in command of Northern black military units.

Eastern Theater, Chancellorsville Campaign At Chancellorsville, Virginia, General Hooker's Army of the Potomac engages General Lee's Confederates in the early part of the day. Later, in the afternoon, Hooker's force of nearly 70,000 men pull away from the Southern forces and all of General Lee's 47,000 troops to take an offensive position. The Potomac Army gathers in an area of rather dense undergrowth known as the Virginia Wilderness where a portion of Lee's army, under the command of General Stonewall Jackson, will make a devastating attack on the Federal army's right flank.

Western Theater, Vicksburg Campaign After having crossed the Mississippi River the previous day, General McClernand's

Above: The Battle of Chancellorsville, May 1863, saw the death of Jackson.

Union troops advance on the Southern position at Fort Gibson. Under the command of Confederate General John Bowen, Southern troops march from Grand Gulf, Mississippi, to attempt to divert McClernand's advance but to no avail. The Federals push steadily forward, resulting in the Southern evacuation of the town of Port Gibson. The way becomes steadily more clear for Grant's forces to march on Vicksburg. The losses at this encounter are tallied at 131 Federals killed, 719 wounded and 25 missing. Confederates report 1150 casualties and 500 taken prisoner.

2 May 1863

Eastern Theater, Chancellorsville Campaign The Army of the Potomac continues to fight at Chancellorsville, Virginia. General Stonewall Jackson takes his Confederates past the Federal right flank to the west and attacks late in the day. This maneuver is aided by General Lee's fire on the Federal left into Union General Meade's men. While regrouping, General Stonewall Jackson is wounded in the arm by his own men; General A P Hill, another Confederate officer, is also wounded – J E B Stuart is now to take command. The Federals are dispersed and pushed back toward Chancellorsville, largely due to General Stonewall Jackson's brilliant outflanking strategy.

Western Theater, Vicksburg Campaign Bayou Pierre, Mississippi, sees fighting as Grant's men push inland to Vicksburg. Colonel Grierson's men are completing their

Above: Union troops attempt to stem a Southern attack during the fighting around the town of Chancellorsville.

600-mile raid, riding hard into Baton Rouge, Louisiana, after having skirmished at several points, including Robert's Ford on the Comite River. The total losses reported for this daring 16-day raid are three killed. seven wounded, nine missing and five men left sick. Grierson estimates that Confederates suffered 100 dead, 500 prisoners taken as a result of his raiders' efforts, and that the South has lost over 50 miles of railroad line and approximately 3000 guns.

3 May 1863

The North In Iowa, Catholic members of the pro-Confederate Knights of the Golden Circle are told by their bishop that they will be excommunicated if they do not resign from this fraternal order.

Eastern Theater, Chancellorsville Campaign Fighting at Chancellorsville, Virginia, continues as the Confederates pound away at Northern positions. The latter are forced to pull back to Chancellor's House as General Lee's troops steadily shell the area from a position known as Hazel Grove. Late in the evening, General Hooker orders General Sedgwick to fire on Confederate positions at

Fredericksburg and the ensuing engagement becomes known as Second Fredericksburg. The Federals at first appear to gain the upper hand, but as they push through the weakened Confederate defense, General Lee opens a new attack on Sedgwick's men at Salem Church, Virginia, halting any further Union advance.

Western Theater, Vicksburg Campaign The Confederate positions at Grand Gulf, Mississippi, are evacuated as a result of General Grant's advance. There is continued skirmishing in the vicinity of Vicksburg as Northern troops encounter Confederates.

4 May 1863

Washington President Lincoln waits in the Federal capital for a word from General Hooker concerning the outcome of the battle at Chancellorsville, Virginia. The president fears the outcome and questions Hooker about the Federal positions at Fredericksburg, Virginia.

Eastern Theater, Chancellorsville Campaign The Federal Army of the Potomac fails to take the offensive at Chancellorsville, and General Lee's Confederates continue to push Sedgwick's troops back, forcing them to cross the Rappahannock during the late evening. Fredericksburg is once again out of the Union's grasp. General Hooker, unwilling to risk another attack, orders the entire Potomac Army to withdraw across the river. At these Chancellorsville engagements, casualties are heavy – the North loses 1606 men, with 9762 injured and another 5919 counted as missing, all of these casualties occurring between 27 April and 4 May. The South reports 1665

Below: Units of Hooker's Army of the Potomac prevent a Confederate breakthrough at Chancellorsville, 3 May 1863.

dead, 9081 wounded and 2018 missing. Among the casualties is General Stonewall Jackson, whose arm has now been amputated as a result of the wound received on 2 May; Davis contacts General Lee by telegraph and tells the victorious general that the nation has 'reverently united with you in giving praise to God for the success with which He has crowned your arms.'

Western Theater, Vicksburg Campaign General Grant pushes into the area south of Vicksburg and minor fighting occurs on the Big Black River.

Naval As part of the Vicksburg campaign, the *Albatross* and several other Union gunboats attack Fort De Russy on Louisiana's Red River. This effort proves fruitless and results in damage to the *Albatross*.

5 May 1863

The North In Dayton, Ohio, Clement Vallandigham, former congressman and a leading Copperhead, or Peace Democrat, having termed the war 'wicked and cruel,' is charged with treason and brought before a military commission by General Burnside, the arresting officer.

Trans-Mississippi In the Utah Territory the Union forces stage an operation, leaving Camp Douglas and intent on subduing pro-South Indians in the vicinity. This expedition heads toward the Bear River in Indian Territory.

6 May 1863

The North Clement Vallandigham is sentenced to close confinement for the duration of the war as a result of his inflammatory statements earlier in the week.

Eastern Theater Despite the defeat of the Federal Army of the Potomac at Chancellorsville, Virginia, General Joseph Hooker makes a public statement of congratulation to the army: 'The men are to be commended on the achievements of the past seven days.' President Lincoln and General Halleck visit Hooker to confer with him on military strategy. As Stonewall Jackson continues to suffer from his wounds, General A P Hill takes charge of II Corps of the Confederate Army of Northern Virginia.

Western Theater, Vicksburg Campaign In Mississippi, Tupelo is the scene of a clash between Union forces under Colonel Corwyn and Southerners commanded by General Ruggles. The latter are defeated and 90 Confederates are taken prisoner.

7 May 1863

Washington Full of concern over the turn of events in Virginia, President Lincoln has returned to the Federal capital after conferring with General Hooker in Virginia. Lincoln writes a letter to Hooker in which he says, 'If possible I would be very glad of another movement early enough to give us some benefit from the fact of the enemies [sic] communications being broken, but neither for this reason or any other, do I wish anything done in desperation or rashness.'

The Confederacy With the victory at Chancellorsville behind them, the Southern leaders turn to Vicksburg, Mississippi, with hope and concern. President Davis contacts the Confederate General John Pemberton saying, 'To hold both Vicksburg and Port Hudson is necessary to our connection with Trans-Mississippi. You may expect whatever it is in my power to do for your aid.'

9 May 1863

The North In a response to General Hooker's congratulatory words to his Army of the Potomac on 6 May 1863, a *New York World* editorial makes the following remarks: 'Whoever knows the facts of the last two weeks will shudder as he reads this order. Whoever does not, let him credit it and believe that his ignorance is bliss.'

Western Theater, Vicksburg Campaign In Mississippi, where Vicksburg is threatened by General Grant's Federals, there is skirmishing near Utica and at Big Sandy Creek. In Louisiana, General Nathaniel Banks' Union troops arrive in Alexandria after having conducted a series of successful raids.

10 May 1863

The Confederacy Since the amputation of his arm, Confederate General Jackson has contracted pneumonia. His death today comes as a terrific blow to the Southern nation; psychologically as well as strategically, Jackson has been an important military figure. Beloved by his men and relied on heavily by General Lee, Jackson dies at the age of 39 at Guinea's Station, Virginia. A note from General Lee to General Jackson dated 3 May 1863, and sent in reference to the latter's injured arm, indicates the depth of Lee's regard for General Stonewall Jackson: 'I cannot express my regret at this occurrence. Could I have directed events I should have been disabled in your stead. I congratulate you upon the victory which is due to your skill and energy.'

11 May 1863

Washington In a continuing current of agitation and strained feelings, President Lincoln is once more caught between opposing political opinions, prompting Secretary of the Treasury Salmon Chase to present his resignation. The chief executive once more refuses to accept Chase's offer to step down.

The North Clement Vallandigham applies in Cincinnati, Ohio, for a writ of habeas cor-

Above: General John Pemberton was ordered to hold Vicksburg for the South by President Jefferson Davis.

pus but is turned down by the United States circuit court there.

12 May 1863

Western Theater, Vicksburg Campaign General Grant's Union troops move closer to Vicksburg, and a division under the command of General John Logan is positioned at Raymond. Logan's Federals are attacked at this point 15 miles from Vicksburg by Confederate forces under the command of General John Gregg. The fighting causes Southern troops to fall back toward Jackson, Mississippi, and each side reports upward of 500 casualties. This skirmish makes clear to General Grant that the South has sufficient

Below: Protected by earth and timber breastworks Union troops enjoy a break from the heavy fighting around Chancellorsville.

troop strength to defend Vicksburg and causes the Union commander to plan preliminary assaults on Confederate positions outside the city.

13 May 1863

Western Theater, Vicksburg Campaign General Pemberton, making preparations for the anticipated attack by Union forces, places Confederates in position at Edward's Station, or Edward's Depot, Mississippi. General Grant's men head toward this point and also toward Jackson, northeast of Vicksburg.

Trans-Mississippi In Missouri there is a Union reconnaissance effort out of Newtonia headed to Centre Creek; this operation lasts until 18 May.

14 May 1863

Eastern Theater There is much concern over the command of the Federal Army of the Potomac. President Lincoln is in contact with General Joseph Hooker, who has done little with the army since Chancellorsville. Lincoln writes to the General saying, 'Some of your troops and Division Commanders are not giving you their entire confidence.'

Western Theater Despite inclement weather, General Grant moves his troops nearer to Jackson, Mississippi, where Confederates have pulled back farther north.

Below: A map showing the movement of Grant's forces before the siege of Vicksburg.

This latter movement is deemed necessary by Confederate General Johnston since he knows his troops are vastly outnumbered. Grant strikes General Gregg's brigade first, and then that of General W H T Walker. By late afternoon, the Southern forces can no longer hold back the Union troops and the latter move in to occupy Jackson, Mississippi, around 1600 hours. To the south, Federal General Nathaniel Banks takes his forces out of Alexandria, Louisiana, heading for Port Hudson, north of Baton Rouge. Port Hudson is considered the second most critical Confederate position on the Mississippi River and its fall is vital to Federal plans.

15 May 1863

The North Union troops break into the office of the *Jeffersonian* at Richmond, Indiana, and wreck the facilities there. This action is precipitated by anti-Union sentiments published by the newspaper.

Western Theater, Vicksburg Campaign Both Confederates and Federals take positions near Edward's Station, Mississippi. General Pemberton has concentrated most of his Southern force here, with a garrison remaining at Vicksburg for the defense of that city. Pemberton is attempting to locate and destroy the Federal lines of communication, an attempt which is fruitless since Grant's strategy of concentrating his troops in the vicinity of Vicksburg precludes the necessity of such communications.

16 May 1863

Western Theater, Vicksburg Campaign The Battle of Champion's Hill, or Baker's Creek, Mississippi, occurs as Grant's Federals clash with Pemberton's Confederates. General McClernand leads his Union forces, attacking the Southern left flank, and McPherson advances on the right of Pemberton's troops. The position at Champion's Hill is held by about 20,000 Confederate soldiers but despite several occasions on which the 29,000 Federals are pushed back, the North ultimately gains possession of the hill. Pemberton's men retreat toward Vicksburg and the Big Black River in Mississippi. This battle at Champion's Hill is considered to be the most severe in the entire Vicksburg campaign. The reports of casualties are an indication of this: Union losses are tallied at 410 dead, 1884 wounded, 187 missing for a total of 2481 altogether out of the original 29,000 men. The Confederacy enters the battle with nearly 20,000 troops and reports 381 killed, approximately 1800 wounded and 1670 listed as missing. This is a total of 3851 casualties for the South.

17 May 1863

Western Theater, Vicksburg Campaign As Pemberton's Confederates continue their retreat, General Grant pursues and a fight at the Big Black River Bridge is the result. A short but fierce encounter, this battle sees Pemberton's men attempt to slow Grant's

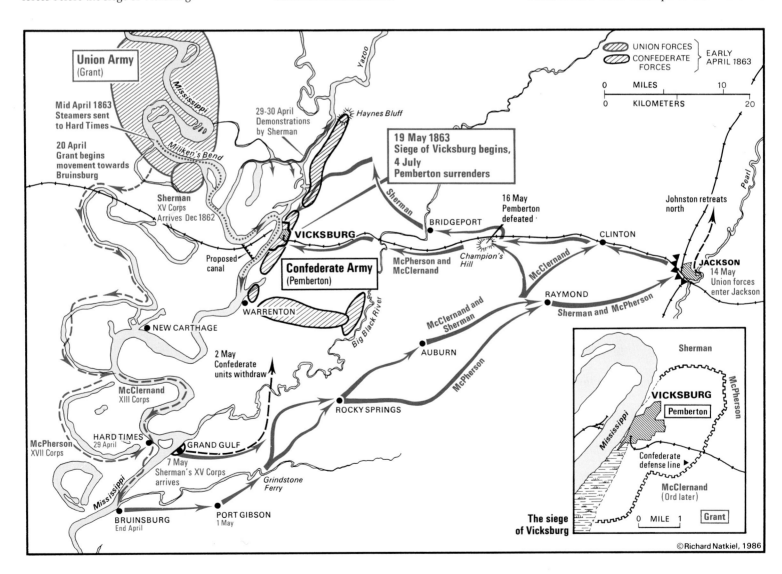

©Richard Natkiel, 1986

Above: Union forces make an abortive attack on strong Southern defenses around the vital city of Vicksburg.

progress by burning the bridges spanning the river, succeeding partially but at a cost of 1700 Confederates taken prisoner by the North. Federals report losses of 39 dead, 237 wounded and three missing out of a fighting force of nearly 10,000. The South stages their defense at this position with about 4000 men. Elsewhere, Union General Nathaniel Banks pushes to a point directly across the Mississippi River from Port Hudson, thereby threatening this vital position.

18 May 1863

The Confederacy Alarmed over the developments at Vicksburg, President Jefferson Davis exhorts civilians and militia in Mississippi to aid General Johnston's efforts and encourages the latter to join forces with Pemberton so as to make an effective attack on Federal forces threatening Vicksburg.
Western Theater, Vicksburg Campaign As General Grant moves his Federals closer to Vicksburg, crossing the Big Black River on reconstructed bridges, General John Pemberton decides to remain with his forces in the city. So begins the siege of Vicksburg, Mississippi, by the Federals.

19 May 1863

Washington The issues surrounding the arrest and imprisonment of Ohio congressman Clement Vallandigham have yet to be laid to rest. Secretary of War Edwin Stanton, carrying out President Lincoln's orders, directs that Vallandigham be sent outside of Federal military boundaries and not be allowed to return.
Western Theater, Vicksburg Campaign Anticipating a relatively easy access to the city, General Grant advances on Confederate fortifications outside Vicksburg, Mississippi. General John Pemberton's troops are well-positioned, however, and the Federals are unable to cut through Southern fortifications. Generals Sherman, McClernand and McPherson all attack with their troops, the result of which is the loss of nearly 1000 Federals in this initial assault on the Confederate positions around Vicksburg.

20 May 1863

Trans-Mississippi In Indian territory there is minor skirmishing between Union and Confederate troops at Fort Gibson.
Naval The Confederacy continues to foil the Union blockade efforts as two Southern vessels make it safely to the harbor at Charleston, South Carolina, from Nassau in the Bahamas. Federal blockaders are able, however, to capture two other Confederate ships, one off the coast of Nassau and one off the mouth of the Neuse River in North Carolina.

21 May 1863

Western Theater, Vicksburg Campaign Federal General Nathaniel Banks moves his troops into position in the area near Port Hudson, Louisiana. The bulk of this force is concentrated at Bayou Sara; other troops are moving along the Clinton Road from Baton Rouge; still others encounter hostile fire from Confederates near Plains Store. These maneuvers of Banks' troops mark the beginning of the siege of Port Hudson.
Naval At Yazoo City, Mississippi, the Confederates destroy a number of workshops in the navy yard and also destroy two steamboats and a gunboat. These actions are completed in the face of an advancing enemy flotilla heading toward the city on the Yazoo River.

22 May 1863

Washington President Lincoln meets with convalescing soldiers at the White House. At this meeting, the president points out that 'the men upon their crutches were orators; their very appearance spoke louder than tongues.'
Western Theater, Vicksburg Campaign Vicksburg, Mississippi, suffers a second attack from General Grant's Union forces. Despite the well-planned assault on Confederate positions there, Grant's men are unable to make any breakthrough. Generals Sherman and McClernand are each able to gain a brief hold at several points, one at Railroad Redoubt, but neither gains a permanent grasp. The Southern defenses are strong and are enhanced by the deep natural ravines surrounding the city. A Northern soldier, R B Scott of the 67th Indiana Volunteers, re-

counts the severity of the attack: 'Every experienced soldier . . . awaited the signal. It came, and in a moment the troops sprang forward, clenching their guns as they started on the charge . . . Twenty thousand muskets and 150 cannon belched forth death and destruction . . . Our ranks were now becoming decimated . . . The charge was a bloody failure.' This second attack on Vicksburg in three days results in heavy losses for the Union: 502 dead, 2550 injured, 147 missing out of a total troop strength of 45,000. Confederates report losses of less than 500 men. The number of casualties makes clear to Grant that direct attacks on the city are fruitless and he concludes that 'The work to be done was to make our position as strong against the enemy as his was against us.'

23 May 1863

Western Theater The Port Hudson, Louisiana, area is the site of fighting as the bulk of General Banks' Federals cross the Mississippi and head toward their goal. Haines' Bluff, Mississippi, sees minor skirmishing. At Vicksburg, the Southern forces continue to man their defenses as General Grant's Federals reinforce their positions.

24 May 1863

The Confederacy President Jefferson Davis is not in complete agreement with General Pemberton's decision to hold Vicksburg, Mississippi. The Confederate president telegraphs a message to General Johnston saying, 'the disparity of numbers renders prolonged defense dangerous.'
Eastern Theater At Fredericksburg, Virginia, the Federal Army of the Potomac, under General Hooker's command, continues to wait, facing the prospect of a clash with General Lee's Army of Northern Virginia.
Western Theater There is some minor reorganization of Union forces in the Murfreesboro area where General William Rosecrans and his men oppose Confederates under General Braxton Bragg at this Tennessee location. In Mississippi, the siege of Southern positions continues to take shape at Vicksburg, as does the siege of Port Hudson, Louisiana. Both of these hold the potential for the defeat of the Confederates in their desire to maintain control of the Mississippi River.

25 May 1863

The North After his sentence of imprisonment had been rescinded by President Lincoln, Ohio congressman Clement Vallandigham is given over to Confederates by Federal military officials in Tennessee. This entire episode is one which provokes outrage from both supporters of Vallandigham in the North and those loyal to the Union who wish to see actions such as his dealt with severely.
Western Theater, Vicksburg Campaign Federal attempts at direct attack being put aside, General Grant now devises a means by which to break through Confederate defenses at Vicksburg, Mississippi. The Union troops there dig a tunnel near the city into which they place, and detonate, 2200 pounds of gunpowder. This explosion is supposed to open up an access route to the city itself, but the Southern troops are waiting in another line of defense to prevent such an entry. General Grant explains: 'The effect was to

Above: General R S Ewell commanded II Corps of the Army of Northern Virginia during the Gettysburg campaign.

blow the top of the hill off and make a crater where it had stood. The breach, however, was not sufficient to enable us to pass a column through. In fact, the enemy had thrown up a line further back.'

Naval The Union navy is successful in capturing two Southern steamboats, the *Red Chief* and the *Starlight*, on the Mississippi River. In another action, the CSS *Alabama* seizes two vessels off the coast of Bahia, Brazil.

27 May 1863

Western Theater, Vicksburg Campaign The Federal siege of Port Hudson, Louisiana, begins as troops under General Banks stage an initial attack on Confederate defenses there. The latter troops are under the command of General Franklin Gardner and num-

ber around 4500. The Union assault is made by approximately 13,000 men, but despite their hopes for an easy victory, Banks' forces are unable to overcome their rather disorganized offensive and the strong repulse made by Gardner's men. The Union reports losses at this action against Confederates at Port Hudson to be 1995 – 293 killed, 1545 wounded, 157 missing. The South tallies casualties to be around 235. Once more, the Union is unable to gain an easy foothold in the vicinity of Vicksburg and Port Hudson.

Naval In an attempt to seize Fort Hill, a Southern position on the Mississippi, Admiral David Porter attacks with the Union gunboat *Cincinnati*. This action, directed by General William Sherman, is unsuccessful as Confederate shore batteries destroy the Union vessel, sinking it and killing or wounding 40 men. There is an attack on Union gunboats at Greenwood, Mississippi. In Georgia on the Chattahoochie River, the CSS *Chattahoochie* explodes by accident, killing 18 men.

28 May 1863

The North In a first for the Union, a regiment of black soldiers leaves Boston. The 54th Massachusetts Volunteers will train at Hilton Head, South Carolina.

29 May 1863

Washington President Lincoln receives a letter from General Burnside in which the latter proffers his resignation as commander of the Department of the Ohio. Burnside takes this step because of the release of Ohio congressman Clement Vallandigham and Lincoln's action rescinding Burnside's imprisonment orders. President Lincoln refuses to accept Burnside's resignation.

30 May 1863

The Confederacy General Robert E Lee and President Jefferson Davis meet to discuss the situation at Vicksburg, Mississippi. The president recognizes that General Johnston's failure to attack Grant's positions has perhaps cost the Confederacy its hold on Vicks-

burg. He says to Lee, 'General Johnston did not . . . attack Grant promptly and I fear the result is that which you anticipated if time was given.'

1 June 1863

The North There is heated opposition to an action taken by General Burnside in the Department of the Ohio. The general calls for the suppression of the *Chicago Times*. This because 'of the repeated expressions of disloyal and incendiary statements.' Citizens of Chicago, Illinois, and the city's mayor, F C Sherman, appeal to President Lincoln to strike down Burnside's orders.

2 June 1863

Washington President Lincoln, reviewing the information that he has concerning Mississippi, wires a message to General Grant asking, 'Are you in communication with General Banks?' It is the opinion of military advisors in Washington that Banks and Grant should combine their forces, but the two generals continue their separate operations.

Eastern Theater In Virginia there is some minor skirmishing around Upperville and Strasburg. General Lee's troops make preparations to move out of their current position in the Fredericksburg area. These Confederate troops of the Army of Northern Virginia number about 89,000 men organized into three corps plus a cavalry unit. The corps are under the command of Generals Longstreet, Ewell and Hill, with J E B Stuart in command of the cavalry's six brigades.

3 June 1863

Eastern Theater, Gettysburg Campaign General Robert E Lee's Confederate Army of Northern Virginia moves out of the Fredericksburg vicinity at the start of a month-long campaign which will culminate in the Battle of Gettysburg, Pennsylvania. Lee has come to the decision to stage an invasion of the North. As these Southern troops advance north, there is skirmishing near Fayetteville, Virginia. The Federal Army of the Potomac, under General Hooker's command, numbers

approximately 122,000 men; it has conducted various reconnaissance efforts prior to this date and Hooker is aware of Lee's intentions. **Western Theater, Vicksburg Campaign** Various maneuvers take place; in Louisiana, Union troops conduct a reconnaissance around Clinton. Minor fighting breaks out at Simsport, Louisiana. General Grant receives some reinforcements in the Vicksburg area from IX Corps stationed until now to the north, in Kentucky.

4 June 1863

Eastern Theater, Gettysburg Campaign General Robert E Lee and his Confederates move toward Culpeper Court House with Generals Ewell and Longstreet and their two corps. General A P Hill and his corps remain in the Fredericksburg area. Union troops conduct reconnaissance efforts for two days, leaving Yorktown, Virginia, and heading for Walkerton and Aylett in that state.

Western Theater, Vicksburg Campaign In Mississippi, Confederates prepare to endure the siege which has been implemented by General Grant's Union forces.

5 June 1863

Eastern Theater, Gettysburg Campaign In the course of a reconnaissance effort in the Fredericksburg area by General Sedgwick's VI Corps of the Potomac Army, there is severe fighting in Virginia. This encounter, known as the Battle of Franklin's Crossing, or Deep Run, sees Union troops clash with Confederates positioned in trenches. The result of this fighting is that although the Federals take 35 prisoners and report six Confederates dead and 35 wounded, the Army of Northern Virginia is still very much in force at Fredericksburg. It is President Lincoln's advice to General Hooker that the Federal Army of the Potomac should concentrate on the portion of Lee's Confederates that is moving out from

Below: Union artillery going into action near the Rappahannock, part of a reconnaissance in force prior to Gettysburg.

Fredericksburg. It is apparent that to attack the Fredericksburg position would be less profitable.

6 June 1863

Eastern Theater, Gettysburg Campaign General Hooker is still attempting to pinpoint General Lee's destination and intention in moving most of the Confederate Army out of Fredericksburg, Virginia. General J E B Stuart and his Confederate cavalry corps stage a review at Brandy Station, Virginia.

7 June 1863

Western Theater, Vicksburg Campaign A serious clash between Federals and Confederates occur as the latter attack the Union troops garrisoned at Milliken's Bend in Louisiana. While Confederates under General McCulloch are successful in pushing the Federals back to the Mississippi, the Union troops, under General Thomas, are aided in their defense of the area by the intervention of two gunboats, the *Lexington* and the *Choctaw*. After the intervention, the Confederates pull back. Losses at this encounter at Milliken's Bend are reported by the Federals at 652 dead and injured, by Confederates at 185 casualties. The Brierfield plantation in Mississippi is burned by Union troops; Brierfield is the home of Confederate President Jefferson Davis.

8 June 1863

Eastern Theater, Gettysburg Campaign General Robert E Lee attends a cavalry review of General J E B Stuart's corps. This occurs at Culpeper Court House, Virginia.

Western Theater, Vicksburg Campaign At Vicksburg, Mississippi, General Grant's troops shell the city; this is a constant, 24-hour bombardment which causes residents to take cover in caves or remain hidden in their houses to avoid the destructive showers.

9 June 1863

Eastern Theater, Gettysburg Campaign In order to gain further information about Confederate positions, General Hooker directs cavalry under the command of General Alfred Pleasonton to conduct a reconnaissance in the area of the Rappahannock River at a location known as Brandy Station, Fleetwood Hill, or Beverly Ford. The battle occurring here between Pleasonton's 11,000 troops and Confederate General J E B Stuart's cavalry forces is considered to be the most severe cavalry fight of the entire war. It results in little real gain for the Federals, although General Hooker obtains some information about Confederate troop strength, movement and positions. Stuart's cavalry manages to hold the location at a cost of some 523 casualties out of nearly 10,000 troops engaged. The Union reports 81 dead, 403 wounded and 382 missing.

10 June 1863

Washington President Lincoln is in communication with General Hooker, advising him as to a course of action for the Federal Army of the Potomac in Virginia. According to Lincoln, the army's best strategy is to 'Fight him when the opportunity offers. If he stays where he is, fret him.'

The North There is a wave of alarm among communities north of the Potomac River as word of Lee's advancing Confederate army becomes available.

Eastern Theater, Gettysburg Campaign The Army of Northern Virginia moves its II Corps under General Ewell out of Culpeper, Virginia, on a northwestern course.

Naval The Federal vessel *Maple Leaf*, loaded with Confederates taken prisoner by Union troops, is forced ashore by its passengers near Cape Henry, Virginia. This group of prisoners is being transferred from Fort Monroe to Fort Delaware, but is successful in making its escape once the vessel reaches the coast.

11 June 1863

The North In Ohio, Peace Democrats submit the name of former congressman Clement Vallandigham for nomination as governor. This despite the fact that Vallandigham, convicted of treason against the Union, has been banished to the Confederacy and has been subsequently transferred by the Southern government to Canada.

Western Theater Once more, Triune, Tennessee, is the scene of skirmishing, this time as General Nathan Bedford Forrest's Confederates clash with Federals in that area of the state. Elsewhere, there is fighting in South Carolina at Little Folly Island and also in Mississippi, near Corinth.

12 June 1863

The North Because of an anticipated invasion and attack on the citizens of Pennsylvania, the governor of that state, Andrew Curtin, calls out the militia. He also requests aid from New York State to repel the assumed influx of Confederates under General Lee.

The Confederacy President Jefferson Davis receives an offer from Vice-President Alexander Stephens, concerning a possible mediation between the Confederacy and the Union. Stephens' suggestion has to do with a diplomatic effort to promote 'a correct understanding and agreement between the two Governments.'

Eastern Theater, Gettysburg Campaign As General Lee's Army of Northern Virginia moves north, passing the Blue Ridge and going into the Shenandoah Valley, the Confederate troops clash with Federals at Newtown, Cedarville and Middletown, Virginia.

13 June 1863

Eastern Theater, Gettysburg Campaign At Winchester, Virginia, there is skirmishing as Confederates under General Ewell push into the area, causing the second Battle of Winchester. Ewell takes over and occupies Berryville, Virginia. There is other fighting near Bunker Hill and White Post, Virginia. At Second Winchester the Federals, under General Milroy, lose 300 men in their encounter with the Southern forces, who report losses of 850 dead or wounded.

14 June 1863

Western Theater Northern General Nathaniel Banks tells Confederates at Port Hudson, Louisiana, to surrender. Failing this capitulation, Banks plans an assault to commence at daybreak. This Federal attack by about 6000 troops is carried out against 3750 Confederates, who hold off the Federals.

Above: Southern cavalry and artillery cross the Potomac into Maryland and Pennsylvania, 11 June 1863.

Trans-Mississippi In Arkansas there is an attack on the USS *Marmora* near Eunice. The town is nearly destroyed by fire following this action as Federals retaliate against the Confederate attack on the vessel.

15 June 1863

Washington In the Federal capital, President Lincoln seeks support from the state militia of Pennsylvania, Maryland, Ohio and West Virginia in the face of the northward advance of Lee's Confederates. The president asks the governors of these states to prvide 100,000 troops. In addition there is an order sent out by the Federal Department of the Navy to disable the CSS *Tacony*, a Southern vessel which has been successful in interfering with Northern shipping along the eastern coastline.

Eastern Theater, Gettysburg Campaign There is a fierce attack on Federal positions at Winchester, Virginia, as General Milroy's 9000 Northern troops attempt to hold the area. General Ewell's Confederates are successful in pushing the Union force back in the direction of Harper's Ferry. In addition to the victory at Winchester, Southern troops also attack Federal positions at Berryville and Martinsburg. At the Winchester battle, Union losses are reported at 95 killed, 348 injured and over 4000 missing or captured; the Confederates losses are 47 killed, 219 wounded, 3 missing. The Confederacy seizes a large quantity of supplies and ammunition: 23 guns, 300 wagons, 300 horses and much

food. The Southern forces continue to press northward, arousing the inhabitants of Maryland and Pennsylvania, and achieving results which provoke Hooker's message to President Lincoln that indicates the Southern invasion is something 'it is not in my power to prevent.' There is a Confederate cavalry raid at Chambersburg, Pennsylvania; J E B Stuart's cavalry acts as a front line unit for General Longstreet's corps that is heading out from Culpeper Court House.

16 June 1863

Eastern Theater, Gettysburg Campaign General Hooker takes his Federal Army of the Potomac and positions it at Fairfax Court House, Virginia, as General Lee and his Confederate Army of Northern Virginia cross the Potomac River.

17 June 1863

Eastern Theater, Gettysburg Campaign Skirmishing continues as General Lee's Confederates push north. The fighting on this day occurs at Point of Rocks, Maryland.

Western Theater, Vicksburg Campaign The siege of Vicksburg continues unabated. Union forces clash with Confederates as the

Below: The CSS *Atlanta* was forced to surrender to Union ironclads after an engagement on the Wilmington River, Georgia.

latter attack gunboats and land positions, the latter occurring today at a point near Commerce, Mississippi.

Naval On the Wilmington River in Warsaw Sound, Georgia, Captain John Rogers, commander of the Federal vessel *Weehawken*, is successful in forcing the surrender of the Confederate ironclad vessel *Atlanta*. The *Weehawken* and the *Nahant*, commanded by Captain John Downes, clash with the *Atlanta*, resulting in several casualties on either side.

18 June 1863

Eastern Theater, Gettysburg Campaign
Further skirmishing breaks out at Aldie, Virginia, as Lee's Confederates push north. There is a Union reconnaissance in the Peninsular area of Virginia.

Western Theater, Vicksburg Campaign
General John McClernand is relieved of his command of the XIII Corps by General Ulysses Grant. This is due to McClernand's repeated acts of insubordination and his apparent unwillingness to cooperate with the rest of the Army. He is replaced by General E O C Ord.

19 June 1863

Eastern Theater, Gettysburg Campaign
Generals Ewell, Hill and Longstreet probe north as the Confederate Army of Northern Virginia continues its invasion. There are encounters between these Southern troops and Union forces, skirmishing breaking out at Middleburg, Virginia, as the North attempts to slow the progress made by Lee's Army.

Western Theater, Vicksburg Campaign
There is continued skirmishing in the area of Vicksburg as the siege continues.

Below: Union batteries lobbing shells into Vicksburg during the siege.

20 June 1863

Washington President Lincoln issues a proclamation which declares West Virginia as the 35th state of the Union.

The North In an effort to provide some defense of the city, citizens in Baltimore, Maryland, erect fortifications to the north and west in order to repel any Confederate raids on the city.

Western Theater, Vicksburg Campaign
Various incidents of skirmishing take place; in Louisiana, at La Forche Crossing there is minor fighting over a two day period. The Federal batteries around Vicksburg, Mississippi, shower that city with shells.

Trans-Mississippi In Missouri, a Union reconnaissance leaves Waynesville. At Government Springs in the Utah Territory Union forces clash with Indians.

21 June 1863

Eastern Theater, Gettysburg Campaign There is fierce but minor fighting in Virginia as General Hooker's Potomac Army encounters Lee's advancing Confederates at Upperville and Haymarket. In Maryland, where Union and Southern troops encounter each other, there are similar clashes near Frederick.

22 June 1863

Eastern Theater, Gettysburg Campaign The fighting continues to be minor and fragmentary as Lee's Army of Northern Virginia pushes on and engages Federals near Aldie, Virginia. At Greencastle, Pennsylvania, Union and Confederate troops clash. As General Lee moves in to Chambersburg, Pennsylvania, citizens in Philadelphia close down businesses and shops.

Naval The CSS *Tacony*, under the command of Lieutenant Charles Read, seizes five

Above: Lieutenant Charles Read commanded the CSS *Tacony* during the capture of five Union vessels off New England on 22 June 1863.

Federal fishing vessels in waters off the coast of New England, proving the fallibility of the Union blockade once again.

23 June 1863

Eastern Theater, Gettysburg Campaign
General Joseph Hooker prepares his Federal Army of the Potomac to cross the river of the same name in Virginia. In Yorktown, Union troops begin a reconnaissance that lasts for five days and heads in the direction of South Anna Bridge.

Above: Union troops, caught in a crater after the detonation of a mine, suffer heavy losses at the hands of Vicksburg's defenders.

Western Theater, Tullahoma Campaign
Under the command of General William Rosecrans, the Federal army begins a major, and a successful, effort to harass Confederates in the Tullahoma, or Middle Tennessee, campaign. By operating against General Braxton Bragg's Confederates in this effort, the Union general prevents Bragg from moving toward Vicksburg with reinforcements. In this way, Rosecrans is supporting General Grant's campaign at Vicksburg, Mississippi.
Trans-Mississippi   In the Nebraska Territory there is fighting at Pawnee Agency. In

Below: Union supply officials weigh bread and meat prior to its distribution at Fairfax Court House, Virginia.

the Nevada Territory, Union soldiers engage Indians in combat near Canon Station. Sibley, Missouri, is the site of minor skirmishing.

24 June 1863

Eastern Theater, Gettysburg Campaign
Sharpsburg, Maryland, sees fighting as Hooker's Potomac Army clashes with troops under the command of Longstreet and Hill. The latter are moving to join forces with Confederate General Ewell, who has arrived in Maryland, and with whom they will advance on Pennsylvania.
Western Theater, Tullahoma Campaign
General Braxton Bragg encounters Federals near Bradyville and Big Springs Ranch in Tennessee, where General William Rosecrans is advancing into the middle of the state. There is also skirmishing at Middleton, Tennessee, and some brief but fierce action at

Hoover's Gap. At the latter engagement, Southern forces report a large number of casualties while the Union lists 45 dead and injured.
Western Theater, Vicksburg Campaign
There is a slight increase in the pressure placed on Confederates at the besieged city of Vicksburg; food is becoming scarcer and the shelling from Federal batteries has been stepped up. A civilian observer, Edward Gregory, describes the hardships suffered by those who had remained at Vicksburg to endure the constant attacks by General Grant's troops: 'Hardly any part of the city was outside the range of the enemy's artillery except the south . . . Just across the Mississippi, seven 11-inch and 13-inch mortars were put in position and trained directly on the homes of the people . . . how people subsisted was another wonder . . . There were some stores that had supplies, and prices climbed steadily, but first nobody had the money, and then nobody had the supplies.' In Louisiana, there is a Confederate raid at Berwick Bay where injured Union soldiers are convalescing. General Taylor's Southern troops, numbering approximately 4000, are easily able to seize the post at Berwick Bay and gain access to much needed supplies.

25 June 1863

The Confederacy   A worried President Jefferson Davis contacts General Braxton Bragg in Tennessee. The president points out the urgent need for reinforcements at Vicksburg, where General Johnston is intent on harassing General Grant's forces to prevent the continued siege of the city. Davis also appeals to General Beauregard, located at Charleston, South Carolina, for additional troops for General Johnston. Davis fears that without these reinforcements, 'the Mississippi will be lost.'
Eastern Theater, Gettysburg Campaign This day marks the start of Confederate General

Surrender of York to Gen. Early and Gen. Gordon. June 28th 1863.

Above: The surrender of York to forces under the command of Southern Generals Early and Gordon in late June 1863.

J E B Stuart's Gettysburg raid (a maneuver that military historians would later criticize as it removed Stuart's Confederate cavalry from the vicinity of the upcoming battle at Gettysburg). Rather than follow strictly the directions provided by General Lee on 22 June 1863, Stuart takes a route around Hooker's rear and flank, avoiding the protection afforded by the Blue Ridge route to the west. Stuart, by this action, crosses the Potomac Army's main supply line and captures upward of 125 Federal wagons and takes more than 400 prisoners. However, although Stuart's raiding does cause some disruption, it will not prevent the concentration of the Federal army at Gettysburg.

26 June 1863

Eastern Theater, Gettysburg, Campaign General Jubal Early and his Confederate forces move into Gettysburg, Pennsylvania, at first encountering some of Hooker's Potomac Army troops and skirmishing with them outside Gettysburg. Although General Hooker wires the president of his intention to move against Lee's Army of Northern Virginia, there is an indication that Lincoln is dubious about Hooker's abilities.

Western Theater, Tullahoma Campaign There is minor skirmishing at Beech Grove, Tennessee. There is a fight between Rosecrans' Federals and Bragg's Confederates at Shelbyville, where the Northern casualty lists show 45 dead, 463 injured, 13 missing. The South reports 1634 casualties, plus many taken prisoner by the North.

Naval After having successfully taken 21 Federal vessels in less than three weeks, Confederate Lieutenant Charles Read in command of the schooner *Archer* attempts to seize the Federal cutter *Caleb Cushing* at anchor in the harbor at Portland, Maine. This attempt is foiled by Federal naval steamers; the *Archer* is destroyed and the Confederates taken prisoner.

27 June 1863

Washington After conferring with General Henry Halleck, President Lincoln decides to remove General Joseph Hooker from his command of the Army of the Potomac. It is decided that General George Meade will replace Hooker; Halleck sends word to Meade

Below: Union troops and civilians abandon Wrightsville and burn the Columbia railroad bridge in the face of Lee's forces.

Above: Union side-wheelers and ironclads in action against Port Hudson, Louisiana, during late June 1863.

of this change. Meanwhile, General Hooker has sent a message to the president concerning the evacuation of Harper's Ferry, Virginia, which Hooker feels is critical. Hooker points out that unless this action is taken he can no longer act as head of the Potomac Army. When Halleck countermands the orders concerning Harper's Ferry, it leads to Hooker's decision to resign from command of the Army of the Potomac.

Eastern Theater, Gettysburg Campaign General Robert E Lee's Army of Northern Virginia moves into Chambersburg, Pennsylvania, after having forced the surrender of York. The Southern army is headed for the state capital at Harrisburg. Elsewhere, J E B Stuart and his cavalry forces encounter Federals near Fairfax Court House, Virginia; in the fighting that ensues, all but 18 of the Union cavalrymen are captured by Stuart's Confederates.

Western Theater, Tullahoma Campaign At Guy's Gap and again at Shelbyville, Tennessee, there is skirmishing between Federal and Confederates. In that same vicinity General Rosecrans' Union forces occupy Manchester, forcing General Bragg to the decision to pull back with his Southern troops to Tullahoma.

28 June 1863

Washington General George Meade is appointed to replace Hooker. President Lincoln and General Halleck learn that, while the newly-appointed Potomac Army chief is uninformed as to the 'exact condition of the troops and the position of the enemy,' he is planning to move the Federal forces toward the Susquehanna River. Both Lincoln and Halleck feel much confidence in Meade, and hope that he will mount an attack on Lee's invading army. There are, at this point, around 100,000 Federal troops concentrated in the area around Frederick, Maryland.

Eastern Theater, Gettysburg Campaign There is skirmishing at Chambersburg, Pennsylvania, where the forces of Generals Longstreet and Hill are positioned. General Ewell is at Carlisle; General Early at York. After learning that the Federal army is north

of the Potomac River, General Lee makes a change in his original plan to march on Harrisburg. The new strategy requires that Hill and Longstreet join Ewell and move on Gettysburg and Cashtown.

Western Theater, Vicksburg Campaign In Louisiana, at Donaldsville, the Southern forces under General Taylor attack local Federals. The latter garrison, under the command of Major J D Bulle, is able to withstand the assault with the help of Federal gunboats. Both Vicksburg, Mississippi, and Port Hudson, Louisiana, continue under siege.

29 June 1863

Eastern Theater, Gettysburg Campaign At Winchester, Maryland, there is a fierce cavalry skirmish between Confederates under J E B Stuart and Union forces under Major N B Knight. The Confederates are attacked by Knight's Federals, but because of Stuart's stronger force, the Southerners repel the assault. At this encounter, the North reports nine casualties; the South, 18 dead and

wounded. General George Meade moves his Union Army of the Potomac toward Gettysburg. General Robert E Lee's forces also push to this point in Pennsylvania.

Western Theater, Tullahoma Campaign General Rosecrans continues to harass Southern forces in Tennessee, skirmishing breaking out at Hillsborough, Decherd and Lexington. Columbia, Kentucky, also sees fighting.

30 June 1863

Washington Despite pressure from supporters of the former Potomac Army chief, President Lincoln refuses to place General George Brinton McClellan back in command of that critical force which is only hours away from battle at Gettysburg, Pennsylvania

Eastern Theater, Gettysburg Campaign Confederate cavalry under General J E B Stuart once more engages Federal cavalry forces, this time at Hanover, Pennsylvania. General Kilpatrick's Federals are able to mount a serious counterattack which nearly results in the capture of Stuart. At this cavalry skirmish, the Union reports 19 killed, 73 wounded, 123 missing. Confederates list nine dead, 50 wounded, 58 missing. General Reynolds' Union troops are sent by General Meade to occupy Gettysburg.

Western Theater, Tullahoma Campaign Fighting continues in the mid-Tennessee area as General Braxton Bragg pulls his Confederates across the Tennessee River in a retreat from Tullahoma. General Rosecrans establishes his Federals at Chattahoochee, Tennessee.

1 July 1863

Eastern Theater, Gettysburg Campaign A three-day battle begins at Gettysburg, Pennsylvania as cavalry forces under Union

Below: Union dead, stripped of their shoes by Southern troops, lie in a field near the town of Gettysburg.

General Buford clash with General A P Hill's Confederate cavalry early in the day. This fighting occurs along the Chambersburg Road but moves closer to Gettysburg proper as the day wears on. Confederate General Ewell's troops join the battle by afternoon, with Longstreet and Hill's men, and make a strong push against the Union XI Corps which is commanded by Federal General O O Howard. This latter force is driven back from Gettysburg in a fierce clash of men and horses, toward the southeast, an area known as Cemetery Ridge and Cemetery Hill. The hard-fighting Federals, entrenched at this position by late in the day, are not harassed further by General Lee's army, however. This gives time for Union General Meade, commander of the Potomac Army, to reinforce Cemetery Hill with more Union troops. It is at this position that Generals Howard and Doubleday are strengthening their fortifications for the next attack by the Confederates. General Robert E Lee wishes that General Ewell make an attack on the Federals at Cemetery Hill immediately, prior to any further reinforcement. However, General Ewell chooses not to advance on the Union forces there on this first day of the Battle of Gettysburg. The Southern Army of Northern Virginia now holds the town of Gettysburg and is waiting for the arrival of General Longstreet's corps prior to making any more offensives against the Northern forces which outnumber them. Casualties at this engagement show that the Federals have suffered a great deal more than General Lee's forces: General O O Howard's Corps sees over 4000 taken prisoner. In addition, Federal General John Reynolds is killed in the midmorning fighting which takes place along the Chambersburg Road by McPherson's Ridge. Meanwhile, the Confederate General Archer

Below: A posed photograph of a dead Southern sharpshooter in position behind a stone sangar at Gettysburg.

is taken prisoner. Archer is the first general officer in the Army of Northern Virginia to be taken by the Federals since General Robert E Lee assumed command of this Confederate force.

Western Theater, Tullahoma Campaign
While fighting continues in Tennessee along the Elk River, near Bethpage Bridge and in the Tullahoma vicinity where Rosecrans' Union troops now are positioned, the major thrust of the Federal campaign against Confederates under General Braxton Bragg is over. The Southern forces are pulling southward toward Chattanooga.

Western Theater, Vicksburg Campaign
There is skirmishing near Edward's Station in the vicinity of Vicksburg, Mississippi, as General Johnston's Confederates continue to fend off the harassing forces of General Grant's Union troops. Inside the city, General John Pemberton's men struggle, under increasingly poor conditions, to continue their defense of Vicksburg.

2 July 1863

Eastern Theater, Gettysburg Campaign The second day of fighting at this critical battle sees Federals positioned at Big Round Top and Little Round Top along Cemetery Ridge. Lee's forces are placed along Seminary Ridge, below the Union lines. Fighting breaks out late in the day as General Longstreet's I Corps pushes against General Daniel Sickles' Federals at the Peach Orchard and along the Emmitsburg Road. Meanwhile, General G K Warren successfully withstands a Confederate assault on Federal positions. Despite Confederate General Hood's forces pressing the Union troops on the Round Tops, the South is unable to do more than gain a slight foothold at the lower sections of these hills; the Federals hold fast to their superior vantage points on the summits. General Ewell's Confederate troops attack Union positions at Culp's Hill and Cemetery Hill, but only General Edward

Above: General Daniel Sickles was involved in some of the heaviest fighting at Gettysburg and lost a leg during the battle.

Johnson's Confederates make any appreciable progress, that at the lower portion of Culp's Hill where they seize some positions not adequately defended by the XII Corps of the Federal Potomac Army. The latter has left this southeast section of Culp's Hill open while concentrating better Union defenses at the Round Tops.

Western Theater, Tullahoma Campaign
While Bragg's Southern troops continue their line of retreat, there is minor skirmishing around Morris' Ford, at Elk River and near Rock Creek Ford, all in Tennessee.

Western Theater, Vicksburg Campaign
There is little change in the situation at besieged Vicksburg, Mississippi, where General John Pemberton remains entrenched with his Confederates inside the city. There is some exchange of artillery fire between Pemberton's and Grant's troops.

3 July 1863

Washington   There is an anxious vigil at the Federal capital as the president awaits information about the Battle of Gettysburg.

Eastern Theater, Gettysburg Campaign This final day of battle at Gettysburg, Pennsylvania, opens with the Federal Army of the Potomac, under the command of General George Meade, preparing for an attack by General Robert E Lee's Army of Northern Virginia. Despite General Longstreet's feeling that a Confederate offensive is risky due to the larger Federal force, General Lee is firmly

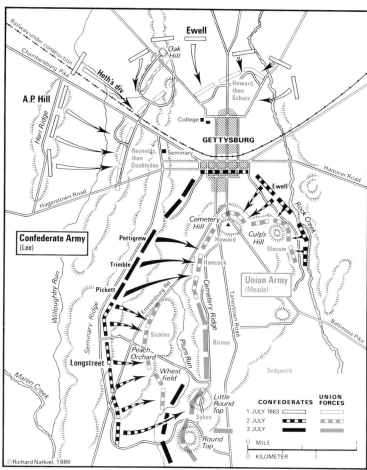

Above left: Fierce fighting around Cemetery Hill during Southern attempts to pierce the Union line at Gettysburg.
Left: The defeat of Pickett's Charge on the last day of the battle ended Southern hopes of victory at Gettysburg.
Above: A trio of ragged Confederate prisoners photographed before their march into captivity.
Above right: The three-day Battle of Gettysburg saw Lee's Army of Northern Virginia defeated by General Meade's forces.

committed to making an assault on the middle of Meade's forces. Accordingly, 15,000 troops are sent to make what will be the final Southern attempt against the Union at Gettysburg. In the early afternoon, Generals Pettigrew, Trimble and Pickett group their men and advance on Federals in the vicinity of the Emmitsburg Road. The Federals are strung out in a line, facing the advancing Confederates, from Culp's Hill to Big Round Top and Devil's Den. The famous Confederate maneuver (later to become known as Pickett's Charge, despite the fact that it is General Longstreet who is in command of this operation and General Pickett's men form only part of the attacking force) does little to save the South's army at Gettysburg, however, and the hand-to-hand combat which ensues sees the death of Confederate General Armistead. The Battle of Gettysburg ends with the Southern forces retreating and attempting to regroup as a counterattack is expected, although it never occurs. General Lee has ventured into a nearly untenable position on this final day of fighting; to send 15,000 men against what he knows to be a larger enemy force is a gamble, and Lee loses it.
Western Theater, Vicksburg Campaign The

situation in Mississippi mirrors that in Pennsylvania: after weeks of siege, the Confederate forces under the command of General John Pemberton display white truce flags. The decision to surrender has been made with understandable reluctance, but the Confederate general ventures forth to meet with Union General Ulysses Grant in order to work out terms of surrender, despite the fact that Grant has already dictated his terms: 'You will be allowed to march out, the officers taking with them their side arms and clothing, and the field, staff and cavalry officers

one horse each. The rank and file will be allowed all their clothing but no other property.' After the six-week siege, there is clearly no alternative for the South; they have almost no food and a continued entrenchment is pointless. The following day, Independence Day, is chosen for a formal surrender, and both North and South are well aware of its significance.

Below: Union artillery is rushed forward to prevent a breakthrough by the Confederates during the final day of Gettysburg.

4 July 1863

Eastern Theater, Gettysburg Campaign The Confederate Army of Northern Virginia now heads slowly back toward Virginia, aided by poor weather as rain engulfs the area making it difficult for Meade's army to follow in pursuit, although the Union commander of the Potomac Army is later criticized for failing to do so. The casualty lists for the three-day encounter at Gettysburg, Pennsylvania, show that both the North and the South suffered terrible losses. The Confederate army reported 3903 dead, 18,735 injured and 5425 missing out of a total of 75,000 men – this means that 28,063, more than one-third of the Confederates at Gettysburg were listed as casualties. The North, having gone into battle with 88,289 men, sustained 3155 dead, 14,529 wounded and 5365 missing, a total of 23,049 casualties.

Western Theater, Vicksburg Campaign The Confederates formally surrender Vicksburg, Mississippi, to the Union army, and nearly 29,000 men under Pemberton's command march out of the city. It is hoped that news of this Union triumph will hasten the end of the Port Hudson siege, and that the entire region of the Mississippi will soon be under the control of the Federal army.

Below: Union troops repulse Pickett's men at the point of the bayonet, inflicting severe losses on Lee's forces.

5 July 1863

Eastern Theater, Gettysburg Campaign Lee's Army of Northern Virginia continues its retreat while Meade lags in pursuit. A few skirmishes, largely fought by cavalry, occur at towns in Pennsylvania and at Smithburg, Maryland.

Western Theater Grant begins to parole the Confederate defenders of Vicksburg, each prisoner signing a pledge not to fight again until he is duly exchanged for a Northern prisoner.

6 July 1863

Eastern Theater, Gettysburg Campaign Minor skirmishes continue along Lee's route of withdrawal, but the Federals cannot put together an organized pursuit. In one action, Federal cavalry officer Buford is repulsed by Lee's advance guard at Williamsport, Maryland.

Western Theater Federal General Sherman moves troops toward Jackson, Mississippi.

7 July 1863

Washington Lincoln is encouraged by news of the fall of Vicksburg but, worried that Lee will escape with his army, writes to Meade urging him to attack without delay.

Eastern Theater, Gettysburg Campaign Lee's army entrenches at Hagerstown, Maryland, ready to cross the storm-swollen Potomac as soon as the waters lower. Minor skirmishes continue in outlying towns and Federal forces move on Maryland Heights.

Western Theater Confederate General Braxton Bragg, driven from west Tennessee by Rosecrans' Army of the Cumberland, gathers his troops around Chattanooga.

8 July 1863

Eastern Theater, Gettysburg Campaign Lee's forces remain at Hagerstown, Maryland, and skirmishes occur at Boonsborough and Williamsport, Maryland. In spite of his recent defeat and present dangerous position, Lee writes to President Davis, 'I am not in the least discouraged.'

Western Theater Discouraged by the fall of Vicksburg, the besieged Confederate defenders of Port Hudson, Louisiana, surrender, leaving the whole of the Mississippi River under Federal control. In his diary, one Port Hudson resident notes that during the six weeks of the siege he and his friends consumed 'all the beef, all the dogs, and all the rats that were obtainable.' The fall of Port Hudson gives the Union over 6000 Confederate prisoners along with large quantities of arms and ammunition. Elsewhere, Confederate raider John H Morgan and 2500 men, beginning a sweep through Indiana and toward Ohio, cross the Ohio River into Indiana meeting only light Federal resistance. Many in Ohio fear that this action will galvanize rising Copperhead sentiment.

9 July 1863

Eastern Theater, Gettysburg Campaign
There is a small skirmish at Beaver Creek, Maryland, but Lee continues to have no substantial opposition.

Western Theater The Confederate leader of Port Hudson, General Gardner, formally surrenders to Federal General Nathaniel Banks. Though the Mississippi is now under Union control, Federal shipping will have continuing troubles with guerrilla attacks. Near Jackson, Mississippi, Sherman closes on General J E Johnston, commander of the Confederate Department of the West.

10 July 1863

Eastern Theater, Gettysburg Campaign
Meade's army begins to move with more determination toward Lee's forces, now gathering in Williamsport, Maryland; skirmishes erupt in several nearby towns, including a serious encounter at Falling Waters.

Western Theater Federal forces prepare for an assault on Battery Wagner, a Confederate defensive position on Morris Island in Charleston Harbor, South Carolina.

11 July 1863

The North Pursuant to the Union Enrollment Act of 3 March, the first names of draftees are drawn in New York.

Eastern Theater, Gettysburg Campaign
Meade begins preparing for an attack on Lee's forces which still await the lowering of the Potomac.

Western Theater Federal forces mount their first attack on Battery Wagner in Charleston Harbor, but are repulsed after gaining the parapets. In Mississippi, Sherman besieges some of Johnston's forces in West Jackson.

Above: The Battle of Boonesborough saw Union cavalry attempt to harry the rear-guard of Lee's Army of Northern Virginia.

12 July 1863

Eastern Theater, Gettysburg Campaign
Meade finally catches up to Lee's army, but engages only in light and ineffective reconnaissance. Lee, building fires to give the illusion of a settled camp, begins to move his troops over the now subdued Potomac on boats and a new pontoon bridge. Meade contemplates an attack the next day, but is dissuaded by his staff.

Western Theater Fighting is seen in Canton, near Jackson, Mississippi, between Sherman's and Johnston's forces. Moving through Indiana, Morgan's raiders meet increased resistance.

13 July 1863

The North, Draft Riots As a result of the first drawing of names for the draft in New York, resentment that has been growing toward the Federal Enrollment Act of 3 March boils over into a violent four-day riot. A mob of over 50,000 people, most of them Irish working men, swarm into the New York draft office, set it afire and nearly kill its superintendent. Over the next few days an evacuated black orphanage and the offices of Horace Greeley's *Tribune* are burned by the rioters. Increasingly, the violence is directed toward blacks, who are attacked, robbed and killed at random; but the rioters also loot businesses, beat to death a Union colonel, and assault the home of the mayor. At length, Federal troops just back from Gettysburg are called in and quell the mob, leaving over 1000 dead and wounded and ending what history will note as one of the darkest homefront episodes of the war and the worst

Above: A representation of the anti-draft riots that broke out in several Northern towns during the second week of July 1863.

race riot in American history. Less serious draft riots break out in Boston, in Troy, New York and other towns in the East and Ohio.
Eastern Theater, Gettysburg Campaign During the night, Lee and his Army of Northern Virginia complete their evacuation from Williamsport over the Potomac, their withdrawal again masked by campfires that also deceive the Union army.

14 July 1863

Eastern Theater, Gettysburg Campaign Finally pressing forward to attack, Meade's Army of the Potomac moves into Southern positions at Williamsport and discovers them

Below: The charge of the 6th Michigan Cavalry Regiment over Southern earthworks during the Battle of Falling Waters, 10 July 1863.

to be abandoned. Thus ends the North's best chance for a quick end to the war. This day Lincoln writes in an unsent letter to Meade, 'Your golden opportunity is gone, and I am distressed immeasurably because of it.' Nonetheless, Lee's last opportunity for an invasion of the North has been stopped.
Western Theater Confederate troops emerge on a sortie from Battery Wagner near Charleston, South Carolina. Clashes are also seen at Iuka, Mississippi, and Elk River in Tennessee.
Naval Federal ships extend their control over the James River in Virginia by taking Fort Powhatan.

15 July 1863

The Confederacy Stricken by the defeats at Gettysburg, Vicksburg and Port Hudson, and the dangerous situations in Charleston and Jackson, President Davis writes to one of his generals, 'The clouds are truly dark over us.'
Eastern Theater, Gettysburg Campaign Lee's army moves southward along the Shenandoah Valley of Virginia, in good condition though short of shoes and supplies.

16 July 1863

The North The Draft Riots subside in New York.
Eastern Theater Morgan's raiders continue their ill-defined exploits in Ohio, meeting with increasing Federal resistance.
Western Theater J E Johnston, fearing Sherman's superior forces, pulls his forces out of Jackson, Mississippi, and leaves the city to Union occupation.

18 July 1863

Western Theater Federal forces mount a second unsuccessful attack on Battery Wagner, South Carolina. After an extensive naval bombardment, a frontal attack is attempted by Federal forces, but the troops are turned back. By the end of the day Federal casualties total 1515 to the defenders' 174.

Losses to the 54th Massachusetts Colored Infantry are especially severe, and their commander, Colonel R G Shaw, is killed. After this action shows that a direct attack against the Battery is inadvisable, a siege is commenced by Federal troops and ships. The Confederates begin moving guns from Fort Sumter to strategic positions within Charleston Harbor.

19 July 1863

Eastern Theater, Gettysburg Campaign In pursuit of Lee, Meade's army crosses the Potomac at Harper's Ferry and Berlin, Maryland.
Western Theater In Ohio, Morgan's raiders, now greatly reduced by skirmishes and desertions, are overwhelmed by Hobson and Shackelford, who kill and capture over 800 of his men. With only 300 men left, Morgan escapes toward Pennsylvania with Hobson in pursuit.

20 July 1863

The North Merchants in New York meet to discuss the relief of black victims of the Draft Riots.
Eastern Theater, Gettysburg Campaign Moving away from the Potomac toward Lee's army, Meade sends parties to take over the passes of the Blue Ridge Mountains. Nearby, skirmishes erupt at Ashby's Gap and Berry's Ferry.

22 July 1863

Eastern Theater, Gettysburg Campaign Meade prepares an assault on Manassas Gap in the Blue Ridge Mountains, Virginia, hoping to open a route for his men into the Shenandoah Valley; there they could intercept Lee's column as it moves south through the valley.

23 July 1863

Eastern Theater, Gettysburg Campaign Federal forces under General W H French push through Manassas Gap only to meet

CHARGE OF THE 6TH MICHIGAN CAVALRY OVER THE REBEL EARTHWORKS NEAR FALLING WATERS

stiff resistance from Confederates; while French is delayed, the Southern corps of Longstreet and Hill move out of reach down the Shenandoah. Meade has thus failed to cut Lee's army in two.

24 July 1863

Eastern Theater, Gettysburg Campaign Meade's forces enter the Shenandoah Valley, Virginia, to find, as they did at Williamsport, that the enemy has gone; Union troops then continue to Warrenton.

Western Theater The Federal siege of Battery Wagner in Charleston Harbor continues with heavy shelling of the stronghold from Union ships. The remnants of Morgan's raiders continue to be harassed by Federal pursers at Washington and Athens, Ohio.

26 July 1863

Western Theater Confederate raider John Hunt Morgan and the last of his men are brought to bay at New Lisbon, Ohio. Since crossing the Ohio River they have averaged 21 hours a day in the saddle and have covered large distances on what was nonetheless a strategically pointless expedition, especially since hoped-for Copperhead support in Ohio and Indiana has failed to materialize. As one commentator later observes, 'This reckless adventure . . . deprived [Morgan] of his well-earned reputation.' Morgan and his officers are sent to Ohio Penitentiary, from which he later escapes.

28 July 1863

Eastern Theater, Gettysburg Campaign Confederate partisan J S Mosby begins a series of daring harassing maneuvers around Meade's army; his raiders strike quickly and disappear.

1 August 1863

The Confederacy The growing incidence of desertion in the Confederate army, combined with the increasingly desperate need for manpower, leads President Davis to offer

amnesty to those absent without leave. He then writes that the citizens of the South have no choice but 'victory, or subjugation, slavery and utter ruin of yourselves, your families, and your country.'

Eastern Theater, Gettysburg Campaign Brandy Station, scene of a June cavalry battle, sees another skirmish between the opposing cavalries of Lee and Meade, as minor encounters continue in the weeks after the major Southern defeat at Gettysburg.

Western Theater Federals begin organizing further troop action in Charleston Harbor, South Carolina, as part of their efforts to recapture Fort Sumter.

Naval Confederate raids on Federal shipping increase on the Mississippi; D D Porter is given command of Union naval forces on the river. Porter has recently been promoted to the rank of rear admiral.

Above: Members of Mosby's raiders rendezvous to plan an attack on a Union supply column in the Shenandoah.

4 August 1863

Western Theater Bombardment continues in Charleston Harbor, as Federals prepare for action the immense 'Swamp Angel,' a 200-pound Parrott gun which fires incendiary shells.

6 August 1863

Naval The British-built CSS *Alabama* captures the Federal bark *Sea Bride* near the Cape of Good Hope.

Below: Union cavalrymen pose for the camera. By the third year of the war, they could take on the South's horsemen on equal terms. Southern units were increasingly short of mounts.

Above: Captain Raphael Semmes standing by the *Alabama's* 110-pounder rifled cannon during the ship's stay in Cape Town, August 1863.

8 August 1863

The Confederacy Lee, dejected and in ill health, writes President Davis offering his resignation as commander of the Army of Northern Virginia. Davis refuses the request, writing, 'our country could not bear to lose you.'

10 August 1863

Trans-Mississippi A Federal expedition to Little Rock, Arkansas, begins as troops led by General Frederick Steele leave Helena, Arkansas.

11 August 1863

Western Theater Federal preparations for an offensive in Charleston Harbor are stopped by heavy shelling from Fort Sumter and Battery Wagner.

12 August 1863

Western Theater Northern artillery, using their accurate Parrott guns, once again commence heavy shelling of the forts in Charleston Harbor, as a new offensive begins.

16 August 1863

Western Theater, Chickamauga Campaign After much delay and official prodding, the Federal Army of the Cumberland under Rosecrans moves eastward from Tullahoma toward the Tennessee River; the goal is Chattanooga and Braxton Bragg's Army of Tennessee. At the same time, Union General Burnside moves down from the Lexington, Kentucky, area toward eastern Tennessee. Rosecrans plans to envelop the Confederates between himself and Burnside; anticipating this strategy, Bragg reorganizes his troops, requesting all available reinforcements. South of Chattanooga, Federal Generals Thomas and McCook are brought up to

threaten Bragg's only railroad link. The stage and the principal actors are now preparing for the complex, protracted, and bloody engagements of the Chickamauga and Chattanooga campaigns in southern Tennessee.

17 August 1863

Western Theater Fort Sumter in Charleston receives its first major bombardment from Union land and naval batteries. Its brick walls begin to fail but the 5009 shells rained on the fort in the next eight days cause few casualties among the defenders and no exploitable breaches in the walls.

18 August 1863

Washington President Lincoln fires a few test rounds of the Union's new Spencer Repeating Carbine, a rifle soon to give Federal soldiers an important advantage over the South's muzzle-loaders.

20 August 1863

Trans-Mississippi In Arizona Territory Colonel 'Kit' Carson moves against the Navaho Indians, who have been engaged in actions against settlers since the United States occupied New Mexico in 1846, after the war with Mexico.

21 August 1863

Western Theater, Chickamauga Campaign Rosecrans' forces reach the Tennessee River outside Chattanooga and begin preparations for the coming offensive.

Trans-Mississippi Around 450 irregular Confederate raiders under William Clarke Quantrill stage a dawn terrorist raid on Lawrence, Kansas, leaving 150 civilians dead, 30 wounded, and much of the town a smoking ruin. In 1862 Quantrill had been denied a commission by Confederate Secretary of War J A Seddon, who termed his notions of war 'barbarism.' For some time the town of Lawrence has been strongly Unionist and abolitionist, thus earning Quantrill's enmity. This strategically pointless raid demonstrates a certain Southern loss of faith in conventional military operations, and many of the South find this and later similar actions disturbing to their sense of divine approval for the Confederate cause: one raider has shouted into the window of a woman whose husband he has just murdered, 'We are friends from Hell!'

22 August 1863

Western Theater In Charleston Harbor, the Swamp Angel, pride of the Federal battery, blows itself up at the 36th round. As one observer later noted, 'The [gun] turned out to have been more destructive to Union gun crews than to Rebel property.'

23 August 1863

Western Theater Union batteries cease their first bombardment of Fort Sumter, leaving it a mass of rubble but still unconquered by the Northern besiegers.

Below: Confederate irregulars terrorize the inhabitants of a Western town. William Quantrill was the most feared leader of guerrillas.

25 August 1863

Western Theater A Union offensive fails to overrun Confederate rifle pits before Battery Wagner in Charleston Harbor.

Trans-Mississippi In the wake of Quantrill's terrorist raid on Lawrence, Kansas, the Federal commander in Kansas City issues a misguided and ineffective anti-guerrilla directive ordering many civilians in the area out of their homes; much property and crops are destroyed, and 20,000 are left homeless. Resentment over these measures is to last for years.

26 August 1863

Western Theater Confederate rifle pits before Battery Wagner are captured in a second Union effort.

29 August 1863

Naval In Charleston Harbor, South Carolina, the experimental Confederate submarine *H L Hunley* sinks on a test cruise, drowning five crewmen. The ship is soon raised and is later to see action.

30 August 1863

Western Theater Heavy Federal shelling resumes on Fort Sumter. Confederates within the fort, meanwhile, are engaged in digging their cannon out of the rubble and moving them into Charleston for the anticipated defense of the city.

1 September 1863

Western Theater Union batteries pour 627 rounds into Fort Sumter near Charleston, reducing its walls to still smaller fragments but not dislodging its defenders.

Chickamauga Campaign Moving toward Chattanooga, Rosecrans' Army of the Cumberland begins a four-day crossing of the Tennessee River largely unopposed by Bragg's Army of Tennessee. Bragg, meanwhile, receives two divisions of much-needed reinforcements.

2 September 1863

Western Theater With no opposition, Federal General Burnside's troops occupy Knoxville, Tennessee, to remain there as a resource for Union forces operating in the vicinity of Chattanooga.

4 September 1863

Western Theater Union General Ulysses S Grant, in a perhaps inebriated state, is fallen on by his horse in New Orleans; the general, soon to be called to Chattanooga, will be partly lame for some weeks.

Chickamauga Campaign In Chattanooga, Rosecrans completes his army's crossing of the Tennessee, still nearly unopposed, and begins to suspect that Bragg is fleeing him. Elsewhere, dwindling supplies of food and clothing result in protests and looting by women in Mobile, Alabama.

5 September 1863

Western Theater, Chickamauga Campaign Rosecrans, convinced that Bragg's Army of Tennessee is evacuating Chattanooga, moves into the Georgia mountains south of the city. Determined to pursue the supposed Confederate retreat, the Union commander takes the risky step of separating his army into three groups in order to go as quickly as possible through three widely-spaced gaps in the mountains.

International Despite Federal protests, British shipbuilders have for some time been constructing vessels for the Confederacy, the most successful of which is the CSS *Alabama*; this ship has been preying on Federal commerce since mid-1862 and has captured or destroyed over 60 Union ships. Finally responding to Washington's protests, the British government on this day seizes in Liverpool's Laird shipyards two newly-built ironclads with ramming spars that have been ordered by the Confederacy. This seizure of the so-called 'Laird Rams' halts the growth of the Confederate navy and ends the last major diplomatic crisis between Washington and Britain during the war.

Below: The ruins of Fort Sumter after three years of war. For much of that time the position was under Union bombardment. Although the fort's walls were smashed, its garrison held out for most of the conflict.

6 September 1863

Western Theater, Chickamauga Campaign
As Federal troops close around this city, General Bragg, perhaps fearing a repeat of the siege of Vicksburg, decides to evacuate Chattanooga. In Charleston, Confederate commander P G Beauregard decides that it would be too costly to fight the coming Union assault on Battery Wagner and Battery Gregg. He evacuates the forts. Fort Sumter, by now nearly a heap of brick, still holds out.

7 September 1863

Western Theater The Federal infantry assault on Batteries Wagner and Gregg finds the enemy evacuated.

8 September 1863

Trans-Mississippi Federal transports and three gunboats from New Orleans enter the Sabine Pass in Texas to attack a small Confederate defensive fort. Within an hour two Union ships have been disabled and one forced to surrender with a loss of some 70 men. The operation is soon abandoned, with the North having sustained a minor but embarrassing defeat that considerably boosts the spirits of western Confederates.
Western Theater, Chickamauga Campaign
Bragg's troops, now numbering some 65,000, march out of Chattanooga and withdraw toward Lafayette, Georgia.

9 September 1863

Western Theater, Chickamauga Campaign
The Federal Army of the Cumberland is now spread in three groups north to south across 40 miles of mountains. The northernmost group, under Crittenden (whose brother is a Southern general), advances through Chattanooga while the others, Thomas in the middle and McCook many miles to the south, pursue what Rosecrans believes to be a fleeing enemy. Indeed, by now the Federal commander is convinced he will chase Bragg to Atlanta if not to the sea. In fact, the Union

Below: A Union encampment at Culpepper, Virginia, occupied by Meade's forces on 13 September 1863 after its evacuation by Lee.

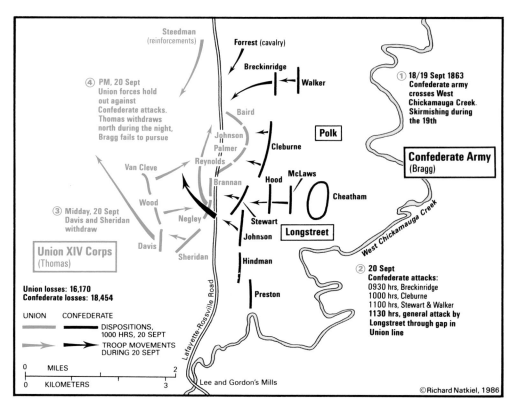

Above: The Battle of Chickamauga saw the Union forces narrowly avoid defeat.

army is racing into a very clever trap. Though some of Bragg's staff, who dislike their harsh and fractious commander and serve him badly, are later to insist he has not planned it, there is little doubt that Bragg has constructed his trap well, and that it has every chance of success: his army, now outnumbering Rosecrans', is gathering at Lafayette, Georgia, and preparing to defeat the widely-separated Federal forces one group at a time.

In Virginia, Longstreet's divisions have departed from Lee's army and are beginning a long railroad journey to reinforce Bragg; they will arrive on 18 and 19 September.

10 September 1863

Western Theater, Chickamauga Campaign
Having created a brilliant trap, Bragg and his staff now proceed to spring it ineptly and too soon. Before the Federals are totally committed, Bragg orders an attack on McLemore's Cove, but it fails to be mounted. During the day both Crittenden and Thomas discover strong parties of the enemy in their paths, and both are able to fall back and regroup. It is soon to become clear to the whole Federal staff that Bragg is by no means retreating.
Trans-Mississippi Federal forces occupy Little Rock, Arkansas, after Confederate forces evacuate; this development poses a serious threat to the Confederate Trans-Mississippi area.

11 September 1863

Western Theater, Chickamauga Campaign
Once again Bragg orders an attack on isolated Federal forces but it fails to materialize.

Knoxville Campaign Burnside, still occupying the city, offers his resignation to Lincoln; the president refuses the resignation and asks Andrew Johnson to form a Union state government.

12 September 1863

Western Theater, Chickamauga Campaign
By this time Rosecrans has realized the perilous position of his armies, divided in the face of concentrated enemy forces. Urgent orders are issued to his wings to move toward the center. McCook's forces to the south begin after midnight an exhausting 57-mile journey through the mountains that will unite them with Thomas on the 17th. Meanwhile, Bragg has ordered General Polk to attack next day a part of Crittenden's forces at Lee and Gordon's Mill on Chickamauga Creek.

13 September 1863

Eastern Theater Weakened by Longstreet's removal to Tennessee, Lee's forces withdraw across the Rapidan River. Meade's army moves from the Rappahannock to the Rapidan, occupying Culpeper Court House.

Western Theater, Chickamauga Campaign
Bragg arrives at Lee and Gordon's Mill expecting to find Crittenden's XXI Corps annihilated by Polk as planned in his orders; instead, he finds that Polk has made no move and that Crittenden has safely concentrated his forces. Yet again, Bragg's plans have been frustrated by his subordinates. His trap has failed. He and his army now wait for reinforcements and for the arrival of the enemy from the west.

15 September 1863

Washington As Meade's advance to the Rapidan is completed, Lincoln writes that the Union army should attack Lee at once.

17 September 1863

Western Theater, Chickamauga Campaign
Union troops move toward concentration around Lee and Gordon's Mill on Chickamauga Creek. By the end of the day the divided forces are within supporting distance of one another. Bragg, now on the east bank of the creek, begins to develop his battle plan: he will turn the Union left flank and get behind Rosecrans' army, cutting off the roads to Chattanooga. The stage is now set for the bloodiest battle of the war in the Western Theater. It is prophetic that the ancient Cherokee Indian name for this creek is *Chickamauga*, meaning 'River of Death.'

18 September 1863

Western Theater, Chickamauga Campaign
Bragg has planned a major attack this day, but cannot get his forces to the west bank of Chickamauga Creek in time. Extensive cavalry skirmishes break out at various locations. The first of Longstreet's forces arrive from Virginia. All day and night Rosecrans is busy concentrating and placing his troops, anticipating Bragg's plan to attack his left and get behind him. Because of the dense woods in the area, broken only by a few small fields, neither commander can determine the strength and position of his enemy; moreover, it is difficult for commanders to observe their own positions.

19 September 1863

Western Theater, Chickamauga Campaign
Dawn finds both fronts solidly facing one another along a six-mile line. A Northern captain describes the feelings of the soldiers before the battle: 'Through that forenoon we saw the constantly moving columns of the enemy's infantry and saw battery after battery as they moved before us like a great panorama. In such moments men grow pale and lose their nerve. They are hungry but they can not eat; they are tired, but they can not sit down. You speak to them, and they answer as if half asleep; they laugh, but the laugh has no joy in it.' The fighting begins almost by accident. Thomas sends one of his divisions to reconnoiter near the creek on the Union left; these troops suddenly encounter the dismounted cavalry of Nathan Bedford Forrest, who return fire and call for infantry help. Soon hostilities have erupted along most of the battle line. Throughout the ensuing day of intermittent but fierce fighting, Bragg throws his strongest efforts against the Union left, pursuing his plan to get behind the enemy and cut them off from Chattanooga. Rosecrans responds by moving division after division to his left, extending his battle line north. By the end of the day losses are enormous on both sides, but neither has gained any significant advantage. The battle grinds to a standstill: dead men blanket the thick woods, wounded men crawl toward the

Below: General Henry Thomas, the 'Rock of Chickamauga,' (mounted, left) stems the Southern onslaught during the battle.

Above: Southern General John Hood was wounded at Chickamauga and subsequently had his right leg amputated.

rear, stretchermen carry hundreds to the overworked field hospitals which are soon marked by bloody heaps of amputated limbs.

During the afternoon Longstreet has arrived with the bulk of his troops; it takes him until 2300 hours to locate Bragg, who gets out of bed for a conference. The plan for the following day is decided upon: Polk will attack at dawn in the north, and the attack will be joined successively by units down the line southward, to climax with an all-out assault by Longstreet on the Union right. Meanwhile, Rosecrans decides on a defensive strategy and his men begin building rough breastworks along the six-mile length of the Union frontline.

20 September 1863

Western Theater, Chickamauga Campaign At dawn, Bragg, unable in the dense forest and morning fog to see his troops, waits for the sound of Polk's attack. After over an hour of inactivity, he sends a messenger to Polk, who is discovered to be comfortably breakfasting in a farmhouse. To the query about his attack, Polk replies, 'Do tell General Bragg that my heart is overflowing with anxiety for the attack – overflowing with anxiety, sir.' This being reported back to Bragg, the commander swears 'in a manner that would have powerfully assisted a mule team in getting up a mountain,' and at about 0930 hours orders his right flank into attack against Thomas on the Union left. Once again the Confederates struggle determinedly to outflank the Federals; but Thomas's men hold at the breastworks and, as it did the previous day, the fighting sways back and forth indecisively. Then at about 1100 there occurs a strange and fatal error.

Union commander Rosecrans, mistaken as to the location of his divisions in the thick brush, orders T J Wood to close up on and 'support' J J Reynolds, whom he supposes to be immediately on Wood's left; Rosecrans' order is thus intended to tighten his battle line. But in fact, there is another whole division between Wood and Reynolds. Wood, taking the order literally, pulls back out of line and moves left toward Reynolds, thereby leaving a gaping hole in the Union line. But before Wood has completed his withdrawal, Longstreet, whether because he has seen the withdrawal or whether through a coincidence fortuitous to say the least, charges in a solid column directly into this gap, with devastating effect.

The Union line has been cut in two, the right wing is in disorderly rout and Thomas's men are being pushed left toward Snodgrass Hill. Thousands of Federals are killed or captured, the rest are running. Along with McCook and Crittenden, a panicky and demoralized Rosecrans flees to Chattanooga, assuming his whole army is being destroyed. But Rosecrans is wrong. On the Federal left Thomas has maintained firm control of his troops, and assumes a virtually impregnable position on Snodgrass Hill. For the rest of the day, Thomas's men desperately turn back wave after wave of attacks, several of them hand-to-hand, as nearly the whole Confederate army swarms up the precipitous slopes. At 1500 hours when Thomas is nearly out of ammunition and is threatened from the rear, he is reinforced from the north by General Granger, who has fortunately violated his morning's orders to keep his Reserve Corps in place. With Granger's men and bullets, Thomas holds the position until nightfall and then withdraws in good order toward Chattanooga. His army's heroic defense has saved the Union forces from utter rout, and General George Henry Thomas will hereafter come to be known as the 'Rock of Chickamauga.'

The battle losses on both sides are staggering. In two days of fighting the Union has 1656 killed, 9756 wounded and 4757 missing, totaling 16,169 casualties; the Confederates have 2132 dead, 14,674 wounded, 1468 missing, totaling 18,274. Both sides have lost about 28 percent of their strength. The battle

is unusual in that the crucial decisions have been taken largely by subordinate officers.

21 September 1863

Western Theater, Chattanooga Campaign As the ragged and demoralized Union army gathers in Chattanooga, Bragg is urged by Longstreet to move quickly against the retreating enemy; but he does not give the orders until 1600 hours, too late to reach the city, thus giving the Federals time to organize their defenses. In Knoxville, Burnside receives a wire from Lincoln: 'Go to Rosecrans with your forces, without a moments delay.' Burnside, pressed by enemy forces, stays.

22 September 1863

Washington Lincoln mourns the death at Chickamauga of his brother-in-law, Confederate General Ben Hardin Helm.
Western Theater, Chattanooga Campaign Bragg orders an attack on Federal positions below Missionary Ridge in Chattanooga; the troops reach the area to find the enemy 'ready to receive and entertain us . . . we expected to be flung against the forts to certain destruction.' Realizing the Federals have now firmly dug in, Bragg cancels the attack. By failing to pursue the Federals before they can reorganize, Bragg has missed his second great opportunity to destroy the Union army. Now, as his forces occupy the commanding heights of Missionary Ridge and Lookout Mountain, his third and final opportunity takes shape. A few days after having thought they were chasing the Confederates to Atlanta, the Federals find themselves defeated and besieged.

Below: General J Reynolds was one of the Union commanders during the costly fighting at the Battle of Chickamauga.

23 September 1863

Washington Lincoln and his cabinet hold an urgent meeting about the crisis in Chattanooga. It is decided to send by rail Hooker's two corps from the Army of the Potomac, still in Virginia, to Alabama in support of Rosecrans. By 25 September the troops are entrained and moving south with extraordinary speed. By 15 November, 17,000 of these and other reinforcements will have arrived at Bridgeport, Alabama, along with thousands of horses and mules.

25 September 1863

Washington Lincoln, angry at Burnside's failure to aid Rosecrans, writes in an unsent letter that he has been 'struggling . . . to get you to assist General Rosecrans in an extremity, and you have repeatedly declared you would do it, and yet you steadily move the contrary way.'

28 September 1863

Western Theater, Chattanooga Campaign Bragg is informed by President Davis that Union reinforcements are on their way. Rosecrans, attempting to justify his handling of the battle – especially in regard to charges that he advanced recklessly and lost his nerve after Longstreet's attack – brings his own charges against subordinates McCook and Crittenden, who are ordered to Indianapolis for a court of inquiry. Eventually the two generals are exonerated, and history will tend to confirm the charges against Rosecrans, who is a hard-working and methodical leader but often excitable and ineffective on the battlefield.

Below: Positioned along the slopes of Snodgrass Hill, Union troops repel a spirited Confederate attack, 20 September 1863.

30 September 1863

Western Theater, Chattanooga Campaign Bragg has thought that Rosecrans might evacuate Chattanooga, but seeing that the Federals show no signs of leaving, he orders cavalry raids by Wheeler on Union lines of communication; these raids continue into October.

2 October 1863

Western Theater, Chattanooga Campaign Hooker's men begin to arrive in Bridgeport, Alabama, eventually to support Union forces in Chattanooga. During the next two days

Above: A Confederate attempt to capture a Union battery at Chickamauga is thwarted by men led by Lieutenant Van Pelt.

20,000 men and 3000 horses and mules will arrive, all having traveled 1159 miles by rail in just over a week. Meanwhile, Confederate cavalry troops continue to raid vital Union supply lines, closing the route between Bridgeport and Chattanooga and forcing Rosecrans to rely on a long, muddy and mountainous wagon road on the north side of the Tennessee River. A later Southern raid on this route destroys in one day 300 wagons

Above: General George Thomas, the hero of Chickamauga, became the commander of the Union forces in Chattanooga on 18 October 1863.

and 1800 mules. Though the Confederates cannot shut off Union supplies entirely, the specter of famine looms for the besieged Army of the Cumberland.

3 October 1863

Western Theater, Chattanooga Campaign Wheeler's cavalry raids continue on troops and supply routes around Chattanooga. A six-day bombardment of Fort Sumter in Charleston Harbor ends with 560 rounds having been fired to no particular effect.

5 October 1863

Western Theater, Chattanooga Campaign Wheeler's cavalry breaks a vital Union supply line by destroying a bridge at Stone's River, near Murfreesboro. The Confederate raiders will be very active in the coming days all around eastern Tennessee. In Chattanooga the famine deepens among Federal troops; draft mules are dying by the hundreds, with cavalry and artillery horses weakening. Soldiers are seen searching in the dust for grains of corn dropped by their animals.
Naval In an attempt to loosen the Federal blockade of Charleston Harbor, the Confederate semi-submersible steamship *David* hits the Federal ironclad *New Ironsides* with a spar torpedo. Damage to the Union ship is extensive but not critical, and two of the *David*'s four crew are captured; the other two crew take the nearly-swamped ship back to Charleston. This is the first successful Southern semi-submersible attack of the war; the only Union attempt at a submersible, the *Alligator*, sank under tow in April 1863, after several unsuccessful trials. In general, the experimental submarines of both sides

throughout the war cause more fatalities to their crews than to their enemies.

9 October 1863

Eastern Theater, Bristoe Campaign Lee, still outnumbered but wishing to capitalize on Meade's loss of Hooker's troops sent to reinforce Alabama, moves his army from the Rapidan to the west and north. He is trying to flank Meade's army and drive them from the west. Over the next month Lee forces Meade to retreat some 40 miles for a time, but achieves little other than to destroy a railroad the Federals have been repairing.
Western Theater, Chattanooga Campaign Wheeler's Confederate cavalry raiders return to Chattanooga having attacked Rosecrans' supply and communication lines all around east Tennessee.

10 October 1863

Eastern Theater, Bristoe Campaign Skirmishes break out around the Rapidan in Virginia as Lee tries to get behind the right flank of the Army of the Potomac.
Western Theater, Chattanooga Campaign Confederate President Davis arrives on the scene near Chattanooga to survey the siege and to attempt mediation in the growing feud between Bragg and his generals.

12 October 1863

Eastern Theater, Bristoe Campaign Amid daily skirmishings, Lee's Army of Northern Virginia continues moving west and north toward Manassas and Washington. Meade slowly withdraws.

13 October 1863

The North Republican Union candidates are successful in a number of state elections. In Ohio Vallandigham, the Canadian-exiled

Copperhead candidate for governor, loses decisively but still receives a surprisingly large vote.

14 October 1863

Eastern Theater, Bristoe Campaign Lee attempts to cut off Meade's withdrawal with an attack under A P Hill on Union corps near Bristoe Station. There ensues a day of inconclusive but costly maneuvering which gains no clear results; though Meade is forced back near the Potomac, his column is not broken. Lee's forces lose 1900 captured and killed to Meade's 548.

15 October 1863

Western Theater For the second time, the Confederate submarine *H L Hunley* sinks during a practice dive in Charleston Harbor, this time drowning its inventor along with seven crew. The ship will be raised yet again.

16 October 1863

Washington The government announces sweeping changes in the organization of its army. The Departments of Ohio, Cumberland and Tennessee are combined into the Military Division of the Mississippi, the whole to be commanded by General Ulysses S Grant. The new commander, still limping from his horse accident, is ordered to leave his post at Vicksburg and go to Illinois; his eventual destination is Chattanooga. Meanwhile, Lincoln encourages Meade, through Halleck, to attack Lee immediately; Meade, however, is not to find during the Bristoe campaign an opportunity that suits him.

Below: The field headquarters of the *New York Herald*, August 1863. The civil war was one of the first widely reported and photographed conflicts of the modern era.

17 October 1863

Eastern Theater, Bristoe Campaign Not wishing to give Meade a chance for an attack, Lee's forces withdraw amid skirmishing from Bull Run and toward the Rappahannock.

Western Theater En route through Illinois to Louisville, Kentucky, Grant is given his instructions by Secretary of War Stanton. Grant has his choice of commanders for the Army of the Cumberland: retain Rosecrans, or replace him with Thomas. Without comment, Grant chooses Thomas; Rosecrans, as a result of his tarnished reputation after Chickamauga, has lost his most important command.

18 October 1863

Western Theater, Chattanooga Campaign General Thomas, succeeding Rosecrans in Chattanooga, declares: 'We will hold this town till we starve.' His army is close to starving as he speaks. Meanwhile, U S Grant officially takes over command of the Military Division of the Mississippi, thus being in charge of the whole area between the Mississippi River and the eastern mountains.

20 October 1863

Eastern Theater, Bristoe Campaign The Army of Northern Virginia gathers on its old line across the Rappahannock, the Bristoe Campaign having accomplished little except to add to the war's casualty statistics; between 10 and 21 October the South has lost 1381 in killed and wounded, the Union 2292 killed, wounded, and captured.

23 October 1863

The Confederacy President Davis removes another of Bragg's quarreling subordinates, General Leonidas Polk, sending him to Mississippi. Late in the day Grant arrives in Chattanooga after an exhausting ride from Bridgeport, during which he has experienced first-hand the difficulties of the Union supply line.

24 October 1863

Washington Once again President Lincoln prods Meade: 'With all possible expedition . . . get ready to attack Lee.'

Western Theater, Chattanooga Campaign In his memoirs, General Grant will describe his first day in Chattanooga: 'The men had been on half rations for a considerable time. The beef was so poor that the soldiers were in the habit of saying that they were living on "half rations of hard bread and *beef dried on the hoof*." It looked, indeed, as if but two courses were open: the one to starve, the other to surrender or be captured. As soon as I reached Chattanooga, I started out to make a personal inspection, taking Thomas with me. We crossed to the north side and reached the Tennessee at Brown's Ferry, some three miles below Lookout Mountain, unobserved by the enemy. Here we left our horses and approached the water on foot. There was a picket station of the enemy on the opposite side, in full view, and we were within easy range, but they did not fire upon us. They must have seen that we were all commissioned officers but, I suppose, they already looked on the garrison at Chattanooga as their prisoners of war. That night I issued orders for opening the route to Bridgeport – *a cracker line*, as the soldiers appropriately termed it.' The plan for the 'cracker line' is partly Grant's and partly Rosecrans' – by various means a river route to Bridgeport is to be opened. Meanwhile, from his position on Missionary Ridge, Bragg has become confident about his advantage over the Union army. His advantage, though, is shortly to be lessened.

26 October 1863

Western Theater, Chattanooga Campaign In the first step to opening the cracker line, Hooker's men from Virginia leave Bridgeport, Alabama, and move across the Tennessee toward Chattanooga. Elsewhere, another major Union bombardment commences in Charleston Harbor.

27 October 1863

Western Theater, Chattanooga Campaign At 0300 hours, 1500 Federals drift silently down the Tennessee River in pontoons to Brown's Ferry; the pontoons are destined to form a bridge for Hooker's men to enter Chattanooga. The plan works – with only light resistance Hazen's men are established on the far shore, the bridge is laid, and Hooker's forces move over it. The cracker line is now open and Chattanooga is reinforced; shortly, supplies will arrive from Bridgeport. Meanwhile, in Charleston Harbor, 625 shots are fired at Fort Sumter, which has now become more a symbol of Confederate resistance (as well as Federal persistence) than a military objective.

28 October 1863

Western Theater, Chattanooga Campaign General Bragg, having failed to prevent the establishment of the Union bridgehead at Brown's Ferry, orders troops under Longstreet to attack on this night an isolated division of Hooker's army at Wauhatchie. This being one of the rare night attacks of the war, the fighting is extremely confused; on both sides the officers scarcely know where the enemy is. After intensive fighting, the Con-

Below: The charge of the 6th New York Cavalry Regiment at the Battle of Brandy Station, Virginia, on 11 October 1863.

Above: The staff and commander of a Union cavalry unit pose for the camera outside their field headquarters.

federates are driven back; each side suffers over 400 casualties. The cracker line will not be seriously challenged again.

29 October 1863

Western Theater   Federal batteries send 2691 shells into Fort Sumter, killing 33 of the defenders. The stepped-up firing will continue for days, but the fort will not surrender.

30 October 1863

Western Theater, Chattanooga Campaign The little Federal steamship *Chattanooga*, built on the upper Tennessee River, arrives in Chattanooga with 40,000 rations and tons of feed. Union soldiers and animals are back on full rations and are no longer quite so firmly besieged. Although no men have starved during the siege, Chattanooga is covered with thousands of dead horses and mules, many of them having starved to death.

2 November 1863

Washington   President Lincoln is invited to the dedication of a new cemetery at Gettysburg and asked to make 'a few appropriate remarks'; actually, his words are intended to be something of a benediction to the main address by orator and statesman Edward Everett. Lincoln, who rarely gets out of Washington these days, accepts the invitation.

4 November 1863

Western Theater, Chattanooga Campaign In a move that dangerously weakens his forces around Chattanooga, Bragg sends Longstreet's corps, including Wheeler's cavalry, to reinforce Confederate troops around Knoxville which is still occupied by Burn-

side's Union army. The decision to send these 20,000 men has in fact been made by President Davis, and is to some extent another response to friction among his generals – Bragg and Longstreet do not get along. This shifting of forces poses an immediate threat to Knoxville; Grant makes a tactical decision not to weaken his own army by reinforcing Burnside, but rather to attack the weakened Bragg as soon as possible and only then to mass his forces against Longstreet. Before he can attack, though, Grant must await the arrival by rail of Sherman's forces, now delayed by the necessity of repairing their own rail route.

6 November 1863

Eastern Theater   Hostilities break out at Droop Mountain, West Virginia, where advancing Federal troops under Brigadier General W A Averell find a Confederate force holding the road. Averell manages to envelop the enemy and scatter them, after which he continues his raiding expedition against the remaining enemy troops and rail links in West Virginia.

7 November 1863

Eastern Theater, Bristoe Campaign   In a maneuver against Lee's Confederate forces, Meade sends troops across the Rappahannock near Kelly's Ford. The first Union attacks do not move the enemy, but at dusk an advance by two Union brigades, including one of the rare bayonet attacks of the war, succeeds in overrunning the Confederate positions and taking a bridgehead. Two Confederate divisions lose 2023 in dead and captured, a figure which shocks the Southern Army. Lee withdraws to the Rapidan, and the contending armies have thus returned to the positions they held at the beginning of the Bristoe campaign. Neither side has gained from their operations.

9 November 1863

Washington   Pursuing one of his favorite pastimes, President Lincoln attends the theater, he enjoys a play called *The Marble Heart*, starring John Wilkes Booth.

10 November 1863

Western Theater   The unconquerable mound of rubble called Fort Sumter has received 1753 Federal rounds since 7 November. This bombardment has so far killed few defenders, but Union batteries keep firing.

12 November 1863

Western Theater, Knoxville Campaign Confederate General Longstreet arrives at Loudon, Tennessee; he and Wheeler are directed to organize an assault on Burnside and his troops at Knoxville.

15 November 1863

Western Theater, Chattanooga Campaign Federal General Sherman arrives, en route to Chattanooga, at Bridgeport, Alabama, with 17,000 men; they have moved 675 miles by boat, rail and foot. Sherman himself joins Grant in Chattanooga for briefings on the impending offensive. Wheeler's Confederate cavalrymen cross the Tennessee River and join Longstreet's infantry.

16 November 1863

Western Theater, Knoxville Campaign   At Campbell's Station near Knoxville, Confederate General Longstreet tries and fails to cut off Burnside's retreat into Knoxville. The Federals are now driven back to the city, but Confederate forces lack the means of mounting a regular siege.

17 November 1863

Washington   President Lincoln begins to write his speech for the dedication of the military cemetery at Gettysburg. Contrary to the later tradition that the speech was written hastily on the train, his address is a carefully-considered statement.

18 November 1863

Washington A special train leaves the capital for Gettysburg carrying President Lincoln, Secretary of State Seward and other notables, including the French ambassador.

19 November 1863

The North, Gettysburg Address A crowd of 15,000 people gathers for the dedication of the military cemetery at Gettysburg. Edward Everett, the main speaker, gives a brilliant two-hour historical discourse on the battle, using information furnished by Meade and other Union officers. After Everett concludes, Lincoln rises and in his high toneless voice gives his 'little speech.' When he has finished, the reception is polite but unenthusiastic; the president considers the address a 'flat-failure.' Over the next few days it receives a few compliments, Everett assuring the president that the speech said more in two minutes than he said in two hours. It is perhaps natural that no one at the time can foresee that these 10 sentences would come to be considered one of the most moving and exquisite utterances in the language.

20 November 1863

Western Theater, Chattanooga Campaign Grant's plans have called for an attack on Confederate positions on the day following, but as Sherman's forces begin to arrive at Brown's Ferry near the city, heavy rains delay preparations for the battle.

Knoxville Campaign Confederate General Longstreet prepares an attack on the salient of Fort Sanders in Knoxville but delays the attack for over a week to await further reinforcements from Chattanooga and to have his plans checked by Bragg's chief engineer.

Below: Lincoln making the Gettysburg Address, 19 November 1863. Its significance was not widely recognized at the time.

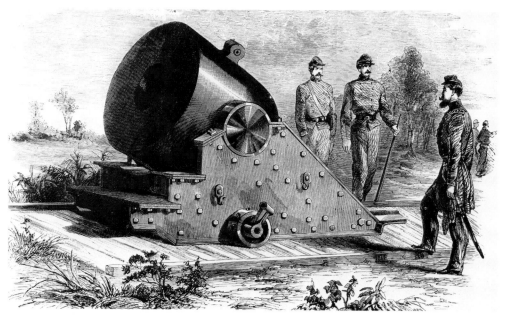

Above: Union gunners stand by to fire a 12-inch mortar, a mass-produced weapon used to pound Southern fortifications.

21 November 1863

Washington Lincoln has become ill with a mild form of smallpox. As he takes to his bed, the president comments, 'At last I have something I can give to everybody.'

Western Theater, Chattanooga Campaign Federal commander U S Grant has developed his plan of battle: Sherman's forces on the Union left wing will attempt to overrun the north end of Missionary Ridge; following this, Hooker will create a 'demonstration' on the right wing, moving part way up Lookout Mountain and diverting troops from the enemy center to meet his advance; after this Thomas will commence the main attack in the center of the Confederate entrenchments on the ridge. Bragg remains sanguine about his position, regarding his army as impregnable: even during the battle he will reassure an anxious bystander, 'Madam, are you mad? There are not enough Yankees in Chattanooga to come up here. Those are all my prisoners.' In accordance with Grant's plan, General Sherman's troops begin moving to the left flank.

22 November 1863

Western Theater, Chattanooga Campaign Changing plans on the eve of battle, Grant now orders Thomas's men to make a 'demonstration' in front of Missionary Ridge on the following day; the main engagement is to begin on 24 November.

23 November 1863

Western Theater, Battle of Chattanooga At dawn Union batteries open up on Missionary Ridge. Confederate cannon return the fire. Soon thereafter, Southern troops on the ridge are entertained by the appearance below their positions of 20,000 Union troops, clad in their best uniforms and marching in perfect ranks, bayonets gleaming, to the vigorous music of military bands. The rebels watch calmly, assuming a grand parade is under way. Suddenly the parade wheels and charges furiously up the slopes: the battle of Chattanooga has begun. In short order Federal troops overrun Orchard Knob, a hill between Chattanooga and Missionary Ridge. Grant orders reinforcements and entrenchments on the Knob, which will become his command post the following day. The Union has established a beachhead on Confederate positions.

24 November 1863

Western Theater, Battle of Chattanooga After midnight, Sherman's troops move across the Tennessee River. One of his men describes the operation: 'My regiment was in Sherman's corps. We had marched twenty miles a day. Now this corps was to form the left of Grant's forces, cross a deep river in the darkness and assault the nearly inaccessible position of Bragg's army. That night we lay in bivouac in the woods close by the Tennessee River. We knew that 116 rude pontoon boats had been built for us and were lying hidden in a creek nearby. We had almost no rations for the army. As for the horses and mules, they had already starved to death by the thousands and were lying around everywhere ... At two o'clock we heard some

Left: A scene from the fighting around Lookout Mountain on 24 November 1863.
Below left: Shrouded by mist, Union troops storm the lightly held Southern positions on the upper slopes of Lookout Mountain.
Above: General Grant (standing, foreground) and his staff on Lookout Mountain plan the next stage of the Battle of Chattanooga.

splashing in the water . . . the boats had come for us . . . Quietly, two by two, we slipped down to the water's edge and stepped into the rude flatboats. "There's room for thirty in a boat," said a tall man . . . who stood on the bank near us in the darkness. Few of us had ever before heard the voice of our beloved commander. Sherman's personal presence, his sharing the danger we were about to undertake, gave us confidence. In a quarter of an hour a thousand of us were out in the middle of the river afloat in the darkness. Silently we sat there, our rifles and our spades across our knees . . . In half an hour we were out on the opposite bank and creeping through the thicket, a spade in one hand and a rifle in the other . . . we formed in line of battle and commenced digging holes for ourselves. We worked like beavers, turn about: no spade was idle for one moment. Daylight found us there, two thousand strong, with rifle pits a mile in length. Other brigades got over the river, pontoons soon were down . . . What a sight for General Bragg when he woke up that morning at his headquarters perch on top of Missionary Ridge!'

By 1300 hours Sherman's forces are across the new pontoon bridge and moving to attack the north end of Missionary Ridge. Meanwhile, Hooker is initiating his 'demonstration' on Lookout Mountain, which is in fact only lightly occupied by Confederates. A dense fog enshrouds the slopes, and Hooker's advance is not discovered until his troops are a few yards away from the enemy. Federals steadily push the few defenders back up the rough and cloud-covered slopes; by noon

a Confederate stand at Craven's Farm has been broken, and Hooker's troops entrench just below the summit. The remaining Confederates withdraw during the night. Hooker's advance, considerably exaggerated as to difficulty, is known to history as 'The Battle Above the Clouds,' on account of the heavy fog that obscures the fighting. On the left wing, Sherman has by 1600 hours encountered only enemy outposts as he seizes what his map tells him is the northern end of Missionary Ridge; he is surprised to discover that he has only occupied an outlying hill – a large and exposed ravine separates him from Missionary Ridge proper. Both he and the Confederates opposite on the ridge begin to strengthen their positions. By the end of the day Union forces are victorious all down the line of battle.

25 November 1863

Western Theater, Battle of Chattanooga
Before sunrise, Hooker sends detachments up the slopes of Lookout Mountain, from which the last defenders have withdrawn during the night; dawn reveals to the Union army below the Stars and Stripes flying at the summit, and soldiers cheer amid their preparations for battle. From his command post on Orchard Knob, Grant orders his wings to advance, Sherman in the north and Hooker in the south, and holds his main attack on the center until the flanks have gained some ground and diverted enemy forces. However, both these attacks soon bog down. Sherman is repulsed on the left as Bragg moves troops and cannon from the Confederate center to resist the attack.

The fighting between Sherman's and Bragg's forces sways back and forth until midafternoon, with Grant moving reinforcements from his center and Bragg moving troops and cannon from his center to resist the attack. Fearing that his main attack on the center is being fatally delayed, around 1500 Grant signals Thomas's men to begin the assault on the heavily entrenched enemy

center at the top of Missionary Ridge. Certain there will be fierce resistance, Grant has ordered his troops to stop halfway up the slope and reorganize. In his memoirs, Grant will describe the attack: 'In an incredibly short time Generals Sheridan and Wood were driving the enemy before them toward Missionary Ridge . . . Our men drove the troops in front of the lower line of rifle pits so rapidly, and followed them so closely, that Rebel and Union troops went over the first line of works almost at the same time . . . The retreating hordes being between friends and pursuers caused the enemy to fire high to avoid killing their own men. In fact, on that occasion the Union soldier nearest the enemy was in the safest position.' This situation results in what seems to observers at the time to be an incomprehensible breach of orders. Rather than stopping to reorganize as ordered, Federal soldiers continue their charge up the ridge without pause; to do otherwise will leave them open to a murderous fire from the crest. Not understanding this, a furious Grant turns and asks Thomas, 'Who ordered those men up the hill?' Thomas speculates that they must have ordered themselves. Grant replies, 'Someone will suffer for it, if it turns out badly.' But the attack, one of the most spectacular of its kind in history, an advance up a heavily-occupied slope into the teeth of the enemy guns, turns out brilliantly for the Union. Shouting 'Chickamauga' as they charge, Federal soldiers overrun line after line of defenses until the rebels on the crest are desperately hurling rocks at the onrushing enemy.

The crest is, therefore, broached and the Confederates are in panic-stricken rout toward Chickamauga. Thousands are captured; Bragg himself barely escapes. Union troops gather at the top, cheering wildly as General Sheridan appears on his horse. 'What do you think at this, General?' someone shouts. 'I think you disobeyed orders, you damned rascals,' Sheridan replies happily. Meanwhile, Hooker is rolling up the Confederate positions to the south; Sherman is still meeting resistance in the north, but those Confederate defenders retreat that night toward where the defeated Army of Tennessee is gathering in Ringgold, Georgia. Grant later writes, 'The victory at Chattanooga was won more easily than expected by reason of Bragg's grave mistakes: first, in sending away Longstreet, his ablest corps commander, [in fact, this was President Davis's order, though perhaps requested by Bragg] . . .; second, in placing so much of his force on the plain in front of his impregnable positions.' Casualties are comparatively low for such a major battle. Union forces lose 5824 from all causes, 10 percent of their 56,359 effectives; the South loses 6667 of 64,165, about the same proportion. While the Confederacy has been bested in yet another major battle, their forces have not been vitally damaged.

26 November 1863

Eastern Theater Skirmishing breaks out around the Rapidan in Virginia as Federal forces begin an offensive against the greatly outnumbered Lee. Meade hopes now to turn the Confederate right flank and force the army back to Richmond.

Western Theater, Chattanooga Campaign
Bragg's retreating Army of Tennessee moves toward Ringgold, Georgia, with Federal troops under Thomas and Sherman in pursuit. Several clashes break out before the Union forces halt.

Knoxville Campaign Outside Knoxville, Confederate General Longstreet prepares his assault on Fort Sanders.

27 November 1863

Eastern Theater Parrying Meade's new initiative, Lee strengthens his right flank, as fighting breaks out near the Rapidan. At Mine Run, Meade finds Lee's forces strongly posted, and his offensive falters; it will not regain momentum in the following days. At Ohio State Penitentiary in Columbus, Confederate raider John Hunt Morgan and some of his officers escape and head south; the future career of Morgan, however, will be of less usefulness to the Confederacy.

29 November 1863

Western Theater, Knoxville Campaign Longstreet finally launches his attack on Federal positions at Fort Sanders (called Fort Loudon by the Confederates), seeking to dislodge Burnside's army from nearby Knox-

Below: Union troops under the command of Thomas begin their assault on Southern positions along Missionary Ridge at Chattanooga.

ville. Rather than beginning with an artillery bombardment, which might have opened a breach in the steep sides of the parapet, Longstreet ill-advisedly commences with an infantry attack. The advance, made in bitter cold, is ineffective; the men are slowed by Union wire entanglements and then bog down in a ditch, lacking the scaling ladders needed to move onto the parapet. Unable to advance or retreat, Longstreet ends the attack, whereupon Federals capture 200 men in the ditch. It is a half-hearted and bungled operation, and the South's last chance to end the Union occupation of Knoxville. Chattanooga has fallen, and Union reinforcements are on the way.

30 November 1863

The Confederacy President Davis accepts the resignation of Braxton Bragg, the defeated commander of the Army of Tennessee. The month ends with a further sinking of Confederate hopes in the wake of a series of crucial defeats. The Confederate victory of Chickamauga is now made worthless; of the Chattanooga campaign only recriminations remain.

1 December 1863

Eastern Theater After the failure of their advance at Mine Run, Meade and the Army of the Potomac withdraw across the Rapidan and set up winter quarters.

2 December 1863

Western Theater Lieutenant General W H Hardee temporarily assumes command of the Army of Tennessee following Braxton Bragg's resignation. Bragg asks his army to support the new commander and suggests Davis consider a new offensive.

3 December 1863

Western Theater, Knoxville Campaign In the face of advancing Union reinforcements, Longstreet abandons his siege of Knoxville and moves his troops toward winter quarters at Greeneville, Tennessee. Thus ends the Knoxville campaign, a major Federal victory largely by default. Burnside, by failing now to pursue Longstreet, obliges Grant to keep a large force in Tennessee until spring.

6 December 1863

Naval In Charleston Harbor, South Carolina, a strong tide breaks over the Union blockade ironclad *Weehawken* and pours into an open hatch; the ship promptly sinks with two dozen of the crew.

7 December 1863

The Confederacy On the same day as the convening of the Union 38th Congress, the fourth session of the Confederate First Congress meets in Richmond. President Davis addresses the body, putting the most hopeful face he can on a discouraging year.

8 December 1863

Washington   At the end of his annual message to Congress, President Lincoln makes his first major statement of reconstruction in a Proclamation of Amnesty and Reconstruction: a full pardon will be given to all Confederates, excepting government officials, high-ranking army officers, those who resigned the US military for the Confederacy, and those who have mistreated white or black prisoners of war (such as by enslaving the latter). All property except slaves will be restored to rebels. Pardons will be conditional on an oath of allegiance to the United

Below: General Meade, commander of the Army of the Potomac in many operations against Lee.

States. Federal statehood will be recognized in any seceded state if one-tenth of the citizens swear allegiance and forswear slavery. The president's statement is received with widespread approval in the North.

Naval   A Northern Copperhead band seizes the Union merchant ship *Chesapeake* near Cape Cod; the vessel is pursued by Federal ships and retaken off the coast of Canada near Nova Scotia on 17 December.

9 December 1863

Western Theater   At his own request, General Burnside is relieved as Federal commander at Knoxville and is succeeded by Major General J G Foster. Burnside has been much criticized for failing to help Rosecrans at Chattanooga and for not pursuing the retreat of Longstreet. It will be said of Burnside that it is to his discredit that he is a poor commander and to his credit that he knows it. Meanwhile on this day, Longstreet, covering his political flank, dismisses several of his staff pending his charges against them (later dismissed) for alleged failures in the Knoxville campaign.

11 December 1863

Western Theater   In a day of comparatively light Federal bombardment of Fort Sumter, a chance shell blows up a powder magazine within the stronghold; 11 are killed and 41 wounded, but the defenders still do not give in to Northern pressure.

14 December 1863

Washington   The widow of Confederate general B H Helm, who was killed in action at Chickamauga, is given amnesty by President Lincoln after she swears allegiance to the Union. Mrs Helm is the half-sister of Lincoln's wife, Mary Todd Lincoln.

Above: A panoramic view of the fighting along Missionary Ridge during the Battle of Chattanooga, a major Union victory.

16 December 1863

The Confederacy   In spite of past differences between them regarding promotion, President Davis names General J E Johnston, formerly in Mississippi, as permanent successor to Bragg as commander of the Department of Tennessee. Bragg's former subordinate, General Leonidas Polk, is given charge of the Army of Mississippi.

25 December 1863

Winter Quarters   Although minor hostilities continue in various theaters, all the military celebrate Christmas as best they can.

Western Theater   In one of a continuing series of raids on Confederate saltworks, Federal troops destroy a factory at Bear Inlet, North Carolina. Skirmishes break out at Fort Brooke, Florida.

Trans-Mississippi   Near Fort Gaston, California, Federal troops engage in skirmishes with Indians.

Naval   Federal vessels see action at John's Island and Stone River, South Carolina, with the USS *Marblehead* being badly damaged by Confederate shore batteries.

31 December 1863

The Confederacy   After a year of setbacks for the Confederate cause, the Richmond (Virginia) *Examiner* observes, 'Today closes the gloomiest year of our struggle.' Few in the South would disagree. The superior manpower and material resources of the North have begun to tell, and the Union army is soon to prepare for the first time a unified strategy for the final conquest of the ailing Confederacy.

These pages: The charge of Union forces against the Confederate defenses at Nashville on 16 December 1864. Although the Northern troops forced the Army of Tennessee to retire, Hood's Southerners were far from beaten.

1864

1 January 1864

Winter Quarters Temperatures plunge below zero from the North well into the South and make for miserable conditions among the soldiers and sailors, but some minor actions are ordered on various fronts.

4 January 1864

The Confederacy In one of a series of increasingly stern orders that create new hardships for the citizens of the South, President Davis authorizes General Lee to commandeer food supplies in Virginia. The Confederate troops and animals in winter quarters are indeed seriously underfed, but the civilian population of the South has also suffered considerable deprivation. Such orders do not improve Davis' popularity.

6 January 1864

Western Theater In another Confederate guerrilla action against Federal shipping on the Mississippi River, the steamer *Delta* is attacked.

Trans-Mississippi Federal Colonel 'Kit' Carson continues his operations against the Navajo in New Mexico Territory, trapping a number of Indians in the Canyon de Chelly. In an infamous action, these Navajo will be forced on the 300-mile 'Long Walk' to Fort Sumner, New Mexico.

7 January 1864

Washington Desertion continues to be a serious problem in the North as well as in the South. Nonetheless, President Lincoln commutes the death sentence of an army deserter, commenting, 'I am trying to evade the butchering business lately.' He will commute a considerable number of such sentences.

8 January 1864

The Confederacy Confederate raider John Hunt Morgan, back from his escape from prison in Ohio, is feted by his government in Richmond.

Below: Members of the North's military railroads construction corps are photographed near the town of Chattanooga.

13 January 1864

Washington Pursuant to his Proclamation of Amnesty and Reconstruction of 8 December, President Lincoln urges Federal officials in Florida and Louisiana to form Union governments 'with all possible dispatch.'

14 January 1864

The Confederacy President Davis writes to General Johnston, now commander of the Department of Tennessee, observing that troops may need to be sent to Alabama or Mississippi. Davis is beginning to consider strategy for the coming year's struggle.

18 January 1864

The Confederacy All white males between 18 and 45 (shortly to be changed to 17 and 50) have been conscripted for service in the Southern army. Today there are protest meetings in North Carolina as opposition grows to the conscription law.

21 January 1864

Western Theater In another response to Lincoln's Proclamation of Amnesty and Reconstruction, pro-Union leaders in Tennessee plan a constitutional convention to set up a government and abolish slavery.

23 January 1864

Washington Lincoln gives his approval to a plan for dealing with freed slaves in which they will be hired for pay to work for their former masters.

25 January 1864

Western Theater Shelling continues on Confederate Fort Sumter in Charleston Harbor, South Carolina, the bombardment having been nearly continuous since 12 August 1863.

27 January 1864

The Confederacy Braxton Bragg is called to Richmond to confer with President Davis, if 'health permits.' Bragg suffers from serious headaches and has been accused of leading battles when both he and his troops would be better off if he were home in bed.

31 January 1864

Washington Implying that he will loosen the requirements stated in his Proclamation of Amnesty and Reconstruction, Lincoln writes to General Banks in New Orleans that Banks is 'at liberty to adopt any rule which shall admit to vote any unquestionably loyal free state men and none others. And yet I do wish they would all take the oath.'

1 February 1864

Washington The turmoil that followed the Enrollment Act of the previous year has to some extent subsided, so there is little resistance when President Lincoln calls for 500,000 additional draftees for the Union Army. A plan to colonize Île à Vache in San Domingo with American blacks is aborted, Lincoln sending a ship to bring back colonists wanting to return. Congress paves the way for Grant's promotion to general in chief of United States Army by reviving the rank of lieutenant general; this action has been ferried through a somewhat reluctant Congress by Grant's patron, Elihu Washburne, who will also assure Lincon that Grant has no presidential ambitions.

Western Theater Hostilities break out along Batchelder's Creek, the beginning of Confederate General Pickett's attempt to recapture New Berne, North Carolina. The attack is called off when Federals draw back to the inner defenses.

2 February 1864

Western Theater A group of Confederate soldiers under Pickett board the US gunboat *Underwriter* in the Neuse River near New Berne, North Carolina. The rebels kill the commander and three of the crew, capturing the remainder. Finding the boilers cold, they set fire to the vessel and, after some skirmishing, abandon the operation on the following day. This marks the end of Confederate efforts to recapture New Berne.

3 February 1864

The Confederacy Declining Southern fortunes in the war inspire increasingly severe actions from the government in Richmond.

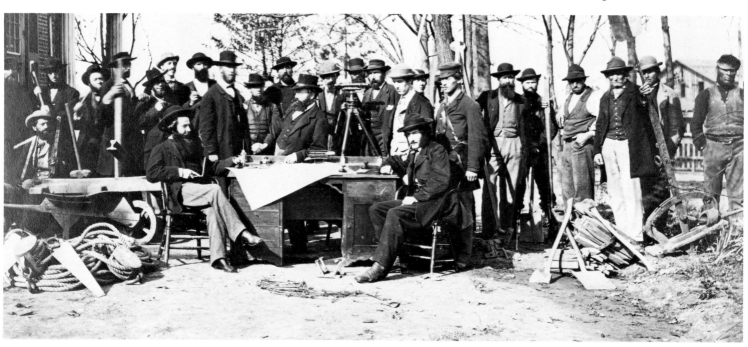

Eastern Theater Federal forces under Meade meet unexpected Confederate resistance on a foray across the Rapidan River in Virginia; held down all day by enemy fire, they retreat during the night.

Western Theater, Meridian Campaign Sherman's forces move out of Jackson, Mississippi, toward Meridian.

7 February 1864

Western Theater, Meridian Campaign General Polk continues his withdrawal before Sherman's advance toward Meridian; skirmishes break out at Brandon, Morton and Satartia, Mississippi. Elsewhere, Union troops take over Jacksonville, Florida, with little resistance from Confederates; over the next few days a Federal expedition will move out from Jacksonville to destroy Southern supply bases.

9 February 1864

Washington President Lincoln sits for several photographs (one of which is later to be used for the US five-dollar bill).

Above: A study of two black sharpshooters taken in the vicinity of Dutch Gap, Virginia.
Right: General Grant captured for posterity. By early 1864 he was poised to take charge of all Union forces in the war.

This day President Davis recommends suspension of writs of habeas corpus for those guilty of dissent of various kinds, spying, desertion and associating with the enemy.
Western Theater, Meridian Campaign After Vicksburg fell, Lincoln turned his attention to Louisiana and Arkansas. In order to drive the rebels entirely out of those states, a campaign is planned on the Red River; but this cannot be implemented until the rising of the river in March. General Sherman is orderd to commence preparations for this campaign. In the meantime, he decides to strengthen the Union position in Vicksburg by destroying the two primary railroads of central Mississippi. He leaves Vicksburg this day with 25,000 men. In conjunction with Sherman's move, a mounted column of 7000 is to leave Memphis, Tennessee, under General W Sooy Smith and attempt to drive Confederate cavalry from northern Mississippi, after which they will sweep down the rail line toward Meridian, Mississippi, and join Sherman around 10 February. The commander of Confederate forces in the area is General Leonidas Polk, formerly under Bragg in Tennessee, with about 20,000 widely scattered forces including cavalry under Nathan Bedford Forrest.

5 February 1864

Western Theater, Meridian Campaign Moving steadily toward Meridian, Mississippi, Sherman's men march into Jackson; minor skirmishes occur along the route.

6 February 1864

The Confederacy The fourth session of the First Confederate Congress continues its work, banning imports of luxuries and circulation of US currency; it also decrees that half of various food and tobacco shipments must be given to the government before ships may leave port.

Above: Union troops survey the wreckage of a derailed train, a victim of an attack by Southern irregulars.

Western Theater In the largest and most dramatic escape of the war, Union prisoners dig their way out of Libby Prison in Richmond, Virginia. Formerly the candle warehouse of Libby and Sons, the large building has been used as a prison for captured Federal officers. While conditions in the camps of both sides are largely poor and growing worse throughout the war, those in Libby Prison are to be exceeded in infamy only by Andersonville. Of the 109 Union officers who escape this day, 48 are recaptured (including their leader, Colonel Thomas E Rose), two drown, and 59 reach Federal lines.

11 February 1864

Western Theater One day after he was originally ordered to have completed his advance in support of Sherman, General

Below: General Meade (fourth from right) and other senior Union commanders meet at Brandy Station, 18 February 1864.

Sooy Smith begins his advance, moving out of Collierville near Memphis, Tennessee. Heavy rains in the swampy countryside have delayed his preparations, and his progress is slow. He will encounter little enemy resistance until he reaches West Point on 20 February. In West Virginia another of the increasingly common incidents of Confederate guerrilla action is seen. Irregulars under Major H W Gilmore throw a train off its tracks, then proceed to rob the civilian crew and passengers.

12 February 1864

Western Theater, Meridian Campaign Now two Federal forces are closing in on Meridian, Mississippi, Sherman's from the west and Sooy Smith's from the north. Engagements break out at Decatur and Chunky Station along Sherman's route.

14 February 1864

Western Theater, Meridian Campaign With little opposition from General Polk, Sherman's army marches into Meridian, Mississippi. Sherman, in a preview of his tactics in Georgia, does considerably more than his

announced plan of dismantling railroad lines. In his own words: 'For five days, 10,000 men worked hard and with a will in that work of destruction . . . Meridian, with its depots, storehouses, arsenals, hospitals, offices, hotels and cantonments no longer exists.' He will spend several days engaged in this rampage (which of course included the railroads) while waiting for the arrival of Sooy Smith, who by now is much overdue. Meanwhile in Florida, a part of Gillmore's army occupies Gainesville.

15 February 1864

The Confederacy President Jefferson Davis becomes increasingly concerned that Sherman will continue from Meridian to Montgomery, Alabama.

16 February 1864

Western Theater, Meridian Campaign Minor fighting occurs between Sherman's and Polk's men at Lauderdale Springs, near Meridian. President Davis' apprehensions about a Federal move on Mobile, Alabama, are increased by Union forays around that city.
Trans-Mississippi A Union campaign against Indians is begun from Fort Walla Walla in Washington Federal Territory.
Naval Federal actions against blockade-runners continue as the Confederate ships *Pet* and *Spunky* are taken near Wilmington, North Carolina.

17 February 1864

The Confederacy The privilege of the writ of habeas corpus is suspended by the Confederate Congress, though this applies only to arrests made by authority of the president or the secretary of war. The Congress also extends the limits of conscription to men between 17 and 50, prompting Vice-President Stephens to write: 'Far better that our country should be overrun by the enemy, our cities sacked and burned, and our land laid desolate, than that the people should suffer the citadel of their liberties to be entered and taken by professed friends.' In short, the vice-president is accusing the president of betraying the most precious ideals of the nation. The hostility between these two men

Above: A favored method of destroying crossties: once weakened by heat, they would bend under their own weight.

is an increasing handicap to the Confederacy. Within the whole South a desperate demand for peace is also simmering.

Western Theater   A watchman on the sloop USS *Housatonic*, one of the largest blockade ships in Charleston harbor, sees 'something in the water' making its way toward the ship. The 'something' is the Confederate semi-submersible ship *H L Hunley*, which is armed with a spar torpedo. On impact the torpedo blows a hole in the *Housatonic*, and both vessels sink, the sloop losing five men and the submarine seven. The tiny *H L Hunley* is long, slim and cigar-shaped, and is hand-propelled by its crew, who lie down along its length; by the time of this, its final sinking, it has, during tests and its single action, drowned at least 33 sailors. Although this event sends trepidation through the Union blockading fleet, effective submarine warfare is still many years in the future.

18 February 1864

Western Theater, Meridian Campaign   In Meridian, Mississippi, Sherman's soldiers continue dismantling the railroads and the town while waiting for their originally intended cooperation group, the cavalry under Sooy Smith, who have just reached the prairie region of eastern Mississippi and are engaged in minor skirmishes around Okolona.

20 February 1864

Western Theater, Meridian Campaign   Giving up his wait for the arrival of Sooy Smith, Sherman begins a slow withdrawal from Meridian back to Vicksburg, Mississippi. His campaign has lost him only 21 killed, 68 wounded, and 81 missing. After he leaves, the Confederates begin repairing the railroad lines he has destroyed.

Florida, Battle of Olustee   In January, President Lincoln has written to Major General Gillmore urging him to bring Florida under Union control and for a state government in time to be represented in the coming Republican presidential convention. After a series

of forays from Jacksonville, the Federals have concentrated some 5500 troops near Olustee, or Ocean Pond, while the Confederates have 5200 infantry and cavalry near Lake City. In the morning of this day a Union cavalry brigade opens the battle at Olustee with a successful advance against Confederate outposts; but then two Federal regiments, after heavy fighting and serious casualties, break and flee in confusion. Other regiments replace the two that have run, holding ground with heavy losses until the rebels have nearly exhausted their ammunition. After dark, Union troops withdraw. Losses are high, particularly to Union black soldiers: a total of 1861 killed, wounded, captured and missing for the Union to the Confederate grand total of 934 casualties.

21 February 1864

Western Theater, Meridian Campaign   Sooy Smith's cavalry runs into the Confederate troops of Nathan Bedford Forrest at West Point, Mississippi; thinking the enemy is stronger than it actually is, Smith precipitously orders a retreat after only light skirmishing. His men withdraw reluctantly.

22 February 1864

Washington   President Lincoln has increasingly run foul of the extreme anti-slavery wing of his party, who are known as the Radical Republicans. Radical Horace Greeley, for example, will call for a new Republican presidential candidate. Secretary of the Treasury Chase has had a series of wrangles with Lincoln and has regularly offered to resign. On this day Chase is seriously compromised by what comes to be called the 'Pomeroy Circular' (named after the Kansas senator who initiated the paper), a Radical paper proposing Chase for president. The secretary admits to Lincoln that he knows of the proposal but denies having seen the circular. Later evidence suggests that he did know of it.

Western Theater, Meridian Campaign   Overtaken by Forrest's pursuing cavalry near Okolona, Mississippi, Sooy Smith's retreating Federals attempt a stand against the enemy, but the 7th Indiana, seemingly about to be overwhelmed by a superior force, breaks precipitously and runs, leaving behind five guns of its battery without firing a shot. A series of delaying actions over a nine-mile line covers the Union retreat until 1700 hours, when a stand is mounted against Forrest's charging cavalry. The Union 4th Mississippi Cavalry mounts a charge against For-

Below: Lieutenant-Colonel Orson H Hart strikes an heroic pose for noted photographer Mathew Brady at Brandy Station, 1864.

Above: Nathan Bedford Forrest, recognized as the most outstanding commander of guerrilla forces in the civil war.

rest which succeeds in checking his advance, but not significantly turning it back. The Union forces then withdraw in great disorder to Memphis.

Meanwhile in Tennessee, Thomas' Army of the Cumberland begins a reconnaissance of Johnston's Army of Tennessee in their winter quarters in Dalton, Georgia. In what will be called the Federal Demonstration on Dalton, Thomas is trying to find out if Johnston has weakened his army by reinforcing Polk and Longstreet.

23 February 1864

Washington   As Lincoln ponders his response to the Pomeroy Circular, the cabinet meets without Chase.

24 February 1864

Washington   Congress approves revival of the rank of lieutenant general, thus paving the way for U S Grant to become general in chief of the Union army. Among several other measures voted by Congress concerning enlistment and the draft, Lincoln approves a plan to free slaves who enlist, while paying their masters compensation.
The Confederacy   In another unpopular move, President Davis appoints General Braxton Bragg to be in charge of 'the conduct of military operations in the army of the Confederacy'; in effect, Bragg is now chief of staff. Longstreet has accused Davis of approving failure and disparaging success; this accusation seems not exaggerated given Davis' continuing support of the inept Bragg and his disparagement of General Joe Johnston and other effective officers.
Western Theater   The Demonstration on Dalton continues as Federals drive the enemy from outposts at Tunnel Hill, Georgia.

25 February 1864

Western Theater   Thomas' forces near Dalton gather and attempt to force a way through Buzzard Roost Gap. Federals under Palmer try for an envelopment in the morning but are held off by a strong Confederate force. Union attempts are later made on the enemy right and center, but both fail and the latter incurs heavy casualties. It finally having become clear that Johnston's forces are by no means weakened, the Federals retreat and the reconnaissance is terminated. Union troops have lost 345 casualties to around 167 for the South.

26 February 1864

Western Theater   In the wake of the Meridian campaign, Sooy Smith's routed cavalry straggle back into Memphis while Sherman's men skirmish around the settlement of Canton, Mississippi.

27 February 1964

The Confederacy   At Andersonville, Georgia (near Americus), Federal enlisted men captured by the South begin to arrive at an unfinished prison compound called Camp Sumter. Built hastily when the numbers of Union war prisoners became unmanageable in Richmond, the prison consists of a 16½-acre log stockade, later enlarged, divided by a stream. Over the next year conditions in the prison will deteriorate until disease and death resulting from poor sanitation, crowding, exposure and inadequate diet become outrageous.
Western Theater   The Federal Demonstration on Dalton, Georgia, finishes with a skirmish near Catoosa Station.

28 February 1864

Eastern Theater   After reports of miserable conditions in war prisons in Richmond and light Confederate forces in the city, President Lincoln and Secretary of War Stanton have authorized a raid that will attempt to seize the Confederate capital by a surprise attack, free the prisoners and distribute amnesty proclamations. Pursuant to this plan, 3500 mounted raiders under General Judson Kilpatrick drive off enemy outposts and cross the Rapidan at Ely's Ford this night. With Kilpatrick is one-legged (from a wound at Gettysburg) Colonel Ulric Dahlgren, a son of the Union navy commander Admiral Dahlgren. Kilpatrick, who has originated the plan for the raid, is a controversial leader; one report states that his 'notorious immoralities set so demoralizing an example to his troops that . . . his surbordinates could only mitigate its influence.' At the same time, Kilpatrick is noted for 'a dare-devil recklessness that dismayed his opponents and imparted his own daring to his men.'

29 February 1864

Eastern Theater   The Kilpatrick-Dahlgren raid takes shape as the two leaders separate at Spotsylvania, Kilpatrick moving with the main body toward Richmond and Dahlgren heading for Goochland with 500 men. During the night the Confederate War Department in Richmond learns of the raid and orders emergency measures.
Trans-Mississippi   In preparation for the impending Red River campaign, Union vessels begin to scout the Black and Ouachita Rivers in Louisiana.

1 March 1864

Washington   Lincoln nominates U S Grant for lieutenant general, the rank recently revived for Grant by Congress.
Eastern Theater   Federal raiders Kilpatrick and Dahlgren close in on Richmond. The Confederate capital is in fact lightly defended by regular forces but, word having arrived of the raiders' approach, a collection of Southern civilians, wounded soldiers and veterans gather to defend the city. Approaching Richmond, Kilpatrick runs into these defenders and takes them to be a major force of the enemy; he has no idea of the whereabouts of Dahlgren, who is supposed to have joined him. After light skirmishing, Kilpatrick decides the Confederate forces are too much

Below: Poor conditions at Andersonville led to the death of many Union prisoners. The camp opened on 27 February 1864.

for him and withdraws across the Chickahominy River to await Dahlgren. Dahlgren, meanwhile, has had problems as well. In the morning he splits his force of 500 men, sending one group under Captain Mitchell down the north bank of the James River to destroy property and enter Richmond. Dahlgren, leading the other body of men, asks the assistance of a black youth to show him a place to ford the river. Deliberately or not, however, the youth leads Dahlgren to an unfordable stretch of the James, delaying the raiders' advance considerably. Outraged and suspecting treachery, Dahlgren summarily hangs the youth before proceeding down the north bank of the James to join his other force at Short Pump, eight miles from Richmond. The party then advances, meeting increasingly stiff resistance, until by nightfall they are within two and one-half miles of the Confederate capital. Despairing of continuing his advance after nightfall, Dahlgren at this point gives up the attempt on Richmond and orders a retreat.

2 March 1864

Washington The Senate confirms Grant's nomination as lieutenant general. Along with being the highest ranking officer, Grant will assume the title of general in chief of the United States Army.
Eastern Theater The forces of the failed Kilpatrick-Dahlgren raid continue their retreat,

Kilpatrick's rearguard still being harassed as he moves away and Dahlgren's men split into two groups, both seeking to join with Kilpatrick. Late in the evening, Captain Mitchell and his men will rejoin Kilpatrick. All day, Confederate cavalry under Lieutenant J Pollard pursue Dahlgren and his group, who are moving north. Late in the day the Confederates circle ahead of Dahlgren and join Captain E C Fox at Mantapike Hill, near King and Queen Court House, where they set up an ambush. Around 2300 hours Dahlgren and his men ride unsuspectingly into the trap. In short order Dahlgren is killed and 92 of his soldiers captured.

Then something is discovered that is soon to make Dahlgren's name notorious. A 13-year-old boy named William Littlepage finds two documents on the Union commander's body. One, signed by Dahlgren and apparently written as an address to his raiders, reads: 'We hope to relieve the prisoners from Belle Isle first, and having seen them fairly started, we will cross the James River into Richmond, destroying the bridges after us, and exhorting the released prisoners to destroy and burn the hateful city; and do not allow the rebel leader, Davis, and his traitorous crew to escape.' The second document, unsigned reads, 'once in the city it must be destroyed, and Jeff Davis and cabinet killed.' Lieutenant Pollard will forward these two documents to Robert E Lee, who will send

photographic copies of them to Federal General Meade with an inquiry as to their origin. A subsequent Federal investigation into the matter leads nowhere, and Meade eventually replies to Lee: 'Neither the United States Government, myself, nor General Kilpatrick authorized, sanctioned or approved the burning of the city of Richmond and the killing of Mr Davis and his cabinet, nor any other act not required by military necessity and in accordance with the usages of war.' Whether Meade's declaration is a fact or a cover-up will never quite be decided, but the affair does damage to the honor of the Union.

4 March 1864

Washington Andrew Johnson is confirmed by the Senate as Federal military governor of Tennessee.
Eastern Theater Kilpatrick and his men raid around the area where Colonel Dahlgren was killed before they return to Meade's army. The Kilpatrick-Dahlgren raid has cost the Federals 340 men and 583 horses, as well as a large number of weapons including Spencer repeating rifles, a gun that has become increasingly important to the Northern army. The Confederates find they cannot use the

Below: The Battle of Olustee, Florida, saw a succession of Union attacks bloodily repulsed by Southern troops who held the field despite their shortage of ammunition.

captured repeaters, however, because they lack the proper cartridges.

Western Theater Most of Federal General Sherman's men return to Vicksburg following their advance to Meridian, Mississippi. Fighting breaks out at Rodney, Mississippi.

5 March 1864

The Confederacy Attempting to reduce excessive profiteering from its blockade-runners as well as to improve its desperately low supplies, the government in Richmond issues orders requiring all vessels to give half their cargo space to government shipments.

8 March 1864

Washington At a White House reception, President Lincoln steps uncertainly up to a short, disheveled-looking military man and inquires, 'This is General Grant, is it?' 'Yes,' Grant replies. The soon-to-be lieutenant general has met his commander in chief for the first time. After a few pleasantries with Lincoln, Grant joins Secretary Seward in the East Room, where the general is obliged to stand on a sofa to shake hands with the cheering crowd. Following the reception, Lincoln, Grant and Secretary of War Stanton confer in the Blue Room, and the president makes some suggestions about Grant's remarks to be made on the morrow: 'Tomorrow, at such time as you may arrange with the Secretary of War, I desire to make you a formal presentation of your commission, as lieutenant general. I shall then make a very short speech, to which I desire you to reply . . . There are two points that I would like to have you make in your answer: first, to say something which shall prevent or obviate any jealousy of you from any of the other generals in the service, and secondly, something which shall put you on as good terms as possible with the Army of the Potomac.'

Below: Troopers of the 3rd Pennsylvania Cavalry Regiment pose with their sabers drawn at their camp near Brandy Station, Virginia.

9 March 1864

Washington In an early-afternnon ceremony attended by the cabinet, U S Grant is officially given his commission as lieutenant general, thus becoming commander of all the Union armies. In some embarrassment, Grant stumbles through a hastily-written speech which makes neither of the points Lincoln has asked him to. Soon afterward Grant and the president have their first private talk, which Grant recounts in his memoirs: 'He stated to me that he had never professed to be a military man or to know how campaigns should be conducted, and never wanted to interfere in them; but that procrastination on the part of commanders, and the pressure from the people in the North and from Congress, *which was always with him*, forced him into issuing his series of Military Orders . . . He did not know that they were not all wrong, and did know that some of them were. All he wanted, or had ever wanted, was some one who would take the responsibility and act, and call on him for all the assistance needed.' It is clear that Lincoln believes he has at last found a commander in whom he can have complete faith. He goes so far as to say to Grant he does not want to know what the general plans to do. After his interview with the president Grant immediately leaves Washington for Brandy Station, Virginia, headquarters of the Army of the Potomac.

10 March 1864

Eastern Theater Grant confers with General Meade, commander of the Army of the Potomac, at Brandy Station. This is the beginning of what will become a close and fruitful association.

Trans-Mississippi, Red River Campaign In the first move of the Federal Red River campaign, General A J Smith's command leaves Vicksburg heading down the Mississippi River toward the Red River which runs through northwestern Louisiana. Smith's troops are escorted by a formidable force in-

Above: The South's General Edmund Kirby Smith had some 30,000 men to oppose the North's forces on the Red River.

cluding 13 ironclads and seven gunboats. This expedition has been planned for some months, and the intention is to establish Union control in Louisiana and eastern Texas. The plans have been largely promoted and drawn by General in Chief Halleck (soon to be demoted), over the objections of Generals Grant, Sherman and Banks, who feel operations against the enemy in Mobile, Alabama, should be given priority. Nonetheless, Banks, as commander of the Depart-

ment of the Gulf, is ordered to coordinate the expedition: he is to take 17,000 troops to link up with 10,000 of Sherman's men and 15,000 of Steele's in Alexandria, Louisiana, or thereabouts. (Steele, commander of the Department of Arkansas, will start so late and proceed so slowly as to miss the campaign.) Opposing the expedition are around 30,000 Confederate troops under Kirby Smith; other obstacles are low water, inhospitable country and the depredations of snipers. From the beginning, Federal efforts will be further hampered by lack of cooperation among the forces and by an insatiable desire for the seizure of valuable cotton by naval and military personnel.

12 March 1864

Trans-Mississippi, Red River Campaign The Federal fleet and troop transports reach the mouth of the Red River and head upriver toward Alexandria, Louisiana.

14 March 1864

Trans-Mississippi, Red River Campaign Moving up the river, Union forces easily overwhelm the partially-completed Confederate Fort de Russy near Simsport, Louisiana, from the land side, capturing 210 prisoners and several guns. Meanwhile, the Federal fleet bursts through a dam nine miles below and proceeds up the river.

15 March 1864

Washington Transferring power from the military to the new civil governor of Louisiana, Lincoln takes another step in his reconstruction of that state, a model for his postwar plans.

16 March 1864

Trans-Mississippi, Red River Campaign Nine Union gunboats have arrived in Alexandria, Louisiana; Federal troops occupy the town and await the arrival of further land forces. Elsewhere, a 10-day Federal reconnaissance begins in Missouri.

17 March 1864

Western Theater Grant and Sherman confer in Nashville, Tennessee, on their plan of attack on General Johnston and the Confederate army in Dalton, Georgia. Formally receiving command of the Union armies on this date, Grant announces, 'Headquarters will be in the field, and, until further orders, will be with the Army of the Potomac.' In short, Grant is turning his primary attention to Lee and his Army of Northern Virginia.

18 March 1864

Trans-Mississippi A convention in Arkansas ratifies a pro-Union constitution and abolishes slavery.

19 March 1864

The Confederacy In Georgia, the state legislature gives a vote of confidence to President Davis and suggests that after any significant Confederate military victory a peace proposal should be made to Washington, the proposal predicated on Southern independence.

Trans-Mississippi, Red River Campaign Federal cavalry under Banks begin to arrive at Alexandria, Louisiana, but the whole force will not be assembled until the 26th. The next few days see small-scale Confederate attacks on the Federal advance guard.

21 March 1864

Trans-Mississippi, Red River Campaign Federal General J A Mower surprises Confederate General Richard Taylor near Henderson's Hill, Louisiana, capturing nearly 250 men, 200 horses and four guns. This action deprives the Confederates for the time being of their means of scouting.

23 March 1864

Washington Back in the capital after conferring with Sherman, Grant prepares for the simultaneous advance of all his armies.

Trans-Mississippi, Red River Campaign Continuing the planned massing of forces, Federal troops under Frederick Steele move south from Little Rock, Arkansas, to join Banks and his forces on the Red River.

24 March 1864

Washington Grant and Lincoln confer at the White House.

Western Theater Confederate cavalry under Nathan Bedford Forrest capture Union City in west Tennessee.

Trans-Mississippi, Red River Campaign Federal General Banks, commander of the

Below: General Nathaniel Banks, commander of the Union's Department of the Gulf, was placed in charge of the Red River campaign.

Department of the Gulf and leader of the campaign, arrives in Alexandria, Louisiana, only to discover two new snags in the operation: first, he is ordered to return Sherman's troops – 10.000 men under A J Smith – to that general by 15 April, for the Atlanta campaign; second, it becomes clear that the river is so low as to make it barely possible for his fleet to move away from Alexandria. Nonetheless, Banks issues orders to his troops for an advance to Shreveport.

25 March 1864

Western Theater Following his capture of Union City in Tennessee, Forrest attacks Paducah, Kentucky, on the banks of the Ohio, entering the city but not capturing the Federal garrison there.

26 March 1864

Western Theater Threatened by cavalry sent by Sherman, Forrest's Confederates withdraw from Paducah, Kentucky, toward Fort Pillow on the Mississippi River.

28 March 1864

The North A group of Copperheads attack Federal soldiers in Charleston, Illinois. In the worst anti-war outbreak since the July 1863 Draft Riots of New York City, five are killed and 20 wounded as more Union troops are called out to quell the disturbance.
Trans-Mississippi, Red River Campaign Confederate troops begin to mass under General Richard Taylor, preparing to resist the advance of Federal forces up the river.

29 March 1864

Washington Responding to press criticism of his handling of Gettysburg, Meade has contemplated requesting a court of inquiry; Lincoln, wishing to avoid the potential divisiveness of such a move, dissuades Meade from the request.
Trans-Mississippi, Red River Campaign Before the arrival of the Federal forces, who are advancing toward Shreveport, Confederates set fire to 10 miles of cottonfields along the riverbank.

3 April 1864

Trans-Mississippi, Red River Campaign The river is rising slightly, but it is still so low that Federal ships have barely been able to pass through the rapids above Alexandria until today, when the last of the 13 gunboats and 30 transports make the passage. Seven gunboats and several large transports remain behind in Alexandria; the supplies largely have to be landed before the rapids, hauled around in wagons, and reshipped. The supply line for this expedition is becoming increasingly difficult and thin. During the day Federal forces concentrate near Natchitoches.

4 April 1864

Washington President Lincoln writes: 'I am naturally anti-slavery. If slavery is not wrong, nothing is wrong . . . And yet I have never understood the presidency conferred upon me an unrestricted right to act officially upon this judgment and feeling.' Concerned about French interests in Mexico and their possible repercussions in Texas – one of the reasons for the Red River campaign – the

House of Representatives passes a resolution saying the United States will not tolerate a monarchy in Mexico. In fact, this monarchy is already decreed; it is to be a puppet regime of France's Napoleon III, who invaded Mexico in 1862. And this regime does in fact have its eye on Texas, though its army will be kept occupied by Juarez until that leader's final victory.

5 April 1864

Trans-Mississippi, Red River Campaign Confederate General Taylor and his army of 16,000 fall back from the Federal advance and group around Mansfield, Louisiana, placing themselves between Banks and his goal, Shreveport. The Federal land forces by this time are marching in a thin line on a single narrow road, encumbered by a wagon train of ammunition and provisions that stretches for 12 miles through the barren, enemy-held wilderness. The Union fighting ships and transports, meanwhile, continue to make poor headway up the low waters of the Red River.

6 April 1864

Western Theater Meeting in New Orleans, a Union convention adopts a new state constitution and abolishes slavery.

7 April 1864

The Confederacy The government orders General Longstreet to move northward and rejoin Lee's Army of Northern Virginia. Longstreet has been in Tennessee since last winter, where he participated in the Chatta-

nooga and Knoxville campaigns. Lee is beginning to prepare his response to Grant's anticipated next move.

8 April 1864

Washington By a vote of 38 to six, the Senate passes the 13th Amendment to the Constitution, abolishing slavery in the United States and all areas under its jurisdiction. While this amendment would have been unlikely before the war, the vote shows that by now the North clearly perceives the importance and moral significance of the gesture.
Trans-Mississippi, Red River Campaign Confederate General Taylor moves his army from Mansfield, Louisiana, forward to Sabine Crossroads to meet the advance of Banks' ground forces, who are moving toward Shreveport. The armies face one another most of the afternoon, reluctant to enter battle. Union Colonel R B Irwin describes the action that ensues: 'About 4 o'clock, when the two lines had been skirmishing and looking at each other for a couple of hours, Taylor suddenly delivered his attack by a vigorous charge of Mouton's division on the left of the Pleasant Hill Road . . . Walker followed astride and on the right of the road, with Bee's brigade of cavalry on his right. The Federal line formed on the cleared slope, about 4500 in all, met with

Below: Soldiers of the Union's 69th New York Infantry Regiment attend Sunday morning mass with members of their families. Religious services in the field were commonplace.

spirit the fierce onset of more than double their numbers, but were soon overcome. The artillery was powerless in the woods . . . Franklin received Banks' orders to move to the front at a quarter-past three. He at once sent for Emory and led forward Cameron, whose division, advancing at the double-quick, arrived on the field, five miles away, an hour later, just in time to witness and for a brief interval to check the disaster, but not to retrieve it. The whole Union line was again driven back. To complete the confusion, a wild panic ensued among the teamsters of the cavalry train, which was close behind. This order of march has been severely criticized, but . . . it did not cause but only aggravated a disaster really brought about by accepting battle at the head of a column 20 miles long, at the hands of an enemy formed in complete order of battle, in a position previously chosen by him, where our artillery could not be used. Taylor's army pursues the retreating Federals, but Emory's division makes a successful stand and covers the retreat, saving the Union army from disaster.

After the Battle of Sabine Crossroads the Federal army withdraws and forms another defensive line at Pleasant Hill; one soldier writes of this withdrawal as 'our skedaddle from the rebs.' The Federals have lost 113 killed, 581 wounded and 1541 missing, for a total of 2235 out of 12,000 engaged – a very high percentage; Southern losses are 1000 killed and wounded out of 8800 engaged.

9 April 1864

Washington General U S Grant begins to issue orders pursuant to his grand strategy of advancing against Southern armies on all fronts: Banks is directed to advance on Alabama; Sherman will move against Johnston and the Army of Tennessee in Georgia; Sigel will move down the Shenandoah Valley in Virginia; Butler will turn toward Richmond; and the Army of the Potomac will advance inexorably against Lee and the Army of Northern Virginia. Grant tells Meade: 'Wherever Lee goes, there you will go also.'

Trans-Mississippi, Red River Campaign At daylight, Confederate General Taylor orders his whole army forward in pursuit of the retreating Federal forces. In the afternoon contact is made with the Union line at Pleasant Hill. The Confederates open their attack around 1700 hours, at first driving back the Union left flank and killing Colonel Benedict, the brigade commander. But as the Confederates turn toward the center, a Federal counterattack repulses them, after which the Union army advances successfully, driving the enemy away in some confusion.

Banks at first wants to continue the advance toward Shreveport but in the absence of support from Steele (who is obstructed by enemy actions in Arkansas), finally decides to withdraw to Grand Ecore, Louisiana. While the day's battle has been technically a Northern victory, it has in fact halted the progress of the Red River Cam-

Above: The Fort Pillow Massacre, perpetrated by Bedford Forrest's command, remains one of the most controversial events of the war.

paign, which has been plagued by problems and mistakes from the beginning. Moreover, General Banks has probably erred in withdrawing now. A report to President Davis from Confederate Trans-Mississippi commander Kirby Smith, who arrives late at night, states: 'Taylor's troops were repulsed and thrown into confusion . . . the Missouri and Arkansas troops . . . were broken and scattered. The enemy recovered artillery which we had taken, and two of our pieces were left in his hands . . . To my great relief I found in the morning that the enemy had fallen back in the night . . . Our troops were completely paralyzed.' But now the Union army faces great difficulties in withdrawing its large force. The end of Federal efforts on the Red River marks the last important operation by either side in Louisiana – Confederate forces will hold the state west of the Mississippi River until the end of the war. The failure of the expedition also means Banks will be delayed in his planned support of Sherman.

10 April 1864

Trans-Mississippi, Red River Campaign The Union expedition under Steele, which had departed Little Rock to aid Banks in Louisiana, returns under Confederate fire to Little

Rock. Taylor's Confederates move back from Pleasant Hill to Mansfield while the Federals gather at Grand Ecore.

11 April 1864

Trans-Mississippi, Red River Campaign The gunboats and transports of the Federal flotilla now face the problem of retreat on the lowering waters of the river. They begin to withdraw to the accompaniment of shelling from Confederate shore batteries and rifle fire. Meanwhile, a pro-Union state government is inaugurated in Little Rock, Arkansas.

12 April 1864

Western Theater Confederates under Nathan Bedford Forrest, on a raiding expedition against Federal operations in Tennessee and Kentucky, surround Union Fort Pillow on the Mississippi in Tennessee. The fort is held by about 557 troops, nearly half of them black. Forrest arrives at midmorning to take command and deploys his men in positions from which they can attack the fort without exposing themselves to fire. This done, he sends an ultimatum to the fort's commander, Major W F Bradford, who at length declines to surrender. The ensuing Southern attack is swift and successful, with only 14 Confederates killed and 86 wounded. But what sends shockwaves through the country, shockwaves that will reverberate for years, are the Union casualties and the disputed reasons for those casualties. Southern accounts claim that the Federal losses – 231 killed, 100 wounded, 168 whites and only 58 blacks captured – occur because the Federals refuse to surrender in the face of certain defeat and try to fight their way out of the fort. The Northern report, which history will in some degree vindicate, states that the fort surrendered almost immediatley, and that what followed was a massacre by Confederates of defense-

Below: By 1864 hospital facilities in the North were far superior to those available in the Confederacy.

less Union troops, especially blacks. Grant, in his memoirs, quotes a portion of a letter by Forrest which states: 'The river was dyed with the blood of the slaughtered for 200 yards ... It is hoped that these facts will demonstrate to the Northern people that Negro soldiers cannot cope with Southerners.' Whatever is the true extent of Southern atrocities in this action, the accusations will inflame the North.

Trans-Mississippi, Red River Campaign Retreating Union gunboats and troop transports are ambushed near Blair's Landing; after a brisk exchange, the Confederates are driven off, losing their commander but inflicting 57 casualties on Union soldiers.

15 April 1864

Western Theater Andrew Johnson, head of the new pro-Union government of Tennessee, makes a speech (in Knoxville) supporting emancipation.

Trans-Mississippi, Red River Campaign Union ships gather along with land forces at Grand Ecore, Louisiana, whence they will depart under enemy fire toward Alexandria.

17 April 1864

Washington In a move that puts increased pressure on the dwindling supply of manpower for the Southern army, Grant decides to exchange no more prisoners with the South until such releases are balanced equally, as they have not been previously. He also announces: 'No distinction whatever will be made in the exchange between white and colored prisoners.' Currently the North holds about 146,634 Southern prisoners.

19 April 1864

Washington Congress authorizes an act permitting the Nebraska Territory to join the Union.

Western Theater The USS *Smithfield*, principal support of the Federal garrison in Plymouth, North Carolina, is rammed and sunk by the CSS *Albemarle*, which then moves

effectively against other Union ships operating in the area.

20 April 1864

Western Theater The Confederate force under R F Hoke that has surrounded the Federal garrison at Plymouth, North Carolina, completes its capture of the city. Federals lose 2500 men and large quantities of supplies. This is the first Southern victory in the area in a while, and it raises Confederate spirits considerably; nonetheless the city has little strategic significance, and Grant has already concluded it is not worth defending – if the major military moves of the summer succeed, Plymouth and nearby Washington, North Carolina, will revert to Federal control naturally. Thus, after Plymouth falls, Grant orders the abandonment of Washington but strengthens the strategically valuable port of New Berne.

21 April 1864

Trans-Mississippi, Red River Campaign Continuing his withdrawal from the disastrous campaign, Federal General Banks moves his land forces out of Grand Ecore and marches 32 miles nonstop to Cloutiersville, Louisiana. Meanwhile, the Federal rear guard is driven from Natchitoches by Confederate cavalry commander J A Wharton, who continues pursuing the Federals as they move toward Cloutiersville. A Southern force under General H P Bee tries to block Banks' retreat near Cloutiersville, but this group is driven off by a Union frontal attack. Federals arrive at the town in good condition but still in serious danger. The vessel *Eastport*, largest of the ironclads in the Federal fleet on the Red River, is refloated after having been sunk by a torpedo on 15 April.

22 April 1864

Washington Following an act of Congress, the phrase 'In God We Trust' begins to be stamped on Federal coins.

The Confederacy Now that black troops are beginning to be used regularly by the Northern army – one example being the soldiers at Fort Pillow – the Confederacy turns its attention to dealing with black prisoners. President Davis writes: 'If the negro [prisoners] are escaped slaves, they should be held safely for recovery by their owners. If otherwise, inform me.'

25 April 1864

Trans-Mississippi, Red River Campaign Banks' retreating army begins arriving at Alexandria, Louisiana. An order arrives from Grant officially terminating the operation, but these orders are to be suspended on 30 April.

26 April 1864

Western Theater Pursuant to Grant's order after the fall of the Federal garrison at Plymouth, North Carolina, Union soldiers begin to pull out of nearby Washington.

Trans-Mississippi, Red River Campaign Federal troops and some of the fleet have arrived relatively unhurt in Alexandria, but the navy remains in an extremely hazardous situation, with several of the ships stuck above the rapids near Alexandria. Union Lieutenant Colonel Joseph Bailey proposes an extraordinary plan for freeing the ships from the river, which by now has fallen in places to three feet in depth: a series of dams will be built to raise the river; when the required seven feet of depth is reached, chutes will be opened for the ships to move through. Meanwhile this day, the ironclad *Eastport*, sunk on 15 April and raised on 21 April, runs aground several times and is finally blown up by its crew above the rapids leading to Alexandria. Immediately thereafter, the crew is attacked by Confederate infantry, who are at length driven off. As Union gunboats proceed down the river they run into Southern artillery, which hits the gunboat *Cricket* with 19 shells; the ship loses 31 of her crew of 50 before escaping. Two Federal pumpboats are also destroyed before the ships move out of range; one, the *Champion 3*, explodes from a hit in the boiler and scalds to death 200 black crewmen. (This type of tragedy is not uncommon in steamships during the war.)

27 April 1864

Washington The plans are made, the armies poised, and Grant issues his orders. He would later describe this event in his memoirs: 'By the 27th of April spring had so far advanced as to justify me in fixing a day for the great move. On that day Burnside left Annapolis to occupy Meade's position between Bull Run and the Rappahannock. Meade was notified and directed to bring his troops forward to his advance; on the following day Butler was notified of my intended advance on the 4th May, and he was directed to move, the night of the same day, and get as far up the James River as possible by daylight, and push on from there to accomplish the task given him. He was also notified that reinforcements were being collected in Washington, which would be forwarded to him should the enemy fall back into the trenches at Richmond. The same day Sherman was directed to get his forces up ready to advance on the 5th. Sigel, at Winchester, was notified to move in conjunction with the others.'

Above: The 26th New York Infantry Regiment on parade outside Fort Lyons, one of many armed camps defending the Northern capital.

28 April 1864

Eastern Theater As they have been since late 1863, Federal batteries continue their shelling of Fort Sumter in Charleston Harbor, sending 510 rounds into the fort over the next seven days in the one-sided battle.

30 April 1864

The Confederacy President Davis reinforces his previous statement about black Federal prisoners: 'Captured slaves should be returned to their masters on proof and payment of charges.' On this same day, Davis' young son Joe dies from a fall off the Confederate White House.

Trans-Mississippi, Red River Campaign One of the most imaginative engineering feats in military history commences as work is begun on the dams that are intended to float the stranded Federal fleet over the rapids above Alexandria on the Red River. The work will be completed in 10 days.

1 May 1864

Washington Brigadier General John P Hatch replaces Major General Q A Gillmore as commander of the Federal Department of the South.

Western Theater Skirmishing breaks out between Sherman's and Johnston's troops at Stone Church, Georgia.

2 May 1864

The Confederacy In his speech at the opening session of the Second Confederate Congress, President Jefferson Davis accuses Federal troops of 'barbarism.'

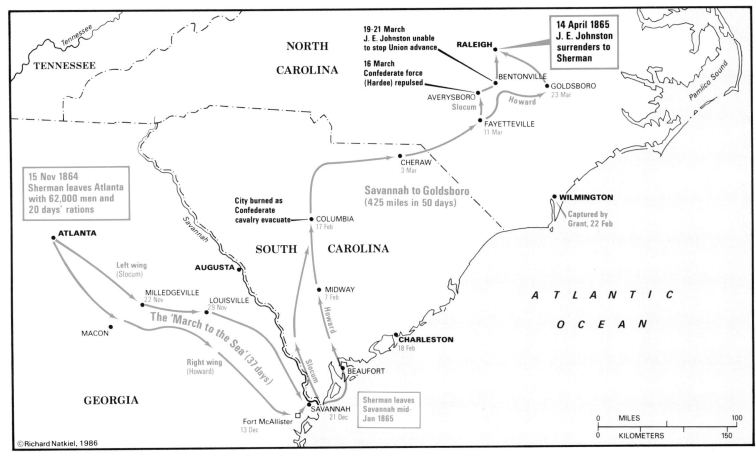

15 Nov 1864
Sherman leaves Atlanta
with 62,000 men and
20 days' rations

19-21 March
J. E. Johnston unable
to stop Union advance

16 March
Confederate force
(Hardee) repulsed

14 April 1865
J. E. Johnston
surrenders to
Sherman

Savannah to Goldsboro
(425 miles in 50 days)

City burned as
Confederate
cavalry evacuate

The 'March to the Sea' (37 days)

Left wing
(Slocum)

Right wing
(Howard)

Captured by
Grant, 22 Feb

Sherman leaves
Savannah mid-
Jan 1865

©Richard Natkiel, 1986

Above: Grant issuing orders during the fighting in the Wilderness, 5 May 1864.
Left: Sherman's March to the Sea, a move that split the Confederacy in two.
Below left: Union troops on the offensive in the Wilderness. The fighting was bitter and confused, made worse by the fires that broke out in the undergrowth.
Below: Cavalry and infantry clash during the Wilderness battle. Grant's attempt to deliver a knock-out against Lee failed, with both sides losing heavily.

Trans-Mississippi, Red River Campaign
Confederates harass Banks' withdrawing army at Well's Plantation, Wilson's Landing and Bayou Pierre as the Federals continue their retreat toward Alexandria, Louisiana. Work continues on the dams that are intended to float the Union fleet down the lowered river. Minor actions are seen at Kneelands Prairie in California, and at Bee Creek, Missouri.

3 May 1864

Eastern Theater, Wilderness Campaign
The Army of the Potomac, still nominally under Meade but in fact directed by Grant, is on the eve of its long-awaited move against Lee's Army of Northern Virginia. A few days before, Grant has written Chief of Staff Halleck: 'The Army of the Potomac is in splendid condition and evidently feels like whipping somebody.' How and where to do the whipping is a subject of contention within the Union staff. Grant wishes to move against the Confederate right flank, using the easy access to water transportation from the junction of the Rappahannock and Rapidan, while Meade wants to attack the Rebel left flank, which will avoid the risk of fighting in the Wilderness and cut off Lee from further northward excursions toward Washington. By attacking across the Wilderness – an area in northern Virginia that takes its name from the dense forest and underbrush that makes it virtually uninhabitable – Grant hopes to cut

Lee off from Richmond, and perhaps capture his whole army. Grant's view prevails, and the Army of the Potomac is ordered to cross the Rapidan on the morning of 4 May.
Trans-Mississippi Steele's forces finally arrive back in Little Rock, Arkansas, after their bungled attempt to aid the also bungled Red River Campaign.

4 May 1864

Washington The House of Representatives passes, over Lincoln's objections, the Wade-Davis Reconstruction Bill, which contains several stiffly punitive measures directed toward the South. If put into law, it will destroy Lincoln's more moderate reconstruction plans; nonetheless, the bill is opposed by extreme Radical Republicans like Thaddeus Stevens, for whom it is insufficiently severe.
Eastern Theater, Wilderness Campaign
The Army of the Potomac crosses the Rapidan toward Lee, its forces 122,000 strong to Lee's contingent of 66,000 hungry and ill-clad men. The Union corps are under the direction of Generals Hancock, Warren, Sedgwick and Burnside. Grant has intended to march through the heavy forest of the Wilderness so as to gain open territory for battle, but he is forced to stop just on the edge of the Wilderness and wait for his supply train to catch up. Lee, who has anticipated Grant's move this time, as he will so often in the future, moves his army up quickly so as to catch the Federals in the Wilderness. This is familiar terri-

tory for the Confederates, and within the tangled trees and brush, uneven ground, and numberless pits and gullies, the superior numbers of the Federal troops will be ineffective and their artillery will be nearly useless. The Confederate forces are carefully positioned, General Ewell on the Orange Turnpike and General A P Hill on the Plank Road; Longstreet's corps and Stuart's cavalry are ordered to move in. During the day there is some fighting in front of the Union advance, but as both armies settle down for the night neither is quite sure of the other's position, and Grant does not yet understand that Lee is going to force him to fight in the Wilderness. Meanwhile, another element of Grant's master plan against the Confederacy is set in motion as troops under General Benjamin Butler assemble near the James River, preparing to move farther upriver toward Richmond.

Western Theater   In Chattanooga, Sherman prepares his part of Grant's plan, readying his troops for their march to Atlanta. There is light, inconclusive skirmishing at Varnell's Station in Georgia.

Trans-Mississippi, Red River Campaign   Harassment of the Union fleet on the river continues as Confederates destroy a steamer and capture two others at David's Ferry, Louisiana.

5 May 1864

Eastern Theater, Battle of the Wilderness   Federal General Warren notifies Grant and Meade of an enemy force – Ewell's – on

Below: Grant studies a map over Meade's right shoulder during a conference at Bethesda Church before the Wilderness campaign.

the Orange Turnpike; thinking that this is only a division, Grant orders Warren to attack. These forces quickly join in a fierce battle, and it becomes clear that Lee's army is opposing the Federals in force. Because of the thick woods, the men often grapple at almost point-blank range; the battlelines become confused in the smoke-filled forest, regiments losing contact with one another. Soldiers and leaders follow the battle by the sound of firing, and often find themselves shooting at an enemy they can see only by the flashing of guns. Late in the afternoon Confederate General Hill's advance along the Plank Road is met by Hancock; a separate and equally desperate contest ensues. Again the fighting is at close quarters, often hand-to-hand with bayonets and clubbed muskets, the artillery silent for fear of doing harm to unseen friendly troops. All day the fighting surges back and forth, but as evening falls nothing significant has been gained by either side, and the forces retire to await the next day's battle. During the night, troops of both sides frequently wander into enemy lines.

Also on this day, General Butler and 40,000 men land at Bermuda Hundred, in the 'bottle' formed by the James and Appomattox Rivers. Though Butler's plan has been supervised by Grant, it is a poor one: Bermuda Hundred is excellent for a defensive position, but is not properly situated for an offensive.

Western Theater   After the Confederates' occupation of Plymouth and Washington, North Carolina, they move against the port of New Berne, which Grant has ordered held at all costs. The attack on New Berne today is turned back by Federal defenders, but the Confederate ironclad ram CSS *Albemarle* roams threateningly on the Roanoke River,

fighting to a draw with seven Federal blockading ships and disabling the USS *Sassacus*.

Trans-Mississippi, Red River Campaign   Confederate shore batteries destroy two Federal wooden gunboats and a transport on the river near Dunn's Bayou. The Union fleet is still marooned above Alexandria.

6 May 1864

The Confederacy   President Davis writes anxiously to General Beauregard, instructing him to meet Butler's threat on Petersburg from the South.

Eastern Theater, Battle of the Wilderness   During the night Grant orders a general attack by Sedgwick, Warren and Hancock, to commence at 0500 hours. Reinforcements are moved up on both sides. Before the Union advance can be launched, however, rebels attack Sedgwick on the Union right flank, and the firing gradually spreads along the line. Federal General Hancock moves against the weak positions of Hill, who has unwisely failed to entrench his forces. Hill's lines are soon enveloped on the Orange Plank Road and are in danger of being routed. But at the critical moment, Longstreet's reinforcements, awaited by Hill since the previous day, make a dramatic appearance, moving down the Orange Plank Road at a trot. Soon the Union advance is checked and the Federals thrown back to their original breastworks; a further Confederate advance captures these works, but is not able to break the Union line.

About 1000, after turning back the Union advance, Longstreet decides to take the offensive against the Federal left flank. He finds an unfinished railroad cut that provides a clear route to the Federal flank and sends four brigades to the attack. Before noon the Federals are overwhelmed by these forces; the Union left is rolled up northward in confusion. But then disaster strikes the Confederate advance, as recounted by Southern General E M Law: 'General Longstreet rode forward and prepared to press his advantage . . . Longstreet and Kershaw rode with General Jenkins at the head of his brigade as it pressed forward, when suddenly the quiet that had reigned for some moments was broken by a few scattering shots on the north of the road, which were answered by a volley from Mahone's line on the south side. The firing in their front, and the appearance of troops on the road whom they failed to recognize as friends through the intervening timber, had drawn a single volley, which lost to them all the fruits of the splendid work they had just done. General Jenkins was killed and Longstreet seriously wounded by our own men.' (This occurs within five miles of where Stonewall Jackson was mortally wounded by his own men a year before.) As he is taken from the battlefield, Longstreet orders General Field to press the attack, but the Confederate forces are in confusion after the accident; Lee comes forward to organize the forces and prepare a new offensive, but the impetus has been lost and the Federals have time to regroup and fortify their positions. A Confederate attack later in the afternoon is halted at the Union breastworks.

Elsewhere during the day Sheridan's and Stuart's cavalry have clashed inconclusively at Todd's Tavern. Confederate General John

Above: Thaddeus Stevens was a radical Republican who opposed the Wade-Davis Reconstruction Bill, believing it was too lenient on the South.

B Gordon, having ascertained that the Federal right flank is close at hand and quite exposed, has spent all day seeking Ewell's permission for an attack. Permission is given by Lee late in the afternoon, and two brigades move out, overlapping the right of Sedgwick's corps. The surprised Federals are driven from a large portion of their works, losing 600 in captured, including Generals Seymour and Shaler. The Union army is now in imminent danger of being cut off from its supply line on the Rapidan. Receiving the increasingly serious, and often exaggerated, reports of this crisis, Grant issues orders with his usual calm demeanor, but, as one of his generals reports: 'when all proper measures had been taken, Grant went into his tent, threw himself face down on his cot and gave way to the greatest emotion . . . [He] was stirred to the very depths of his soul . . . and not till it became apparent that the enemy was not pressing his advantage did he recover his perfect composure.' Had Gordon attacked earlier in the day he might have pressed his advantage home; but the Confederate move is halted by darkness.

Casualties in the two days of fighting have been staggering: the North has lost 2246 killed, 12,037 wounded, and 3383 missing, a total of 17,666 of 100,000 engaged; the Confederate losses, from the usual incomplete records kept on Southern casualties, are something over 7500 of 60,000 engaged; the Union losses are thus more than twice the Confederate, but the North has lost only a slightly larger percentage of its army than has the South. Although the troops do not yet know it as they entrench in the evening, the Battle of the Wilderness is over. But the tragedy is not quite over as darkness falls. Brush fires have broken out in the thick woods; several times during the day the fighting has stopped by mutual consent while soldiers of both armies work side by side to move their wounded out of the burn-

ing woods. During the night the forest fires rage, and while the entrenched armies listen to the screams of the trapped, 200 Federal wounded die in the flames.

Between the James and Appomattox Rivers, meanwhile, Butler's troops begin their entrenchment on a three-mile line north to south across the neck of the peninsula formed by the two rivers. The Federals are within sight of the steeples of Petersburg, seven miles away; Richmond lies fifteen miles to the north. At this point the Confederates have less than 10,000 men in the area around Petersburg and Richmond; the Federal force is four times that number. A small force of Confederates under Beauregard repel 1000 Union troops who, on Butler's orders, attempt to cut the Richmond and Petersburg Railroad line. This is the first action in Butler's campaign on Richmond.

7 May 1864

Eastern Theater, Wilderness Campaign By dawn the weather around the Wilderness is rainy, the troops not moving out of their en-

Above: Using a makeshift stretcher, a group of Union soldiers rescue a wounded comrade from the fires of the Wilderness.

trenchments. Early in the morning a reporter observes the following: 'Grant and Meade had retired a little from the crowd and stood by the roadside in earnest conversation – Grant, thoughtful, a cigar in his mouth, a knife in one hand and a stick in the other, which he was whittling to a point. He whittled slowly toward him. His thoughts were not yet crystallized. Suddenly he commenced on the other end of the stick, whittled energetically from him, and word was at once sent to General Warren and the other corps to move in the direction of Spotsylvania.' Grant, sure that Lee is retreating south, has decided on the bold stroke of attempting again to flank Lee on the Confederate left, moving round the Army of North Virginia

Below: A Confederate firing line, supported by an artillery battery, prepares to receive a Union attack in the Wilderness.

Above: Philip Sheridan became the finest Union commander of cavalry in the war, launching many attacks on Southern supply lines.

toward Richmond. But Grant is doubly mistaken; Lee has not retreated, and the Federal flanking movement is no surprise. On this morning Lee observes to General Gordon: 'General Grant is not going to retreat. He will move his army to Spotsylvania . . . I am so sure of his next move that I have already made arrangements to march by the shortest practicable route, so that we may meet him there.' During the day marching orders are issued to both armies. The Battle of the

Below: The Bloody Angle at Spotsylvania saw some of the heaviest fighting of the whole war, losses were high on both sides.

Wilderness has been a draw, and the race to the vital Confederate crossroad of Spotsylvania has begun.

To the south in Virginia, another effort by 8000 of Butler's men on the Richmond and Petersburg Railroad is rebuffed at Port Walthall Junction by a force of some 2700 Confederates. Federals are already beginning to refer to their campaign as a 'stationary advance.'

Western Theater, Atlanta Campaign Since November of 1863 the two great armies of the West have been stationary, Sherman's Federals in Chattanooga and Johnston's Army of Tennessee in nearby Dalton, Georgia. As part of Grant's overall plan, Sherman has been ordered 'to move against Johnston's army, to break it up and to get into the interior of the enemy's country as far as you

Above: The Battle of Yellow Tavern, 11 May 1864. The action saw the death of 'Jeb' Stuart, a victim of a shot fired at close range by a Union trooper.

can, inflicting all the damage you can against their war resources.' Sherman's success in his mission, surpassing all expectations, will leave him with a reputation as perhaps the greatest Federal commander of the war. Sherman's first goal in his disruption of the Confederacy is the vital supply, manufacturing and communications center of Atlanta. He has assembled a conglomeration of several armies, including the stolid but effective General Thomas's Army of the Cumberland, McPherson's Army of the Tennessee and Schofield's Army of the Ohio, a total of over 100,000 men. His opponent, leader of the Confederate Army of Tennessee, is General J E Johnston, an erratic but effective leader whose fine strategic sense is often offset by poor administrative work and lack of attention to detail. Johnston is also liable to quarrel with superiors, and has never been liked by President Davis. His subordinates include corps commanders Hardee, Hood and, soon to arrive, Polk; including Wheeler's 2000 cavalry, Johnston's forces number about 62,000. This day Sherman begins his advance with a move toward Johnston's left flank, the enemy's defenses in Dalton, Georgia, being too strong to attack directly. Pursuing this strategy, a corps under Palmer drives Confederate outposts from Tunnel Hill, pushing them to Buzzard's Roost.

8 May 1864

Eastern Theater, Spotsylvania Campaign Warren's troops, exhausted from four days of fighting in the Wilderness, arrive at the end

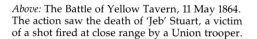

Above right and right: The Battle of Spotsylvania involved some of the worst action of the civil war, particularly around a line of breastworks known as the Bloody Angle.

Above: Union General Warren oversees the construction of a line of earthworks across the Weldon Railroad to trap Lee.

of their long forced march to find that, instead of being in retreat toward Richmond, the rebels are in their path and ready to fight in force. The Confederates have won the race to Spotsylvania. Warren's Federal cavalry arrive at Spotsylvania about 0800 hours and clash with Stuart's cavalry, who are blocking the Brock road. Stuart immediately calls for assistance from Anderson, whose men are resting nearby. Soon the head of Warren's column is thrown back. Frustrated by their unexpected collision with the enemy, Meade and Sheridan have a violent quarrel in the afternoon, Meade accusing Sheridan's cavalry of being in the way of Warren's forces and crucially impeding them. Sheridan replies that he did not order the cavalry into position, that Meade himself must have done it; the cavalry officer concludes by telling Meade to order the cavalry himself. Following this quarrel, Sheridan convinces Grant to let him make a raid around Lee's army that will disrupt supply lines, take on Jeb Stuart and join Butler in moving on Richmond. Thus begins Sheridan's Richmond Raid.

It is clear to both armies that battle is about to be resumed. Meanwhile, Sedgwick arrives to reinforce Warren and in the late afternoon forces of the two generals assault Anderson's right wing, but the Confederates, aided by the arrival of Ewell's men, repulse this attack with heavy losses on the Union side. Both sides now begin building entrenchments and await the remainder of their forces.

Western Theater, Atlanta Campaign   Sherman's men probe the forces of the Army of Tennessee in several locations around Confederate positions on Rocky Face Ridge. Union troops move on the Confederates at Buzzard Gap, and a similar unsuccessful attempt is made along the Lafayette-Dalton road at Dug Gap.

9 May 1864

Eastern Theater, Spotsylvania Campaign
The armies continue their entrenching operations on a day of light fighting. Lee has laid his lines out to utilize the brows of the slopes in the open fields. In the middle of his east-to-west lines is a curved salient of breastworks that looks somewhat like a horseshoe. It will be known to history as the 'Bloody Angle.' During this day the Union loses one of its finest leaders when corps commander General John Sedgwick is felled by a Southern sharpshooter. (Sedgwick's last words, addressed to a dodging soldier, are, 'They couldn't hit an elephant at this distance.') Also during the day, Sheridan's cavalry leaves on their Richmond raid, pursued by Stuart's cavalry. Sheridan's men damage Southern supply lines at Beaver Dam Station.

Elsewhere, Butler again lumbers into action in the direction of Petersburg, sending his whole army against communication lines and the railroad, some of which are destroyed. Finding the enemy strongly entrenched at Swift Creek, Generals Smith and Gillmore suggest to Butler that they place a pontoon bridge across the Appomattox. This plan could bring considerable Union strength against Petersburg, but it is summarily rejected by Butler, whose criticism of the plan is to stop advice from his staff.

Western Theater, Atlanta Campaign   Five Federal assaults are repulsed from the crest of Dug Gap by Johnston's men. Federal cavalry are also driven back from Poplar Place with heavy losses. Sherman's General McPherson routs a small Confederate force at Snake Creek Gap and presses on nearly to Resaca, bringing his men behind Johnston's lines.

However, finding strong defenses at Resaca, McPherson pulls back to Snake Creek Gap, for which he is severely criticized by Sherman. While he has failed to cut Johnston's line of retreat, McPherson's effort will convince the Army of Tennessee to abandon Dalton.

Trans-Mississippi, Red River Campaign
The Union gunboat *Lexington* passes through a gap in a Union-built dam above Alexandria, the first ship of the flotilla to make it through the rapids. During the next few days the rest of the fleet will follow.

10 May 1864

Eastern Theater, Spotsylvania Campaign
Lee has directed solid breastworks and entrenchments to be made all along his line, but he faces battle with two of his three corps commanders out of action – Longstreet is wounded, replaced by Anderson, and an ailing A P Hill is replaced by Jubal Early. During the day the Union corps of Warren, Hancock and Wright (who has replaced Sedgwick) are thrown against the Confederate left and left-center; all of these attacks are repulsed with heavy Federal losses. Meanwhile, Sheridan finishes his work at Beaver Dam Station, having destroyed two locomotives, over 100 railroad cars, 10 miles of track, medical stores and a large quantity of rations. Sheridan's subordinate, General George Custer, releases 378 Union prisoners who had been taken in the Battle of the Wilderness. Sheridan's men move on toward Richmond; Confederate cavalry commander Jeb Stuart rides to intercept them.

In southeast Virginia, Federal General Butler's men destroy a few more railroad tracks before being ordered back into their 'bottle,' the defenses on the peninsula at Bermuda Hundred. The withdrawal allows Beauregard time to send six brigades to defend nearby Drewry's Bluff.

Western Theater, Atlanta Campaign   Polk's corps from Mississippi is en route to reinforce Johnston's Confederates as the commander learns of McPherson's penetration of his defenses at Snake Creek Gap. Sherman, meanwhile, decides to move his whole army through the vulnerable gap.

11 May 1864

Eastern Theater, Spotsylvania Campaign
On a day of heavy rain there is no fighting. Movements along Federal lines lead General Lee to wonder if Grant is not beginning yet another flanking movement. To prepare his response to that possibility, Lee orders artillery moved from his left and center, including the horseshoe salient; thus his potentially strongest defensive position is left without artillery. It is on that position that Grant orders Hancock to move at dawn tomorrow. During the day Grant also writes to Chief of Staff Halleck, 'I . . . propose to fight it out on this line if it takes all summer.' In Blacksburg, in southwest Virginia, Federals skirmish during a raid on Confederate railroads. But there is fighting elsewhere today. Jeb Stuart and his cavalry reach Yellow Tavern in the morning and position themselves to block Sheridan's way to Richmond. Sheridan's cavalry arrive before noon and mount a few probing attacks on the Confederate line. In the late afternoon the Federals attack in force. During this attack General Jeb Stuart, at the

age of 31 one of the most colorful and effective of Southern cavalry leaders, is mortally wounded while firing at the enemy from his horse; he dies in Richmond the following day. Federals also mortally wound General James B Gordon and drive the Rebel cavalry back. But the engagement gives the Confederates time to strengthen Richmond, and Sheridan, realizing that it would be unwise to move on the Confederate capital, begins to ride south toward the James, to link up with Butler.

12 May 1864

Eastern Theater, Spotsylvania Campaign
At 0400 hours on what is to become one of the bloodiest days of the war, Confederates within the horseshoe salient hear the sound of commands and jumbled voices from the Federal lines. Suddenly through the torrential rain a wave of 20,000 Federals charges directly at the front of the salient; the defenders see only a solid wall of blue pouring toward and then over their breastworks, which are taken with little resistance. Federals capture over 2000 enemy, including many from the Stonewall Brigade, several officers and 20 cannon, which have been moved up this morning only to be captured. The remaining Confederates fall back to a second line of breastworks on the neck of the salient, and, regrouping there, begin to pour a murderous fire into the advancing Federals while Lee, realizing the imminent danger to his whole army, quickly moves up reinforcements under General Gordon.

By 1000 the Confederates have moved into place every man that can be spared from the

entire army, and the Federals are driven back to a stand on the north side of the horseshoe salient. There follows a truly terrible day of fighting, with both sides making a series of fruitless and costly attempts to advance.

During the night, Lee orders his forces out of the salient. In the fighting for this small piece of territory the Union has suffered 6800 casualties to the South's 5000, and the salient has earned its historic name of 'Bloody Angle.' At the end of the day a Yankee soldier says simply, 'This has been the most terrible day I have ever lived.'

To the southeast, Sheridan, riding to join

Above: A pencil sketch showing the center of the Union position at Spotsylvania Court House, Virginia, on 9 May 1864.

Butler, is attacked by troops moved out from Richmond to trap him against the Chickahominy River. Below Richmond, Federal General Butler begins advancing toward Confederate positions at Drewry's Bluff, which is being steadily strengthened by General Beauregard.

Below: The death of Sedgwick during the Battle of Spotsylvania, 9 May 1864.

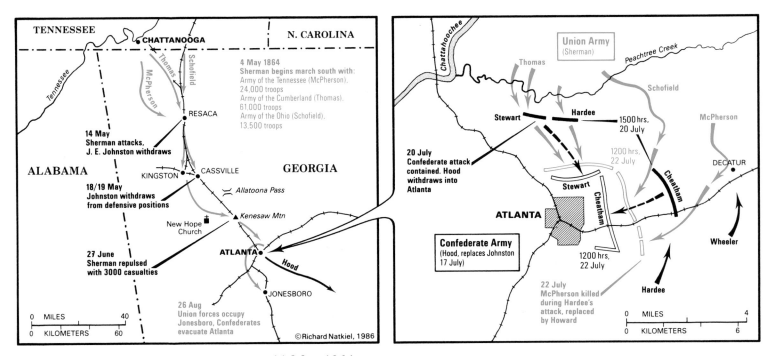

Above: The movement of the rival forces during
the Atlanta campaign.

Western Theater, Atlanta Campaign
During the night General Johnston moves
the Army of Tennessee out of Dalton, establishing new defenses north and west of Resaca, Georgia, just in front of Sherman's
advancing forces. The two generals have
established the pattern of the whole campaign; as if in a formal dance, Sherman will
move his superior forces to one flank or the
other of his enemy, and Johnston will execute
a graceful retreat.

13 May 1864

The North Horace Greeley, reflecting the
feelings of many Northern Republicans dissatisfied with Lincoln, writes in his New York
Tribune: 'Our own conviction is . . . that it is
advisable for the Union Party to nominate for
President some other among its able and true
men than Mr. Lincoln.'
Eastern Theater, Spotsylvania Campaign
Union troops shift to the south and east,
again sidling toward Richmond around the
right flank of the enemy. There is no fighting,
but both sides deal with their wounded and
dead.
   Along the Chickahominy, Sheridan
escapes from Southern attackers and moves
toward Butler, who is this day engaged in
slowly moving his forces into position at
Drewry's Bluff.
Western Theater Skirmishes break out as
the armies of Sherman and Johnston move
into position around Resaca, Georgia. In
Charleston Harbor, South Carolina, yet
another major Federal bombardment begins
on Fort Sumter.
Trans-Mississippi, Red River Campaign
The last Federal gunboats move past the
dams erected on the river, heading toward
the Mississippi while Banks' troops march
out of Alexandria toward Simsport. It has
been a notable recovery from what has otherwise been a humiliating failure for the North.
Meanwhile, Confederates under Jo Shelby
begin a series of raids north of the Arkansas
River that will go on through the month.

14 May 1864

Eastern Theater, Spotsylvania Campaign
Grant has orderd an attack on Lee's right
flank today, but slow preparations and heavy
rain give Lee time to oppose the attack and it
is canceled. Meanwhile, Sheridan's cavalry
make contact with Butler's forces. Another
element of Grant's master plan takes shape in
Virginia's Shenandoah Valley; German-born
General Franz Sigel (who often leads Ger-
man-American troops, thus the slogan 'I
fights mit Sigel') moves south toward the
Confederate cavalry of General J D Imboden.
Rebel reinforcements under Breckinridge are
on the way.
Western Theater, Atlanta Campaign There
is heavy fighting all along the line as Sherman's men unsuccessfully try to crack Johnston's defenses around Resaca, Georgia. By
the end of the day the lines have not significantly changed, and Johnston is confident
enough of his defenses to stay where he is.

15 May 1864

Eastern Theater, Spotsylvania Campaign
The only action today is a skirmish at Piney
Branch Church. During the night the Federals entrench across from the Confederate
right flank. Meanwhile, Sigel moves his army
of 6500 men south down the Shenandoah
Valley, one of the primary storehouses of
Southern food supplies. Sigel runs into Imboden's cavalry, who delay his advance until
the arrival of Confederate reinforcements
under Breckinridge at New Market. By 1100
hours Sigel's forces have been pushed back
about a half mile. A series of costly but increasingly effective Southern assaults follow,
and at 1600 Sigel orders a general retreat. Of
5150 engaged, the Federals lose 93 killed, 482
wounded and 256 missing, totaling 831
casualties; the Confederates lose approximately 42 killed, 522 wounded and 256 missing, totaling 820 from about 5000 engaged.
   Elsewhere, Butler has planned an attack on
Drewry's Bluff today, but delays it to arrange
his defensive measures, which include
stringing wire entanglements between
stumps in his front, this being among the first
uses of these entanglements in war (they

have been tried, with little success, by Burnside in Knoxville). There is not enough wire,
however, to extend the obstacles as far as is
needed.
Western Theater, Atlanta Campaign A
second day of sharp fighting round Resaca
begins with a clash between the advancing
Federal corps of General Hooker and advancing Confederates under General Hood.
During a day of heavy but inconclusive fighting Sherman is unable to break through the
Confederate defenses. However, Johnston
learns that the Federals have crossed the
Oostenaula River and are moving on his rear
and accordingly he immediately orders
another retreat. Southern forces pull back.

16 May 1864

**Eastern Theater, Battle of Drewry's
Bluff** In an early morning of thick fog with
visibility about 15 feet, 10 hastily assembled
brigades of Confederates under General
Beauregard attack Butler's lines on the right;
Federals under General K A Heckman repulse five charges before they are overwhelmed and Heckman captured along with
400 men. Other Union troops on the right
become disorganized in the fog; but the fighting on the Federal left is inconclusive, the
center holds, and wire entanglements are
devastatingly effective in stopping advancing Confederates. Nonetheless, Butler at
length gives up and orders a retreat in what is
by now a heavy rainstorm. Beauregard has
planned a pursuit but it does not take shape;
thus is lost the opportunity to strike a serious
blow at the enemy. By next morning the Federals will be safely back at Bermuda
Hundred; there they will be, in Grant's
phrase, 'bottled up' by Beauregard to the east
and by the James and Appomattox Rivers to
the north and south. Thus, in two days, two
major elements of Grant's master plan have
failed miserably, the Red River campaign
having previously done likewise; Grant himself has been stymied by Lee. Only Sherman
in Georgia is fulfilling his assigned role. Furthermore, in Virginia Butler has lost over
one-quarter of his 15,800 men engaged since
12 May, to Beauregard's 2506 of 18,025 en-

gaged. Butler's bumbling exploits are to continue, but he is so influential in the North that Lincoln is afraid to relieve him until after the presidential election.

18 May 1864

Eastern Theater, Spotsylvania Campaign A new Federal attack is mounted at 0400 hours on the strengthened breastworks that were at the neck of the Bloody Angle and are now the Confederate left (Lee's lines now stretch north-south). After brief fighting the attempt is abandoned, as is an ensuing effort by Burnside on the Federal left. Following this, Grant once more begins sidling to his left, trying to get around Lee's right flank. Sheridan has begun a hazardous journey from near Richmond to rejoin the Army of the Potomac.

19 May 1864

Eastern Theater, Spotsylvania Campaign Trying to find if Grant is again moving to the Confederate right, Lee sends General Ewell to make contact at Harris' Farm. The armies meet and the rebels are repulsed but reinforcements help Ewell to hold out until dark. In the Spotsylvania campaign now drawing to a close, Federal casualties have been 17,500 out of 110,000 engaged; Grant's losses since the beginning of the Wilderness campaign have been over 33,000. Confederate losses at Spotsylvania are uncertain.

Western Theater, Atlanta Campaign Johnston again stops his army near Cassville, Georgia, with Sherman in pursuit. Deciding to strike at the Federals, Johnston orders General J B Hood, his best combat leader and worst enemy on his staff, to mount an assault on the Union center. But Hood, brilliant as a leader but blundering as a strategist, turns from his attack to face a supposed Federal threat on his right. He is mistaken about the threat, and his move spoils the timing of Johnston's plan. Finding the Union forces moving around both his flanks, Johnston again withdraws to the south.

Trans-Mississippi, Red River Campaign The failed Federal expedition comes to an end as troops cross the Atchafalaya River on a bridge made of steamboats. Elsewhere, Shelby's cavalry continue their raiding in Arkansas.

20 May 1864

Eastern Theater Grant sends Hancock's corps along the railroad toward Hanover Junction in Virginia, hoping to draw Lee's army into an offensive; the Federals with their greatly superior numbers could crush Lee before he entrenches. But once again Lee second-guesses his foe, and moves to entrench across Grant's path in Hanover Junction. The armies are again racing to the east and south, toward Richmond.

22 May 1864

Eastern Theater In the morning Confederate General Ewell arrives ahead of Grant's forces at Hanover Junction and begins to entrench; Anderson arrives at noon. Grant is still moving the main body of his force.

Western Theater, Atlanta Campaign Sherman again flanks Johnston's army, going around the Confederate left at Altoona and heading toward Dallas, Georgia.

Above: Cavalry crossing the North Anna River, Virginia, the scene of heavy fighting between 23-25 May 1864.

23 May 1864

Eastern Theater General A P Hill arrives early and adds his troops to the Confederate entrenchments on the south side of the North Anna River between Hanover Junction and the water. Lee arranges his army in a wedge, with the point on the river. In the afternoon Federals under Warren cross the stream to the north and are engaged by Hill, who advances slightly in severe but indecisive fighting. Meanwhile, Hancock's corps have moved southward to the north bank to confront the right side of the Confederate wedge opposite. Now the Union army is split in two,

Below: A panoramic view of Union positions near Spotsylvania as seen from the headquarters of General Warren.

Above: The three-day Battle of Cold Harbor saw both sides lose heavily for little tangible military advantage.

and Lee thus has a rare opportunity to deal Grant a serious blow. But on this day Lee is ill, delirious with fever and confined to his tent. During the day the Confederates receive reinforcements led by Pickett, Hoke and Breckinridge, the latter fresh from his defeat of Sigel near Richmond.

24 May 1864

Eastern Theater The Battle of the North Anna River continues. Federal General Warren is reinforced on one side of the Confederate wedge while Hancock crosses the river toward the other side. Meanwhile, Burnside arrives on the north side of the river and begins to cross amid skirmishing at Ox Ford, the point of the Confederate wedge on

Below: In an attempt to outflank Lee's forces around Cold Harbor, Grant dispatched his troops across the Pamunkey River.

the opposite bank. Now the Union army is split into three parts, but Lee is still feverish and not able to direct his troops in pressing this advantage. Sheridan arrives back at the Army of the Potomac after his cavalry raid completely around Lee's army, during which he has not moved on Richmond but has nonetheless destroyed vital supplies, won four engagements and killed Jeb Stuart.
Western Theater, Atlanta Campaign Realizing that Sherman is moving around him toward Dallas, Georgia, General Johnston orders his forces out of Altoona toward Dallas in order to remain in front of the Union army. Fighting breaks out at several nearby towns, with Southern cavalry under Wheeler harassing Federal supply wagons.

25 May 1864

Eastern Theater The Battle of the North Anna River continues. Grant begins a series of fruitless attempts to find a vulnerable point in the Confederate lines.
Western Theater, Atlanta Campaign Johnston's army awaits Sherman's approach,

Hood at New Hope Church on the road from Altoona, Polk on his left, Hardee on his right. Federals under Hooker attack Hood's corps, but are turned back after two hours by murderous fire from 16 cannon and 5000 rebel muskets. Union losses are heavy.

26 May 1864

Washington Major General J G Foster assumes command of the Federal Department of the South.
Eastern Theater Failing to find a weakness in Lee's entrenchments, Grant and Meade late at night move the Army of the Potomac northward back across the river and for the fourth time begin sidling around Lee's right, this time toward Hanovertown, 18 miles away. In the Shenandoah the new Federal commander of the Department of West Virginia, General David Hunter, heads toward Staunton with 16,000 men. Opposing this move is Breckinridge's replacement, General W E 'Grumble' Jones.
Western Theater, Atlanta Campaign After a day of skirmishing along their line of advance, Sherman's men halt for the moment and begin entrenching in the New Hope-Dallas area.

27 May 1864

Eastern Theater Early in the day, Federals, led by Sheridan's cavalry, put two pontoon bridges across the Pamunkey River and occupied Hanovertown. Cavalry skirmishes erupt in several locations as the rest of the Army of the Potomac moves into Hanovertown during the day. To the south, Lee begins moving to head off the Federals.
Western Theater, Atlanta Campaign Heavy fighting is seen around the New Hope-Dallas line as the opposing forces jockey for position. Sherman loses 1400 casualties in an unsuccessful attempt to turn the rebel right. Confederate losses are light. In the evening Johnston directs Hood to attack the end of the Federal left flank the next morning.
Trans-Mississippi Confederate raider Jo Shelby, campaigning in Arkansas, is named commander of Confederate troops north of the Arkansas River.

28 May 1864

Eastern Theater Lee's Army of Northern Virginia hurries to get in front of Grant, moving toward Cold Harbor as the Federals cross the Pamunkey River near Hanovertown.
Western Theater, Atlanta Campaign Hood, ordered to attack around Sherman's left flank, reports to Johnston that the Union flank is guarded by entrenchments at right angles to the front. Johnston cancels the attack.

29 May 1864

Eastern Theater Having crossed the Pamunkey River, Grant and Meade's Army of the Potomac march southwest toward Richmond. Between them and the Confederate capital stretch Lee's lines.

30 May 1864

Eastern Theater Grant's forces begin arriving at the north bank of the Totopotomoy River, facing Lee's line across the river and north of the Chickahominy. The Federals are now within 10 miles of Richmond. Another day's skirmishing is seen in the area. Federals are reinforced by two corps under the contentious General W F 'Baldy' Smith.
Western Theater Confederate raider John Hunt Morgan, in action again after his escape from a Federal war prison in Ohio, begins attacking Sherman's distant supply lines in Kentucky.

31 May 1864

The North A group of Radical Republicans hostile to Lincoln's conduct of the war, emancipation and reconstruction meets in Cleveland, Ohio, to nominate their own presidential candidate, General John Charles Frémont.
Eastern Theater Grant, still trying to move around Lee's right, sends some of his forces south toward Cold Harbor. Lee moves again to cut him off. Skirmishes again mark the day's fighting.
Western Theater, Atlanta Campaign The running battle between Sherman's forces and Johnston's Army of Tennessee has by now claimed about 9000 casualties on each side during May. Hostilities continue around the New Hope-Dallas area.

1 June 1864

Eastern Theater, Battle of Cold Harbor Lee begins to shift forces to meet Grant's new threat, moving men out of Richmond north to the rivers near Cold Harbor. Before dawn Lee moves against Federal troops holding the important road junction of Cold Harbor, wishing to turn Grant's flank before he can attack the Confederate left. But two badly-managed Southern attacks are repulsed, partly by Sheridan's cavalry using the new Spencer repeating rifles. Lee then orders reinforcements to his right flank, and three strong Federal advances against the right and center are turned back late in the day, Smith on the Federal side having been delayed in moving up by a mistake in orders. The attacks show that the Confederates have dug in with their usual efficiency and are able to direct a heavy fire all along their lines. Grant moves Hancock's corps southward to his left and orders an attack tomorrow morning.
Western Theater, Atlanta Campaign The

success of Sherman's advance toward Atlanta is absolutely dependent on his ever-lengthening supply line, and his careful planning and protection of that line are to mark the entire campaign. This day the vital connection between Chattanooga and the Federals' current position near Dallas, Georgia, is secured by General George Stoneman's cavalry, who capture Altoona Pass and its railroad line. Now Sherman will begin moving his troops away from the Dallas area northwestward to his lifeline along the railroad. At the same time, Sherman orders operations to protect the distant reaches of his supply line, particularly against the depredations of General Forrest, who is now gathering his forces in Tupelo, Mississippi. Sherman says, with his customary ferocity: 'That devil Forrest . . . must be hunted down and killed if it costs 10,000 lives and bankrupts the Federal treasury.' To this end, Union General S D Sturgis is sent with 3000 cavalry, 4800 infantry and 18 guns to deal with Forrest; Sturgis today leaves Memphis and heads toward Ripley, Mississippi. Meanwhile, rebel raider John Hunt Morgan is active against Sherman's supply lines in Kentucky, today engaging in a skirmish near Pound Gap.

2 June 1864

Eastern Theater, Battle of Cold Harbor Grant's general assault on Lee's lines, ordered for the early morning, is delayed by slow troop movements, fatigue and supply problems. After a heavy rain begins in the afternoon, the attack is again delayed until tomorrow morning. Union soldiers see all too clearly what such a charge directly on strong fortifications will entail. Walking through the troops in the evening, General Horace Porter discovers an awesome sight: 'I noticed that many of the soldiers had taken off their coats and seemed to be engaged in sewing up rents in them. On closer examination it was found that the men were calmly writing their names and addresses on slips of paper and pinning

Above: The fighting at Cold Harbor was characterized by a series of fruitless attacks as both sides sought to outflank each other.

them on the backs of their coats, so that their dead bodies might be recognized and their fate made known to their families at home.' After an abortive attack during the day, Lee's officers during the evening carefully lay out and strengthen their defenses for the expected attack. In the Shenandoah Valley, Sigel's replacement General David Hunter sees action against Confederates under W E Jones at Covington, Virginia. Hunter, ordered by Grant to do what Sigel failed to do and sweep the valley, is headed south for Staunton with 16,000 men, opposed by Jones's 8500 infantry and cavalry.

3 June 1864

Eastern Theater, Battle of Cold Harbor Grant has determined to make a decisive blow on Lee's army, hammering his lines in a direct assault like the one that initially overran the Bloody Angle at Spotsylvania. The charge is to be led by the corps of Hancock, Wright and Smith, later to be reinforced by Warren and Burnside, on the center and right of Lee's lines under Anderson and Hill. The attack is intended to be pressed regardless of cost. It begins at 0430 hours, countless thousands of Union soldiers rising from their entrenchments and marching straight toward the fortifications of the enemy. Then, 'there rang out suddenly on the summer air such a crash of artillery and musketry as is seldom heard in war.' The dead and wounded fall in waves like mown wheat. For a short time the Confederate breastworks are reached, but then a murderous countercharge sends the Federals back.

Within the space of a half hour 7000 Federal troops are killed and wounded, their bodies blanketing the ground before the enemy breastworks. Each of the three Union corps commanders complains to Meade that the other two have failed to protect his troops

Above: Sheridan's cavalry launch a furious but ultimately unsuccessful attack on Southern positions at Trevilian Station, 12 June 1864.

from enfilade fire; this is because the three corps have attacked on diverging lines toward the defenses, thus opening their flanks to fire. Incredibly, after the devastated troops have fallen back from the first attack, the order comes from Grant for a second general assault, this time by corps without reference to others, thus sacrificing unity of attack. This charge is mounted raggedly, with many troops holding back, and it is repulsed, leaving fresh heaps of dead and wounded. Finally Grant orders a third advance. This order is essentially ignored. In the evening Grant admits, 'I regret this assault more than any one I have ever ordered.' A later commentator puts it more directly: 'Cold Harbor represents a horrible failure of Federal generalship.' But the failure continues. A Union observer writes: 'The groans and moaning of the wounded, all our own, who were between the lines, were heartrending.' These wounded are simply to be abandoned. For three days Grant will make no effort to propose a truce to collect his wounded; to go out between the lines without a truce is suicidal, though some Confederates risk their lives to bring in nearby Union wounded. Not until 7 June will Union stretcher parties actually be sent out. By this time all but two men of those thousands have died, horribly, of wounds, thirst, hunger and exposure, all in full sight of both lines. The reason for this callous abandonment is

partly, perhaps, the tradition that says the first commander asking permission of the enemy to bring in wounded is the loser, and Grant will not admit to being the loser.

When Grant calls off the attack at noon, Federal killed and wounded for 3 June total around 7000, added to the 5000 casualties of 1 and 2 June. The day's Confederate losses are probably under 1500. Grant will observe in his memoirs: 'No advantage whatever was gained from the heavy loss we sustained.' A Northern observer notes that the Army of the Potomac 'has literally marched in blood and agony from the Rapidan to the James.' The

men have marched, slept, and fought for one month in the same blood- and sweat-stiffened uniforms; the roads of their march are strewn with the carcasses of 6000 horses. Federal casualties in the month of incessant campaigning have been 50,000, 41 percent of their original strength; the South has lost 32,000, 46 percent of its strength, and these losses are irreplacable.

Below: The Southern city of Petersburg, a rail center, was the major objective of Grant's forces during the summer of 1864; it finally fell on 3 April 1865.

4 June 1864

Eastern Theater The armies of Grant and Lee lie quietly in their entrenchments, listening to the groans and entreaties of the Union wounded. Hunter's Federals, moving down the Shenandoah, skirmish at Port Republic and Harrisonburg, Virginia.

Western Theater, Atlanta Campaign Realizing that Sherman is flanking him again, moving northeast toward the Atlanta-Chattanooga railroad, Johnston during the night moves the Army of Tennessee out of the New Hope-Dallas area toward his already-made lines in the mountains before Marietta. There are engagements at Big Shanty and Acworth, Georgia.

5 June 1864

Eastern Theater Confederate General W E Jones makes his stand against Hunter's advance toward Staunton, Virginia, turning 5000 men toward Hunter's main body. But the Federals drive Jones back to his defenses at Piedmont, where he is pounded by Union artillery. A series of attacks and counterattacks ensues, which finally sends the Confederates into a rout during which Jones is killed. Hunter loses 780 men to the South's 1600, of whom 1000 are taken prisoner. Tomorrow Hunter will enter Staunton unopposed.

7 June 1864

The North The National Union Convention – essentially the Republican Party but with some Democrats who support the war – opens in Baltimore with Lincoln the unanimous candidate for president, but with some question about the vice-presidency and with the anticipated wrangles between Radical and mainstream Republicans.

Eastern Theater The opposing armies still lie in their entrenchments at Cold Harbor, Union men finally moving out to pick up their dead; only two of the wounded have survived since the battle of 3 June. Grant and his staff are despondent at their failure to overwhelm Lee; clearly, the direct-assault tactic will not work. Grant slowly accepts the inevitable next move – he must move his army south across the James to threaten Petersburg, the back door to Richmond. As a diversion for his coming move, Grant sends Sheridan's cavalry west to join Hunter at Charlottesville and operate against railroads from there to Hanover Junction. This will become known as Sheridan's Trevilian raid (so named after a town where some of the action occurred).

8 June 1864

The North By a large majority Lincoln is nominated for president by the National Union Convention in Baltimore. In a surprising move never quite explained – Lincoln claims he is neutral on the issue – Democrat Andrew Johnson of Tennessee is nominated for vice-president over the incumbent Hannibal Hamlin. It is perhaps felt that a Southern Democrat who supports the war will be useful to the ticket. The party platform calls for reunification, pursuing the war to its end, no compromise with the South and a constitutional amendment forbidding slavery.

Western Theater Sherman's men gather around the Western and Atlantic Railroad,

ready to close in with Johnston before Marietta, Georgia. Sherman has increasingly to weaken his forces to protect his supply line, now including the railroad back to Chattanooga. In Kentucky, John Hunt Morgan captures a Federal garrison at Mount Sterling, and in the action his raiders help themselves to $18,000 from the local bank.

9 June 1864

Eastern Theater General Benjamin Butler makes yet another mismanaged attempt on Petersburg. Beauregard sends the Federals packing, despite having only 2500 defenders to Butler's 4500 troops.

Western Theater Confederate raider Morgan and his men are routed from Mount Sterling, Kentucky.

10 June 1864

The Confederacy The Confederate Congress authorizes military service for all ages from 17 to 50.

Eastern Theater A Union force of 8000 men under General S D Sturgis, sent by Sherman to take care of Forrest, meet their assigned foe at Brice's Crossroads in Mississippi. The Confederate leader has learned the preceding evening of this advance, and beats the Federals to the crossroad. While his pickets hold the enemy, Forrest moves up his artillery and men, and when the Federals arrive in strength, tired from a forced march in fierce heat, they find themselves immediately under attack. Forrest pressures both Union flanks, which begin to give way late in the afternoon. Finally the Federals panic and run, leaving behind so much equipment that the Confederates have trouble getting around it to chase the fleeing enemy. Sturgis has been defeated by a force less then half as large as his own and has lost 227 killed, 394 wounded and 1623 captured, plus leaving 16 of his 18 guns and his entire supply train of 250 vehicles. Forrest reports losing 492 of 3500 engaged. It is one of 'that devil' Forrest's finest moments. At the end of the day the Federals are still running and rebels still pursuing. Elsewhere, Morgan's increasingly riotous raiders burn a Federal

Above: A number of pontoon bridges built across the James River allowed the four corps of Grant's command to close on Petersburg.

depot and stables in Lexington, Kentucky. In Georgia, Sherman's men move toward Johnston's mountain positions northwest of Marietta.

11 June 1864

Eastern Theater General Robert E Lee has dispatched his nephew, General Fitzhugh 'Fitz' Lee, and General Wade Hampton, Stuart's successor as cavalry commander, to stop Sheridan's depredations in Virginia, in fact a diversion from the planned movement of the Army of the Potomac on Petersburg. Hampton makes contact with Sheridan near Louisa. During the ensuing fight, Hampton is told that Federals are in his rear; these prove to be Custer's men, who have with their usual boldness struck between Hampton's and Fitz Lee's columns, capturing for the moment many Confederate horses and vehicles. Hampton turns to attack Custer with his own column, and after a confused battle Custer is fought back to Trevilian Station, by which time other Federals have driven Fitz Lee to Louisa. Elsewhere in Virginia, Hunter's men engage in depredations in and around Lexington, including burning the Virginia Military Institute. Robert E Lee dispatches General Jubal Early to deal with Hunter.

Western Theater Fighting off Forrest's men, Sturgis and his beaten Federals straggle back toward Memphis, where they will arrive on 13 June. Following this debacle, Sturgis will finish the war 'awaiting orders.'

Naval The CSS *Alabama*, most successful of Confederate seagoing raiders, sails into Cherbourg, France, for a period of much-needed refitting.

12 June 1864

Eastern Theater, Petersburg Campaign After several days of careful and secretive preparations, the four corps of the Federal Army of the Potomac pull quietly out of their positions at Cold Harbor and steal toward the

Above: Union troops attempt to storm the
defenses outside Petersburg, 18 June 1864.
All of the attacks were easily repulsed.

James River on roads and bridges, several of
which have been built within the week – including a massive pontoon bridge across the
James, 2100 feet long, to be built in a half day
on 14 June. By 16 June the entire army will
have been moved to the south shore of the
James. Meanwhile, Warren's corps stays
behind to screen the movement on the left
flank. In this brilliantly planned and executed
maneuver, Grant seems for once to have out-
smarted Lee, who does not discover the
move for several days, thus leaving largely
undefended the goal of Grant's march –
Petersburg. At Trevilian Station Sheridan
mounts a furious attack against Hampton's
entrenchments, but the attack is thrown back
with heavy losses. Sheridan decides at length
that he will not try to join Hunter in the valley
as planned, but will move to rejoin Grant.
After their repulse, Sheridan and his men
begin moving back the way they came,
having lost 1007 casualties of 8000 engaged
(Confederate losses are uncertain but probably comparable.)
Western Theater Confederate raider Morgan and his 1300 men, having the previous

day taken Cynthiana, Kentucky, are met and
defeated in that town by 1500 Federals under
General Burbridge. The Confederates lose
nearly half their party. Morgan and his remaining troops flee toward Abingdon, Virginia, where he arrives on 20 June. In Mississippi, Forrest continues his pursuit of
Sturgis.

13 June 1864

Eastern Theater, Petersburg Campaign
Lee, realizing the Federals have moved but
not yet certain of the import of the move,
guesses wrongly that the enemy's object is
Richmond. Lee therefore moves southward
to cut off approaches to the capital; this will
have no effect on Grant. The Army of the
Potomac smoothly continues its massive
movement.

14 June 1864

Eastern Theater, Petersburg Campaign As
the Army of the Potomac nears completion of
its crossing of the James, Grant sends
General W F 'Baldy' Smith's corps by water to
Bermuda Hundred to join Butler in his
'bottle.' Grant goes along himself to plan an
attack on Petersburg by Butler and Smith.
Lee still does not perceive Grant's move and
thus has not reinforced Petersburg.

Western Theater, Atlanta Campaign
During a conference of Johnston's staff at
their position on the summit of Pine
Mountain near Marietta, Georgia, Federal
Parrott guns send a few shells toward the
summit from Sherman's new position
nearby. One of the shells hits General Leoni-
das Polk and kills him instantly.
Naval The USS *Kearsarge* moves toward
Cherbourg, France, to blockade the raider
CSS *Alabama*.

15 June 1864

Washington The House votes 95 to 66
against a joint resolution abolishing slavery.
The North Notorious Copperhead Clement
L Vallandigham returns to Dayton, Ohio,
from Canada to add his voice to the Democratic election efforts.
Eastern Theater, Petersburg Campaign
Having urgently requested reinforcements
from Lee, Beauregard's messenger is told by
Lee that Beauregard is in error in thinking a
large force of Federals are south of the James.
Ironically, at that same moment Beauregard's
force of some 5400 defending Petersburg is
under assault by W F 'Baldy' Smith's whole
corps of 16,000 men. Lee still does not understand Grant's move, and Petersburg is thus
in serious danger. But the Federals have had

a day of mishaps: Smith's attack, scheduled for early morning with reinforcement from Hancock, is delayed until 1900 hours by Smith's slowness; meanwhile, Hancock is being delayed by a combination of faulty maps, hazy orders from Grant and an unnecessary stop for provisions. Nonetheless, Smith's attack in the evening makes good headway, not surprising since his force is three times the enemy's. When Hancock finally arrives, he suggests that both he and Smith use the moonlit night to press the attack on Petersburg. Success is in fact very likely. Then, making one of the great blunders of the war, 'Baldy' Smith decides against this. Instead, he asks Hancock to occupy the captured trenches while he withdraws. Hancock, though he is senior to Smith, agrees, thus perhaps prolonging the war by many months. During the night, Beauregard decides to abandon his position facing Butler in Bermuda Hundred and use the men to reinforce Petersburg.

Western Theater, Atlanta Campaign Sherman's corps under Thomas, McPherson and Schofield close in amid skirmishes on Johnston's position near Marietta, Georgia.

16 June 1864

Eastern Theater, Petersburg Campaign Confederate commander Beauregard, having pulled in most of his Bermuda Hundred line, now has 14,000 men to defend Petersburg. By now the entire Union Army of the Potomac except for Wright's corps is across the James and at the door of Petersburg. Grant and Meade, arriving in the morning, direct the day's renewed assaults, which by late evening have with many losses captured several positions. Meanwhile, in the afternoon Federals overrun the remaining 1000 Confederates at Bermuda Hundred. Lee, still not aware of the threat to the city, sends replacements not to Petersburg but to Bermuda Hundred.

17 June 1864

Eastern Theater, Petersburg Campaign Another series of Federal attacks on Petersburg make slow and costly headway, and late in the day Beauregard actually recaptures

some positions. During the night the defenders pull back into a tighter and tougher position. Lee, perceiving at last the Federal threat, orders Hill and Anderson to Petersburg. Meade orders another attack for tomorrow.

18 June 1864

Eastern Theater, Petersburg Campaign During the day a series of badly-coordinated assaults are launched against Petersburg as Confederate reinforcements begin to arrive from Lee. All the early Federal efforts meet with costly repulses. A major Union attack beginning at 1400 hours makes some progress but is terribly costly – in 30 minutes one regiment loses 632 of 900 engaged, the highest casualties of any Union regiment in a single battle during the war. As the fighting ends with darkness, Grant gives up the idea of making an assault. In four days of storming the entrenchments, the North has lost 1688 killed, 8513 wounded, and 1185 captured and missing, a total of 11,386 casualties of 63,797 engaged; Confederate losses are unknown in the 41,499 engaged by the end of the day. The opportunity of taking Petersburg when it was weak has been lost; reinforcements have arrived along with Lee himself, and the city is now effectively impregnable. The only course hereafter is a siege, and Grant begins preparations to that effect. Grant has over 110,000 men to work with, to Beauregard's 50,000, and the North holds two rail lines and several roads. But poor Union leadership will mark the ensuing siege, and so will the continuing brilliance of Lee's defense. Meanwhile outside Lynchburg, Hunter is repulsed in an attack on Breckinridge and some of Early's corps. Finding Early is moving toward him in force, Hunter retreats, eventually to end up in Parkersburg and Martinsburg, Virginia. Having dispensed with Hunter, Early is now freed for other excursions.

19 June 1864

Naval As crowds of observers watch from nearby cliffs and from a British yacht, the CSS *Alabama* under Captain Raphael Semmes sallies out near Cherbourg, France, to meet the

USS *Kearsarge* under Captain John A Winslow. A fierce battle ensues, the ships circling closer and closer while blazing away with their cannon. At length the *Alabama* is crippled and limps toward shore, striking its colors as it settles. The English yacht, the *Deerhound*, is given permission by Captain Winslow to pick up survivors as the *Alabama* goes down. While the men watch from the *Kearsarge*, the yacht picks up a number of sailors, including Captain Semmes, and proceeds to steam rapidly out of reach; thus the defeated captain and some crew make a getaway to neutral England. The Confederates have nine killed and 21 wounded to the Union ship's three wounded. This ends the high-seas career of the Southern commerce raider *Alabama*, which has taken 65 Federal merchant ships in the course of the war.

21 June 1864

Eastern Theater, Petersburg Campaign Wishing to extend his siege into a semicircle around Petersburg and cut Southern supply lines, Grant orders General Birney (who has replaced the wound-troubled Hancock) to seize the Weldon Railroad, and General Wright to cut the road to Lynchburg. Later in the day, Grant and the visiting President Lincoln tour the siege lines on horseback. Lincoln's visit to the area will conclude tomorrow after a talk with General Butler.

22 June 1864

Eastern Theater, Petersburg Campaign Pursuing their previous day's orders from Grant, Generals Birney and Wright move out on their separate operations around Petersburg. But both are met by Confederate divisions under A P Hill. Birney is attacked and driven back with 2962 casualties including 1600 prisoners, in an engagement on the Jerusalem Plank Road. Meanwhile, Wright's forces are blocked and Federal cavalry under Wilson are turned back amid heavy skirmish-

Below left: The fighting around Petersburg between the 15th and 18th of June.
Below: The destruction of the Southern *Alabama* by the USS *Kearsarge*, 19 June 1864. The battle took place off the French coast.

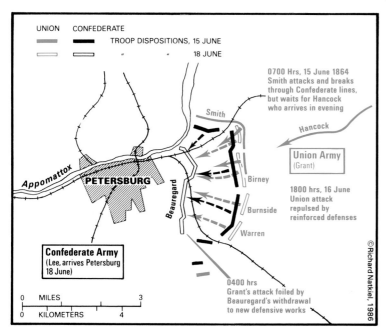

©Richard Natkiel, 1986

ing after destroying some railroad track. Although these Union efforts to extend the siege lines have largely failed, Federal forces do next day gain a foothold on the Jerusalem Plank Road.

Western Theater, Atlanta Campaign Sherman's men have now closed in on Johnston's positions northwest of Marietta, Georgia. Today Confederate General Hood makes a determined but unsuccessful attack on the Federals near Zion Church.

23 June 1864

Eastern Theater, Petersburg Campaign Union cavalry briefly hold a section of the Weldon Railroad near Petersburg, but are driven off. Federal cavalry under Wilson, moving against Confederate supply lines on the South Side Railroad, are in action at Nottoway Court House. Federal cavalry commander Sheridan moves toward Grant's army with a huge wagon train. In the Shenandoah, Confederate General Jubal Early moves north from Lynchburg while skirmishing with Hunter's retreating army.

Western Theater, Atlanta Campaign Two weeks of rain have kept action down between the armies of Sherman and Johnston near Marietta. As the rains end Sherman begins to gather his forces for a new effort. After his highly successful flanking maneuvers, Sherman has decided on a general assault on the strongly entrenched Confederates.

25 June 1864

Eastern Theater, Petersburg Campaign Based on an innovative plan by mining engineer Colonel Henry Pleasants, enthusiastically supported by Burnside and approved without enthusiasm by Grant, Federals begin digging a tunnel toward the Confederate earthworks at Petersburg. Eventually the mine is to be filled with powder and a crater blown in the Confederate fortifica-

Below: Union infantry and artillery wait for the order to assault the Confederate lines around Petersburg.

tions. The 511-foot shaft will be completed on 23 July. Also today, after a skirmish with Confederate cavalry on 24 June, Sheridan's cavalry and wagon train are back from their Trevilian raid and nearing reunion with the Army of the Potomac.

27 June 1864

Washington Lincoln formally accepts the nomination for president.

Eastern Theater, Petersburg Campaign At Staunton, Virginia, Confederate General Jubal Early organizes his army of 10,000 into two corps. Early plans an invasion of the North.

Western Theater, Atlanta Campaign The day has arrived for Sherman's general assault on Johnston's positions at Kennesaw Mountain near Marietta, Georgia. Sherman will describe the results in his memoirs: 'About 9 o'clock AM of the day appointed, the troops moved to the assault, and all along our lines for 10 miles a furious fire of artillery and musketry was kept up. At all points the enemy met us with determined courage and in great force . . . By 11:30 the assault was over, and had failed.' In three major uphill assaults into a hail of shot and shell, the Federal troops capture not one breastwork. A Southern soldier will recollect: 'A solid line of blue came up the hill. My pen is unable to describe the scene of carnage that ensued in the next two hours. Column after column of Federal soldiers were crowded upon that line. No sooner would a regiment mount our works than they were shot down or surrendered. Yet still they came . . . I am satisfied that every man in our regiment killed . . . fivescore men. All that was necessary was to lead and shoot. In fact, I will ever think that the reason they did not capture our works was the impossibility of their living men to pass over the bodies of their dead.' Federal losses in the battle are 1999 killed and wounded and 52 missing, over 2000 casualties out of a total of 16,229 attackers; Confederates numbered some 17,733, their losses 270 killed and wounded and 172 missing.

30 June 1864

Washington Radical Republican Secretary of the Treasury Salmon P Chase, after a number of wrangles with Lincoln, submits another in a series of resignations. This time, to Chase's apparent surprise, Lincoln accepts the resignation and begins looking for a new secretary.

Eastern Theater, Early's Washington Raid Putting in motion his projected invasion of the North, Confederate General Jubal Early moves his army to New Market, Virginia.

2 July 1864

Eastern Theater, Early's Washington Raid Early's column heads north toward the Potomac, meeting little resistance as it moves into Winchester, Virginia.

Western Theater, Atlanta Campaign Realizing that, after his failed assault, Sherman is returning to his flanking tactics, Johnston pulls his army back south of Marietta, again to lines already prepared. In Charleston Harbor, South Carolina, Federal troops establish a beachhead on James Island prior to further attacks on the city's defenses.

3 July 1864

Eastern Theater, Early's Washington Raid The Confederates meet forces under Franz Sigel and over two days drive them back near Harper's Ferry. Panic begins to spread among civilians north of the Potomac.

Western Theater In Charleston, two Union attacks on Confederate forts on the outskirts of the town are turned back.

4 July 1864

Washington Receiving the radically-inspired Wade-Davis Bill just passed by the Senate, with its punitive plans for reconstruction, Lincoln pocket-vetoes the measure. In the storm of protest that follows, Lincoln will stand firmly by his more lenient policies, which he is now putting into effect in Louisiana and Arkansas.

Western Theater, Atlanta Campaign Finding Sherman about to get between his army and Atlanta, Johnston again pulls back, this time to the Chattahoochee River northwest of Atlanta.

5 July 1864

Eastern Theater, Early's Washington Raid Avoiding Sigel's forces at Harper's Ferry, Early begins crossing the Potomac into Maryland at Shepherdstown. As consternation breaks out in Washington, Grant and Chief of Staff Halleck begin to take Early seriously, dispatching reinforcements on the morrow. Meanwhile, militia are called up to defend Maryland.

Western Theater Another Federal expedition against Confederate raider Forrest commences; Union troops leave LaGrange, Tennessee, under command of General A J Smith.

6 July 1864

Eastern Theater, Early's Washington Raid The Confederates finish crossing the Potomac and easily capture Hagerstown, Maryland, where $20,000 is demanded of the citizens, nominally in reparation for Hunter's raids in June.

7 July 1864

Eastern Theater, Early's Washington Raid Federal reinforcements arrive in Washington and Baltimore as Early's 'invading army' skirmishes in several places around Middletown.

Western Theater In Charleston Harbor, Federals are driven from their beachhead on James Island. In 10 days of fighting in the area, Union forces have lost 330 to the South's 163. Still another Federal bombardment begins on the rubble of Fort Sumter.

8 July 1864

Western Theater, Atlanta Campaign Against the wishes of President Davis, Johnston responds to new Union flanking movements by ordering the Army of Tennessee back south of the Chattahoochee River to the gates of Atlanta. Tomorrow Bragg will arrive, sent by Davis for consultation. Sherman is rapidly accumulating forces and supplies for the assault on Atlanta, and orders operations on Southern railroad lines between Columbus, Georgia, and Montgomery, Alabama; these are carried out by 22 July.

9 July 1864

Eastern Theater, Early's Washington Raid Arriving at the Monacacy River near Frederick, Early finds in his path a force of 6000 Federals under General Lew Wallace. A series of largely unplanned Confederate

Below: As the *Alabama* sinks beneath the waves, an English yacht moves in to pick up survivors from the stricken vessel.

attacks eventually routs the hastily-assembled Union forces, many of whom are inexperienced and untrained. Confederate casualties are around 700 of 14,000 engaged; Union casualties are put at nearly 2000, most of them 'missing.' Rather than wasting forces in pursuit, Early presses on toward Washington, stopping to demand a $200,000 levy in Frederick. By now Washington is seriously worried: 'long guns sprouted with bayonets are going about in company with short clerks . . . and every body is tugging some sort of death-dealing tool.'

Above: The scene on the deck of the *Kearsarge* during the encounter with the *Alabama* – the crew of a cannon prepare to fire.

10 July 1864

Washington Lincoln, seemingly unperturbed by Early's approach, tells a group in Baltimore: 'Let us be vigilant but keep cool. I hope neither Baltimore nor Washington will be sacked.' Nevertheless, Early's deep thrust toward the Northern capital provokes widespread fear among the civilian population in and around Washington.

Above: Union artillery provides covering fire as Sherman's men launch their attack on Kennesaw Mountain, Georgia.

11 July 1864

Eastern Theater, Early's Washington Raid By noon Early's army arrives at Silver Springs, Maryland, on the outskirts of Washington. Confederates spend the day reconnoitering for the proposed attack tomorrow. Skirmishing flares at Frederick and at Fort Stevens near Washington, where the president and his wife are sightseeing the battle; Lincoln at one point is under fire as he looks over the parapets. But Early begins to observe reinforcements moving into the capital from Grant's army – Wright arrives with a corps during the day. Many of the rest of the defenders are raw troops, however. Finally, during the night Early decides to give up the attack. Whether he could have actually taken the capital remains uncertain but some of his soldiers are sure he could have, and a correspondent inside the city observes: 'I have always wondered at Early's inaction. Washington was never more helpless. Our lines . . . could have been carried at any point.'

12 July 1864

Eastern Theater, Early's Washington Raid Having decided to give up his assault on Washington, Early's men skirmish on the outskirts before pulling out at night. During action at Fort Stevens, Lincoln again stands up to watch, prompting an officer to shout, 'Get down, you fool!' Before their withdrawal, the Confederates burn the home of Postmaster General Montgomery Blair.

13 July 1864

Eastern Theater Early's forces retreat toward the Potomac at Leesburg; in pursuit is a force of 15,000 under General Horatio Wright.
Western Theater In their campaign to stop General Forrest and his raids on Sherman's all-important supply lines, Federals under A J Smith near their quarry at Tupelo, Mississippi. Forrest's men move up for an attack, and there are minor actions during the day.

14 July 1864

Eastern Theater Early's forces safely cross the Potomac at Leesburg; Wright informs Washington that he does not advise pursuing the enemy into Virginia.
Western Theater At Tupelo, Mississippi, Smith has established strong entrenchments on his front, and against these Forrest and General S D Lee throw a series of assaults that are turned back with heavy losses. The Confederates withdraw by noon while the Federals stay in their positions all day; an evening attempt by Forrest to envelop the enemy left is also unsuccessful. Of Smith's 14,000 men, there are 674 casualties to Forrest's 1347 of 9500 engaged. Plans are made to renew the battle tomorrow.

15 July 1864

Western Theater A further Southern assault on Smith's entrenchments is repulsed with little loss to either side. A worse problem is the heat, from which many soldiers are collapsing. Around noon a further Confederate advance reveals that Smith, worried about short supplies, is retreating. The Confederates follow amid skirmishing but are repulsed, Forrest being slightly wounded. While this action at Tupelo has been nominally a Federal victory, it has been a defensive one when the point was to mount an offensive. Thus Forrest is still fully at large, though Smith does manage to protect the Nashville to Chattanooga railroad.

16 July 1864

Eastern Theater Early and his men are moving with little immediate opposition back toward the Shenandoah Valley, where they will engage in a busy summer's raiding.
Western Theater, Atlanta Campaign Johnston works on his fortification around Atlanta, planning to attack the enemy if opportunity presents. Sherman's army is moving across the Chattahoochee on pontoon bridges; McPherson is sent on a wide enveloping movement through Decatur, Georgia.

17 July 1864

Eastern Theater, Atlanta Campaign A telegram arrives from President Davis relieving the cautious Johnston from command of the Army of Tennessee, and replacing him with General John Bell Hood. Although Hood has the reputation of being a fighting commander, he faces immense difficulties in holding on to Atlanta.

19 July 1864

Eastern Theater Federals catch up with Early's forces near Berryville and a sharp series of skirmishes ensues in the area. After a repulse at Berry's Ford and the news of Union troops threatening his supply train, Early retreats toward Strasburg.

Western Theater, Atlanta Campaign Sherman closes his forces on Atlanta, McPherson on one wing moving through Decatur to the east, Thomas on the other wing pushing across Peachtree Creek to the north, and Schofield advancing in the center. Sherman finds such feeble resistance that he wonders if the Confederates are evacuating. But Hood is readying his forces to fall on Thomas.

20 July 1864

Eastern Theater Federals continue to harass Early's retreat on Strasburg, Virginia. There are many fierce, small-scale engagements. At Stephenson's Depot, near Winchester, a division of Confederates under S D Ramseur are defeated by Federal General W W Averell, who captures 250 men. But Early's main body is till intact.

Western Theater, Atlanta Campaign Sherman's men are today introduced to what will be Hood's tactics for the remainder of the campaign. Federal General Thomas's Army of the Cumberland is resting in the afternoon after crossing Peachtree Creek, when Confederates under Hardee attack in force. The fighting is desperate and often hand-to-hand. Soon Thomas moves up cannon and as they begin firing he directs his resistance from the front, arranging a devastating enfilade fire. After two hours of frantic assault, the Confederates fall back with losses of 4796 from 20,000; Federal losses are about 1779 from the same number engaged. Hood has failed in his first test, and Thomas has preserved the reputation he gained as the 'Rock of Chickamauga.'

Below: One of many Union assaults on the lines of Southern breastworks on the slopes of Kennesaw Mountain. The Union attacks were repulsed with heavy losses.

Above: Southern General Jubal Early led an inspired raid against Washington in mid-1864, but stopped short of the Northern capital when larger Union forces closed in.

21 July 1864

Eastern Theater, Atlanta Campaign Determined to press an offensive, Southern commander Hood sends Wheeler and Hardee toward McPherson's Army of the Tennessee; these Federals are in an exposed position near Decatur, from where they are moving to form Sherman's left wing around the south of Atlanta. Sherman's middle and right under Schofield and Thomas are in position.

22 July 1864

Western Theater, Battle of Atlanta About noon McPherson and Sherman are conferring when firing is heard from the left; McPherson rides off to investigate the action. After a 15-mile march, Hardee has made his attack, which is intended to flank McPherson and get in the rear of the Union forces. A furious assault initially causes consternation in the Federal ranks, but McPherson arrives just as a successful counterattack is mounted. Having seen this success, the general is riding to direct other positions when he is intercepted by Confederate skirmishers, who silently signal him to surrender. McPherson tips his hat to the enemy and bolts; he is shot from his horse and killed instantly. New charges by the Confederates then gain some ground, but by 1500 hours these attacks are being halted. Realizing this, Hood orders General Cheatham to make another attack closer to the Federal center. This action makes some headway before being repulsed by a Federal counterattack. Meanwhile, Confederate cavalry under Wheeler are moving unsuccessfully against Federals in Decatur.

As evening falls, Hood's men have made no gains; failing for the second time to dislodge Sherman, they sink back to their entrenchments. Federal casualties for the day are 430 killed, 1559 wounded, 1733 missing, for 3722 casualties out of over 30,000 engaged. Sherman, now in effect besieging Atlanta, will next turn his attention to Hood's supply lines.

24 July 1864

Eastern Theater At Kernstown, Virginia, Jubal Early's army attacks a group of Federals under General George Crook. A rout ensues, and the Federals flee to Bunker Hill, West Virginia, with 1185 casualties to light losses for the Confederates. Early's cavalry will pursue Crook northward on the 25th, when the Federals will repulse their pursuers at Williamsport on the Potomac.

25 July 1864

Eastern Theater, Petersburg Campaign Grant attempts to tighten his hold on the city by sending forces against the railroads leading toward Richmond.

27 July 1864

Eastern Theater, Petersburg Campaign Work having been completed as of 23 July on the mine under the Confederate entrenchments, preparations are being made for its detonation on 30 July. The mine is being filled with 320 kegs of powder, and Burnside's black troops are engaged in special training for the assault, when they will run through the crater blasted into Southern positions. In the northern Shenandoah, Early's men destroy Union rail lines and prepare to recross the Potomac.
Naval The Union navy under Admiral Farragut engages in reconnaissance preparatory to an attack on Mobile Bay, Alabama.

28 July 1864

Eastern Theater, Atlanta Campaign Following up Stoneman's and McCook's raids around Atlanta, Sherman sends Howard and the Army of the Tennessee south of Atlanta to move against the vital railroads supplying the city from the south. Again the aggressive Hood takes the offensive, sending corps under General S D Lee against the Federals at Ezra Church. Howard digs in and repulses the enemy, and Hood's third sortie is turned back with losses of up to 5000. But the Federals have been prevented from cutting the railroad.

29 July 1864

Eastern Theater Once more Early crosses the Potomac west of Williamsport and spreads consternation into Maryland and Pennsylvania. His men are engaged in fighting at Harper's Ferry, West Virginia, Hagerstown and Clear Spring, Maryland and Mercersburg, Pennsylvania.

30 July 1864

Eastern Theater, Petersburg Mine Assault It is perhaps significant that two of the most incompetent Federal generals of the war, Butler and Burnside, are both attracted to novel methods of warfare. One of Butler's pet ideas, the wire entanglements used at his otherwise deplorable Drewry's Bluff action, has at least proved effective. Burnside's mine, planned by Colonel Pleasants to blow a crater into the enemy works through which an attack can be mounted, is in fact an innovative idea of possibly great consequence in the siege of Petersburg. Today after a month's work the detonation is scheduled and the troops are ready. However, the previous day Meade with Grant's approval has decided that the black troops of Ferrero's IX Corps, the only ones specially trained to pursue the mission, are not to lead the attack, since if it fails the Union will be accused of callously misusing its black soldiers (which, given the experimental nature of the operation, is very possibly the case). After this rebuff, Burnside is chagrined and proceeds with some indifference, drawing straws to select who will lead the assault (Ledlie, 1st Division, loses) and being a little hesitant about final preparations and instructions. The explosion is set for 0300 hours. At that moment every Federal eye strains toward the fortifications. Nothing happens. An investigation by two volunteers finds the fuse has gone out. They relight it. At 0445 one of the largest explosions ever seen on the American continent sends flames, earth, cannon, bodies and parts of bodies 100 feet into the air in the midst of a mushroom-shaped cloud. When all this has descended and settled, there is a crater 170 feet long, 60 to 80 feet wide and 30 feet deep stretching well into the Southern positions. At least 278 Confederates have been killed in the explosion or smothered in the debris. For the time being the defenders have fled the area as Union

Below: Confederate troops attempt to storm hastily constructed Union defenses during the Battle of Ezra Church, 28 July 1864.

attackers descend into the hole. Finding themselves in a maze of trenches and pits, the men falter. Meanwhile, their commander, Ledlie, is cowering in a bombproof shelter behind his lines. Soon the Confederates collect themselves and in an exemplary manner begin to train their artillery into the hole; finding themselves somewhat sheltered from this fire, the ostensible attackers are even less disposed to pursue their assault. By the time 15,000 men have been herded into the crater, the enemy fire has become truly murderous and the Federal attackers are only interested in hiding. The Union army is now quite literally at the feet of the enemy. Finally, in desperation, the black troops originally slated to head the attack are ordered in; after dispatching them, their commander, Ferrero, joins Ledlie in the bombproof shelter. The black troops advance quickly and resolutely, followed by not one white soldier, and are cut to pieces on the other end. The whole inglorious affair ends with a confused melee of surviving Union soldiers rushing devil-take-the-hindmost back to their own lines. The North has lost 3748 casualties of 20,708 engaged, the Confederates about 1500 of 11,466.

Also on this day, Confederate cavalry from Early's forces ride into Chambersburg, Pennsylvania, and offer not to burn down the town if $500,000 in cash or $100,000 in gold can be raised, to help the raiders meet expenses and serve as more 'reparations' for Hunter's Federal raids in the Shenandoah. The sum is not obtainable, however, and the town is duly put to the torch. The rebels

move on west to McConnellsburg, pursued at some distance by Averell.

Western Theater, Atlanta Campaign Sherman's raiders Stoneman and McCook, engaged in disrupting operations on Confederate supply lines around Atlanta, both run into trouble. Stoneman and 700 men are captured by the enemy on the outskirts of Macon; McCook has to fight his way out of a Confederate encirclement at Newman, and loses 500 men and many supplies.

1 August 1864

Eastern Theater, Valley Campaign Grant gives cavalry commander Philip H Sheridan the mission of clearing the enemy, especially Early, out of the Shenandoah Valley. Early's cavalry leader McCausland is now seriously threatened by Averell's pursuit.

3 August 1864

Western Theater, Atlanta Campaign Sherman dispatches A J Smith for another crack at Forrest. Smith leaves today for Oxford, Mississippi, preparing for a movement on Columbus.

Naval Preparing for the naval move on Mobile Bay, Federal troops attack, but do not yet capture, Fort Gaines on Dauphin Island, one of the Confederate forts guarding the bay. Meanwhile, Federal Admiral Farragut's fleet is ready to move.

5 August 1864

Washington Furious at Lincoln's pocket-veto of their punitive reconstruction bill, Senator Benjamin Wade and Representative

Above: Union forces launch an attack in the wake of the explosion of a mine under the Southern defenses around Petersburg.

H W Davis issue what is called the Wade-Davis Manifesto, proclaiming 'their right and duty to check the encroachments of the Executive on the Authority of Congress.' At issue is whether Lincoln or Congress will control reconstruction.

Naval, Battle of Mobile Bay At 0600 hours Admiral David Farragut's fleet begins to run past the three Confederate forts into the important Southern port of Mobile Bay and head for the Confederate defending ships – the mighty ironclad ram *Tennessee* and three wooden gunboats under Admiral Franklin Buchanan. Soon the Federal ships come under fire from Fort Morgan and the gunboats, and are also heading toward a treacherous maze of underwater mines (known as torpedos at this time). After 0700 Federal ironclad *Tecumseh* is sunk by a torpedo, and it is after this that the 63-year-old Farragut, standing high in the rigging of his flagship *Hartford*, is supposed to have exclaimed, 'Damn the torpedos, full speed ahead!' Whether or not this was said, the Union fleet does just that, led into the bay by the *Hartford* with little further damage from the forts or from torpedos. After repeatedly being rammed and shelled, the CSS *Tennessee* is disabled and surrenders, and the bay is secured. Federals have lost 145 killed (including 93 drowned in the *Tecumseh*), 170 wounded, and four captured. The Confederates lose few killed and wounded, but 270 men are taken

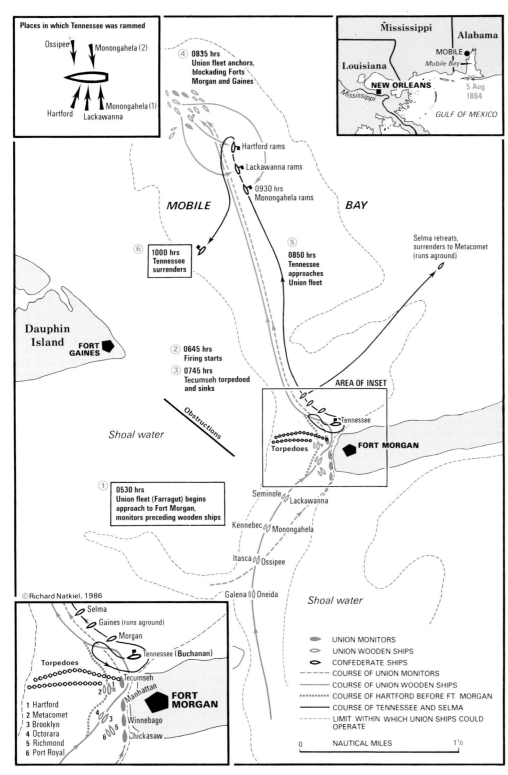

Places in which Tennessee was rammed

Ossipee — Monongahela (2)

Hartford — Lackawanna — Monongahela (1)

④ 0835 hrs
Union fleet anchors,
blockading Forts
Morgan and Gaines

Hartford rams

Lackawanna rams

0930 hrs
Monongahela rams

MOBILE   **BAY**

⑥ 1000 hrs
Tennessee
surrenders

⑤ 0850 hrs
Tennessee
approaches
Union fleet

Selma retreats,
surrenders to Metacomet
(runs aground)

**Dauphin
Island** FORT
GAINES

② 0645 hrs
Firing starts

③ 0745 hrs
Tecumseh torpedoed
and sinks

AREA OF INSET

Shoal water

Obstructions

Tennessee

Torpedoes

FORT MORGAN

① 0530 hrs
Union fleet (Farragut) begins
approach to Fort Morgan,
monitors preceding wooden ships

Seminole
Lackawanna

Kennebec Monongahela

Itasca Ossipee

©Richard Natkiel, 1986

Galena Oneida

Shoal water

Selma

Gaines (runs aground)

Morgan

Torpedoes

Tennessee (Buchanan)

Tecumseh

1 Hartford
2 Metacomet
3 Brooklyn
4 Octorara
5 Richmond
6 Port Royal

Manhattan

**FORT
MORGAN**

Winnebago

Chickasaw

UNION MONITORS
UNION WOODEN SHIPS
CONFEDERATE SHIPS
— — — COURSE OF UNION MONITORS
———— COURSE OF UNION WOODEN SHIPS
•••••••• COURSE OF HARTFORD BEFORE FT. MORGAN
———— COURSE OF TENNESSEE AND SELMA
— — — LIMIT WITHIN WHICH UNION SHIPS COULD
          OPERATE

0   NAUTICAL MILES   1½

Mississippi Alabama
MOBILE
Mobile Bay

Louisiana

NEW ORLEANS   5 Aug
                            1864
Mississippi

GULF OF MEXICO

Above: The Battle of Mobile Bay, 5 August 1864,
ended in a significant Union victory.

(including Admiral Buchanan) and all ships
sunk or captured. Besides removing a valuable port from the Confederacy, the action
gives the Union army a staging area for
planned operations against Mobile. Federal
bombardment from the water will lead to the
fall of Forts Gaines and Powell over the next
few days; Fort Morgan will hold out until the
end of the month.

7 August 1864

Eastern Theater Part of Early's cavalry
under McCausland are finally attacked in
force by W W Averell at Moorefield, West
Virginia. Federals capture 420 men.

9 August 1864

Eastern Theater, Petersburg Campaign
The siege remains quiet, and the defenders
have already repaired the damage to their
works caused by the Federal mine detonated
on 30 July.
Valley Campaign Sheridan prepares to
move from Halltown and Harper's Ferry,
West Virginia, to confront Early. Elsewhere,
rebel raider John S Mosby steps up his activities in the Federal-held part of Virginia.
Western Theater, Atlanta Campaign As
the siege of Atlanta continues, opposing
commanders Sherman and Hood probe, raid
and search for ways in and out. On Mobile
Bay Federal troops begin a siege of Fort Morgan, the last remaining Confederate works
on the bay.

10 August 1864

Eastern Theater, Atlanta Campaign Confederate commander Hood dispatches much
of his cavalry under Wheeler to raid Sherman's rail lines above the city. Wheeler will
be active until 10 September in various locations but this action is in fact another blunder
by Hood. Sherman already has the supplies
he requires for the moment, and now the
Confederate army is without cavalry.

12 August 1864

Eastern Theater, Valley Campaign Sheridan moves toward Early, who is entrenched
south of Winchester along Cedar Creek,
where there is a small skirmish during the
day. Small actions will go on until Sheridan
withdraws on 14 August. It will be some
weeks before the antagonists do much more
than follow in one another's footsteps.
Naval In a week of heavy raiding the Confederate crusier *Tallahassee* takes six Union
vessels off New York and seven off Sandy
Hook, New Jersey.

15 August 1864

Eastern Theater, Valley Campaign After
further skirmishing with Early near Cedar
Creek, Sheridan withdraws toward Winchester pending the arrival of supplies.
Western Theater, Atlanta Campaign
Wheeler's Confederate cavalry raid Sherman's supply lines on Tennessee railroads.
Naval Confederate raider *Tallahassee* takes
six more Federal ships off New England; four
more will be captured on the 16th.

17 August 1864

Eastern Theater, Valley Campaign Early's
forces pursue the withdrawing Sheridan; a
sharp action breaks out near Winchester,
Virginia.

18 August 1864

Washington Grant refuses a second Confederate request to exchange prisoners, thus
cutting off Confederate reinforcements but
also condemning to slow starvation many
Federal prisoners in the South, who can
scarcely be fed by their captors when the
Confederate army is itself hungry.
Eastern Theater, Petersburg Campaign In
the first action since the mine disaster, Federals move to extend their lines around the
city. A corps under Warren occupies a mile of
the important Weldon Railroad, fighting successfully at Globe Tavern, Yellow House and
Blick's Station before being halted by the
enemy in the evening.
Western Theater, Atlanta Campaign Hoping to force the enemy out of Atlanta, Sherman sends two brigades under General
Judson Kilpatrick to raid Hood's lines of communication south of the city. Strong Confederate resistance will interfere with this
raid, and Kilpatrick returns to Decatur on 23
August having had little success.

19 August 1864

Eastern Theater, Petersburg Campaign
Warren's infantry is attacked by Confederates under A P Hill south of Petersburg, and
the Federals with heavy losses are forced
back to their position at Globe Tavern. However, the North still controls the important
Weldon Railroad.

Valley Campaign Sheridan and Early continue skirmishing around Winchester.

21 August 1864

Eastern Theater, Petersburg Campaign In a final desperate attempt to dislodge Federals from the much-needed Weldon Railroad, A P Hill attacks Warren's forces south of Petersburg. The attack fails and the South has lost 1600 of the 14,000 in action around the railroad; Federal casualties are 4455 of 20,000.

Valley Campaign Early and R H Anderson have planned a dual attack on Sheridan today, but it fails to develop and the day sees minor skirmishing in several places around Charles Town. At night Sheridan withdraws to strong positions near Harper's Ferry.

Western Theater General Forrest makes another bold move, taking Memphis, Tennessee, for the day and capturing several officers; Federal Generals Hurlbut and Washburn barely escape. Smith tries and fails to cut off Forrest's retreat, and then is called back. Forrest is now free to operate against Sherman's supply lines. Nearly two months of attempts against him have largely resulted in Federal embarrassments such as this.

23 August 1864

Naval Fort Morgan falls, the last of the three Confederate forts on Mobile Bay. Now the Union controls one of the last two major ports that had been left for Southern blockade-running. Only Wilmington, North Carolina, now remains.

25 August 1864

Eastern Theater, Petersburg Campaign After several days of destroying track along the Weldon Railroad, Hancock's Federals are assaulted at Ream's Station by a reinforced A P Hill, who drives them back from the railroad in heavy fighting. Federals lose 2742 men, mostly in captured and missing, and

Below: Union ironclads and gunboats run the gauntlet of Confederate shore batteries during the action at Mobile Bay.

many armaments. Hill's men then withdraw to Petersburg, and the rail line remains broken.

Valley Campaign With Sheridan entrenched on the Potomac, Early leaves a force to hold him there and resumes his roaming in West Virginia, threatening a new invasion of Maryland and Pennsylvania.

Naval CSS *Talahassee* pulls into port at Wilmington, North Carolina, having captured 31 Union vessels in three weeks.

27 August 1864

Western Theater, Atlanta Campaign The time has come to begin the final act of the Atlanta campaign. Sherman pulls two corps out of his trenches on a wide circuit of the city. The Confederates think Sherman is retreating; the message 'the Yankees are gone' is telegraphed all over the South. But Sherman's men are moving to choke off Hood's

Above: David Farragut leads the Union forces at Mobile Bay from the rigging of his flagship, the *Hartford*.

last rail lines into the city, especially the Macon Railroad at Jonesboro. Several previous expeditions have failed to accomplish this task but this effort will not fail.

29 August 1864

The North The Democratic National convention meets in Chicago, with the keynote address given by Copperhead activist Clement Vallandigham. Another speaker proclaims: 'Four years of misrule by a sectional, fanatical and corrupt party have brought our country to the verge of ruin.'

Eastern Theater, Valley Campaign Sheridan is on the move again against Early, winning an engagement at Smithfield crossing on the Opequon Creek.

Trans-Mississippi A Confederate expedition prepares at Princeton, Arkansas, under General Sterling Price. Its object is to retake Missouri.

30 August 1864

The North As expected, the Democratic National Convention prepares to nominate General George B McClellan for president. The Peace Democrat and Copperhead dominated platform asserts that, 'justice, humanity, liberty and the public welfare demand that immediate efforts be made for a cessation of hostilities.' The platform also assails Lincoln's 'usurpation of extraordinary and dangerous powers not granted by the Constitution' and says, 'the aim and object of the Democratic Party is to preserve the Union and rights of the State unimpaired.'

Western Theater, Atlanta Campaign Sherman's Generals Thomas and Howard cut one of Hood's two remaining rail lines, the Montgomery and Atlanta, in two places. Schofield is moving toward the second, the Macon and Weston Railroad. Still thinking that Wheeler's raids have forced Sherman to retreat for lack of supplies, Hood orders an attack on the Federals at Jonesboro.

Above: A view of the Confederate entrenchments just north of the Georgia Railroad on the outskirts of Atlanta.

31 August 1864

The North   In the convention at Chicago General McClellan is nominated as the Democratic candidate for president.

Western Theater, Atlanta Campaign Hood's attack on Howard's Army of the Tennessee near Jonesboro is turned back with heavy losses – 1725 Southern casualties to Howard's 170. Meanwhile, Schofield cuts the Confederates' last railroad line at the town of Rough and Ready, Georgia. During the night Sherman orders General Slocum to try to enter the city on 1 September. In more ways than military, Atlanta is doomed.

1 September 1864

Eastern Theater, Valley Campaign Elements of Sheridan's army clash with Jubal Early's Confederates at Opequon Creek.

Western Theater, Atlanta Campaign General Hood and the Army of Tennessee evacuate Atlanta. Unable to carry off the munitions and stores, the Confederate rearguard blows up the much-needed supplies as they leave, sending billows of smoke and fire into the night air and shock waves reverberating to Union lines on the outskirts of the city. In Jonesboro, Union troops renew their counterattack against the enemy and, at the end of the day, Hardee withdraws his men to Lovejoy Station, where they rendezvous with the army leaving Atlanta.

2 September 1864

The Confederacy   Worried over the South's chronic shortage of manpower, General Lee suggests to Jefferson Davis that Confederate leaders replace white laborers in the army with black slaves to free a greater number of whites for combat service. Lee also argues that stringent new regulations governing exemptions and a more vigorous enlistment policy are necessary to offset the constant losses to battle and disease.

Western Theater, Atlanta Campaign Led by General Henry Slocum's XX Corps, Federal troops begin to move into Atlanta in the morning. Sherman informs Lincoln of the successful completion of his four-week siege of the city with terse exultation: 'So Atlanta is ours, and fairly won.'

3 September 1864

Washington   President Lincoln, responding to the news from Sherman of the fall of Atlanta, and also in recognition of Admiral Farragut's victory at Mobile Bay in August, declares 5 September a national day of celebration.

Eastern Theater, Valley Campaign Answering Lee's request to return troops on loan from Richmond, Jubal Early sends General Richard H Anderson's corps toward the Confederate capital. At Berryville, though, they run into a part of Sheridan's army and, after some hard fighting, retreat to the shelter of the main body of Confederate troops at Winchester.

4 September 1864

Western Theater   Union troops commanded by General A C Gillem surround the celebrated Confederate raider, John Hunt Morgan, while he and his men are bivouacked at Greenville, Tennessee. Morgan, the commander of the Department of Southwest Virginia since his escape from an Ohio penitentiary last year, is less successful this time in eluding his captors and he is shot and killed as he tries to flee from the trap. One hundred Confederates are killed in the action and another 75 are taken prisoner.

Naval   A 60-day bombardment of Fort Sumter, at Charleston, South Carolina, ends.

5 September 1864

Eastern Theater, Valley Campaign   Though General Early yesterday moved his army south from its former position, Confederate troops continue to clash with the enemy along the Opequon Creek.

Western Theater   Following the procedure President Lincoln had outlined for the re-admission of the state to the Union, those citizens of Louisiana who have taken the loyalty oath renouncing secession go to the polls and ratify a new constitution abolishing slavery in the state.

6 September 1864

Naval   Federal ships again open fire on Fort Sumter. This latest bombardment will continue for the next nine days.

7 September 1864

Eastern Theater, Valley Campaign   Sheridan's and Early's armies continue to skirmish near Winchester, Virginia.

Western Theater   General Sherman issues an order for the evacuation of all civilians

Below: A Northern cartoon showing the dangers of compromise with the South – Jefferson Davis shakes hands with a wounded Union soldier.

from Atlanta. The order will provoke an angry exchange between the Union general and General Hood, as well as protests from the citizens of the town, but Sherman remains obdurate.

Trans-Mississippi Fighting occurs at Centralia, Missouri, between Federal soldiers and Confederates.

8 September 1864

The North General George B McClellan formally accepts the Democratic nomination for president. In his letter of acceptance, however, McClellan refuses to accept that part of the Democratic platform which labels the war a failure: 'I could not,' he writes, 'look in the face of my gallant comrades of the army and navy, who have survived so many bloody battles and tell them that their labor and sacrifice had been in vain.' Although he separates himself from the Copperhead faction of the party by this remark, McClellan makes it clear that his own ideas concerning the basis for peace between North and South are considerably different from those of the Republicans. In contrast to their demand for the unconditional surrender of the Confederacy and recognition of emancipation, the Democratic nominee insists only on reunion, and maintains that when 'any one State is willing to return to the Union, it should be received at once, with a full guarantee of all its constitutional rights.'

Naval Following up last month's victory at Mobile Bay, Federals destroy over 50 Confederate furnaces at Salt House Point.

Below: A scene of the destruction that greeted Sherman's men when they entered Atlanta on 2 September 1864.

Above: Dejected Southern prisoners trudge into captivity after being defeated by Union troops under Howard at Jonesboro.

9 September 1864

Trans-Mississippi Federals clash with the enemy near Warrensburg, Missouri, and in Arkansas Confederates attack the *J D Perry* at Clarendon.

10 September 1864

Western Theater Grant sends Sherman a telegram urging him to begin a new drive against the enemy as soon as possible. Although no definite decision has yet been made as to what Sherman's next move will be, both Union generals still see Hood's army as the primary target.

11 September 1864

Western Theater Generals Sherman and Hood enter into a 10-day truce to allow for the removal of civilians from Atlanta. A citizens' committee in the occupied city draws up and presents a formal protest to Sherman against his policy of removal. The Union leader, however, will answer the petition with characteristic bluntness: 'You might as well appeal against the thunderstorm,' he will tell them, 'as against these terrible hardships of war.' In the next 10 days, 446 families will leave the city to take up residence either to the north or south.

12 September 1864

Eastern Theater, Valley Campaign President Lincoln, anxious to break the stalemate between Sheridan and Early's army, suggests to Grant the possibility of 'quietly but suddenly' transferring troops to Sheridan to allow him to strike at the enemy.

13 September 1864

Eastern Theater, Valley Campaign The two armies in the Valley continue to skirmish with engagements today at Bunker Hill and at two fords at Opequon Creek.

14 September 1864

Eastern Theater, Valley Campaign After one unsuccessful attempt already, General Richard H Anderson's corps leave Early's army to rejoin Lee at Petersburg. The loss of these troops substantially weakens the Confederate forces in the Valley.

16 September 1864

Eastern Theater, Siege of Petersburg South of the James River, General Wade Hampton and his force of Confederate cavalry engage a

group of Federals herding cattle and, after defeating them, lead over 2400 head of beef back to the hungry army at Petersburg.

Valley Campaign Generals Grant and Sheridan meet at Charles Town, West Virginia, to discuss the military situation at Winchester. Sheridan, who is aware that some of Early's troops have recently left the area for Richmond, proposes offensive action against the Confederates. Grant approves the plans for ousting Early's force.

Western Theater With some 4500 men, General Nathan B Forrest leaves Verona, Mississippi to operate against Sherman's supply and communication lines. Until the beginning of November, Forrest will continue to harass Union outposts in northern Alabama and Tennessee.

17 September 1864

The North John C Frémont, who had been nominated as a candidate for president in the spring by a convention of Radical Republicans dissatisfied with Lincoln's handling of the war, announces his intention to withdraw from the race. Though he still feels that Lincoln's administration is a failure, he fears a Democratic victory would lead to either a recognition of the Confederacy or at the very least a re-establishment of slavery. To prevent this and to work for emancipation, he pledges his support to Lincoln.

Eastern Theater, Valley Campaign Though outnumbered by more than three to one, Jubal Early begins to move his troops northward in the direction of Sheridan's army in order to operate against the Baltimore and

Below: The Battle of Winchester ended when Sheridan's men stormed the breastworks held by Jubal Early's troops.

Ohio Railroad. In West Virginia there is some fighting around Buckhanon.

18 September 1864

Eastern Theater, Valley Campaign After encountering enemy cavalry, Confederate troops in the valley under General Early fall back slightly toward Winchester again. The 12,000 man force, however, is somewhat widely scattered and in poor defensive position. Informed of this, Union General Sheridan decides to attack the Confederates in the morning.

19 September 1864

The North, The Lake Erie Conspiracy Two Confederate agents put into action their plan to capture the US gunboat *Michigan* and then free Confederate prisoners being held at Johnson's Island on Lake Erie. Once freed, they hope to organize the men into an army which will operate in the area. Captain John Yates Beall of the Confederate navy, accompanied by a band of men he had recruited across the border in Canada, commandeers the steamer *Philo Parsons* and the *Island Queen*, but the other agent, Charles H Cole, who had managed to plant himself on board the *Michigan*, is discovered and arrested before he can give the signal to his cohorts to board the ship. Beall scuttles the *Philo Parsons* and escapes but later will be captured and hanged as a spy.

Eastern Theater, Valley Campaign Sheridan attacks the Confederates at Winchester. In the morning, bottlenecks develop as the Union troops try to cross the Opequon to engage the enemy and for a time it appears as though the outnumbered Southern army might successfully repulse the attack. As the day progresses, however, Sheridan is able to

bring a larger number of his troops to bear against the Confederate breastworks. By the end of the day the Federals are forcing Early's troops into a full retreat. Union losses are 653 killed, 3719 wounded and 618 missing. The Southern army leaves 3000 of their wounded in Winchester as they flee the city and suffer the loss of another 2000 taken prisoner during the day. News of the victory will be greeted with jubilation throughout the North but particularly by Republicans who see battle victories as indispensable if they are to win the political elections in November. Referring to the battle and its impact on the political climate of the North, Republican James Garfield will write that 'Phil Sheridan has made a speech in the Shenandoah Valley more powerful and valuable to the Union cause than all the stumpers of the Republic can make.'

Trans-Mississippi General Sterling Price leads a cavalry force of 12,000 men into Missouri. Since the failure of the Federal Red River expedition last April, Confederate authorities and General Edmund Kirby Smith had talked of launching a campaign to recover Missouri for the Confederacy. The South, however, will never be able to marshal a force necessary to implement such an ambitious plan, and Price's raid is to be the last offensive move by the South into Missouri. They cross into Missouri from Indian Territory. Just before entering the state, the Confederates capture a Federal supply train near Cabin Creek and then continue their advance northward.

20 September 1864

Eastern Theater, Valley Campaign A Union cavalry force pursues Early's fleeing troops as they move southward after yester-

Above: Abandoned Southern trenches outside Petersburg. On 29 September troops under General Stannard captured Fort Harrison.

day's defeat. The Union horsemen clash with the Southern rearguard at Middletown, Strasburg and Cedarville.

Trans-Mississippi As Price's Confederate cavalry moves toward St Louis, fighting occurs with Federals at Keytesville and on the Little Black River in Missouri.

21 September 1864

Eastern Theater, Valley Campaign General Early's troops dig in at Fisher's Hill after halting their retreat from Winchester. Sheridan's army, following the Confederates, fortifies its own positions just north of Fisher's Hill.

22 September 1864

Easter Theater, Valley Campaign After following Early's fleeing army for two days, Sheridan again throws his troops against the enemy at Fisher's Hill. The battle develops into a complete rout and the Southerners plunge into headlong retreat further up the Valley. 'I do not think there ever was an army so badly beaten,' Sheridan gloats in his message to Grant of the battle. Despite the exaggeration, Fisher's Hill is both decisive and one-sided. Federal losses in the battle are only 528, while the Confederates lose 1235 men as well as 12 artillery pieces. It will be almost a month before Early's troops are again prepared to fight.

Trans-Mississippi There is skirmishing at Patterson and Sikeston, Missouri.

23 September 1864

Eastern Theater, Valley Campaign Though Confederate cavalry battles Federals at Mount Jackson, Front Royal and Woodstock, Sheridan's army does not follow Early's troops up the Valley.

Western Theater General Nathan Forrest and his cavalry force attack a Federal garrison at Athens, Alabama. Forrest's raid into northern Alabama is part of a concerted Confederate effort to harass Sherman's line of communications to Atlanta.

24 September 1864

Eastern Theater, Valley Campaign Having defeated Early in two decisive battles and forced his army to retreat up the Valley, Sheridan begins to turn his attention to destroying the vast food resources of the Shenandoah Valley. 'If the war is to last another year,' Grant has written Sheridan, 'we want the Shenandoah Valley to remain a barren waste.'

25 September 1864

Western Theater, Franklin and Nashville Campaign Jefferson Davis arrives in Palmetto, Georgia, where he talks with General John B Hood about campaign strategy against Sherman in Atlanta. To the north, General Forrest attacks Federal railroad lines, capturing Sulfur Branch Trestle in northern Alabama. There is also fighting today at Johnsonville, Tennessee, and near Henderson, Kentucky.

Trans-Mississippi Price's men skirmish with the enemy at Farmington and Huntsville, Missouri.

26 September 1864

Eastern Theater, Valley Campaign Elements of Sheridan's cavalry harass Early's army near Port Republic, Virginia.

Western Theater Now in Tennessee, Forrest and his troops assault a Federal garrison near Pulaski.

27 September 1864

Trans-Mississippi Sterling Price and his cavalry force continue their advance northward through Missouri. At Pilot Knob, they attack a Federal garrison under the command of Thomas Ewing Jr. The Union forces, though badly outnumbered, beat off the attack, inflicting some 1500 casualties, and then escape under cover of darkness. Meanwhile, a small band of Confederate guerrillas led by 'Bloody' Bill Anderson ride into Centralia, Missouri, looting and burning many of the town's buildings. They then capture a train as it pulls into the town and kill over 20 unarmed Federals on board. Later the band ambushes a column of Union cavalry sent out to intercept the raiders, killing another 100 enemy soldiers.

28 September 1864

Western Theater There is scattered fighting at Brownsville, Mississippi, and at Wells Hill and Rheatown, Tennessee.

29 September 1864

Eastern Theater, Siege of Petersburg Grant orders an attack on Forts Harrison and Gilmore, enemy fortifications in front of the Petersburg-Richmond lines. Troops under General George Stannard succeed in capturing Fort Harrison but the move against Fort Gilmore fails and that outpost remains in Confederate hands. Meanwhile, south of Petersburg, 16,000 Federal soldiers try to extend Union lines westward to capture Boydton Plank Road and the Southside Railroad, two important routes leading into that city.

Valley Campaign Elements of Sheridan's and Early's armies clash near the town of Waynesborough.

Trans-Mississippi Federals fight Price's advancing cavalry at Leasburg and Cuba, Missouri.

30 September 1864

Eastern Theater, Siege of Petersburg Confederate troops commanded by General Richard H Anderson try to retake Fort Harrison, lost to the Federals in yesterday's action. The assault fails. In the two days of fighting af the fort, Federal losses are 929 killed or wounded and 1756 missing. The Confederates lose a total of 2800, including 300 prisoners. Fighting also continues southwest of Petersburg, near Peebles' Farm, as a vigorous counter attack by Ambrose P Hill pushes back the advancing Federal columns.

1 October 1864

Eastern Theater, Siege of Petersburg Fighting continues around Peebles' Farm as Union troops try to extend their lines encircling Petersburg. In the Valley, meanwhile, General Sheridan prepares to move his army north to Cedar Creek from its present position in Harrisonburg. Also a Federal expedition into southwest Virginia and east Tennessee fights two small engagements at Clinch Mountain and Laurel Creek Gap in Tennessee.

Western Theater, Franklin and Nashville Campaign General Hood moves his army around Atlanta to strike Sherman's railroad line, assaulting Union troops at Salt Springs. In support of Hood's army General Forrest and his cavalry continue to hit at positions in

Above: Sherman directs his assault troops from Kennesaw Mountain during the renewed fighting around Atlanta.

Sherman's rear. Forrest and his men skirmish with Federal troops at Athens and Huntsville, Alabama, and also capture a number of Union blockhouses at Carters Creek Station in Tennessee.

Naval The *Condor*, a British blockade-runner, is grounded near Fort Fisher, North Carolina, as it is being chased by the USS *Niphon*. On board the *Condor* is Mrs Rose O'Neal, a Confederate spy, who to avoid capture tries to escape in a small boat with her secret dispatches and $2000 in gold. The boat capsizes in the heavy seas and Mrs O'Neal drowns.

2 October 1864

The Confederacy President Davis gives General Pierre Gustave Toutant Beauregard command of the two armies in the west under Hood and Richard Taylor. Beauregard is to direct the overall strategy and coordinate the activities of the two armies but is not to interfere with field operations when visiting either of them.

Eastern Theater, Siege of Petersburg Four days of fighting at Peebles' Farm comes to an end as the Confederates withdraw to their entrenchments. Between 30 September and the end of this day, Union forces have succeeded in extending their lines three miles westward.

Valley Campaign Skirmishing takes place between elements of Jubal Early's army and that of Sheridan at Mount Crawford and Bridgewater. In southwest Virginia, a Federal raid designed to destroy Confederate salt mines in the region is repulsed near Saltville. After the engagement, the Southern defenders put to death over 100 prisoners, most of whom are blacks. Although Lee will order a full investigation when he hears of the atrocity, only one man will be brought to justice, and he primarily for the murder of a white officer.

Trans-Mississippi General Sterling Price, still moving northward through Missouri, occupies the town of Washington in the face of growing Southern resistance.

3 October 1864

Eastern Theater, Valley Campaign Confederate cavalry hit at Sheridan's army near Harrisonburg.

Western Theater, Franklin and Nashville Campaign The Army of Tennessee continues to disrupt Sherman's supply lines forcing him to send more troops from Atlanta to protect his trains. Meanwhile, General George Thomas, whom Sherman had directed to Nashville to protect that city from a possible attack by Hood's army, reaches the city and begins to prepare its defenses.

Trans-Mississippi Sterling Price's men engage Federal troops at Hermann and Miller's Station, to the west of St Louis. Though the citizens of that town had been considerably alarmed by the Confederate raid into Missouri, Price's foray has caused Union officials to deploy General A J Smith's corps, originally intended to reinforce Thomas in Tennessee, to St Louis to meet the new danger to the Trans-Mississippi area.

4 October 1864

Western Theater, Franklin and Nashville Campaign There is more action between Confederate and Union forces in Georgia, with engagements at Acworth, Mom's Station and near Lost Mountain. General Sherman moves his headquarters to Kennesaw Mountain to place himself in a better position to strike against Hood's army.

Trans-Mississippi Price, unwilling to strike directly at freshly reinforced St Louis begins to swing his troops to the west and away from the city. The raiders engage Federal forces at Richwoods, Missouri.

5 October 1864

The Confederacy Jefferson Davis gives a speech in Augusta, Georgia. He attempts to rekindle the spirit of the people by assuring them that he has never been more confident that with determined and vigorous effort, the

Below: General John Bell Hood, one of the South's ablest commanders, confronted Sherman around Franklin and Nashville.

South can drive the enemy from its territory.
Western Theater, Franklin and Nashville Campaign In an attack that will later gain much publicity, Confederate troops under General Samuel G French strike a Federal position at Altoona, Georgia, hoping to destroy a railroad bridge there. General Sherman sends the commander at Altoona a message telling him to hold his position ('General Sherman says hold fast. We are coming.'), and though promised reinforcements never arrive, the Federals fight a heroic defense, beating off the enemy attack. Federal losses are 706, while the Confederates lose 799.

6 October 1864

Eastern Theater, Valley Campaign Though twice severely beaten last month, Confederates in the Valley still refuse to give up completely. Cavalry under Confederate General Thomas L Rosser hit General George Custer's cavalry at Brook's Gap, near Fisher's Hill. Custer's troops succeed in beating off the attack.
Western Theater General Forrest continues to plague Union forces in Sherman's rear, fighting an engagement with Federals at Florence, Alabama.

7 October 1864

Eastern Theater, Siege of Petersburg Confederate troops north of Richmond try to push back Federal troops and the two sides clash on the roads leading to Darbyville and New Market. The attack fails, though, as the Southerners are forced to retreat.
Valley Campaign Sheridan's cavalry continues its work destroying crops and rounding up livestock. Sheridan writes Grant that so far his men have burned 2000 barns filled with wheat, hay and farm implements, destroyed in excess of 70 flour mills, driven off 4000 head of livestock and killed over 3000 sheep to feed the army. When he is through, he adds, the area between Winchester and Staunton 'will have little in it for man or beast.'
Western Theater, Franklin and Nashville Campaign Elements of Hood's and Sherman's armies collide at Dallas, Georgia, as the Confederate general tries to maneuver his troops toward Alabama.
Naval The USS *Wachusett* traps and then captures the CSS *Florida* at the Brazilian port of Bahia. The Brazilians protest and even fire at the USS vessel, but it still makes off with its prize. To mollify the Brazilians, Secretary of State William H Seward will later condemn the Union captain's action as unlawful.

8 October 1864

Eastern Theater, Valley Campaign Union and Confederate cavalry skirmish at Tom's Brook and in the Luray Valley.
Naval The Confederate *Shenandoah*, or *Sea King*, sails from London and on 19 October will be commissioned as a roving commerce destroyer.

9 October 1864

Eastern Theater, Valley Campaign After suffering Confederate cavalry attacks for the past few days, Sheridan turns his cavalry divisions led by George Custer and Wesley Merritt against the enemy's horsemen. The Confederates flee up the Valley after an en-

gagement in which they lose 300 prisoners and suffer another 57 casualties. There is also fighting in Fauquier Country, Virginia, just to the east of the Valley.
Trans-Mississippi Sterling Price and his men continue northwestward away from St Louis capturing the Missouri towns of Boonville, Russellville and California.

10 October 1864

Eastern Theater, Valley Campaign Sheridan withdraws his army north to Cedar Creek. At the same time his VI Corps starts out toward Washington.
Western Theater, Franklin and Nashville Campaign Hood's and Sherman's men skirmish near Rome, Georgia, as the Confederate army continues to move westward. Meanwhile, a Federal expedition tries to attack General Forrest at Eastport, Mississippi, by ferrying soldiers up the river by boat. The Confederates, however, disable the Union vessel, and the Northern troops are left stranded, able to do little more than make good their escape.

11 October 1864

Western Theater, Franklin and Nashville Campaign Sherman concentrates his troops at Rome, Georgia, after receiving word that Hood's army is just south of the city. Federal and Southern troops clash along the road between Atlanta and Flat Creek. Farther north, Confederate cavalry raid Fort Donelson, the site of a black recruiting station, but are driven off by Northern soldiers after a brief battle.
Trans-Mississippi Sterling Price and his men continue to slash their way northwestward through Missouri, skirmishing with Federals at Boonville and Brunswick.

12 October 1864

Western Theater, Franklin and Nashville Campaign Parts of Hood's and Sherman's armies clash at Reseca, La Fayette and on the Coosaville Road near Rome, Georgia, while farther north there is some fighting at Greeneville, Tennessee.
Naval Rear Admiral David D Porter assumes command of the North Atlantic Blockading Squadron relieving acting Rear Admiral Samuel P Lee. Porter, who was only a lieutenant at the outbreak of war, won renown for the role he played at New Orleans, and with Grant at Forts Henry and Doneslon and at Vicksburg.

13 October 1864

Eastern Theater, Valley Campaign Taking advantage of Sheridan's withdrawal to Cedar Creek, Jubal Early moves his army back to its old position at Fisher's Hill. Fighting breaks out as the advancing Confederates probe enemy lines. Farther north, John S Mosby and his band of partisan rangers derail a passenger train near Kearneyville. They rob two Federal paymasters on board of nearly $173,000 and then burn the train before making their escape.
Western Theater, Franklin and Nashville Campaign Hood's troops seize control of the railroad north of Reseca, Georgia, leading to Tunnel Hill, and there are a number of isolated engagements with Union detachments along the rail line.

Above: Joseph Shelby was one of the most daring Southern guerrilla leaders and gained fame for the capture of Glasgow, Missouri.

14 October 1864

Eastern Theater, Valley Campaign Sporadic fighting continues between elements of Early's and Sheridan's armies as the two forces probe each other's lines at Cedar Creek.
Trans-Mississippi Sterling Price calls on the people of Missouri to help him redeem the state. His men fight Federal soldiers near Glasgow. There is also an action at Danville, Missouri.

15 October 1864

Trans-Mississippi Shelby's 'Iron Brigade,' part of Price's cavalry, captures the town of Glasgow, Missouri, forcing the surrender of more than 400 Federals under the command of Colonel Chester Harding Jr. Shelby's men also occupy Sedalia after 700 defenders flee the town.

16 October 1864

Eastern Theater, Valley Campaign General Philip Sheridan leaves his army at Cedar Creek for a conference with President Lincoln and General Grant on the military situation in the Valley.
Western Theater Elements of the two armies in northern Georgia continue to clash as the Confederates harass the Union supply lines.
Trans-Mississippi In Missouri, Price and his men reach the town of Ridgely and occupy it as they continue to move northwestward along the Missouri River.

17 October 1864

Western Theater General Beauregard assumes command of the Confederate armies east of the Mississippi. In northern Georgia General Hood and his army move toward Gadsden, Alabama, breaking off, for

Above: Members of the band of the US 107th Colored Infantry Regiment pose for a photograph outside their camp.

the most part, their attacks on Sherman's supply lines. The Confederate general hopes that by heading north and eventually into Tennessee, he will be able to force Sherman to do the same, thus freeing Georgia of the invading army.

Trans-Mississippi Fighting continues with Federals both to the rear and in front of Price as the cavalry rides toward Lexington in northwest Missouri. Federal forces are now closing in on the Confederate raiders from three directions: General Samuel R Curtis, commander of the Department of Kansas, approaching from the west; Alfred Pleasonton and his cavalry pursuing from the rear; and General Alfred J Smith coming up from the south. The Confederate cavalry burns Smithville as it passes through the town and also occupies Carrolton during the day.

18 October 1864

Eastern Theater, Valley Campaign General Jubal Early and his staff plan an all-out attack on the Federals at Cedar Creek to be launched in the morning.

19 October 1864

The North A small group of Confederate raiders, led by Lieutenant Bennet H Young and composed mainly of escaped prisoners, crosses the Canadian border and descends upon the small Vermont town of St Albans. The men rob three local banks of over $200,000 but resistance by local citizens prevents them from carrying out their plans to burn the town. Eleven of the raiders escape back over the border where they will later be arrested and then released by Canadian officials after that government decides it lacks jurisdiction.

Eastern Theater, Valley Campaign Concealed by Three Top Mountain and early morning fog, the three divisions of Early's corps attack the left flank of the Union army commanded by General George Crook. Completely surprised, the Federal flank falls back in disarray with one division forming a new

line north of Middletown while the rest regroup to the west of the town. General Sheridan, on his way back from a conference in Washington, has spent last night in Winchester. He hears the sound of battle and meets streams of stragglers retreating down the Valley Pike as he rides toward Cedar Creek. Turning his men around, he gallops on, arriving at the front at about 1030 hours. Meanwhile the Confederate charge slows to a stop as soldiers fall out of line to loot the enemy's camp. The Confederates fail to follow up their surprise attack and at 1600 the Union forces counterattack, forcing them to flee in disorganized retreat. Although Union casualties are higher (5665 for the North compared to an estimated 2910 for the South), they decisively win the battle, forcing the enemy from the field.

20 October 1864

Washington President Lincoln formally establishes Thanksgiving as a national holiday.

Eastern Theater, Valley Campaign In the wake of General Early's defeat at Cedar Creek, elements of Sheridan's army strike at the Confederates as they retreat toward Fisher's Hill.

21 October 1864

Trans-Mississippi There is more fighting between Federals and advancing Confederate troops under Sterling Price at the Little Blue River. The Union troops again fall back to the west.

22 October 1864

Western Theater, Franklin and Nashville Campaign General Hood's army is in Gadsden, Alabama, preparing to go to Guntersville and from there on to Tennessee. General Sherman's troops are in Gaylesville, Alabama, just west of Rome, Georgia. From this position, the Union general feels he can protect both Chattanooga and Atlanta from the Confederates.

Trans-Mississippi Deciding that his best chances of survival lie in defeating the various enemy forces closing in on him before they can unite, General Price orders

Shelby's troops to attack the Federals in front while John S Marmaduke holds off the enemy to the rear. After Shelby's men have completed their work, Price plans to turn his entire force around to meet Alfred Pleasonton's pursuing cavalry. Shelby hits the enemy and, finding an exposed flank, forces the Northerners under General Samuel Curtis to fall back to Bush Creek near Westport, where they form a new line.

23 October 1864

Trans-Mississippi Following up its success of yesterday, Shelby's cavalry again strikes at General Curtis' troops, now near Westport, Missouri. The Federals check this assault, though, and launch a powerful counterattack. While this is going on, Pleasonton's Union cavalry breaks through General Marmaduke's rearguard defense, forcing the harried Southerners from the field. Pleasonton then closes in on Shelby's Confederates from the rear, who in turn are forced to retreat. The Battle of Westport, involving some 20,000 Federal troops and over 8000 Confederates, results in about 1500 casualties for each side and will mark the end of the last serious threat to Union control of Missouri.

24 October 1864

Trans-Mississippi Sterling Price retreats south along the border between Kansas and Missouri with a long train of plunder which his men have captured in their month-long raid through Missouri. After some delay, the bulk of the Union cavalry pursues the fleeing Confederates.

25 October 1864

Western Theater, Franklin and Nashville Campaign Elements of Hood's army, still in northern Alabama, clash with Union troops near Round Mountain, in Turkeytown and on the Gadsden Road.

Trans-Mississippi Federal cavalry catch up with Price's retreating columns at Marais des Cygnes, Kansas. In the fight that ensues, they capture two Confederate generals (including John Marmaduke), four colonels and 1000 men. The Southerners also lose ten pieces of artillery in the engagement.

26 October 1864

Western Theater, Franklin and Nashville Campaign The Army of Tennessee arrives at Decatur, Alabama, which is held by Federal troops. Hood had originally hoped to launch his invasion of Tennessee from here but finds that General Forrest and his cavalry have been delayed. After some artillery fire against Federal positions at Decatur, Hood moves his army farther west.

Trans-Mississippi Union troops ambush and kill the notorious 'Bloody' Bill Anderson near Richmond, Missouri. Anderson had once ridden with William Quantrill.

27 October 1864

Eastern Theater, Siege of Petersburg General Grant orders an assault on enemy positions to gain control of the Boydton Road and Southside Railroad southwest of Petersburg. A strong defense under the leadership of General Ambrose P Hill, however, frustrates the Union drive. Unable to get necessary reinforcements, the Federals withdraw,

Above: Sheridan arrives at Cedar Creek to save the beleaguered Union forces from defeat.

leaving the transport lines still in the hands of the Confederates. The assault involves over 40,000 Federal troops and 20,000 Southerners, with the former suffering 1194 killed or wounded and 564 missing. Confederate casualties are not recorded.

Naval During the night, an expedition of 15 men led by Lieutenant William B Cushing ascends the Roanoke River in a steam craft and blows up the Confederate ram *Albemarle* by smashing through its protective log boom and then exploding a torpedo against the *Albemarle*'s hull. For planning and executing this bold scheme, Cushing will be promoted to the rank of lieutenant commander.

28 October 1864

Trans-Mississippi Troops under General Samuel Curtis again catch up with Price's fleeing troops and attack the Confederates at Newtonia, Missouri. The timely arrival of Federal reinforcements during the engagement again forces Price to withdraw.

29 October 1864

Western Theater Cooperating with Abraham Buford, who had built a trap for Federal boats on the Tennessee River near Fort Heiman and Fort Henry, General Forrest and his men capture the steamer *Mazeppa*. Meanwhile, Hood, still waiting for Forrest to join his army so he can launch his planned invasion into Tennessee, continues to move his army westward.

30 October 1864

Western Theater, Franklin and Nashville Campaign The Army of Tennessee moves into Tuscumbia, Alabama. The Confederates also cross the Tennessee River and seize the town of Florence. Forrest, continuing to operate against Federal vessels, captures two transports and the gunboat *Undine* from the enemy. Meanwhile, Federal troops move from Chattanooga to Pulaski, Tennessee, as

Below: General Sheridan leads his cavalry in a charge against Confederate positions at Cedar Creek, 19 October 1864. Although the North lost heavily, the Southern forces retreated.

Above: The Confederate port of Savannah was the main objective of Sherman's March to the Sea which began on 16 November 1864.

General George Thomas prepares to meet an invasion into Tennessee.
Naval   The CSS *Olustee* runs the Federal blockade outside Wilmington, North Carolina, and begins to prey on enemy shipping.

31 October 1864

The North   Nevada enters the Union as the 36th state. Although Lincoln was considerably reassured by the elections held earlier in the month in Pennsylvania, Ohio and Indiana, he still believes the presidential election will be very close. Nevada, which is felt to be safely Republican, can now contribute three electoral votes to the election because of its statehood.
Naval   Seven Federal vessels under the command of William H Macomb capture Plymouth, North Carolina.

1 November 1864

Western Theater, Franklin and Nashville Campaign   General Alfred J Smith, who has been in Missouri to check Price's invasion, moves his men to Nashville, where they will reinforce General George Thomas. Thomas is preparing his defenses to meet a threatened attack by Hood's army. Meanwhile, General Forrest takes his makeshift navy of captured Federal vessels up-river to Reynoldsville Island, just south of Johnsonville, Tennessee, where he prepares another ambush.

2 November 1864

The North   Secretary of State William H Seward warns the mayor of New York of rumors that Confederate agents in Canada are planning to set fire to New York City on election day.
Western Theater   Federals recapture the *Venus* from Forrest just south of Johnsonville, Tennessee. The *Venus* is one of the boats that Forrest's men had taken at their 'trap' downstream a few days earlier.

3 November 1864

Western Theater   The Federal IV Corps arrive in Pulaski, Tennessee. These troops had been sent by General Thomas to strengthen the detachment of troops already at the town against the threatened invasion by the Confederate Army of Tennessee.

4 November 1864

Western Theater   Federal gunboats close in on Forrest's ambush station at Reynoldsville Island, from the north and south, forcing the Confederates to burn the captured *Undine* to prevent its recapture. Forrest then moves his force to the outskirts of Johnsonville where they shell a Federal naval supply depot causing heavy damage.

6 November 1864

The North   Colonel Benjamin Sweet and his men arrest close to 100 men in Chicago on charges of plotting against the US. Confederate agents and Copperhead sympathizers, according to the alleged plans, were to release prisoners being held at Camp Douglas on election day. The prisoners then would seize the polls, stuff the ballot boxes and burn the city of Chicago. Although the plot will never be entirely substantiated, many of those arrested are heavily armed, and at the home of one of the conspirators a large cache of arms and ammunition is found.
Trans-Mississippi   Price's men, who have now retreated out of Missouri, fight Federal troops at Cane Hill, Arkansas. There is also fighting between Union soldiers and Indians in the Nebraska Territory.

8 November 1864

The North   It is election day in the North. President Lincoln is elected to a second term over General George B McClellan. With Tennessee war-governor Andrew Johnson as his new running mate, Lincoln wins over 55 percent of the popular vote and carries every participating state except Delaware, Kentucky and New Jersey. His strongest support comes from the soldiers on active duty who

give 'Old Abe' 119,754 out of slightly more than 154,000 votes. In the electoral college, Lincoln gets 212 votes to McClellan's 21.

9 November 1864

Western Theater   General Sherman in Kingston, Georgia, issues preliminary orders in preparation for a 'march to the sea.' Although Hood had hoped that by invading Tennessee he could draw Sherman northward, the Union general believes that Thomas' troops in and around Nashville will be able to handle the Army of Tennessee.

10 November 1864

Washington   President Lincoln addresses a crowd at the White House gathered to help him celebrate his recent victory at the polls. He tells the audience that he believes the results vindicate Americans' belief in democracy, and urges a united effort to save the country.
Eastern Theater, Valley Campaign   Despite his recent defeat at Cedar Creek, Jubal Early moves his shattered army down the Valley toward Sheridan to continue harassing the Federals.
Western Theater, March to the Sea   Destroying all property which might be of use to the Confederates, Sherman's army leaves Kingston for Atlanta. He also gives orders for the destruction of railroad lines around Atlanta as well as those going north from Reseca, Georgia.

11 November 1864

Western Theater   Union troops in Rome, Georgia, destroy everything that might be of military use in that city and then move south to join the rest of the army at Atlanta. Meanwhile, skirmishing continues between Federals and elements of Hood's army near Shoal Creek, Alabama; and in eastern Tennessee there is fighting at Russellville.

13 November 1864

Eastern Theater, Valley Campaign   Early moves his army back to New Market and part of his troops set off for Richmond and Petersburg to reinforce General Lee's troops.
Trans-Mississippi   There is fighting between Indians and Federal soldiers near Fort Larned, Kansas, while in Missouri Northern troops scour Pemiscot County in search of enemy guerrillas.

14 November 1864

Western Theater, March to the Sea   With Sherman's army now returned to Atlanta, soldiers continue their work tearing up railroad lines, burning bridges and destroying anything else of use to the enemy. Meanwhile, in Tennessee, General John M Schofield arrives in Pulaski to assume command of the forces in that city, the first line of defense against Hood.

15 November 1864

Western Theater, March to the Sea   Confederate militia and Federals clash around Atlanta while other Northern soldiers complete the destruction of the city in preparation for the march to Savannah. In northern Alabama, Hood's army continues to skirmish with Federals near Shoal Creek on the Tennessee River.

16 November 1864

Western Theater, March to the Sea About seven in the morning, General William T Sherman and his army leave Atlanta for Savannah carrying 20 days rations with them. By and large, however, the 62,000-man army is to live off the land, foraging liberally throughout the Georgia countryside. Sherman has also instructed his division commanders that they should take any livestock that they might deem necessary from the inhabitants and if they meet resistance 'should order and enforce a devastation more or less relentless.' To oppose them, the Confederates have about 13,000 men including 3000 state militia under the command of George W Smith and a 10,000-man cavalry force led by Joseph Wheeler. These troops are concentrated around Lovejoy Station. Sherman's army marches out in two wings, the right heading down the Macon Railroad toward Lovejoy Station while the left wing moves along the Georgia Railroad toward Augusta. By deploying his troops along two diverging paths, Sherman hopes to deceive the enemy as to his true destination. As the right wing approaches Lovejoy Station, the Confederates there, except two cavalry brigades, move south toward Macon. The Union cavalry defeats the remaining troops, pursuing them to Beaver Creek station where they capture 50 prisoners. In northern Alabama, Hood's army continues to battle Federal units at Shoal Creek as General Forrest and his cavalry finally arrive to reinforce the Army of Tennessee. Forrest's cavalry were intended to compensate for the loss of Wheeler's troops now harassing the Federals in Georgia. In eastern Tennessee, Breckenridge and his raiders skirmish with Federals at Strawberry Plain before he withdraws toward southwest Virginia.

17 November 1864

The Confederacy Jefferson Davis writes a letter to several Georgia state senators denouncing all plans involving individual states negotiating for peace with the North.
Western Theater, March to the Sea The two wings of Sherman's army continue to diverge, one going east and the other south. There is some fighting along the way at Towalega Bridge. Davis meanwhile orders General William J Hardee to assume command of all troops in Georgia. To the north, there is increased fighting in northern Alabama with clashes occurring at Maysville and at New Market.

18 November 1864

Western Theater, March to the Sea At Macon, Georgia, President Davis orders Howell Cobb, commander of the Georgia reserves, to get out every man he can to oppose Sherman's army. He also tells him to employ black slaves to help obstruct roads in the path of the Federal army.
Trans-Mississippi Even with Price driven from Missouri, Confederate bands and guerrilla units continue to harass Federal troops. Today there is fighting at Fayette between the two sides.

19 November 1864

Trans-Mississippi Federal soldiers continue to battle Indians in the Nebraska Territory, today at Plum Creek Station.
Naval President Lincoln lifts the Federal blockade at Norfolk, Virginia, and at Fernandina and Pensacola, Florida. These ports are now under the control of Union forces.

20 November 1864

Western Theater, March to the Sea Sherman's troops continue their progress, fighting enemy cavalry, home-guards and state militia at Clinton, Walnut Creek, East Macon and Griswoldsville, Georgia.

21 November 1864

Western Theater, Franklin and Nashville Campaign Hood moves his Army of Tennessee out of Florence, Alabama, northeastward toward Tennessee. His force includes 30,000 infantry and 8000 cavalry. The Confederate general had originally hoped to launch his invasion from Decatur as long as three weeks ago but for a variety of reasons (including the belated arrival of General Forrest and his cavalry) he delayed. During this period General Thomas has had time to improve his defenses and strengthen his army in and around Nashville as well as to reinforce Federal outposts at Pulaski and Columbia, Tennessee. Now on the move,

Below: General Sherman reviews the cavalry of Kilpatrick outside the town of Marietta, Georgia, on 15 November 1864.

Above: A rendition of the campaign in Georgia. The march involved the wholesale destruction of Southern property and industry.

though, Hood plans to place his army between that of General Schofield in Pulaski and the body of Federals to the north.
March to the Sea   General William J Hardee arrives in Macon to oversee the defenses of Georgia. From the disposition of the two wings of the enemy's army, he decides that Augusta or Savannah and not Macon must be the objective of the Northern army. He orders General Smith to move his troops eastward to oppose the advance of the Federal right wing. General Wheeler, meanwhile, is to continue to use his cavalry to strike at the enemy's rear columns.

22 November 1864

Western Theater, Franklin and Nashville Campaign   Hood's army moves northeastward toward Columbia, hoping to capture that city and cut off Union General Schofield's troops in Pulaski from the rest of the Federals to the north. Schofield, however, realizing what is afoot, begins to evacuate his troops northward to Columbia.
Western Theater, March to the Sea   In Millegeville, the Georgia state legislature issues a call for troops to check Sherman's invasion and then flees the state capital just before Sherman's left wing, commanded by General Henry W Slocum, occupies the city. The Georgia state militia attacks the Union right wing in a vain effort to halt its progress.

23 November 1864

Western Theater, Franklin and Nashville Campaign   Skirmishing breaks out at Fouche Springs, Henryville and Mount Pleasant, Tennessee, as Hood's army continues to march toward Columbia.
Western Theater, March to the Sea   In Georgia, the two wings of Sherman's army reunite in Millegeville, where there is more fighting between Federals and state militia. Fighting also takes place at Ball's Ferry and at a railroad bridge belonging to the Georgia Central over the Oconee River.

24 November 1864

Western Theater, Franklin and Nashville Campaign   The front column of General Schofield's troops under the command of General Jacob D Cox arrives in Columbia, Tennessee, just in time to help Federals already there drive off General Forrest's Confederate cavalry. By the end of the day, the rest of Schofield's men arrive and dig in south of the Duck River.

25 November 1864

The North   Southern arsonists, acting under orders from agents in Canada, set fire to 10 hotels in New York City, including the Belmont, Metropolitan, Saint James and Astor House. Alarms also go off in two downtown theaters and a fire is set at Barnum's Museum. Strangely, none of the fires does serious damage and all are quickly extinguished. Later R C Kennedy will be arrested and executed for setting the blaze at Barnum's Museum.
Western Theater, March to the Sea   Cavalry under General Joseph Wheeler battle Federals outside Sanderson, Georgia, before the Federals succeed in occupying the town.

26 November 1864

Western Theater, Franklin and Nashville Campaign   Hood's Army of Tennessee arrives outside Columbia only to find Federal troops well-entrenched both south and north of the Duck River.
March to the Sea   Fighting continues between Confederates and elements of Sherman's army at Sanderson, Georgia.
Trans-Mississippi   The Nebraska Territory is again the scene of fighting between Federal soldiers and Indians, this time near Plum Creek Station and at Spring Creek.

27 November 1864

Eastern Theater, The Siege of Petersburg   The steamer *Greyhound*, General Benjamin Butler's floating headquarters, blows up on the James River, apparently an act of Southern sabotage. In West Virginia, Federal soldiers skirmish with the enemy at the town of Moorefield.

Western Theater, Franklin and Nashville Campaign   Believing that Hood's army will attack from south of Columbia, General Schofield moves his troops north of the Duck River in the evening, burning the bridges behind him and digging in to prepare for the assault.
March to the Sea   At Waynesboro, Georgia, Sherman's march is interrupted as the Confederate cavalry strike at the Union army.

28 November 1864

Eastern Theater, Valley Campaign   Confederate General Thomas L Rosser leads his cavalry on a raid into Maryland where they destroy a bridge on the Baltimore and Ohio Railroad and then retreat back up the Valley into Virginia.
Western Theater, Franklin and Nashville Campaign   With troops under Stephen D Lee staying at Columbia to create the impression that an attack will come from the south, General Hood moves the rest of his troops east of that city, planning to cross the Duck River north of the Federal army and cut off its retreat. During the afternoon Forrest's cavalry cross the river about 10 miles north of the Federals near Spring Hill, driving the Union cavalry north toward Franklin.
Western Theater, March to the Sea   Fighting in Georgia occurs along Sherman's advance at Buckhead Church and Buckhead Creek. There are also cavalry engagements at Davisborough and Waynesboro.

29 November 1864

Western Theater, Franklin and Nashville Campaign   Having been driven off to Franklin by enemy cavalry, General James H Wilson, Schofield's cavalry commander, sends back word to his commander at Columbia that the enemy has crossed at Spring Hill and the Federal army is in danger of being cut off to the north. Schofield still believes that he is to be attacked from the south but he does send some troops up to Spring Hill to investigate Wilson's report. Meanwhile, in the morning hours, Confederate infantry begin to cross over the Duck River north of the Federal army, with more following in the afternoon. Reports of these activities come back to Schofield from his reconnaissance troops and around 1500 hours the Union general starts his army north to Franklin. Although Confederate troops arrive at Spring Hill before him and Hood himself is on hand over an hour before dark, Schofield somehow manages to get his whole army past the enemy during the night.
Trans-Mississippi, Sand Hill Massacre   Colorado militia under the command of Colonel John M Chivington descend upon the Cheyenne village at Sand Creek, Colorado Territory, without warning, killing almost one-third of its residents and torturing and mutilating many of their victims. A large proportion of the dead are women and children. For some time previous, there have been raids by Indians against gold miners and other settlers in the area. Although the Cheyenne, under the leadership of Chief Black Kettle, deny that they were involved in the raids and are under the protection of the Federal garrison at Fort Lyon, Chivington and his men decide to launch a reprisal on the settlement for the past attacks. The massacre

will be later officially condemned by the Federal government.

30 November 1864

Western Theater, Franklin and Nashville Campaign Escaping the trap the Confederates had planned for him, General Schofield arrives in Franklin with his 32,000-man force in the morning. The Union general deploys his troops in a long arc south and west of Franklin (nestled in a bend of the Harpeth River) while he works to get his supply train north of the river. The Confederates are slow to pursue the Federals but by 1530 hours the Army of Tennessee has arrived south of the city and launches a full-scale assault over two miles of open field and against entrenched positions. Bloody hand-to-hand fighting develops as the Southerners several times reach the enemy lines only to be repulsed with heavy losses. While the infantry assaults are in progress, cavalry units from the two armies also fight each other both to the west and to the east of the city. On both flanks, however, the Confederates are ultimately forced to withdraw. At 2100 Hood finally calls off his attacks and, during the night, Schofield withdraws his men across the river and toward Nashville. During the battle, 27,939

Union soldiers are engaged in fighting while the Confederates have 26,897 men in the field. Northern casualties are 2326, including 1104 missing, while the South loses 6252 men of whom 702 are missing.

Western Theater, March to the Sea In Georgia, Sherman continues his march southeastward with a skirmish at Louisville. At Hilton Head, South Carolina, Federal troops launch an attack aimed at cutting the Charleston and Savannah Railroad. The Georgia militia, however, meets these troops at Honeyhill and forces them to withdraw.

1 December 1864

Western Theater, Franklin and Nashville Campaign Schofield's army reaches Nashville where it joins the troops already there under the command of General George Thomas. Hood's army follows quickly on the Federals' heels and encamps southeast of the city. Both sides are preparing themselves for battle around Nashville.

2 December 1864

Western Theater, Franklin and Nashville Campaign Too weak to attack the strong Federal lines after its severe losses at Franklin, Hood's Army of Tennessee begins to for-

tify its own position southeast of Nashville. The Union lines, carefully prepared by Thomas during the last month, ring the Tennessee capital extending north on both sides to the Cumberland River. During the day, Confederate cavalry carry out raids against isolated positions on the Federal lines.

3 December 1864

Western Theater, March to the Sea The four corps of Sherman's army continue their march toward Savannah. They meet some resistance during the day from Southern soldiers at Thomas Station.

4 December 1864

Western Theater, March to the Sea Federal cavalry under General Hugh J Kilpatrick are struck by Confederate cavalry as they guard railroad wrecking crews near Waynesboro, Georgia. After some sharp fighting, the Federals finally force the enemy to retreat. More fighting breaks out at Statesborough, Lumpkin Station, along the Georgia Central Railroad, and on the Little Ogeechee River as the

Below: The Battle of Franklin ended when Hood's Confederates were unable to pierce the defense lines held by General Schofield's troops.

Above: By early December 1864, Hood's men had been forced back into Nashville, a city circled by strong Union entrenchments.

badly outnumbered Confederates continue to harass the enemy army.

Franklin and Nashville Campaign Around Nashville, Confederate cavalry strike at enemy outposts at White's Station and Bell's Mills. During the next week Confederate horsemen will have little opposition in the area, as General George Thomas busies his cavalry in rounding up horses for several thousand soldiers without mounts.

Below: Kilpatrick's cavalry launch their final charge against Southern troops guarding a vital railroad near Waynesboro, Georgia.

5 December 1864

Western Theater, Franklin and Nashville Campaign General Hood sends Nathan B Forrest with his cavalry and a division of infantry to Murfreesboro where they are to operate against some 10,000 Federal troops garrisoned there under the command of General L H Rosseau.

6 December 1864

Western Theater, Franklin and Nashville Campaign General Grant, who has been urging Thomas to attack the Confederates as soon as possible ever since they arrived south of Nashville, now sends him a direct order to 'attack Hood at once.' Many of Thomas' cavalrymen, though, are still without mounts and he has been delaying until enough

horses can be found. He warns Grant that an attack would be risky without cavalry. Confederates, meanwhile, launch a raid from Paris, Tennessee, to Hopkinsville, Kentucky.

7 December 1864

Western Theater, Franklin and Nashville Campaign In Murfreesboro, General L H Rosseau orders Robert L Milroy to make a reconnaissance in force against enemy troops commanded by General Forrest, who has been sent by Hood two days earlier to operate against Federals in the Murfreesboro area. Milroy defeats Forrest's men, forcing them from the field and capturing over 200 men and 14 guns.

8 December 1864

Eastern Theater, Siege of Petersburg Skirmishing takes place along Hatcher's Run, south of Petersburg, as Federal expeditions scout that area.

Western Theater, March to the Sea In Georgia, Sherman's army, nearing Savannah, skirmishes at Ebenezer Creek and near Bryan Court House.

Naval General Benjamin Butler takes 6500 men down the James River to Fort Monroe to join a naval expedition aimed at destroying Fort Fisher and closing the vital Southern port of Wilmington.

9 December 1864

Eastern Theater, Siege of Petersburg More fighting takes place between Federal reconnaissance troops and the Confederates along Hatcher's Run, south of Petersburg.

Western Theater, Franklin and Nashville Campaign Grant issues an order replacing General George Thomas with John Schofield as commander of Union troops in Nashville.

The general in chief suspends the order, however, when Thomas tells him that he had intended to attack on 10 December but a severe storm of freezing rain has forced him to alter his plans. To the south, fighting breaks out at the Ogeechee Canal, at Monteith Swamp and at Cuyler's Plantation.

10 December 1864

Eastern Theater, Siege of Petersburg Skirmishing occurs at Fort Holly, near Petersburg.

Western Theater, March to the Sea General William T Sherman and his army of 60,000 men arrive south of Savannah. In and around the city there are 18,000 well-entrenched Confederates under the command of General William J Hardee. The Southerners have flooded the rice fields around Savannah so that there are only five narrow strips of land over which a Federal attack could be launched. Sherman, surveying the situation, rejects an assault and instead decides to besiege the city. His army, now stationary, must worry about providing itself with necessary supplies. Although his men have adequate food, forage for horses is a daily concern. For this reason, Fort McAllister, located on the coast south of Savannah, is of vital importance. If the Federals can capture this fort, it will reopen contact with the navy and allow for the provisioning of Sherman's army. In Knoxville, a Federal expedition sets out under the command of General George Stoneman aimed at destroying enemy salt and lead mines in southwest Virginia and eliminating enemy troops in the area.

Naval Union troops capture and burn the Confederate steamer *Ida* on the Savannah River.

11 December 1864

Western Theater, Franklin and Nashville Campaign Thomas is again bombarded by messages from Grant telling him to strike the

Below: Fort Monroe, Virginia, was the target of a Union operation begun on 8 December 1864.

Above: A Confederate 100-pounder gun in position at Fort Fisher, a work defending the seaways near Wilmington.

enemy. He replies that he will do so as soon as weather permits.

Western Theater, March to the Sea Along the coast of Georgia, Federal soldiers rebuild the King's Bridge, which the Confederates destroyed, in preparation for an attack on Fort McAllister.

12 December 1864

Western Theater, Franklin and Nashville Campaign In Nashville, Thomas sends General Halleck a message telling him he will attack as soon as the ice on the ground melts sufficiently to allow troop movements. In eastern Tennessee, General George Stoneman and his cavalry force skirmish with the enemy at Big Creek near Rogersville.

13 December 1864

Western Theater, March to the Sea Federal troops charge across a field strewn with mines and other obstacles and capture Fort McAllister from the 230 Confederates garri-

soning the fort. The fall of Fort McAllister to Northern troops reopens communication and supply lines to Sherman's army. In Tennessee, meanwhile, part of General Stoneman's force defeats Confederate troops commanded by General Basil W Duke at Kingsport.

Franklin and Nashville Campaign Today also, Grant orders Major General John Á Logan to proceed to Nashville to assume command of the army in that city. Grant himself leaves for Washington, intending to go on to Nashville to speed up operations there. While these proposed changes in the Union command are in the works, Confederates attack a railroad train near Murfreesboro.

Naval A naval expedition designed to reduce Fort Fisher, sails from Fort Monroe for the North Carolina port of Wilmington.

14 December 1864

Western Theater, Franklin and Nashville Campaign General Thomas wires Washington that he plans to attack Hood's army on the 15th. To the east, Stoneman's Union raiders again encounter the enemy, this time at Bristol, Tennessee. After a fight they capture 300 Confederates.

Naval US naval vessels begin a bombardment of Forts Rosedew and Beaulieu on the Vernon River. The action will continue for a week.

15 December 1864

Western Theater, Franklin and Nashville Campaign Union troops at Nashville attack the Army of Tennessee. Using troops commanded by General James B Steedman to hit the enemy's right and divert Hood's attention in that direction, General Thomas throws the bulk of his army's strength at the Confederate left in an attempt to envelop it from the west. Outnumbered two to one, Hood's army also fights the battle without the aid of most of its cavalry (which is away at Murfreesboro). During the day, the Confederates gradually contract their lines as the

Above: Union officers and their families stand for the camera on top of a new railroad bridge.

Union assault pushes them from their original positions and to the south. The Federals gain considerable ground but by nightfall the enemy army, though bruised, is still intact. Thomas believes the enemy will withdraw, however, during the night. General Stoneman's raiders, meanwhile, again strike the enemy at Abingdon and Glade Springs, Virginia.

16 December 1864

Western Theater, Franklin and Nashville Campaign Morning finds the Confederate army still drawn up southeast of Nashville. After some initial probing, the Union army follows up its successes of yesterday by basically repeating the same battle plan. With Steedman's troops again holding the Confederate right, the bulk of the Northern army is thrown against the enemy's left. As Union soldiers finally succeed in turning the left flank, the Confederate center also collapses and Hood's shattered army flees in disorganized retreat. The right flank fights off the Federals with a desperate rearguard action as the Southern army plunges south toward Franklin. Close to 50,000 Federal troops see action in the two days of fighting while the Confederates have only slightly more than 23,000 in the field. Casualties are surprisingly light (387 killed, 2562 wounded and 112 missing for the Federals; probably not more than 1500 killed and wounded for the South). However, General Thomas reports capturing 4462 enemy soldiers. What is more, the battle effectively destroys the fight-

ing capacity of the Confederacy's Army of Tennessee and it will be the last major battle it will fight during the war.
Western Theater, March to the Sea In Georgia, Sherman's troops skirmish at Hinesville. To the east, Stoneman's cavalry capture Wytheville, Virginia, during the day and also fight the enemy at Marion.
Trans-Mississippi Fighting is reported during the day at Dudley Lake in Arkansas.

17 December 1864

Western Theater, Franklin and Nashville Campaign In Tennessee, Union cavalry under General James H Wilson pursue the fleeing Army of Tennessee, skirmishing with its rearguard at Hollow Tree Gap, the West Harpeth River and Franklin. The Confederates are still without most of their cavalry as Forrest's men have not yet rejoined the army. General James Chalmer's cavalry units, which were badly cut up at Nashville, are the only horsemen available to help fend off the Federals.
Western Theater, March to the Sea In Savannah, General William J Hardee receives word from Jefferson Davis that Lee cannot spare troops from the trenches around Petersburg to reinforce him against Sherman. Sherman, meanwhile, sends the Confederate commander at Savannah a message demanding the surrender of his troops.

18 December 1864

Washington President Lincoln issues a call for 300,000 additional troops to help put down the rebellion.
Western Theater, Franklin and Nashville Campaign At Spring Hill, Federal cavalry again skirmish with Hood's retreating army.

Western Theater, March to the Sea In Savannah, Hardee refuses Sherman's demand for a surrender of the Southern troops in the city.
Naval A fleet of ships commanded by Rear Admiral David Porter joins General Benjamin F Butler's force of 6500 men and together they sail toward Wilmington, North Carolina, where they hope either to capture or destroy Fort Fisher and thus close the port to Confederate blockade-runners.

19 December 1864

Eastern Theater, Valley Campaign In response to Grant's orders, General Sheridan sends General Alfred Thomas A Torbert with 8000 men to operate against the Virginia Central Railroad. They will meet strong resistance from Southern troops along the line and will withdraw on 23 December. Although Early and Sheridan remain in the Shenandoah, their armies are considerably reduced as troops on both sides have been sent off to reinforce the armies in Petersburg.

20 December 1864

Western Theater, Franklin and Nashville Campaign In Tennessee, elements of General Thomas's army pursuing Hood's army pause to build a bridge over the rain-swollen Rutherford Creek and then continue on the trail of the Confederates. The two sides skirmish at Columbia.
Western Theater, March to the Sea As the Federal left moves to encircle Savannah and cut off the Confederates' escape route, General Hardee moves his army out of the city northward toward South Carolina, where he hopes to be reinforced by troops in that state.

21 December 1864

Western Theater, March to the Sea Federal troops occupy the city of Savannah. Tomorrow, Sherman will send Lincoln his memorable message: 'I beg to present you, as a Christmas gift, the city of Savannah.' In southwest Virginia, Stoneman and his cavalry, after accomplishing their mission to destroy enemy salt and lead mines and drive enemy troops from the region, begin to withdraw back toward east Tennessee.

23 December 1864

Western Theater, Franklin and Nashville Campaign Hood's army continues its retreat southward and Federal cavalry continue their pursuit. Both yesterday and today skirmishing occurs between the two sides in the vicinity of Columbus, Tennessee.
Naval After battling storm-tossed seas for several days, Rear Admiral Porter's fleet arrives off Wilmington. General Benjamin F Butler, commander of the landing force, has his men pack an old ship with over 200 tons of gunpowder and then explode it near Fort Fisher, hoping the fort will be destroyed in the blast. The plan fails, though, as the explosion does little but wake the fort's sleepy inhabitants.

24 December 1864

Western Theater, Franklin and Nashville Campaign There are slight skirmishes between Federals and Hood's retreating army near the towns of Lynnville and Richland Creek, Tennessee.
Naval The naval armada under Rear Admiral Porter begins its bombardment of Fort Fisher. By depriving the Confederates of this fortress, the Union command believes it can effectively shut the last major port available to Confederate blockade-runners. During the day, troop transports also arrive. The plan is to storm and capture the fort after the naval bombardment has sufficiently weakened its defenses.

25 December 1864

Western Theater, Franklin and Nashville Campaign Federals skirmish with elements of the Army of Tennessee at Richland Creek, Devil's Gap and White's Station, Tennessee. The Confederates finally reach the Tennessee River.
Naval With close to 60 ships bombarding the fort, Federal troops commanded by General Butler land north of Fort Fisher and

move to within 75 yards of the fort, capturing Half Moon Battery as they advance. A strong fire from the 500 Confederates garrisoning the fortress checks the Union advance, though, and the Federals never renew the attack. Instead, after hearing that Confederate reinforcements (which General Lee had sent on 18 December) are within five miles of the fort, Butler decides an assault will be too costly and he withdraws his men. They will be transported back to Hampton Roads.

26 December 1864

Washington President Lincoln sends a message to General Sherman congratulating him on his success in Savannah and also for Thomas's victory at Nashville. The president admits that he had been apprehensive about the march to the sea, but deferred to the general's judgment. For that reason, he explains, all the honor for the victory must go to Sherman himself.
Western Theater, Franklin and Nashville Campaign Hood's army begins to cross the Tennessee River. There is some fighting at Sugar Creek. The retreat of the Confederates back over the Tennessee both symbolically and effectively brings to an end Hood's bold plan to take his army all the way to the Ohio River.

27 December 1864

Western Theater, Franklin and Nashville Campaign The Confederate Army of Tennessee finishes crossing the Tennessee River and then marches toward the town of Tupelo, Mississippi.

Above: Southern troops abandon Savannah to Sherman's command on 21 December 1864.

28 December 1864

Washington President Lincoln, disappointed by the Federal failure at Fort Fisher, asks Grant for his comments on the ill-fated expedition. The general in chief, who has been calling for Butler's dismissal since summer, is very decided on whom he feels is responsible for the 'gross and culpable failure.'

30 December 1864

Washington In a cabinet meeting, President Lincoln suggests that Butler should be relieved of his command of the Army of the James. Butler's superiors have long felt that he is militarily inept, but Lincoln until now has hesitated to relieve this politically influential general. The expedition to Fort Fisher, however, is an embarrassment to the administration and – some will later explain – in the wake of the recent election, Lincoln's position is less tenuous.
The Confederacy Francis P Blair, an aging but still powerful political figure from Maryland, writes to Jefferson Davis asking for a meeting with the Confederate leader in Richmond. Blair hints broadly that he is interested in exploring possible avenues for peace. This interview will lead directly to the Hampton Roads Conference next month between Lincoln and Confederate Vice-President Alexander Stephens.

Below: The naval yards at Savannah were burnt before they could fall into Northern hands.

These pages: Lincoln delivers his inauguration address after taking his oath from the newly appointed Chief Justice Salmon P Chase on 4 March 1865.

1865

1 January 1865

Eastern Theater, Siege of Petersburg A work crew under the direction of General Butler sets off a large charge of gunpowder on the James River designed to clear away the last remaining portion of a canal being constructed to allow Federal vessels to bypass a large bend in the river. The huge explosion fails to clear the ditch, however, and the ambitious project will remain uncompleted.

Trans-Mississippi Union soldiers, trying to clear Arkansas of its troublesome and ubiquitous guerrilla bands, skirmish with the enemy at Bentonville.

3 January 1865

Western Theater, Carolinas Campaign General Sherman transfers a portion of his army north to Beaufort, South Carolina, in preparation for his campaign through the Carolinas. Skirmishing breaks out along the way at Hardeeville, South Carolina.

4 January 1865

Naval Union troops leave from Bermuda Hundred for a new assault on Fort Fisher. Although most of the 8000 soldiers on this latest expedition against the Confederate fortress at Wilmington, North Carolina, have also been on the unsuccessful mission in December, General Alfred H Terry rather than Butler is now commanding the men who are to launch the land assault against this important enemy position.

Western Theater Union troops operating against the Mobile & Ohio Railroad skirmish with the enemy at Ponds in Mississippi.

5 January 1865

Washington President Lincoln issues a pass through Union lines to James W Singleton. Singleton, like several others, hopes that through unofficial channels he may be able to instigate peace negotiations between the two governments and bring an end to the fighting. Although Lincoln doubts that a peace can be negotiated through the auspices of the Confederate government consistent with the North's demand for reunion, he does not interfere with Singleton's mission and, to the extent of issuing the safe conduct pass, condones the unofficial peace-feeler.

6 January 1865

Washington In the House of Representatives, debate turns to the proposed Constitutional amendment abolishing slavery. Although passed by the Senate at the last session, it had failed to receive the necessary two-thirds vote in the House. The fall elections have increased the Union-Republican majority in the 39th Congress, but it is not scheduled to sit until December of 1865 and Republicans are anxious that the amendment pass before that time. They now set to work to convince enough Democrats to change their vote so that the amendment can be passed in the House and sent to the states for ratification.

The Confederacy Jefferson Davis writes a letter to Alexander Stephens, his continuous and outspoken vice-president, criticizing him for actively working to undermine the people's confidence in their president. Stephens, a long-time critic of the Confederate chief executive and currently active in the

Above: Southern General Beauregard was placed in overall command of Confederate troops in Florida, Georgia and South Carolina in 1865.

Georgia peace movement, has accused Davis of secretly favoring the re-election of Lincoln over McClellan in the recent Northern presidential race.

Trans-Mississippi Federal soldiers skirmish with a group of Confederates at Huntsville, Arkansas.

7 January 1865

Washington The War Office issues an order relieving General Benjamin F Butler of command of the Army of the James and of the Department of Virginia and North Carolina. Major General Edward Ord is named to fill the vacated posts.

Eastern Theater, Valley Campaign More troops from General Philip Sheridan's dwindling army leave the Shenandoah Valley to reinforce the Union army besieging the city of Petersburg.

Trans-Mississippi Federal soldiers battle Indians in the Colorado Territory at Julesburg and Valley Station.

Naval The Danish ironclad *Sphinx* sets sail from Copenhagen to Quiberon Bay, France. The Confederate government has already secretly bought the *Sphinx,* and it will become the CSS *Stonewall.*

8 January 1865

Naval The army forces of General Alfred Terry join up with a large naval fleet commanded by Rear Admiral Porter off the coast of Beaufort, North Carolina. This Federal expedition is aimed at seizing the Confederate position known as Fort Fisher.

9 January 1865

Washington Moses Odell, a Democratic representative from New York, comes out in favor of the proposed constitutional amendment abolishing slavery. Odell will be one of the key Democrats whose vote will make its passage possible.

Western Theater, Franklin and Nashville

Campaign Hood's Army of Tennessee, after its long retreat from Nashville, arrives in Tupelo, Mississippi. In Tupelo, Confederate officials hope somehow to reassemble the broken army after its disastrous campaign in Tennessee. Davis also hopes to be able to transfer troops from Hood's army to reinforce Hardee's men opposing Sherman in the Carolinas.

Carolinas Campaign Secretary of War Edwin Stanton arrives in Savannah, Georgia, to confer with General Sherman on military matters. Stanton also plans to investigate charges made against Sherman of his alleged 'criminal' mistreatment of black freedmen.

10 January 1865

Washington Debate continues in the House of Representatives on the fate of the proposed constitutional amendment abolishing slavery throughout the country. Fernando Wood of New York, arguing against the amendment, tells Congress that passage of the amendment would destroy any chances for securing peace with the South.

Trans-Mississippi Federal soldiers battle Confederates near Glasgow, Missouri.

11 January 1865

Eastern Theater Riding in icy cold weather and deep snow, Confederate General Thomas L Rosser leads 300 men from his cavalry unit on a daring raid into West Virginia. The raiders attack unsuspecting Ohio troops stationed in Beverly, killing or wounding 25 Federals, and then retire with 583 prisoners.

12 January 1865

The Confederacy Francis P Blair, an important Maryland political figure, meets Jefferson Davis in Richmond to discuss possible avenues for peace between North and South. Blair's personal scheme calls for the two sides to join together to expel the French from Mexico. Such a course he feels would not only root out a dangerous incursion against the Monroe Doctrine, but would also help revive a feeling of brotherhood between North and South. Although the scheme does not meet the approval of either Davis or Lincoln, the Confederate president does promise to send a representative to discuss peace with Lincoln. This meeting will take place on 3 February.

Western Theater Davis sends a message to General Richard Taylor urging him to send troops from Tupelo, Mississippi, to reinforce Hardee in his operations against Sherman in the Carolinas. Meanwhile, in Savannah, Secretary of War Edwin Stanton calls a meeting of about 20 of 'the most intelligent of the Negroes' in that city to ask them how they feel blacks could best maintain their newly acquired freedom. Their spokesman, Garrison Frazier, tells Stanton that blacks should be placed on land to farm until they can afford to buy it. He also tells Stanton that because of deepseated prejudice against them, he feels his people would be better off living by themselves rather than among whites. Because of charges concerning Sherman's alleged mistreatment of blacks, Stanton also asks the group what their attitude is toward Sherman. Instead of complaints, however, Frazier tells Stanton, 'We have confidence in General Sherman, and think that what concerns us could not be under better hands.'

13 January 1865

Naval Just after midnight, Admiral Porter's fleet of 59 ships begins its bombardment of Fort Fisher. Having reinforced the fort since the last attack in December, the Confederates now have close to 2000 soldiers and 47 guns in and around the fort itself and another 6000 men at the northern end of the peninsula, commanded by General Braxton Bragg, to oppose any attempted landing by the enemy. In midafternoon, however, Union troops under the command of General Terry establish a beachhead north of Fort Fisher and during the night dig in opposite Bragg's force and prepare to fend off any attack from that quarter.

14 January 1865

Western Theater, Carolinas Campaign Some troops under Sherman's command move from Beaufort to Pocotaligo, South Carolina. In Tupelo, Mississippi, General Pierre G T Beauregard assumes temporary command of the Army of Tennessee; this force will be turned over to General Richard Taylor on 23 January.

Naval General Terry's troops continue to prepare for their attack on Fort Fisher while they also work to secure their position against Bragg's Confederates. With Admiral Porter's fleet pounding away at the fort itself, Colonel William Lamb, commanding the Southern garrison there, sends urgent appeals to Bragg to turn his men loose on the Federal landing expedition which is to the north of the fort.

15 January 1865

Naval At 0800 hours, Admiral Porter's powerful armada opens up again on Fort Fisher, this time at point-blank range. Throughout the morning, the Federals pour a withering fire at the fort and its defenders. In midafternoon, Northern troops launch a twin attack against the fortress: one, composed of 2261 sailors and marines, strikes from the ocean side; the other, 3300 of General Terry's 8000-man landing force, assails the fort from the northwest. The remaining 4700, meanwhile, remain entrenched opposite General Bragg's Confederates to prevent them from interfering in the operation. The fort's defenders repel the assault from the sea but are unable to resist the land attack and at 2200 are forced to surrender. Confederate casualties are about 500, while the combined Union losses are 1341. The Federals, however, take over 1900 prisoners, including General William H Whiting and Colonel William Lamb. Bragg will come under severe criticism from both these men for failing to attack the landing party during the operations.

16 January 1865

Washington Back in Washington, Francis P Blair gives President Lincoln a detailed report on his recent discussion with Jefferson Davis over possibilities for peace between North and South. Later, Lincoln will turn down Blair's scheme for a combined effort to expel France from Mexico, but the Marylander's trip between Richmond and Washington does succeed in getting both sides to agree to meet with one another.

The Confederacy In a move that is widely seen as a direct challenge to Davis' control over military matters, the Confederate Senate passes a resolution (by a vote of 14 to 2) advising the president to appoint Lee as general in chief, to give Joseph Johnston his old command of the Army of Tennessee and to make Beauregard overall commander in Florida, Georgia and South Carolina.

Naval At Fort Fisher, two drunken sailors, looking for loot in the newly captured fortress, stumble into a magazine with their torches and explode 13,000 pounds of gunpowder. Twenty-five Federals die in the blast and another 66 are wounded. Some Confederates, captured in last night's battle, are also killed in the explosion. Meanwhile, Davis, learning of the loss of the fort, sends General Bragg a message urging him to retake the fort if at all possible.

Western Theater To provide for the 10,000 black refugees that had followed his army through Georgia on its March to the Sea, General Sherman issues *Special Field Order Number 15*. The order sets aside all abandoned or confiscated land along the coast of Georgia, including islands, for the settlement of freedmen. Families are to be given 'possessory title' to not more than 40 acres until Congress regulates their title. Although Sherman will later insist that the order was intended as nothing more than a temporary war measure, and almost all of the land will eventually revert to its former owners, many blacks hope this order represents the determination of the government to make land available to the new freedmen.

Below: Confederate batteries in Fort Fisher come under fire from gunboats of Admiral David Porter's fleet, 15 January 1865. Later, after heavy infantry assault, the fort fell.

Above: Sherman's troops move through a swamp during their advance from McPhersonville, South Carolina, on 1 February 1865.

19 January 1865

The Confederacy After much prodding from Davis, General Robert E Lee agrees to accept the position of general in chief of all the armies of the Confederacy. Davis is anxious to head off mounting criticism of his control of the armies by acceding to Congress' 'advice' to appoint Lee as military commander of all Confederate forces.

Western Theater, Carolinas Campaign General Sherman issues orders commanding the units of his army to begin their march into South Carolina. Heavy rains will delay the march until early February, but some troop movement commences.

20 January 1865

Western Theater, Carolinas Campaign Sherman's army in the vicinity of Savannah continues preparations for its northward march.

Trans-Mississippi There is a fight near Fort Larned, Kansas, between Federal troops and Indians.

21 January 1865

Western Theater, Carolinas Campaign General Sherman moves his headquarters out of Savannah toward Beaufort, South Carolina.

23 January 1865

The Confederacy To help mollify elements in Congress critical of his handling of military matters, Davis signs into law a bill passed by Congress last week creating the position of general in chief. Both Congress and Davis are agreed that Lee is to fill the new post.

Western Theater In Mississippi, General Richard Taylor assumes command of the Army of Tennessee. Because many of the troops formerly with this army have been transferred east to reinforce General Hardee in South Carolina, the Army of Tennessee now has fewer than 18,000 soldiers.

Naval Eleven Southern ships set sail down the James River, hoping to attack the Federal squadron off the coast. Four of the ships, however, run aground and the Confederates are forced to abandon the project.

26 January 1865

Western Theater, Carolinas Campaign Although Sherman intends to march his army to Goldsboro, North Carolina, he wants to deceive the enemy as to his real objective. To do so, he sends an expedition out toward Charleston to create the impression that his army will head in that direction. The troops skirmish with the enemy near Pocotaligo, South Carolina. Farther west, there is also fighting near Paint Rock, Alabama.

27 January 1865

Western Theater Fighting breaks out between Union and Confederate troops in DeKalb County, Alabama.

28 January 1865

The Confederacy To represent the South in the upcoming peace talks with President Lincoln, Jefferson Davis appoints Vice-President Alexander Stephens, Robert M T Hunter, president *pro tempore* of the Senate, and Assistant Secretary of War John A Campbell.

Western Theater, Carolinas Campaign There is skirmishing along the Combahee River in South Carolina between elements of Sherman's army and defending Confederates.

30 January 1865

Western Theater, Carolinas Campaign Reinforcements from the Army of Tennessee from Tupelo, Mississippi, begin to arrive in Augusta, Georgia. Altogether some 4000 soldiers will arrive from Tupelo to help General Hardee defend the Carolinas against Sherman's army. Meanwhile, fighting breaks out between the two sides at Lawtonville, South Carolina, as elements of Sherman's army continue their activities in the lower part of the state. In Kentucky, there is fighting at Chaplintown, as Confederates harass Union troops in the state.

31 January 1865

Washington By a vote of 119 to 56, the House of Representatives passes the proposed constitutional amendment abolishing slavery throughout the United States. The amendment will now go to the states. It must be ratified by three-fourths of them before it will become a part of the Constitution. A critical question is whether any of the states formerly or presently in rebellion should be included in ratification calculations. A number of Republicans believe that the rebellious states must first be accepted into the Union as new states, and until they are, should have no influence over the ratification process. This view, of course, improves the chances for adoption of the amendment. Today also, Lincoln gives Secretary of State William H Seward instructions concerning his upcoming conference with the Confederate peace commissioners. President Lincoln insists that recognition of Federal authority is a necessary precondition to peace, while Davis still clings to independence as the only basis of negotiations.

1 February 1865

The North   Illinois ratifies the 13th Amendment, becoming the first state to do so since its passage in the House of Representatives yesterday.

Western Theater, Carolinas Campaign After having been delayed for almost two weeks by heavy rains, Sherman's Union army sets out in earnest on its march through the Carolinas. By again dividing his army – his right wing making a feint toward Charleston while the left wing moves in the direction of Augusta – Sherman hopes to confound the enemy as to his true objective. As the army begins its march through South Carolina, many of the soldiers seem determined to make the state, which they see as the heart and soul of secession and rebellion, suffer for its treason. Aside from the official work of destruction, the Federals also burn and destroy much private property. Although such destruction is against orders, Sherman seems to have anticipated South Carolina's fate in a letter he had written to General Halleck in December: 'The whole army is burning with an insatiable desire to wreak vengeance upon South Carolina,' he wrote. 'I almost tremble

at her fate, but feel that she deserves all that seems in store for her.'

2 February 1865

Washington   President Lincoln leaves the capital for Hampton Roads, Virginia, where tomorrow he plans to meet with Confederate peace commissioners.

The North   Rhode Island and Michigan become the second and third states to ratify the 13th Amendment.

Western Theater, Carolinas Campaign Hindered by fallen trees and burned bridges, Union troops under General Sherman continue their march through South Carolina. To oppose them, the South has 22,500 soldiers brought in from various theaters of the war. About 12,500 of these are concentrated in and around Augusta, Georgia, and the remainder lie between Port Royal Sound and Charleston on the Carolina coast. With the two wings of the Federal army aimed in different directions, the Confederates are unaware that its true objective is Columbia.

3 February 1865

Washington   President Lincoln and Secretary of State Seward meet with Stephens, Hunter and Campbell on board the *River Queen*, off Hampton Roads, to discuss possibilities for peace between North and South. The talks, which last about four hours, produce no positive results, however, as the Confederate agents want an armistice first and all talk of reunion postponed until later, while Lincoln insists on recognition of Federal authority as an essential first step toward

peace. The president also informs the Southerners of the recent passage of the 13th Amendment in Congress and expresses confidence that it will soon be ratified by the states.

The North   Maryland, New York and West Virginia ratify the 13th Amendment. To date, six states have done so.

Western Theater, Carolinas Campaign   As Sherman's right wing continues to move in the direction of Charleston, Federal troops battle Confederates at Rivers' Bridge and at Dillingham's Cross Roads beside the Salkehatchie River.

4 February 1865

Washington   President Lincoln returns to the White House after his unsuccessful peace mission to Hampton Roads, Virginia.

Western Theater, Carolinas Campaign Fighting occurs along Sherman's advance at Angley's Post Office and Buford's Bridge.

5 February 1865

Washington   President Lincoln presents a plan to his cabinet pledging the Federal government to pay $400,000,000 to the slave states if they lay down their arms before 1 April. The cabinet, though, is united in opposition to the scheme and the matter drops.

Eastern Theater, Siege of Petersburg   In another attempt to extend his lines westward, General Grant orders part of his army

Below: The scene in the House of Representatives after the passage of the resolution to abolish slavery, 31 January 1865.

to move in the direction of Boydton Plank Road to stop Confederate wagon trains from using that road to supply Petersburg. This movement, which will continue for the next three days, will be the last major move by Grant to push his lines westward prior to the final assault.

6 February 1865

The Confederacy Davis also reports to Congress on the meeting at Hampton Roads between Lincoln and the three Confederate peace commissioners. Lincoln, he says, insists upon unqualified submission as his terms for peace.

Eastern Theater, Siege of Petersburg Heavy fighting occurs south of Petersburg, near Dabney Mills, as Confederate troops led by General John Pegram attack the positions Union troops had taken up on 5 February. Federals repel the attack and Pegram is killed in the assault.

Western Theater, Carolinas Campaign Fighting takes place at Fishburn's Plantation, on the Little Salkehatchie and near Barnwell as Confederates continue to operate against Sherman's advancing columns in South Carolina.

7 February 1865

The North Maine and Kansas both ratify the 13th Amendment. In the Delaware legislature, however, it fails to receive enough votes for passage.

Eastern Theater, Siege of Petersburg In the third day of action around Hatcher's Run, south of Petersburg, Union troops fall back

Below: Fires break out in the city of Columbia, South Carolina, after it has been occupied by Sherman's troops.

from the Boydton Plank Road after Confederate reinforcements arrive on the scene. In three days, the Union troops have succeeded in extending their lines to Hatcher's Run at the Vaughan Road crossing. The movement costs the North 1512 casualties. Southern casualties during the action are unreported.

Western Theater, Carolinas Campaign Fighting swamps and swollen rivers, Sherman's troops continue their progress toward Columbia. Some fighting takes place during the day at Blackville, South Carolina.

8 February 1865

Western Theater, Carolinas Campaign At Williston on the Edisto River and along the banks of the South Edisto, Sherman's Union troops again battle Confederates. Sherman responds to a complaint from Confederate cavalry leader Joseph Wheeler that Union soldiers are ruthlessly destroying private property along their path: 'I hope you will burn all cotton and save us the trouble,' Sherman tells Wheeler. 'All you don't burn I will. As to private houses occupied by peaceful families, my orders are not to molest or disturb them, and I think my orders are obeyed. Vacant houses being of no use to anybody, I care little about. I don't want them destroyed but do not take much care to preserve them.'

9 February 1865

The Confederacy General Robert E Lee assumes the position of general in chief of the Confederate armies. He suggests a pardon be given all deserters who report back to their commands within 30 days. Davis approves the plan.

Western Theater, Carolinas Campaign General John M Schofield assumes his duties as commander of the Department of North

Carolina and troops under his command arrive at Fort Fisher in preparation for an assault on Wilmington. Schofield's assignment is to move his troops westward, restoring communications, to provide Sherman's army with a shorter supply line than would be necessary if it were to continue to draw provisions from Savannah. Sherman's army, still marching northward, skirmishes with the enemy at Binnaker's Bridge and at Holman's Bridge in South Carolina.

10 February 1865

Western Theater, Carolinas Campaign There is fighting around Charleston Harbor at James Island and at Johnson Station. Confederates in the city are still not sure whether Sherman's army intends to attack them and are forced to maintain defenses against both land and sea assault.

11 February 1865

Eastern Theater, Siege of Petersburg Some fighting occurs near Williamsburg, Virginia.

Western Theater, Carolinas Campaign Sherman's army reaches the Augusta and Charleston Railroad, thus placing itself directly between Confederate forces in and around Augusta and those on the coast of South Carolina near Charleston. Some action takes place at Aiken, Johnson's Station and around Orangeburg, South Carolina. In Charleston, General William J Hardee, who is now separated from potential reinforcements from the west, still believes the Federal army intends to strike at that city.

12 February 1865

Washington The electoral college meets and, by a vote of 212 to 21, Lincoln is declared president. Although Tennessee and Loui-

Above: The scene in Columbia after the fires had died down. Large areas of the city were destroyed in the conflagration.

siana had both voted in the November election, Vice-President Hannibal Hamlin, presiding over the college, does not present the votes of these states.

Western Theater, Carolinas Campaign
Sherman's army repulses Southern defenders at the Orangeburg Bridge on the North Edisto River and continues its northward march toward Columbia.

13 February 1865

International Lord John Russell complains to US commissioners of United States activities on the Great Lakes. Britain and Canada are particularly upset at the military buildup in that area. The Lincoln administration, however, believes it is necessary to counter raids by Confederate agents operating out of Canada. The Saint Albans raid of October 1864, in particular, has generated a good deal of animosity between the US and its northern neighbor. The raid not only originated in Canada but the Canadian government later released the perpetrators from jail for lack of jurisdiction.

14 February 1865

Western Theater, Carolinas Campaign
Sherman's troops cross the Congaree River and then both wings turn toward Columbia, South Carolina. Meanwhile, Jefferson Davis urges General Hardee, who is still expecting the Union army to attack Charleston, to delay evacuating that city as long as possible. He does, however, leave the final decision to Hardee and Beauregard who, he admits, are better aquainted with the situation.

15 February 1865

Western Theater, Carolinas Campaign
Fighting flares up along the Congaree Creek and Savannah Creek and also at Bates Ferry on the Congaree River as Confederates try to slow Sherman's march toward Columbia. There is also fighting during the day at Red Bank Creek and Two League Cross Roads in South Carolina. In addition to the continuing attacks by Southern cavalry, the Union army must contend with deep swamps and rain-swollen waterways.

16 February 1865

Western Theater, Carolinas Campaign
Sherman's army arrives at the Congaree River just south of Columbia, South Carolina. Both General Beauregard and Confederate cavalry leader Wade Hampton are in the city during the day, but are powerless to resist the Northern army. Beauregard tells Lee that there is nothing to be done to save the state capital and then in midafternoon leaves Columbia. To the east, in Charleston, General William J Hardee makes preparations to evacuate his troops from that city. With Sherman's army between him and potential reinforcements in Augusta, and with a formidable threat from the sea as well, Hardee's position is clearly untenable.

17 February 1865

Western Theater, Carolinas Campaign In the morning, town officials of Columbia, South Carolina, ride out to surrender the city formally to the Union General William T Sherman and his army. As the remainder of the Southern cavalry flee the capital, the Northern troops occupy it and the officers and staff settle into a few of the fine mansions that grace the city. Some time during the night fire breaks out in a number of homes and, though many of the town's 20,000 residents battle the flames, the wind-fanned blazes quickly spread to neighboring structures. By morning two-thirds of Columbia will lie smoldering in ashes. Sherman is quick to blame the fleeing enemy soldiers for the fires, but for residents of the town and for Southerners in general, the burning of Columbia will long stand as a symbol of the savage cruelty of Sherman's marauding army. Among the homes destroyed during the night is the magnificent mansion of General Wade Hampton, commander of the Southern cavalry opposing Sherman's march. Meanwhile, General Hardee evacuates Charleston, moving his troops northwestward to Cheraw, South Carolina. After the long siege Fort Sumter finally falls into Federal hands.

Above: Casually dressed members of the 23rd New York Infantry Regiment have a photograph taken with their black servants.

18 February 1865

The Confederacy In a letter to Mississippi Congressman Ethelbert Barksdale, General Lee endorses the idea of arming slaves to help the South win independence. The idea, which has gained considerable support in the Confederate Congress since its new session opened in November, was recently incorporated in a bill introduced by Barksdale in the Confederate House of Representatives. Lee tells Barksdale that he believes blacks would make efficient soldiers, but they should fight as free men.

Western Theater, Carolinas Campaign General Sherman orders the destruction of all railroad depots, supply houses and industries in Columbia not already destroyed in yesterday's fire. Near Wilmington, North Carolina, Federal forces bombard Fort Anderson from the sea while troops under the command of General Jacob Cox land south of the city and then begin to move westward hoping to outflank Confederate troops there. To the west, Confederates raid Fort Jones, Kentucky.

Naval After several days of refitting, the CSS *Shenandoah* leaves Melbourne, Australia.

19 February 1865

Western Theater, Carolinas Campaign As Union troops try to outflank Confederate forces in Wilmington, North Carolina, by marching around the city from the south, fighting breaks out along the way, including one action at Town Creek. The Federal navy meanwhile, continues its bombardment of Fort Anderson, and during the night the Southern garrison evacuates that place. In Columbia, South Carolina, as Union soldiers finish their work of destroying everything of military use in that city, units of Sherman's army begin their march northward toward Goldsboro, North Carolina. In Alabama, Federals continue an expedition aimed at Selma and encounter enemy soldiers.

20 February 1865

The Confederacy The Confederate House of Representatives passes a bill authorizing the use of slaves as soldiers. Since Jefferson Davis's November message to Congress calling for the increased use of slaves as laborers in the military, debate in the South has increasingly turned to suggestions of actually arming the blacks.

Western Theater, Carolinas Campaign General Jacob Cox's Union troops continue their flanking maneuver on the east bank of the Cape Fear River near Wilmington.

21 February 1865

The Confederacy The Confederate Senate votes to postpone consideration of the House bill authorizing the arming of slaves.

Eastern Theater, Siege of Petersburg General Lee writes Secretary of War John Breckenridge that if it becomes necessary to abandon Richmond, he will move his army to Burkeville, Virginia, where it could stay in contact with Confederate troops in the Carolinas, and possibly join forces for a combined assault on either Grant's or Sherman's army if the opportunity occurs.

Western Theater, Carolinas Campaign General Braxton Bragg orders the evacuation of Southern troops from Wilmington, North Carolina, the last major Confederate port. With enemy pressure from the sea, and Union General Jacob Cox's troops closing in from the west, the Confederates in the city begin destroying all supplies there which they cannot carry with them. Meanwhile, there is fighting at Eagle Island and Fort Strong as Federals keep up pressure on the enemy.

22 February 1865

Western Theater, Carolinas Campaign Union troops enter the city of Wilmington, which General Braxton Bragg's troops had evacuated last night. In their campaign against the city, the North lost 200 casualties. Farther south, there is fighting at Camden, South Carolina, and again on the Wateree River as Sherman's army continues its march northward.

23 February 1865

Western Theater, Carolinas Campaign Fighting again erupts near Camden, South Carolina, between elements of Sherman's army and Confederate troops.

24 February 1865

Western Theater, Carolinas Campaign As Union troops continue to wreak their vengeance on South Carolina as the birthplace of secession through unofficial acts of destruction, General Sherman complains to Confederate cavalry General Wade Hampton of the murder of Union foragers by Southern soldiers. Hampton will reply that while he is unaware of the specific episode to which Sherman refers, he has ordered his men to shoot on sight any Northerners caught burning people's homes. And, he will tell Sherman, 'This order shall remain in force so long as you disgrace the profession of arms by allowing your men to destroy private dwellings.' More fighting occurs between the two sides at Camden, South Carolina.

26 February 1865

Western Theater, Carolinas Campaign Sherman's troops again encounter the enemy, today at Lynch Creek and Stroud's Mill, South Carolina. The Federal XX Corps reaches Hanging Rock.

27 February 1865

Eastern Theater, Valley Campaign In response to Grant's orders, Sheridan sends a 10,000 men cavalry force under General Wesley Merritt to destroy the Virginia Central Railroad and James River Canal. They are then to take the city of Lynchburg, Virginia.

Western Theater, Carolinas Campaign There is fighting along Sherman's path at Mount Elon and Cloud's House, South Carolina. Southern troops also skirmish with Northerners at Spring Place, Georgia.

28 February 1865

Western Theater, Carolinas Campaign Rocky Mount and Cheraw, South Carolina, are the scene of fighting as Sherman's troops continue their march toward North Carolina.

1 March 1865

Eastern Theater, Valley Campaign Union cavalry engage the enemy at Mount Crawford.

2 March 1865

Eastern Theater, Siege of Petersburg Lee, as general in chief of the Confederate forces, sends a message through the lines to General Grant suggesting that the two of them hold a 'military convention' to try to reach 'a satisfactory adjustment of the present unhappy difficulties.' Lee's peace overture is the result of a conversation between General James Longstreet and General Edward Ord in which the latter reportedly said that the Union general in chief would respond favorably to such an invitation.

Valley Campaign At Waynesborough a Union cavalry force led by General George A Custer attacks the remnant of Jubal Early's Confederate army and completely routs it, breaking up and scattering the shattered enemy force. Although Early and his staff manage to escape, more than 1000 Southern soldiers are taken prisoner. The Federals herd their prisoners and over 200 wagons of supplies northward down the Shenandoah Valley with an escort and then head toward Charlottesville, Virginia. Meanwhile, Jubal Early and those of his command who had managed to escape capture, begin to make their way back to Richmond. The Battle of Waynesborough marks the end of the last campaign in the Shenandoah Valley.

Western Theater, Carolinas Campaign The Federal XX Corps, one of the four corps of Sherman's army, reaches Chesterfield, South Carolina, after battling Southern troops at nearby Thompson's Creek.

3 March 1865

Washington Congress passes an act setting up the Bureau of Refugees, Freedmen and Abandoned Lands. The body, which will be known more commonly as the Freedmen's Bureau, is to have overall supervisory powers over those in the South dislocated by the war and in need of temporary assistance. A large part of its responsibility will be in aiding and providing work for the newly freed black population. After passing this important reconstruction bill, the 38th Congress adjourns.

Eastern Theater, Siege of Petersburg General Grant receives instructions from President Lincoln concerning Lee's peace overture of yesterday. The president directs his general in chief not to have any conference with Lee unless it is to accept the surrender of his troops 'or on some minor or purely military matter.' All political questions, Lincoln makes it clear, are to be settled by him personally. Tomorrow, Grant will relay the substance of this message to General Lee, thus completely laying to rest all talk of peace negotiations between the two commanding generals. To the west, Sheridan's troops, now riding east toward Petersburg, occupy the town of Charlottesville, Virginia.

Western Theater, Carolinas Campaign Sherman's troops enter Cheraw, South Carolina, while Confederate defenders fall back across the Pee Dee River. The Federal advance, however, is interrupted during the day by fighting at Thompson's Creek and Big Black Creek.

4 March 1865

Washington President Lincoln is inaugurated for his second term of office, taking his oath from the newly appointed Chief Justice Salmon P Chase. Before taking the oath, Lincoln delivers an inaugural speech in which he tells the audience: 'Fondly do we hope – fervently do we pray – that this mighty scourge of war may speedily pass away. Yet, if God wills that it continue, until all the wealth piled by the bondman's two hundred and fifty years of unrequited toil shall be sunk,

Below: Elements of the 1st Tennessee Artillery Battery detrain before going into action against Southern troops.

Above: General Wade Hampton led Southern cavalry in a series of lightning raids against Union headquarters late in the war.

and until every drop of blood drawn with the lash, shall be paid by another drawn with the sword, as was said three thousand years ago, so still it must be said "the judgements of the Lord are true and righteous altogether."' With an eye to the future, the president then gives the crowd his view of a proper peace: 'With malice toward none; with charity toward all; with firmness in the right, as God gives us to see the right, let us strive on to finish the work we are in; to bind up the nation's wounds . . . to do all which may achieve a just, and a lasting peace, among ourselves, and with all nations.'

7 March 1865

Western Theater, Carolinas Campaign
Federal troops commanded by General Jacob Cox work to repair railroad lines running from New Berne to Goldsboro, North Carolina. Cox and his immediate superior, General John M Schofield, plan to meet Sherman's army at Goldsboro; by restoring the rail lines to that city, they will provide a short supply line to Sherman's men from the North Carolina coast. Reinforcements arrive at Kinston, North Carolina, today from the Confederate Army of Tennessee. Generals Braxton Bragg and Johnston hope to use these

new men with those already under Bragg's command to launch an attack on Union General Cox's force moving westward.

8 March 1865

Eastern Theater   Sheridan's cavalry force, still moving eastward to join up with Grant in Petersburg, fights the enemy at Duguidsville, Virginia.
Western Theater, Carolinas Campaign
Using the troops just arrived from the Army of Tennessee to supplement his own force, General Braxton Bragg attacks Federals under the command of General Jacob Cox just outside of Kinston, North Carolina. One brigade of new Federal recruits break under the Confederate assault, but their battle-hardened comrades repulse the Southerners. Fighting will continue for the next two days as Bragg tries to destroy Cox's Federals before they can link up with Sherman's army moving north toward Goldsboro.

9 March 1865

Washington   Lincoln accepts the resignation of John P Usher as secretary of the interior. It will take effect on 15 May.
The North   Vermont ratifies the 13th Amendment abolishing slavery in the United States.
Western Theater, Carolinas Campaign
Confederate cavalry under the command of Generals Wade Hampton and Joseph

Wheeler launch a surprise attack on General Judson Kilpatrick at Solemn Grove and Monroe's Cross Roads in the late evening. Many of the Federals are caught in their beds, and Kilpatrick only narrowly avoids that fate himself. The Union soldiers, however, rally and beat off the attackers. Fighting continues outside of Kinston, as Confederate General Bragg tries to defeat Union General Cox's troops before they can link up with Sherman's advancing army. Cox, however, is bolstered by reinforcements rushed to his aid from the east, while Bragg fails to receive additional troops that he had been promised. The Federals are able successfully to maintain their positions.

10 March 1865

Western Theater, Carolinas Campaign
Bragg withdraws his troops to Kinston, North Carolina, after failing to defeat or turn back Federal troops advancing westward from New Berne. From Kinston, Bragg will move to Goldsboro where he plans to unite his forces with those of Joseph Johnston in preparation for an attack on part of Sherman's advancing columns. At Monroe's Cross Roads, South Carolina, General Judson Kilpatrick's men counterattack the enemy after being surprised in camp by them last night. The Federals defeat the Southern cavalry of Hampton and drive them off.

11 March 1865

Eastern Theater   Sheridan's cavalry reaches Goochland Court House on its way to rejoin Grant in Petersburg.
Western Theater, Carolinas Campaign
Sherman's army arrives at Fayetteville, North Carolina, where he plans to rest for a couple of days.
Trans-Mississippi   Fighting takes place today at the Little Blue River in Missouri as well as Washington, Arkansas.

12 March 1865

Western Theater, Carolinas Campaign
Soldiers in Sherman's army busy themselves in Fayetteville destroying all machinery, industries and transport facilities which might be of use to the Confederates. Sherman plans to remain in Fayetteville until 15 March and then head his army toward Goldsboro after making a feint toward Raleigh. He orders General Schofield, who is marching troops in from the east, to take them directly to Goldsboro. To the west, fighting takes place at Morganza Bend, Louisiana.

13 March 1865

The Confederacy   The Confederate Congress sends to Davis the bill calling for the arming of black slaves for use in the Southern armies. The law, as finally passed, leaves to the states the ultimate decision on whether the black soldiers should be freed, but it is the consensus that they will be liberated. Davis immediately signs the bill into law, but at the same time chastises Congress for its delay and calls for more legislation designed to close conscription loopholes.

14 March 1865

Eastern Theater   General Sheridan, still on his way to Petersburg with his cavalry, engages the enemy at the South Anna Bridge in

Virginia. In West Virginia, Federal expeditions near Moorefield and Philippi comb those areas for bands of Confederates.

Western Theater, Carolinas Campaign General Jacob Cox's troops reach Kinston, North Carolina, on their way to Goldsboro where they will join up with Sherman's army. Cox's men are repairing railroad lines along their path to provide Union troops operating in the state with a short supply line to the coast.

15 March 1865

Western Theater, Carolinas Campaign As General Sherman moves his troops out of Fayetteville, fighting erupts along his advance at Smith's Mills and on the Black River. The Federal army moves northward in three columns, with the left wing commanded by General Henry Slocum making a feint toward Raleigh. The Confederate commander, Joseph Johnston, meanwhile, is trying to concentrate his troops north of Sherman's advance and hopes to defeat the segments of the Union army before they can unite.

16 March 1865

Western Theater, Carolinas Campaign Union General Slocum's advancing column meets enemy troops blocking its path on a bridge near Averasborough, North Carolina. The Federals attack the Confederate troops, pushing them back but failing to completely sweep them out of the path. During the night, however, the Confederate commander, General Hardee, withdraws his troops to Bentonville where they rejoin the main body of Southern troops under Johnston. In the Battle of Averasborough, the Federals lose 682 men while Confederate casualties are near 865.

17 March 1865

Western Theater, Mobile Campaign Troops led by General Edward R Canby, commander of the Department of West Mississippi, begin their campaign to capture the city of Mobile, Alabama. Canby has some 45,000 men under his command, while the Confederate garrison defending the city numbers about 10,000. The Federals plan to approach the city from two directions, with one column advancing from Pensacola while the other winds its way up the east side of Mobile Bay from Mobile Point.

18 March 1865

Western Theater, Carolinas Campaign As Sherman's left wing, commanded by General Henry Slocum, approaches the city of Bentonville it skirmishes with Wade Hampton's Confederate cavalry. Hampton is trying to slow the Union troops' advance long enough to give Johnston time to concentrate his force at Bentonville.

Mobile Campaign Some 1700 Federal troops feint to the west side of Mobile Bay to create the impression that the attack will come from that direction. In fact, the main Union assault is to take place on the eastern side of the bay.

19 March 1865

Eastern Theater After completing its mission to destroy the Virginia Central Railroad and the James Canal, Sheridan's Union cavalry arrives at White House on the Pamunkey River. Soon, Sheridan plans to join Grant's army south of Petersburg.

Western Theater, Carolinas Campaign As the left wing of Sherman's army, commanded by General Henry Slocum, marches toward Bentonville, it again fights Wade Hampton's cavalry, pushing the Confeder-

Above: Union General Judson Kilpatrick narrowly avoided capture at the hands of Hampton's men on 9 March 1865.

ates back as it advances. Joseph Johnston's 20,000 men then counterattack the Federals, forcing the latter to fall back and entrench. Slocum's men manage to repulse several more full-scale assaults before nightfall. Meanwhile, as word of the battle reaches the other two columns of Sherman's army on the

Below: A contemporary rendering of the scene at Sherman's headquarters during his drive south.

Above: General George Pickett. His defeat at Five Forks on 1 April sealed the fate of Lee's remaining troops.

right, they turn west to concentrate against the enemy. During the night, after failing to overwhelm the enemy, Johnston has his men fortify their positions opposite the Federals. To the east, General Schofield and his Union troops marching toward Goldsboro, North Carolina, from the coast, engage several enemy forces at the Neuse River Bridge and also near Cox's Bridge.

20 March 1865

Western Theater, Carolinas Campaign With both Johnston's Confederates and Slocum's Union troops dug in at Bentonville, the rest of Sherman's army arrives and concentrates against the Southern force. Johnston had hoped that he could defeat Slocum's 30,000 before the remainder of the Northern troops could come to his support. Now his Confederates, numbering 20,000, face an enemy army of nearly 100,000. During the day, some skirmishing takes place, but neither side launches an all-out assault. To the west, General George Stoneman leads a cavalry force of 4000 Union soldiers from Jonesborough in east Tennessee toward North Carolina. Stoneman's raid, which is designed in part to destroy enemy transport lines, is also intended to aid Sherman's campaign.

21 March 1865

Western Theater, Carolinas Campaign While some of his troops attack the enemy lines, Sherman sends another force around the rear of Johnston's army to capture Mill Creek Bridge and cut off the Confederates' retreat. Johnston, however, detects the maneuver and blocks the Federals while at the same time holding off the frontal attacks. During the night, he withdraws his troops to Smithfield. Despite the disparate manpower of the two forces, those engaged during the day are fairly balanced, with about 16,127 Federals seeing action compared with 16,895 Confederates. In the three days of fighting, the Federals suffer 1646 casualties while Johnston loses 2606. Bentonville will be the last major attempt by the Confederates to check Sherman's advance.

22 March 1865

Western Theater, Raid to Selma General James H Wilson leads a force of Union cavalry south from the Tennessee River toward Selma, Alabama. Selma is one of the last remaining manufacturing centers left to the Confederacy. By depriving the South of its munitions factories, Union officials believe they can significantly handicap the enemy war effort. Thanks to the efforts of the North's numerous blockade squadrons operating along the coast, the South is already short of raw materials.

23 March 1865

Washington President Lincoln leaves the national capital for City Point, Virginia with his wife and son. In addition to a conference with Grant and Sherman, Lincoln hopes the trip will provide some time for rest and relaxation. Lincoln will stay close to the front lines until 8 April.

Western Theater, Carolinas Campaign Sherman's army reaches Goldsboro, North Carolina, joining Schofield's Union force which has come into the city from the coast. The Union march from Savannah to Goldsboro, some 425 miles, has been accomplished in 50 days and will give Sherman a reputation as one of the greatest generals.

24 March 1865

Washington President Lincoln arrives at Fort Monroe to confer with Grant.

Eastern Theater, Siege of Petersburg Confederates prepare to launch a full-scale attack on the Union right. Lee hopes that, by capturing Fort Steedman, he can cut the Federal supply line to City Point and perhaps force Grant to contract his lines.

Naval The CSS *Stonewall* leaves Ferrol, Spain, and encounters two Union frigates. The Northern wooden vessels refuse the *Stonewall*'s challenge to fight.

25 March 1865

Eastern Theater, Siege of Petersburg Confederate troops led by General John B Gordon launch a full-scale assault on Fort Steedman and nearby Federal lines. Union troops are caught completely by surprise and the Southern troops easily capture the Federal stronghold as well as the enemy entrenchments next to the fort. The initial success quickly evaporates as Northern troops counterattack later in the day and drive the Confederates out of all their newly acquired positions, including the fort itself. During the day the North suffers close to 1150 casualties, while the South loses nearly 4000, many of whom are taken prisoner.

Western Theater, Mobile Campaign General Edward Canby's Union troops arrive outside of Spanish Fort, after marching along the east side of Mobile Bay. Spanish Fort is one of the important fortifications protecting the city of Mobile.

26 March 1865

Eastern Theater, Siege of Petersburg In the wake of the failure at Fort Steedman, Lee tells Davis that he doubts that it will be possible to prevent Grant's and Sherman's armies from joining up and it would be unwise for the Army of Northern Virginia to remain where it is until the two Union forces do connect. Meanwhile, Sheridan's Union cavalry arrives at the Petersburg front to reinforce Grant's army.

Western Theater, Mobile Campaign Fighting takes place at Spanish Fort as Federals prepare to lay siege to that crucial Southern fortification.

27 March 1865

Washington At City Point, Virginia, Lincoln confers with Generals Grant and Sherman (who has come up from Goldsboro, North Carolina, for the talks) and Admiral David Porter. The discussions will continue through the 28th. It is at these talks, Sherman will later say, that Lincoln discusses the topic of reconstruction. According to Sherman, Lincoln tells him that as soon as Southerners lay down their arms, he is willing to grant them full citizenship rights. (The general will refer to this discussion of reconstruction to justify the peace agreement he makes with General Johnston in April.)

28 March 1865

Western Theater, Raid to Selma Wilson's Union cavalry fight Confederates at Elyton, Alabama, as it continues to move toward Selma. In North Carolina, Stoneman's cavalry fights at Snow Hill and Boone after crossing into that state from east Tennessee.

29 March 1865

Eastern Theater, Appomattox Campaign In what will develop into the final major campaign in the Civil War, Grant sends the newly arrived cavalry under Sheridan, together with some infantry units, to try to envelop the Confederate right flank to the southwest of Petersburg. If successful, Grant can not only cut the Southside Railroad, an important Confederate supply line, but also threaten the Southern escape route to the west. Anticipating such a move, Lee sends Generals George Pickett and Fitzhugh Lee to block any such Federal movements. The two sides clash at the crossing of Quaker and Boydton Roads and also on the Vaughan. The Federal advance, however, slows in the evening as rains hamper movement.
Western Theater As Stoneman's cavalry continues its penetration of North Carolina, it battles Confederates at Wilkesborough.

30 March 1865

Eastern Theater, Appomattox Campaign Heavy rains interfere with Union plans to outflank the enemy on the right of the Confederate siege lines, but both sides continue to mass troops in the area. Fitzhugh Lee's Southern cavalry is successful during the day in repulsing an advance at Five Forks.
Western Theater, Raid to Selma Wilson's expedition of Federal troops battles enemy cavalry from General Forrest's command at Montevallo, Alabama. Tomorrow, the Federals will destroy important iron and coal works near that town.

31 March 1865

Eastern Theater, Appomattox Campaign As the rains end, Union troops under the command of Generals Sheridan and Gouverneur Warren assault enemy positions around White Oak Road and Dinwiddie Court House, southwest of Petersburg. Outnumbered nearly five to one in the area, Confederates succeed in repelling the Federal advance; but in the evening, feeling the Union force is too powerful, General Pickett moves his troops back to Five Forks. Although it is not yet absolutely determined, the fact is that this move is the beginning of the end for the Confederate forces, because their retreat from the defenses of Petersburg will soon force Lee to abandon the nearby capital of the Confederacy and this will lead to the surrender at Appomattox.

1 April 1865

Eastern Theater, Appomattox Campaign Convinced that the loss of Five Forks would threaten the Confederate line of retreat,

General Lee sends Pickett a message commanding him to hold that position 'at all costs.' Federal troops under the command of General Sheridan and Gouverneur Warren (whom Sheridan relieves during the day for allegedly moving too slowly) completely overpower and crush Pickett's troops, however, not only seizing the vital Southern position but isolating Pickett's command from the remainder of the Southern army. Southern troops engaged in the action are probably fewer than 10,000; the Federals, on the other hand, have about 53,000 men available, with about 27,000 of these seeing action during the day. Northern casualties are estimated at 1000 while almost half of the Confederate troops are captured.
Western Theater, Carolinas Campaign Fighting occurs at Snow Hill, North Carolina, between elements of Sherman's army and Southern defenders.
Mobile Campaign General Edward Canby's operation against Mobile, Alabama, leads to fighting today at Blakely. The Union monitor *Rodolph*, one of the fleet supporting Canby's expedition, hits a torpedo in Blakely River and sinks.
Raid to Selma Wilson's Union cavalry force continues to move toward Selma, engaging enemy cavalry at several points between Randolph and Trion. General Forrest, who is directing the Southern resistance to Wilson's operations, is trying to delay the Federals long enough to allow reinforcements to arrive at Selma.

Below: Southern troops and civilians abandon Richmond, Virginia, to the flames in the face of strong Union pressure.

Naval After several days of operations against Northern whaling vessels in the Pacific, the CSS *Shenandoah* arrives at a harbor in the Eastern Carolines.

2 April 1865

The Confederacy While attending church in Richmond, Jefferson Davis receives a message from General Lee telling him that he will have to evacuate the Confederate capital immediately because the Confederate troops are being forced to abandon the defense of Petersburg. Davis quietly leaves the church and in the evening he and several members of his cabinet board a special train bound for Danville, Virginia. Back in the capital, factories, warehouses and arsenals are destroyed and whole sections of the city gutted by flames as Confederate soldiers prepare to abandon the place to Federal troops.

Eastern Theater, Appomattox Campaign Learning from Confederate deserters that Lee has severely weakened his defense to reinforce his right flank at Five Forks, General Grant orders a full-scale assault on the Confederate siege lines. The Federals break through at several points but the most crucial success comes when General Horatio G Wright's VI Corps seizes Southern entrenchments around Fort Fisher and rolls up the right flank. During the night Lee, who had already told Davis in the morning that the army would have to evacuate its position, leads his troops out of Petersburg and toward Amelia Court House. James Longstreet's and John B Gordon's troops hold Petersburg until the rest of the army can make its escape. During the day 63,299 Federals engage 18,579 Confederates, with the former suffering 3361 casualties; Southern casualties are not recorded, but include among the dead General Ambrose P Hill.

Western Theater, Mobile Campaign Federals, already besieging Spanish Fort, now begin to lay siege to Fort Blakely. Both forts are important positions in the Confederate fortifications protecting Mobile.

Below: After many months of siege, Petersburg finally fell to Union forces under Grant on 3 April 1865.

Raid to Selma After breaking through strong defensive fortifications held by 5000 Southerners under Forrest's command, Federal troops occupy the city of Selma, Alabama. Forrest and General Richard Taylor, both in the city, narrowly avoid capture but the Union troops bag some 2700 Confederate prisoners and a large store of enemy supplies.

3 April 1865

The Confederacy Jefferson Davis and members of his cabinet arrive in Danville, Virginia, after fleeing Richmond last night.

Eastern Theater At 0815 hours Union General Godfrey Weitzel formally accepts the surrender of Richmond. After four years of repeated threats from the enemy, the Confederate capital has finally fallen to Federal troops. Richmond is not just important as the seat of government, however, but is a vital manufacturing center as well. The Tredeger Iron Works, located in Richmond, has been the South's most important munitions factory. To the south, Union troops have also occupied the city of Petersburg.

Western Theater, Raid to Selma Wilson's Union cavalry clash with elements of Forrest's command outside Tuscaloosa, Alabama. To the north, there is also fighting between Union and Confederate troops at Mount Pleasant, Tennessee.

4 April 1865

Washington President Lincoln goes to Richmond and is cheered by crowds of Union soldiers and Richmond blacks as he tours that city after traveling up the James River from City Point, Virginia. Lincoln has been with Federal troops around Petersburg since 24 March and was on hand to witness Grant's final assault on Lee's defensive lines on 2 April.

The Confederacy From Danville, Virginia, Jefferson Davis issues a proclamation to the people of the South admitting the great loss the Confederacy has suffered in the fall of Richmond; he tells them that while the struggle is entering a new phase, they should not abandon the fight.

Eastern Theater, Appomattox Campaign

Lee's army clashes with pursuing Federals at Tabernacle Church and Amelia Court House. Hoped-for supplies do not arrive at the latter place and Lee is forced to feed his army off the surrounding countryside. Meanwhile, Sheridan's cavalry arrives at Jetersville, on the Danville Railroad, cutting off the possibility of further retreat by the enemy along that line. Lee's army is now effectively trapped between Meade's troops from the east and Sheridan's from the south and west.

5 April 1865

Washington In Richmond, President Lincoln confers with Confederate Assistant Secretary of War John Campbell on the subject of peace. The president tells Campbell (who had been one of the three Confederate agents at the Hampton Roads Conference in February) that he will not back down on the abolition of slavery and to secure peace the South must first submit to the authority of the Federal government. In Washington, Secretary of State William H Seward is severely injured in a carriage accident. Seward will still be confined to bed over a week later when the president is assassinated.

Eastern Theater, Appomattox Campaign Without supplies and with further retreat along the Danville Railroad blocked, Lee moves his army toward Farmville where he hopes to be able to feed his hungry forces. As the Army of Virginia moves westward, it skirmishes with Federals at Amelia Springs and Paine's Cross Roads.

6 April 1865

Eastern Theater, Appomattox Campaign As Lee's army approaches Farmville, it accidently diverges into two segments, each heading off in a different direction. The Federals, in pursuit of the fleeing Confederates, strike the divided enemy at Sayler's Creek, completely overwhelming each of the two wings. In the battle, the Confederates lose almost one-third of their total strength as prisoners (close to 8000 are captured during the

Below: A lone Union infantryman surveys the ruins of Richmond with the Southern White House in the distance.

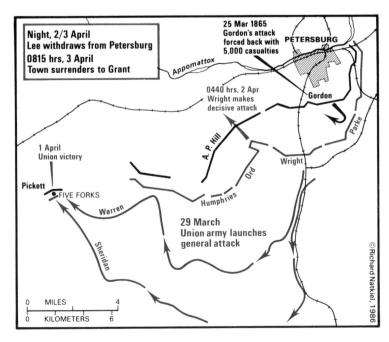

battle). Federal losses, meanwhile, are recorded as about 1180.

Western Theater, Raid to Selma At Lanier's Mills, Sipsey Creek and King's Store, Alabama, Wilson's Union cavalry continues to battle several elements of Forrest's command.

7 April 1865

Washington Hearing through General Sheridan that Lee might surrender if pressed, President Lincoln tells Grant: 'Let the *thing* be pressed.'

Eastern Theater, Appomattox Campaign Grant sends General Lee a message asking him to surrender his army to prevent 'any further effusion of blood.' Lee responds to the message by inquiring what would be the terms of such a surrender. Meanwhile, heavy fighting at Farmville delays the Confederate army's flight. Although the Federal assaults are repulsed, Sheridan's cavalry is allowed enough time to circle around the south of the Army of Northern Virginia and place itself directly in the path of the Southern army's final retreat.

International The US opens negotiations with Britain over claims resulting from damage inflicted by the CSS *Alabama*. Since the *Alabama* was built in Britain, the US government holds Britain accountable for such damage as inflicted by the *Alabama* during the course of the war.

8 April 1865

Washington President Lincoln, who has been in the Petersburg-Richmond area since the end of last month, returns to the capital.

Eastern Theater, Appomattox Campaign General Grant writes Lee that his one condition of surrender is 'that the men and officers surrendered shall be disqualified from taking up arms against the Government of the United States until properly exchanged.' Although his staff is divided on the question, Lee turns down the idea of surrender for the time being and in the evening decides to try to break through Union troops blocking his path at Appomattox Court House.

Western Theater, Mobile Campaign Following a heavy bombardment, Federals charge Spanish Fort, an important Confederate fortification protecting Mobile. After an initial repulse, the Union troops succeed in breaking through the Southern defenses. The Confederate garrison manages to avoid capture, however, by slipping out of the fort during the night.

9 April 1865

Eastern Theater, Appomattox Campaign In the early morning, the Confederate Army of Virginia launches an attack on Federal troops blocking their path to the south. The Confederates succeed in breaking through the Federal cavalry but are unable to pene-

Above: Joyous crowds greet President Lincoln as he visits the former residence of Jefferson Davis on 4 April 1865.

trate the infantry units behind it. The Union infantry instead begins to advance against the Southerners while other Northern troops in the rear begins to push in Lee's rearguard. As the morning wears on, Lee realizes that further resistance is futile, so he orders that a white flag (actually, a towel is used) be carried through the Union lines with a request for a cease fire until he can work out terms of surrender with Grant. In the early afternoon, the two generals in chief meet at the home of a Wilbur McLean in Appomattox Court House. Lee agrees to turn over all munitions and supplies (sidearms excepted) to the Federal army and to send his soldiers home where they could not return to fight until 'properly exchanged' (that is, until a Union prisoner is exchanged for each, an eventuality both generals know will never take place). Grant writes down the terms of surrender in his own hand and, at Lee's request, adds: 'let all men who claim to own a horse or mule take the animals home with them to work their little farms.' After signing the surrender, Lee mounts his faithful old horse Traveler and rides back to his men, whom he then tells: 'Go to your homes and resume your occupations. Obey the laws and become as good citizens as you were soldiers.'

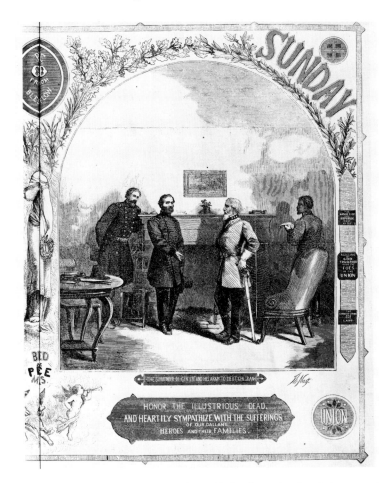

Western Theater, Mobile Campaign Federal forces capture Fort Blakely, another important fortification guarding Mobile, Alabama.

10 April 1865

Washington A brass band leads 3000 people to the White House as news of Lee's surrender sweeps through the city. Called on to make a speech, Lincoln tells the crowd that he will do so tomorrow. Lincoln then asks the band to play 'Dixie' remarking that it had always been a favorite of his, and although the South had claimed it as theirs, it now belongs to the Union.

The Confederacy Learning of Lee's surrender at Appomattox, Davis and those members of his cabinet who had followed him to Danville set out for Greensborough, North Carolina, where they hope to be more secure from Federal cavalry.

Eastern Theater General Robert E Lee gives his formal farewell to the Army of Northern Virginia. Applauding their valor and courage, Lee tells his men that he feels the time has arrived when any more sacrifice by them could produce nothing that would compensate for the loss that would be suffered. He tells them to go home until properly ex-

Above left: With his exhausted troops virtually surrounded, Lee was forced to seek peace terms with Grant at Appomattox Court House on 9 April 1865. By all accounts the meeting was amicable. Both men desired a swift end to hostilities.
Above: A picture taken after the surrender ceremony with General Robert E Lee (center).
Below: Union troops standing outside Appomattox Court House after the meeting of Grant and Lee had ended.
Right: The front page of the *New York Times* announces the surrender of Lee. However, other Southern commanders did, for a time, continue the struggle.

The New-York Times.

VOL. XIV.....NO. 4225.   NEW-YORK, MONDAY, APRIL 10, 1865.   PRICE FOUR CENTS

HANG OUT YOUR BANNERS

UNION

VICTORY!

PEACE!

Surrender of General Lee and His Whole Army.

THE WORK OF PALM SUNDAY.

Final Triumph of the Army of the Potomac.

The Strategy and Diplomacy of Lieut.-Gen. Grant.

Terms and Conditions of the Surrender.

The Rebel Arms, Artillery, and Public Property Surrendered.

Rebel Officers Retain Their Side Arms and Private Property.

Officers and Men Paroled and Allowed to Return to Their Homes.

The Correspondence Between Grant and Lee.

OFFICIAL.

WAR DEPARTMENT, WASHINGTON,
April 9, 1865—9 o'clock P. M.

This department has received the official report of the SURRENDER, THIS DAY, OF GEN. LEE AND HIS ARMY TO LIEUT.-GEN. GRANT, on the terms proposed by Gen. Grant.

Details will be given as speedily as possible.

EDWIN M. STANTON,
Secretary of War.

THE PRELIMINARY CORRESPONDENCE.

FROM THE PACIFIC COAST.

THE VICTORY.

Thanks to God, the Giver of Victory.

Honors to Gen. Grant and His Gallant Army.

A NATIONAL SALUTE ORDERED.

Two Hundred Guns to be Fired at the Headquarters of Every Army, Department, Post and Arsenal.

[OFFICIAL]

WAR DEPARTMENT, WASHINGTON, D. C.,
April 9, 1865—9.30 P. M.

Lieut.-Gen. Grant:

Thanks be to Almighty God for the great victory with which he has this day crowned you and the gallant armies under your command.

EDWIN M. STANTON,
Secretary of War.

FROM RICHMOND.

REJOICINGS.

Continued on Eighth Page.

Died,

NEAR THE SOUTH-SIDE RAIL ROAD,

ON SUNDAY, APRIL 9th, 1865,

The Southern Confederacy,

AGED FOUR YEARS.

CONCEIVED IN SIN, BORN IN INIQUITY, NURTURED BY TYRANNY, DIED OF
A CHRONIC ATTACK OF PUNCH.

ABRAHAM LINCOLN, Attending Physician.

U. S. GRANT, Undertaker.

JEFF DAVIS, Chief Mourner.

EPITAPH.

Gentle stranger, drop a tear,
The C. S. A. lies buried here:
In youth it lived and prosper'd
    well,
But like Lucifer it fell;
Its body here, its soul in — well
E'en if I knew I wouldn't tell.

Rest C. S. A., from every strife,
Your death is better than your
    life;
And this one line shall grace your
    grave—
Your death gave freedom to the
    slave.

Jas. B. Rodgers, Pr., 52 & 54 North Sixth St.

Above: A hand bill published shortly after Lee's surrender at Appomattox celebrates the defeat of the South.

changed and then bids them good-bye: 'With an increasing admiration of your constancy and devotion to your country, and a grateful rememberance of your kind and generous consideration of myself, I bid you an affectionate farewell.'
Western Theater, Carolinas Campaign General Sherman marches toward Raleigh, North Carolina, where most of Joseph Johnston's force of Confederates is located.

11 April 1865

Washington Lincoln addresses a crowd gathered outside the White House on the subject of reconstruction. Although he defends the newly created state government in Louisiana, he admits that he would have preferred the vote to be given black soldiers as well as the 'most intelligent' of that race. He also tells his audience that reconstruction plans must remain flexible. This is to be Lincoln's last speech.
Western Theater, Carolinas Campaign Sherman's troops continue their march toward Raleigh, battling the enemy at Smithfield, Pikeville and Beulah, North Carolina.
Mobile Campaign Confederates abandon Fort Hugar and Fort Tracy, the last remaining

fortifications blocking Union troops from Mobile, Alabama. During the night, Confederates also pull out of Mobile itself.

12 April 1865

Eastern Theater At Appomattox Court House, a formal surrender ceremony takes place – although neither Lee nor Grant attend. General Joshua Chamberlain of Maine, who had distinguished himself in the last days of fighting, is accorded the honor of accepting the arms and flags of the Confederate Army of Northern Virginia. Chamberlain has his Union troops lining the roads; as the Confederate column, led by General John B Gordon, approaches, Chamberlain gives the command, 'Carry arms!' and the surprised Gordon orders the same, 'honor answering honor.' The Confederate units then fold and lay down their flags and stack their arms. For all practical purposes, the war is over.
Western Theater, Carolinas Campaign Sherman's troops battle Southern resistance in the outskirts of Raleigh, North Carolina. Meanwhile, General Stoneman and his Union cavalry, riding eastward through North Carolina, capture the city of Salisbury and take over 1700 enemy soldiers prisoner.
Mobile Campaign Federal troops occupy the city of Mobile, Alabama. The campaign against Mobile has cost the Federals 1578 casualties and came at a time, Grant would

later write, 'when its possession was of no importance.'
Raid to Selma Wilson's Union cavalry occupy Montgomery, Alabama, after skirmishing on Columbus Road.

13 April 1865

Washington As part of a demobilization program, Lincoln halts the draft and reduces requisitions for war supplies.
Western Theater, Carolinas Campaign Sherman's army occupies Raleigh, the state capital of North Carolina, on its way to Greensborough, now the temporary seat of the Confederate government.

14 April 1865

Washington After conferring with his cabinet and General Grant during the day, Lincoln goes to the play, *Our American Cousin*, at Ford's Theater. He is accompanied by his wife and by Clara Harris, daughter of a senator, and her fiancé, Major Henry Rathbone. About 2200 hours that evening, John Wilkes Booth enters the president's box through the door in the rear. Booth is an actor in a family of famous actors, but where the other Booths sympathize with the North, John has long supported the Confederacy. Always an egomaniac and somewhat unstable, he has already failed at a plot to kidnap Lincoln. Now Booth walks up to the president and shoots him behind the ear; he stabs Rathbone and then hurls himself over the balcony onto the stage, breaking his left leg on impact and yelling (according to some) *Sic semper tyrannus!* ('Thus be it ever to tyrants!'). Booth then exits from a side door and rides off on a horse. The president is carried out of the theater to a house across the street where doctors examine him and pronounce his wound mortal.

Meanwhile, Lewis Payne (or Powell), an accomplice of Booth's, forces his way into the home of Secretary of State William Seward, still in bed recuperating from his carriage accident. Payne stabs Seward several times, but Seward's son and a male nurse fight off Payne who manages to escape. As news of the attacks on Lincoln and Seward reach the townspeople, Washington is seized by panic. (As it is, Booth's fellow conspirator who has been assigned to kill Vice-President Johnson has lost his nerve.) Secretary of War Edwin Stanton quickly declares martial law throughout the District and sets a dragnet to round up all suspects. Booth and another of his conspirators, David Herold, succeed in fleeing the city and during the night will reach the home of a Dr Samuel Mudd, who will set Booth's broken leg. (Later Mudd will be found guilty of aiding Booth but he will insist that he knew nothing of the events of this evening and was simply doing his duty as a doctor.)

Western Theater, Carolinas Campaign Sherman, marching with his army from Raleigh toward Durham Station, receives a message from Confederate commander Joseph Johnston requesting a temporary cessation of hostilities until a peace can be worked out. To the south, at Fort Sumter, South Carolina, during the day Federal officers and a number of distinguished guests hold a flag-raising ceremony at the fort where

Above: John Wilkes Booth, a Southern sympathizer, carried out the assassination of Lincoln at Ford's Theater on 14 April 1865.

the war had begun four years before (and which had returned to Federal control only on 17 February). General Robert Anderson, who had surrendered the fort to the Confederates in 1861, is on hand to see the Stars and Stripes again raised over Fort Sumter.

Naval The CSS *Shenandoah* leaves the East Caroline Islands in the Pacific and heads toward the Kurile Islands.

15 April 1865

Washington At 0722 hours, with his son Robert, Senator Charles Sumner, Secretary Stanton, and others gathered at his bedside, President Lincoln dies. Andrew Johnson takes the oath at 1100 and assumes the office of president.

The Confederacy Jefferson Davis and members of his cabinet leave Greensborough, North Carolina, on horseback, accompanied by a small bodyguard. Tomorrow they will arrive at Lexington.

Eastern Theater Some fighting takes place in West Virginia.

16 April 1865

Washington John Wilkes Booth and David Herold arrive at Rich Hill, Maryland, southeast of Washington.

Western Theater, Raid to Selma Wilson's Union Cavalry moves eastward into Georgia, capturing the city of Columbus and West Point. Before crossing the border, the Northern cavalry skirmishes with the enemy at Crawford and Opelika, Alabama.

17 April 1865

Washington Lincoln's body is brought to the East Room of the White House where it will lie in state until the funeral ceremony on

Below: Andrew Johnson took the oath of office to become Lincoln's successor as president at 1100 hours on 15 April 1865.

19 April. Southeast of the city, Booth and Herold arrive at Port Tobacco on the banks of the Potomac where they hope to find some means to cross the river into Virginia.

Western Theater, Carolinas Campaign Generals Sherman and Johnston meet at Durham Station to discuss peace. Unlike the talks between Grant and Lee, this conference looks beyond the surrender of Johnston's army to questions involving a peace settlement between North and South.

18 April 1865

Western Theater, Carolinas Campaign Generals Sherman and Johnston meet again to discuss peace and sign a broad political peace agreement. It not only calls for the cessation of all hostilities, but also promises a general amnesty for all Southerners and pledges the Federal government to recognize all the state governments of the South as soon as their officials take an oath of allegiance. Both men realize that the agreement will have to receive approval from their governments, but Sherman apparently is unprepared for the severe criticism that he will be subjected to because of his central part in the agreement.

19 April 1865

Washington Funeral services are held for the dead president in the East Room of the White House. Afterward a long and solemn funeral procession escorts the casket to the Capitol rotunda where the public will view it during the day.

Above: One of the final dramas of the war was the surrender of General Johnston to Sherman at Durham Station on 17-18 April 1865.

The Confederacy   Davis and his party arrive in Charlotte, North Carolina, where they will spend the next few days. Here, the Confederate president hears of Lincoln's assassination for the first time. General Wade Hampton writes to Davis suggesting that the Confederacy continue its struggle from west of the Mississippi.

Trans-Mississippi   General John Pope writes to Confederate General Edmund Kirby Smith suggesting a surrender of all Southern troops west of the Mississippi on the same terms given General Lee.

20 April 1865

The Confederacy   Lee writes Jefferson Davis telling the Confederate president that he is opposed to the continuation of hostilities through guerrilla warfare and recommends an end to all fighting. For some time, Davis has believed that partisan warfare should be the second stage of Southern resistance to the North.

21 April 1865

Washington   The casket bearing the body of President Lincoln is taken from the Capitol rotunda and put on board a special funeral train bound for Springfield, Illinois.

Eastern Theater   John S Mosby, the famed 'Gray Ghost,' disbands his troops. Most of the partisans then go in to the nearest Federal outpost and apply for parole.

22 April 1865

Washington   After several days of hiding our near Port Tobacco, Booth and Herold finally are able to cross the Potomac in a small fishing craft.

Western Theater   Wilson's Federal cavalry is still active, taking the town of Talledega, Alabama, during the day.

23 April 1865

Western Theater   Stoneman's and Wilson's cavalry are still active, with Stoneman's troops fighting a skirmish near Henderson,

North Carolina, while Wilson's men clash with Confederates at Munford's Station, Alabama.

24 April 1865

Washington   Federal troops under the direction of Secretary of War Stanton continue their search for Booth and any other persons connected with Lincoln's assassination or the attack on Seward. Booth and Herold arrive at Port Conway, Virginia.

The Confederacy   Unaware what response the Sherman-Johnston peace agreement has received in Washington, Davis sends Johnston his approval of the plan. Even after Lee's surrender, Davis had for a time held out hope that the struggle might continue, and as late as yesterday he had told his wife that he thought a return to the Union would bring oppression to the South.

Western Theater   Grant arrives in Raleigh, North Carolina, where he informs Sherman that his peace agreement with Johnston has been rejected by President Johnson. Sherman is particularly stung by criticism that he exceeded his authority in agreeing to such terms as are included in the peace package. The Union generals immediately notify Johnston that the truce will end in 48 hours.

25 April 1865

Washington   Federal soldiers pursuing Booth and Herold trace the two fugitives to the farm of Richard H Garrett, south of the Rappahannock River in Virginia.

Western Theater   Generals Johnston and Sherman agree to meet again to discuss peace.

Below: Lincoln's funeral cortege moves through central Washington on its journey to Springfield, Illinois. Vast crowds turned out to pay their respects to the former president.

26 April 1865

Washington In the early morning, Federal soldiers following Booth and Herold surround the Garrett barn and call out to the two fugitives to surrender. Herold comes out but Booth refuses. The soldiers then set fire to the barn and as it begins to burn a shot is fired. Booth falls mortally wounded. He is dragged from the barn and dies soon afterward. (Whether the gunshot was fired by a soldier or self-inflicted will never be completely settled.) Booth's body is taken back to Washington for an autopsy and will be buried at Arsenal Penitentiary.

The Confederacy Davis meets with his cabinet in Charlotte, North Carolina, and they agree to leave the state to try and get across the Mississippi.

Western Theater General Johnston surrenders his army of nearly 30,000 men on terms virtually the same as those given Lee. Sherman, however, does agree that the Federal government will provide transport home to those soldiers who need it.

27 April 1865

Western Theater The *Sultana*, a steam-powered riverboat, catches fire and burns after one of its boilers explodes. On board are some 2031 passengers, mostly Federal soldiers recently released from Southern prisoner of war camps. At least 1238, and perhaps more, die in the mishap, the worst ever on the Mississippi.

28 April 1865

The North Lincoln's funeral train reaches Cleveland, Ohio, where over 50,000 citizens view the president's body.

29 April 1865

The Confederacy Davis and those members of his cabinet who are still traveling with him reach Yorksville, South Carolina.

Below: Lewis Wallace, better known as the author of *Ben Hur*, was one of the men appointed to conduct the trials of the Lincoln conspirators.

30 April 1865

Western Theater Generals Edward Canby and Richard Taylor meet near Mobile, Alabama, and agree to a truce to arrange for the surrender of all Confederate troops in Alabama and Mississippi. The armies of Taylor and Edmund Kirby Smith are the only large bodies of Southern troops which have still not surrendered.

1 May 1865

Washington President Johnson orders the appointment of nine army officers as commissioners in the trial of those accused of conspiring to kill President Lincoln.

The Confederacy Jefferson Davis and his party, still moving south, reach Cokesbury, South Carolina. Davis hopes to be able to get to the coast of Florida and from there go by boat to Texas.

2 May 1865

Washington Accusing the Confederate government of complicity in the murder of Lincoln, President Andrew Johnson offers a $100,000 reward for the capture of Jefferson Davis.

The Confederacy President Davis, a number of cabinet members and their armed escort reach Abbeville, South Carolina. With the rejection of the first Sherman-Johnston peace agreement by President Johnson, the course that Davis and his advisors should pursue is extremely uncertain. That they are fugitives is sure. But whether they should surrender themselves to Federal authorities, seek refuge in a foreign country or try to maintain the struggle from west of the Mississippi is still unsettled. Davis seems to favor the last option but his cabinet advisors disagree.

Above: David Herold, seen here in captivity at Washington Naval Yard, was apprehended by Union troops in Virginia.

3 May 1865

The North Lincoln's funeral train reaches Springfield, Illinois, where tomorrow the president will be buried.

The Confederacy Judah P Benjamin, Davis' secretary of state, separates from the small band of fugitives fleeing toward Texas. Benjamin will eventually escape to Britain.

4 May 1865

Western Theater Richard Taylor, commander of Confederate troops in Alabama, Mississippi and east Louisiana, surrenders to General Edward Canby at Citronelle, Alabama. Canby offers Taylor substantially the same terms as Grant gave Lee. In addition, though, Taylor is allowed to maintain the use of railways and transport ships to return his men to their homes.

Trans-Mississippi West of the Mississippi, Confederate forces are still officially at war. There is fighting near Lexington, Missouri.

5 May 1865

The North Connecticut ratifies the 13th Amendment, abolishing slavery in the United States.

6 May 1865

Washington Secretary of War Edwin Stanton appoints the commissioners to conduct the trial of those accused of conspiring to assassinate Lincoln. Among those appointed are David Hunter, Lew Wallace (who will later write *Ben Hur*) and August Kautz. Joseph Holt, the judge advocate-general of the army, is to be the chief prosecutor.

Above: A view of the grand parade of the Army of the Potomac on 23 May 1865, part of the victory celebrations in the North that took place after the South's surrender.

8 May 1865

Trans-Mississippi Federals clash with Confederates near Readsville, Missouri.

9 May 1865

The Confederacy Jefferson Davis, still moving southward with his small party of fugitives, joins forces with his wife at Dublin, Georgia. Meanwhile, Northern troops, who have been searching for the Confederate president, begin to close in on Davis and his fellow-travelers.
Western Theater General Nathan B Forrest disbands his troops.

10 May 1865

Washington President Johnson tells the people of the country that armed insurrection against the authority of the Federal government can be considered 'virtually at an end.'
The Confederacy President Davis, his wife, Postmaster-General Reagan, and Burton Harrison, the president's secretary, are captured by the 4th Michigan Cavalry near Irwinville, Georgia. The prisoners are escorted to Nashville, Tennessee, under heavy guard. From there, Davis will be sent to Richmond, Virginia.
Western Theater General Samuel Jones surrenders his command at Tallahassee, Florida. To the north, William Clarke Quantrill, the most notorious of all Confederate guerrillas, is mortally wounded near Taylorsville, Kentucky. He and a small group of followers have been looting in that state recently. (Included among those who rode with Quantrill during the war are Frank and Jesse James and Cole Younger, among the most celebrated outlaws the West will produce.)

11 May 1865

Trans-Mississippi General M Jeff Thompson, the famous Southern military leader of the Missouri-Arkansas region, surrenders the remnant of his command at Chalk Bluffs,

Arkansas. Thompson is given the same terms that Grant gave Lee at Appomattox.
Naval The CSS *Stonewall* sails into Havana harbor, Cuba.

12 May 1865

Washington President Johnson appoints General Oliver O Howard to head the Bureau of Refugees, Freedmen and Abandoned Lands. The Freedmen's Bureau will oversee the care of Southern refugees in the postwar period and also be charged with helping the newly freed blacks adjust to their freedom. Under the Bureau's supervision, too, are extensive tracts of land confiscated by the Federal government during the war. The eight defendants charged with conspiring to assassinate Lincoln plead not guilty today.
Trans-Mississippi Federals under the command of Colonel Theodore H Barrett attack and capture the Southern camp at Palmitto Ranch on the Rio Grande. Fearing a counterattack, the Union troops abandon the ranch in the evening.

13 May 1865

Trans-Mississippi The Confederate governors of Arkansas, Mississippi and Louisiana meet with Edmund Kirby Smith, overall commander in the Trans-Mississippi area, and advise him to surrender under terms which they outline for him. Others in the western part of the Confederacy, including Jo Shelby, threaten to arrest Smith unless he continues the struggle against the North. In the second day of fighting at Palmitto Ranch, in Texas, Northern troops return to the Southern encampment, again driving away enemy resistance. Later in the day, however, Confederates led by Colonel John S Ford launch an attack on the Federals there and force them to withdraw. The Battle of Palmitto Ranch is to be the last significant land battle of the war.

17 May 1865

Washington General Philip Sheridan is appointed commander of the district west of the Mississippi and south of the Arkansas River. Because of Sheridan's reputation for

wholesale destruction, stemming from his campaign in the Shenandoah Valley, there is considerable Southern resistance to this appointment.

19 May 1865

Naval The CSS *Stonewall* surrenders to Federal officials in Havana harbor.

22 May 1865

Washington President Johnson declares that as of 1 July all Southern seaports except four in Texas will be opened for trade. Also effective that date, all restrictions on civilian trade east of the Mississippi will be lifted except on contraband of war.
The Confederacy Jefferson Davis arrives at Fort Monroe, Virginia, where he is put in chains and locked in a cell. Although Davis will never be brought to trial, many Northerners at this time, especially in the wake of Lincoln's assassination, are inclined to feel vindictive toward the Southern leader.

23 May 1865

Washington The nation's capital holds a grand review for the Army of the Potomac. As General George Meade's army marches past throngs of cheering Washingtonians, the flags in the city fly at full mast for the first time in four years.
The North The loyal government of Virginia (also known as the Pierpont Government) moves to Richmond, Virginia, the state capital. During the war, the pro-Union government of this state has been located in Federally-controlled northern Virginia.

24 May 1865

Washington Washington officially receives the North's other major army as the grand legions of William T Sherman march through the streets of the capital. Many are struck by the contrast between the polished Army of the Potomac and this more casual army from the west.
Trans-Mississippi Federals continue to operate against guerrilla bands in the west, with some skirmishing near the town of Rocheport, Missouri.

25 May 1865

Western Theater In Mobile, Alabama, close to 20 tons of gunpowder captured from the Confederacy explodes, destroying buildings and boats along the docks of the city. There are some 300 casualties resulting from the blast.

26 May 1865

Trans-Mississippi General Simon B Buckner, as agent for General Edmund Kirby Smith and General Peter J Osterhaus, a representative of General Edward Canby, meet to discuss the surrender of all Confederate troops west of the Mississippi. The two agree on terms basically the same as those offered Lee at Appomattox. Smith will approve these terms on 2 June. Smith's force is the last major body of Southern troops to surrender. Some of these Trans-Mississippi Confederates, most notably Jo Shelby and the remnants of his Iron Brigade, will refuse to accept defeat and instead will cross over the border to Mexico in the hope of continuing the struggle.

27 May 1865

Washington With only a few exceptions, President Johnson orders the release of all persons held in prison by the Northern military authorities.

29 May 1865

Washington President Johnson issues a proclamation giving a general amnesty to those who have participated in the rebellion against Federal authority. Excepted from the provisions of the general amnesty are several special classes of Southerners, principally those who own more than $20,000 worth of property and those who held high rank in either the Confederate government or military; these must apply individually to the president for a pardon. (The president will be very liberal in granting these individual pardons.) An important implication of the executive action is that, once an oath is taken, all property rights, except those in slaves, will be fully restored. The large tracts of confiscated lands now held by the Federal government (much of it being farmed by black freedmen) will be turned over to the former owners.

Right and far right: Two of the men implicated in the Lincoln plot – Michael O'Laughlin and Samuel Arnold.
Below: The execution of the Lincoln conspirators at the Old Penitentiary, Washington.

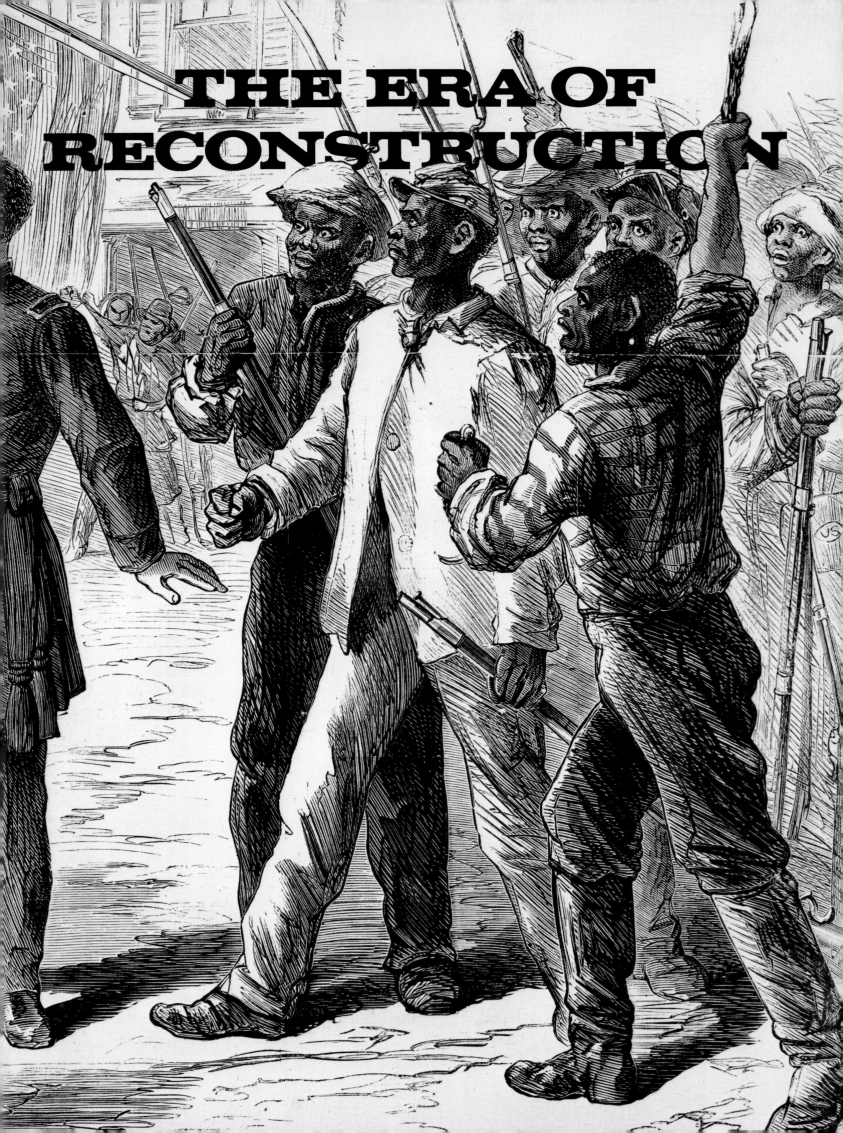

THE ERA OF RECONSTRUCTION

June 1865

The military phase of the Civil War is now coming to an end as several Confederate units surrender. On 23 June, the last formal surrender of a large Confederate force occurs in Oklahoma Territory when the Cherokee leader Brigadier General Watie surrenders a battalion formed by Indians. The Confederate raider CSS *Shenandoah* continues to capture Union whalers in the Bering Sea. President Johnson is moving to impose the peace and union as quickly as he can. He declares released all Confederate prisoners of war, except for navy officers over the rank of lieutenant and army officers over the rank of captain, if they will take an oath of allegiance. He lifts trade restrictions throughout the United States, except for the contraband of war, and declares an end to the Federal blockade of the Southern states in existence since April 1861. And in an effort to restore pro-Union governments before Republicans in Congress can intervene, Johnson names provisional governors to six of the former Confederate states and restores to the Union the state of Tennessee since it has reorganized its own government. But bitter feelings are inevitably revived when on 30 June the eight alleged conspirators in the assassination of Lincoln are found guilty by the military commission. Four are to be imprisoned, and four are to be hanged.

July 1865

On 7 July, the four alleged conspirators are hanged at the Old Penitentiary in Washington, DC. There has been considerable public protest over the case of Mrs Mary Surratt, whose guilt seems to come down to little

Below: A drawing reflecting the role of the Freedmen's Bureau in improving the educational standards of the black population.

more than that she kept the boarding-house where Booth hatched his plot, but President Johnson refuses to intervene. The other convicted conspirators are imprisoned on an island off Key West, Florida. (Michael O'Laughlin dies of yellow fever in 1867; Dr Samuel Mudd is pardoned in 1868 because of his work in the epidemic; and Edward Spangler and Samuel Arnold are pardoned in 1869.) The execution and imprisonment of the assassination conspirators somewhat placates those seeking revenge but it by no means satisfies many others.

August 1865

Confederate General Jo Shelby, refusing to surrender to the Federal government, leads a force of about 1000 Confederate men to Mexico City where his offer to Emperor Maximilian to form a 'foreign legion' is turned down. However, Maximilian provides them with a large tract of land near Vera Cruz, and many of them settle there. The Confederate raider CSS *Shenandoah,* sailing from the Bering Sea toward San Francisco, is informed by a British ship that the war has ended. President Johnson proclaims that as of 1 September articles previously considered war contraband may be traded with the former Confederate states.

October 1865

President Johnson paroles Vice-President Alexander Stephens and four other high-ranking Confederate leaders who have been in prison since their government collapsed. Johnson also proclaims an end to martial law in Kentucky. At Morant Bay, Jamaica, a British colony, free blacks riot and kill 21 white and black people before British troops reassert command. When word of this incident reaches the United States, it feeds the fears of Southerners about the freed blacks.

November 1865

Mississippi adopts laws regulating labor service, vagrancy and such matters, the first of the post-war black codes by which the South moves to restrict the opportunities of blacks. The Confederate raider CSS *Shenandoah* surrenders to the British at Liverpool, England. Captain Henry Wirz, commander of the former Confederate prison at Andersonville, Georgia is hanged after being found guilty of charges of cruelty to Federal prisoners of war held in the prison.

December 1865

The United States Congress convenes and, under the control of Republicans, sets about undoing the conciliatory policies of President Johnson. It forms the Joint Committee on Reconstruction, and it rejects the senators and representatives elected by the former Confederate states. With 27 states having approved it, the 13th Amendment to the Constitution – abolishing slavery – is formally put into effect.

February 1866

Congress passes legislation that broadens the powers of the Freedmen's Bureau, including a provision that anyone accused of interfering with the civil rights of a freed person will be tried by a military court. President Johnson vetoes this as unconstitutional, but Congress will override his veto in July. Although this legislation is the Republicans' attempt to counter the efforts of President Johnson and use the Freedmen's Bureau for political purposes, the fact is that the former Confederate states are beginning to enact a series of discriminatory and restrictive black codes to keep the former slaves from participating in a free society. Union attempts to improve the lot of recently freed blacks are far from fully effective.

April 1866

President Johnson issues a proclamation stating that 'the insurrection which heretofore existed in [the Confederate states, except for Texas, since its government is not yet formed] is at an end and is henceforth to be so regarded.' Congress adopts a Civil Rights Act, previously vetoed by President Johnson on the grounds that it interfered with the rights of states, guaranteeing citizenship to all native-born individuals (except for untaxed Indians).

May 1866

Six ex-Confederate veterans in Pulaski, Tennessee begin an informal organization known as the Ku Klux Klan. Almost from the end of the fighting, several groups of Confederate men had begun to form vigilante groups they named 'The Pale Faces,' 'The White Brothers,' and such. These men were determined to oppose the attempts of freed blacks to claim their rights, and the Ku Klux Klan at first is only one of many such local groups.

June 1866

Congress adopts the 14th Amendment, which states that all laws governing citizenship extend to blacks. But another section prohibits former office-holders who engaged in 'insurrection or rebellion' from holding any office (unless Congress, by a vote of two-thirds of both houses, removes this restriction). Furthermore, no state can be restored to the Union without accepting this amendment. Although the extension of citizenship rights to the blacks will have a long-term benefit, the immediate goal and impact of this amendment is the Republicans' desire to prevent the return of the Democrats in the Southern states and to the national Federal government.

August 1866

President Johnson, in a proclamation declaring the end of the insurrection of Texas, takes the occasion to conclude: 'I do further proclaim that the said insurrection is at an end and that peace, order, tranquillity, and civil authority now exist in and throughout the whole of the United States of America.' In effect, this marks the official end of the Civil War, but extremists on both sides of the political spectrum continue to stir up discontent.

November 1866

In the congressional elections, many voters find themselves forced to choose between radical Republicans or compromise Democrats. President Johnson is forced to support many Democratic candidates, and this allows the Republicans to intensify their efforts to portray him as sympathetic to the Southern cause. As a result of the elections, the radical Republicans strengthen their hold on their party and the national government. In Indianapolis, Indiana, Union veterans from 10 states and the District of Columbia meet to form a national organization, the Grand Army of the Republic. Although nominally a nonpolitical organization, the GAR will become increasingly supportive of the Republican Party's policies, and the Republicans in return will enact legislation favorable to the Union veterans.

Above: Members of President Andrew Johnson's impeachment committee pose for the camera in March 1868.

March 1867

It is almost two years since the war ended on the battlefield, but a Republican-controlled Congress decides to punish the South by undoing the policies of President Johnson. Congress passes the first Reconstruction Act, which divides the South into five military districts to be headed by general officers. These military governors, furthermore, are to take their orders from the commander of the army, who at this time is General Grant, not from the President. The first assignment for these military governors is to register voters and supervise the election of conventions to draft new state constitutions. These conventions will soon draft constitutions that give the vote to blacks while disqualifying former Confederate leaders, and many white Southerners will thus begin to boycott the formal elections. Congress also passes the Tenure of Office Act, which requires the president to obtain the approval of the Senate for removing any official whose appointment originally required Senate approval. Johnson recognizes this as an infringement on the traditional balance of powers and vetoes it, but Congress overrides his veto.

April – May 1867

The Supreme Court rules in two cases – *Georgia v. Stanton* and *Mississippi v. Johnson* – that it has no jurisdiction to stop enforcement of the Reconstruction Acts passed by Congress. This effectively leaves the former Confederate states under the rule of the Republican-controlled government.

May 1867

In Nashville, Tennessee, local Ku Klux Klans assemble to form an organization that they see as the 'invisible empire of the South' – the premise being that the newly freed blacks, 'carpetbaggers' and others are forming an

'empire' that must be fought. Former Confederate General Nathan Bedford Forrest accepts the post of Grand Wizard of the Empire, and the Democrats of Tennessee, quickly recognizing the Klan's potential, support it in the desire to gain backing in forthcoming elections. Jefferson Davis, after serving two years at Fort Monroe, is released on bail.

July 1867

Congress passes another supplement to the Reconstruction Act, this one assigning to the military governors the right to replace and select state officials.

August 1867

President Johnson has become increasingly bothered by his relationship with his Secretary of War Edwin Stanton who, as a radical Republican, has been actively working against the president's policies. Johnson now calls for Stanton's resignation, but Stanton – citing the Tenure of Office Act – refuses to resign, so Johnson suspends him.

February 1868

President Johnson decides to make a test case on the constitutionality of the Tenure of Office Act and thus, having reinstated Stanton in January, dismisses him. This is what Johnson's enemies have been waiting for. On 24 February the House of Representatives votes to impeach President Johnson for 'high crimes and misdemeanors.' There are 11 articles in the impeachment resolution, but basically it comes down to one issue: the removal of Stanton. Secretary Stanton, with the support of the Senate, declares he will 'con-

Above: A cartoon showing President Grant as the peacemaker between the North and South. His terms in office were blighted by scandal.

tinue in possession until expelled by force,' assigns a guard to his office, and remains in the War Department building night and day.

March – May 1868

On 5 March the Senate convenes as a court to hear the charges against President Johnson. Presiding is Chief Justice Salmon Chase; although a friend of many of the radical Republicans, he will preside over the trial with fairness and insistence on legal procedures. The prosecution is led by Representatives Benjamin Butler and Thaddeus Stevens, and they will attempt to ignore all legal restraints and to appeal to sheer partisan prejudice. (At one point Butler will wave a bloodied shirt that he alleges belonged to a Northerner beaten by Klansmen – this to prove the 'crime' of Johnson's reconstruction policies.) Johnson himself does not attend but he is ably defended by distinguished lawyers who demolish the prosecution's arguments.

May 1868

In the votes on the articles of impeachment, the Senate divides 35 to 19 for conviction – but a two-thirds majority is required, so President Johnson is acquitted by one vote. Johnson would have been convicted had not seven Republicans risked their political careers by voting to acquit. Secretary of War Stanton resigns, but the radical Republicans remain in control of their party and at their convention this month they gain the nomination for General Grant. Decoration Day is inaugurated, primarily through the efforts of former General John A Logan, for the purpose of decorating the graves of Civil War veterans.

June 1868

Seven former Confederate states are readmitted to the Union by Congress now that their governments are reorganized under the Reconstruction Acts.

July 1868

The Democratic Party, recognizing that Johnson is now a liability, nominates Horatio Seymour, governor of New York, as its presiden-

tial candidate. The 14th Amendment, having been ratified by three-fourths of the states, comes into force.

August 1868

Thaddeus Stevens, the representative from Pennsylvania who has been almost fanatical in his desire to reconstruct the South by his principles, dies. His passing takes some of the steam out of the radical Republicans' zeal to punish the Confederacy, but it by no means ends the excesses of the Reconstruction.

September 1868

The legislature of Georgia expels its black members, so military government is reimposed. Increasing numbers of blacks are now being elected to state and local offices, but only in South Carolina will they gain a majority in either house and they never control a state government nor do they try to repeal laws such as those against mixed marriages or enact laws that punish white people. However, most Southerners greatly resent the presence of blacks in any position of authority, and they wait or work to remove them and their carpetbagger protectors.

November 1868

Ulysses S Grant wins the Federal presidential election.

December 1868

President Johnson, even though a 'lame-duck' president, issues a proclamation that pardons all former Southerners except some 300 Confederate leaders, but Congress will proceed to enact laws that nullify much of the effect of this executive clemency.

January 1869

The Johnson-Clarendon Convention, an agreement settling various Anglo-American disputes, is concluded. But since the chief issue involves the damage done to Northerners' shipping by the *Alabama* and other Confederate ships that had been constructed or outfitted in Britain, the Senate will vote in April to reject ratification and press for better terms. General Forrest, having had second thoughts about the goals of the Ku Klux Klan, tries to disband the organization and resigns as Grand Wizard, but the local Klans continue.

February 1869

Congress proposes a 15th Amendment to the Constitution. This one will guarantee the right to vote to every citizen, regardless of race or any previous condition of servitude.

March 1869

Grant is inaugurated president and proceeds to establish an administration that is marked from the outset by ill-advised appointments to various high offices. Grant is a decent if naive man and allows those around him to go much their own way. In matters to do with the South, he has no sympathy for either the extreme anti-black element nor for the punitive approach of the radical Republicans, but the net effect of his moderation will be the reestablishment by white Southerners of their own rule and the denial of rights to the blacks.

January – March 1870

Three more ex-Confederate states – Virginia, Mississippi and Texas – are restored to the Union after they have ratified the 15th Amendment, which becomes the law of the land in February. Yet in practice blacks are increasingly being denied their right to vote. So, too, free public education for all children is now officially established throughout the South through the Federal laws, but black children are forced into segregated schools.

May 1870

Congress passes a Ku Klux Klan Act, aimed specifically at the Klan's efforts to deny blacks their right to vote. Popularly known as a 'force bill,' it provides heavy penalties for anyone interfering with citizens exercising their right to vote under the 15th Amendment.

July 1870

Georgia, having ratified the 15th Amendment, is readmitted to the Union, the last of the Confederate states to be so.

December 1870

When the third session of the 41st Congress convenes, it is the first time since 1860 that representatives from all the states are present.

April 1871

Congress passes another Ku Klux Klan Act, which declares that any acts by armed groups, including those like the Ku Klux Klan, may be treated as rebellion and put down by military force. The president is even empowered to suspend the writ of habeas corpus in enforcing the 15th Amendment.

May 1871

Secretary of State Hamilton Fish secretly works out the Treaty of Washington with Canada and Britain. The dispute over the boundary line between Canada and the United States in the far west is to be decided by the Emperor of Germany and the issue of fishing privileges of Canadians and Americans is to be settled by a special commission. The most touchy issue, that of the claims resulting from the action of the Confederate raiders such as the *Alabama,* is to be settled before a special tribunal which is to meet in Geneva, Switzerland. The tribunal meets first in December 1871, and in September 1872 it awards $15,500,000 to the United States for the depredations committed by these ships.

May 1872

The Grant administration is becoming increasingly tarnished and many Republicans are among the most disillusioned by Grant's lack of leadership. A group calling itself the Liberal Republicans holds a convention and nominates as their presidential candidate Horace Greeley, editor of the New York *Tribune* and nationally known for his outspoken views on many public issues. In July Greeley also receives the nomination of the Democratic Party and in September he receives the nomination of the Liberal Colored Republicans. Congress adopts an Amnesty Act that removes restrictions from former Confederates and restores their political privileges such as holding public office.

June 1872

President Grant is nominated for re-election by the Republican Party.

November 1872

Despite the scandals that are marking Grant's administration, and despite Greeley's hard campaigning, Grant wins easily. Greeley is so devastated by his political and personal setbacks that he goes insane and dies by the end of November. (His electoral votes will be divided among other candidates.)

April 1873

The Supreme Court rules that the 14th Amendment applies to barring states from interfering with the rights of blacks as citizens of the United States, not to protecting property rights. But this apparently idealistic ruling is actually a side issue of the cases under review, which involve slaughter-houses in Louisiana adversely affected by a monopoly created by the state legislature, and not everyone in America's 'gilded age' will support the court's ruling.

November 1874

The Democrats gain a majority in the House of Representatives in the national elections, thus signaling the end of the grip held by the Radical Republicans. In the South, white Southerners are once again taking control of the political parties and governments. Even many blacks have become disillusioned by events and are voting for Democrats.

March 1875

Congress adopts a Civil Rights Act that guarantees all citizens, regardless of race, equal enjoyment of public facilities such as trans-

Below: Members of the Ku Klux Klan captured by Federal authorities in 1870. This racist group was made a proscribed organization.

port, restaurants and hotels. It also declares that no one may be excluded from jury service on the basis of race. In the course of debating this bill, Representative Benjamin Butler, one of the last of the diehard radical Republicans, proposes an amendment that would compel the racial integration of all schools in the South, but President Grant has this amendment removed. And in 1883, the Supreme Court will find the entire act unconstitutional.

November 1875

Mississippi votes for its state legislature, and with most blacks and Republicans too intimidated to vote, the Democrats win a majority in both houses. There had been disorder in the state almost from the beginning of the term of Governor Adelbert Ames, a Northerner and Republican and a holdover from the Reconstruction days. Wanting to have Federal troops to stop the whites who were attacking blacks, Ames had appealed to President Grant. The attorney general replied that 'the whole public are tired of these annual autumnal outbreaks in the South,' but he refused to call out the troops. The Democratic legislature will take its revenge on Ames by threatening to impeach him in January 1876, but he resigns in March and leaves the state. A United States Senate committee will later investigate this episode and label it 'one of the darkest chapters in American history,' but the fact is that the nation at large has little interest in pursuing the subject.

June 1876

The Republican Party nominates Rutherford B Hayes, governor of Ohio, as its presidential candidate. The Democratic Party nominates Samuel J Tilden, governor of New York, as its presidential candidate. The Democrats campaign on the issue of the need to reform the

Above: Rutherford Hayes became president on 5 March 1877.

government after the years of Grant's administration. The Republicans campaign by reminding voters that those responsible for the Confederate rebellion were Democrats.

November 1876

Tilden wins the popular vote by a margin of 250,000 over Hayes, but there are disputes over the voting of Florida, Louisiana, South Carolina and Oregon so that neither candidate can claim a clear majority.

January – March 1877

Since this presidential deadlock is not anticipated in the Constitution, Congress sets up an Electoral Commission of five Supreme Court justices, five senators, and five representatives. The intention was to have seven Republicans, seven Democrats, and one Independent, but in the end there are eight Republicans. The voting over the disputed electoral votes is on strictly partisan grounds so that all are awarded by votes of eight to seven to Hayes. On 2 March Hayes is declared the winner and the next day President Grant allows him to take the oath of office privately so as to forestall any further challenge by the Democrats. On 5 March Hayes is inaugurated in the public ceremony. Only later will it come out that Republican leaders visited the disputed Southern states and got Democratic leaders to acquiesce in Hayes' election in return for which the Republicans promised that Hayes would withdraw the Federal garrison under the Reconstruction Acts and generally ignore the enforcement of the 14th Amendment, which guaranteed the civil rights of the blacks. Hayes also agrees to appoint a Southerner to his cabinet.

April 1877

President Hayes resolves a disputed election between two rivals for the governorship of South Carolina by awarding the office to the candidate of the 'redeemers,' the old guard of white Southerners, and withdrawing the Federal troops from the state. Then on 24 April Hayes removes the Federal troops from Louisiana, the last of the former Confederate states to be governed with Northern support. Reconstruction is over.

INDEX

ACKNOWLEDGMENTS

The author and publishers would like to thank David Eldred for designing the book, Sam Elder for proof-reading and Ron Watson for compiling the index. The following photographic agencies provided material for this book:

Aldus Archive: pages 33(below), 52-53, 115(top), 118(top).
Anne S K Brown Military Collection, Brown University Library: pages 34(left), 35, 36, 37(top left & right), 40(top), 44(top), 48(both), 56(top), 64(top), 69(below), 70(top), 75, 79, 82(top), 84(top), 87, 88(both), 92-93, 96, 97, 104(both), 113(below), 119(below), 121, 122(below), 123(top), 128(both), 129(below), 130(top), 133(top), 149, 150, 156(top right), 157(top), 158, 162(below), 163, 164(top), 170, 175(below), 178, 183(top), 185, 188(below), 191, 202(top).
Bettmann Archive: pages 162(top), 186.
Bison Picture Library: 6(top right), 10(top), 14(below), 27, 28, 29(both), 37(below), 59, 60(below), 64(below), 65, 81, 82(below), 89(top), 100, 104(top), 107(top), 109, 114(top), 116(top), 127, 145, 152, 153(below), 166, 170, 198, 202(below).
Chicago Historical Society: pages 26(below), 50(below), 68, 73(below), 74(top), 76(top), 116(below), 117(below), 119(top), 135(below), 169(below), 206.
Courtesy Mr Raymond Baylees: page 60(top).
Harper's Weekly: pages 44(below), 98(below).
Historical Society of Pennsylvania: pages 57, 84(below).
John Hay Library, Brown University: pages 6(top left), 210.
Library of Congress: pages 6(below left & right), 8-9, 11(both), 12(both), 13(top), 14(top), 15(all 3), 16(both), 17(top), 18(both), 19(both), 20-21, 22, 24, 25, 26(top), 30(below), 31, 32(both), 34(right), 39, 40(below), 41,

42(top), 43, 45(both), 47, 50(top), 51, 54, 55(both), 56(below), 58(below), 61, 63(below), 66, 67(both), 69(top), 70(below), 71, 72(top), 73(top), 74(below), 76(below), 77, 78(top), 80, 83(top), 85, 86(both), 89(below), 90, 91, 94, 95(below), 98(top), 99, 102(below), 103, 107(below), 110, 111, 112(top), 114(below), 115(below), 117(top), 120, 122(top), 123(below), 124(below), 125, 130(below), 131, 132, 133(below), 134(below), 136, 137(both), 138-39, 140, 141, 142(below), 143(below), 144(below), 146(both), 147, 151, 154, 155(top right & left), 156(top left & below), 159(top), 161(both), 164(below), 165, 168, 169(top), 172(top), 173, 176(both), 177(both), 179, 180(below), 181, 184, 188(top), 189(both), 191(top), 194, 195, 196, 199, 201, 202, 204, 205, 208(all 3), 209, 211(both), 212(both), 213(both), 214, 215(all 3), 216-17, 218, 219, 220(both).
Museum of The Confederacy: pages 72(below), 106(below), 126, 148, 182.
New York Public Library: pages 78(below), 134(top), 159(below), 180(below).
Norfolk Southern Corporation: pages 142(top), 143(top).
Peter Newark's Western Americana: pages 153(top), 157(below), 167, 183(below), 187.
Rutherford B Hayes Presidential Center: pages 155(below), 172(below), 220.
US Defense Dept: page 30(top).
US Dept of The Interior: pages 13(below), 17(below).
US Military Academy Archives: page 141(below).
US National Archives: pages 49, 106(top), 192-93, 200, 207.
US Naval Historical Center: pages 83(below), 113(top), 191(below), 197.
US Navy: pages 10(below), 42(below), 46(top), 58(below), 63(top), 95(below), 102(top), 112(below), 124(top), 175(top).
VMI Museum: pages 38, 129(top).
Virginia State Library: page 62.
Weidenfeld Archive: pages 33(top), 118(below).